The Radical Persuasion, 1890–1917

The Radical Persuasion 1890–1917

Aspects of the Intellectual History and the Historiography of Three American Radical Organizations

Aileen S. Kraditor

Louisiana State University Press
Baton Rouge and London

To my mother
and to the memory of my father

Copyright © 1981 by Louisiana State University Press
Manufactured in the United States of America

Designer: Patricia Douglas Crowder
Typeface: VIP Palatino
Typesetter: G&S Typesetters, Inc.
Printer and Binder: Thomson-Shore, Inc.

LIBRARY OF CONGRESS CATALOGING IN PUBLICATION DATA

Kraditor, Aileen S
  The radical persuasion, 1890–1917.

  Includes bibliographical references and index.
  1. Radicalism—United States—History.   2. Socialist
Party (U.S.)   3. Socialist Labor Party.   4. Industrial
Workers of the World.   I. Title.
HN90.R3K7   324.273'7   80-18996
ISBN 0-8071-0767-0   0-8071-0864-2 (pbk)

Published with the assistance of a grant from the National
Endowment for the Humanities.

Contents

Preface

This book is a study of the Socialist Labor Party, the Socialist Party of America, and the Industrial Workers of the World. The project began, in about 1968, as the third in a series of studies of American dissenting movements (my first two having been on the woman suffrage movement, 1890–1920, and the abolitionist movement, 1834–1850). Very soon, however, an unlooked-for, subsidiary purpose began to take form: the hypotheses I was testing had implications for my concurrent rethinking of my own philosophy, including my interpretation of American history. The conventional approach to past radical movements has come out of the world view that I was finding less and less persuasive as the 1970s went by. Therefore my critique of that approach to radical history and historiography is necessarily a critique of my own earlier work as well.

The manuscript for this book was completed in December, 1977. Since then, many books and articles relevant especially to Chapter X have been published. Some of them—as well as a few published earlier that I had been unaware of—offer interpretations similar to mine. Where such works are not cited in the notes the reason is that I worked out my interpretations independently of them. Wherever there was the slightest chance that a work had influenced my thinking it is cited as a source.

I gratefully acknowledge permission from the Past and Present Society, Corpus Christi Society, Oxford, England, for permission to quote from my article "American Radical Historians on Their Heritage," which first appeared in *Past and Present: A Journal of Historical Studies* (August,

1972). I owe a debt of gratitude to Michael Fellman, Merle Goldman, Stanley B. Haber, Eric Schneider, and a friend who prefers to remain anonymous. Some criticized the manuscript (most disagreeing with its point of view), and others helped in various ways to push it along the road to publication. Louise L. Stevenson committed an act of friendly retribution for the critical jobs I did on her papers when she was my student, and the manuscript was much improved by her meticulous editing.

Boston University gave me two consecutive years of unpaid research leave; the National Endowment for the Humanities and the John Simon Guggenheim Memorial Foundation provided the wherewithal for me to take those years off from teaching. A Radcliffe Institute Fellowship, without stipend, afforded me access to Harvard's incomparable libraries. The staff of Wellesley College Library was unfailingly helpful to this constant visitor from the neighborhood. Ms. Dorothy Swanson of the Tamiment Library suggested the arrangement that permitted me to use its magnificent microfilm collection at home. To all these institutions and people, my thanks.

A special acknowledgment is due to a beloved friend who did not live to see the outcome of her contributions to this project. Doris W. Dashew discussed all the ideas in it with me from their inception, and some of them originated in the course of conversations in a way that makes it impossible for me to say who thought of them first. The last such conversation took place on August 31, 1977, the day before she died. The usual disclaimer, that the author alone is responsible for the final result, is not quite fitting here, for this book is almost as much hers as mine.

The Radical Persuasion, 1890–1917

I   Introduction

I

This book scratches the surface of an enormous subject—the intellectual history of American radical movements. Since little work has been done in this field, in contrast to the large literature on the institutional history of radical movements, the topics I have chosen to explore should not be interpreted as comprising what I would consider the complete list of the most important elements of a comprehensive intellectual history of these movements between 1890 and 1917. This work omits, for instance, the views of the members of the radical organizations concerning religion. In the discussion of the topics included, I emphasize the members' attitudes toward their organizations, and their theories rather than their strategies and tactics. Each of the topics, both those included and those omitted here, should be the subject of several whole books.

When radicalism ceased being the framework of my perceptions (starting about 1968), it became itself, in a new way, an object of historical study for me, with respect to both my own history and that of the United States. The resulting insights into the nature of my own increasingly past radicalism yielded insights into the nature of the thinking and role of past American radical movements. Instead of assuming that they saw American social reality accurately, I discovered that their perceptions had become possible objects of open-ended analysis, and instead of automatically perceiving their contemporaries through the radicals' eyes, I could now consider the startling notion of looking at those radicals through their contemporaries' eyes.

One crucial discovery that many historians have made independently is that a vast area of historical subject matter had been ignored by Old Left historians: the beliefs, values, and living patterns of the overwhelming majority of nonelites. Such people do, of course, appear in Old Left histories, but they are fictions, either Victims or Battlers for Freedom. Ordinary people live only in relation to the enlightened minorities and to their oppressors, waking to the truth or misled into acting contrary to their own interests. The results of this school of historiography resemble those of the Progressive school that divided the nation into The People and The Interests, even though the theory they start with is different. At the time I began to wonder about that silent— in radical histories—majority, "the new social history" and "the new political history" had already produced enough works to indicate that the data ignored by radical historians would thoroughly refute their a priori assumptions. Since, for a time, I still considered myself a radical, I turned to the New Left historians' pioneering work, which rejected the Old Left's "elitist" bias. Eventually, however, it became clear to me that their work too was hobbled by certain assumptions, chiefly the assumption that the "self-activity" of the unorganized majority of the working class was essentially anticapitalist. Instead of studying data about the workers' lives and belief-systems without preconceptions about their meaning, New Left historians have generally studied them in the light of their own need to find seeds of radicalism that could be made "relevant" to present radical praxis. Both of the Lefts thus give us a choice between a passive majority needing a vanguard in possession of radical theory and an active majority inevitably producing radical theory. Neither treats John Q. Worker's life and belief-system as having had meaning other than in relation to capitalist oppression and the historically assigned mission to destroy it.

But if the majority of workers spent most of their lives not striking or rebelling, had as complex a life in the "private sphere" as the new social history discovered, and considered their ethnicity, religion, and community and kinship networks as important as the new political history showed they did, was that assumption of both schools of radical historiography correct? Perhaps it is wrong to assume that the lives of the nonelites were, in all spheres, so tightly meshed with a system of economic and political power that that "system" provides the framework within which all important aspects of the workers' lives are best understood.

The most productive work in social history has been done by historians who do not begin with the "system" paradigm (except in the history of slave societies, to which it is applicable), who do not search the data primarily for seeds of revolt or of the ideological hegemony of the ruling class, but who consider the possibility that when workers constructed belief-systems, life-styles, and relationships partly without reference to the structure of economic and political power, they were manifesting an accurate perception of the partial autonomy of their lives. I believe those historians are on the right track. Hence, I shall argue that what radicals perceived as a "System" was actually what I shall call a "Society," with "social space" that allowed a variety of institutions, life-styles, values, aspirations, and beliefs to exist independently of the interests and needs of the rulers of the economy. "Society" is not the opposite of "System" in the sense of substituting a collection of closed, island communities for the highly integrated network of the System. The Society model includes interdependent and mutually influencing institutions, communities, and ideological currents, with unequal power and influence. It acknowledges the existence of class and other conflicts within, as well as between, those components of the Society, some of those conflicts extending beyond the boundaries of the components within which they originated. But it also takes account of the partial autonomy of those institutions and communities and belief-systems, and of the limits of their influence. It implies a criticism of the System model for exaggerating the synchronic at the expense of the diachronic shapers of social formations.

In sum, if a new approach comes out of the discovery that ideological assumptions have distorted perceptions of current and past reality, questions about perception itself assume new importance. These include questions concerning the relationship among three things: the mode in which reality is perceived, the resulting picture of reality, and the objective reality. So long as a historian employs past radicals as the eyes through which he looks at their society on the assumption that they perceived it accurately, he cannot treat *their* standpoint as a hypothesis to be tested and perhaps disproved.

The inquiry gradually shaped itself around one central question:

how accurately did American radicals perceive the world in the late nineteenth and early twentieth centuries? That was the period in which the foreign-born majority of industrial workers were using the aforementioned social space to construct new belief-systems and living styles by combining their Old Country heritages with American ingredients. And it was the period in which what are generally considered the conditions for successful radical propaganda and agitation were present: theories, movements to propagate them, a big and concentrated working class to hear the messages, and very widespread dissatisfaction with the distribution of wealth and power. Yet none of the movements converted anything near the number of workers they needed. These considerations suggested the possibility that the radicals' perception of the worker was erroneous in the same way that later radical historians' perception of him has been, and for the same reasons: their System-thinking made them see him only with reference to the System, its rulers and gravediggers, and the doctrinal needs of the radicals' own movements. The inquiry into the radicals' writings led me to mountains of documents never quoted or cited in the secondary literature or anthologies of sources. That discovery piqued my curiosity about another matter: when the historic record as seen through the eyes of a historian who asks open-ended questions[1] is compared with the historic record as seen through the eyes of a radical historian, what do the discrepancies between the two depictions reveal about the latter's perceptions of reality? On this point I could get some help from my own recollections. As an alumna of the Old Left I could switch back and forth between two modes of perception and compare them. Both my own ideological journey and the discoveries I made in the early stage of work on this book therefore led me to make it a running commentary on the radical historiography of American radicalism as well as a study of certain aspects of past American radicalism.

In due course a number of propositions took shape, two concerning conclusions and two concerning assumptions. Among the "conclusions" that it seems sensible not to require the data to yield are: a) that the reason American workers failed to convert in large numbers to radicalism was either that they were ideologically dominated by the capitalists and their agents or that they were intimidated by threats of force or unemployment; and b) that the belief-systems that the various radical movements offered the workers "reflected" the latter's interests better than the workers' own belief-systems did. And among the starting assumptions that it seems wise not to make are: a) that to inquire into the nature of a past radical's belief-system is to discredit it[2]; and b) that the only things in the historical record that call for explanation are things that the historian disapproves of, because radicalism is "natural" among nonelites in a class society and does not need to be accounted for.[3]

II

This book, then, deals with three "worlds": those of John Q. Worker, of American society in general between 1890 and 1917, and of the radicals. Chapters II and III discuss some obstacles to our entering imaginatively into the first two worlds. The chief obstacles are the assumptions that determine the questions that radical historians—and many liberal historians—ask: that American society was a System and that some sort of radicalism was and is the normal ideology for workers in an industrialized capitalist society. The alternative approach offered in Chapter IV argues that both the radicals and the workers in the 1890–1917 period should be perceived as participants in a protracted response to and debate about the changes occurring in American society. The advent of the industrial revolution in the United States, culminating in the large-scale industrialization and urbanization that started in the 1880s, in time forced Americans to confront, in thought, the obsolescence of customary norms governing class relations. I give the name "shake-up period" to the 1890–1917 period because that was when the cumulative impact of the changes during the two previous generations and the need for new norms had become too obvious to ignore. The ideological and cultural resources that all sides brought to bear on their responses were as specific to their generation as were the dislocations that evoked them.

Section 2 deals with the world of the radicals and approaches it by way of their perceptions of their society, of John Q. Worker, and of themselves. (I originally intended to make Jane Q. Worker a major personage as well, but as Chapter V points out, the radicals had little to say about the special circumstances of working women—or of blacks—and tended to oppose special recognition of any distinctions whatever within the working class, except between the skilled and unskilled.) The core of the research was a page-by-page reading of some of the chief periodicals and convention proceedings of the three organizations; the Socialist Labor Party is mostly ignored after about 1902 because of its insignificance once the Socialist Party of America was in the field.

Most of the writers of these documents of course were leaders at various levels, journalists, orators, candidates for office, those who both influenced and reflected the thinking of members who belonged voluntarily and who could resign or demote the spokesmen if they disagreed. In the absence of a complete content analysis of the literature to note the frequency of words and concepts with all their variations and subtleties, I have relied on impressions built up from the reading of thousands of pages of propaganda, convention debates, and other sources. Where a certain document is used to illustrate a point, it is because it meets one of two criteria: it expresses a view that appears often enough to indicate that it played a large part in the thinking of at least an important minority of the subjects, or the writer or speaker was influential enough in one of the three movements for his views to have had significance. The reader is entitled to question the accuracy of my perception of those patterns; therefore I made it easy to check them by furnishing more footnote citations for critical themes and subthemes than are customary and by inserting a "Documentary Excursus" at each of six places to give the reader the flavor of the relevant sources. Only a few of the items in the documentary excursi have been quoted or cited in the familiar literature, and even they take on new meaning when placed among others of the same sort.[4] The economic problems of publishing what is in any case a large book have forced me to omit most of the multiple citations from this volume. Readers who wish to obtain additional supporting evidence for those points accompanied hereafter by the expression "see Supplement" may consult a manuscript in the Boston University Library, which includes a "Supplement" containing those citations.

The radicals' speeches and writings are used here mainly as revelations, both conscious and unconscious, of how they perceived themselves and John Q. Worker. They are all taken from published sources because, since the critical task of all radical movements in a democratic society was mass conversion of the workers, it is their public rhetoric that best reveals both the images that the movements wanted to project to the public and the images that they did project. The wished-for and actual images differed in a way that enables the historian to reconstruct the patterns of perception, including self-perception. Even if there is a difference between the ideas that a person expressed publicly and those he expressed only in private letters and conversation, it is the public record that is more informative for the sort of analysis that this book undertakes. When one adopts a particular line of argument because he expects his audience to find it persuasive, he has a mental picture of that audience's mind. For example, if he appeals primarily to its interests, we infer two things: first, that he believes his audience will be more receptive to an appeal to its interests than to something else it values, and second, that he believes it defines its interests as he does. (These points apply, of course, only in contexts in which the speaker or writer had a choice of approaches.)

Suppose that, upon studying that intended audience, we find that the propagandists' image of it was false, wholly or in part. We should then inquire whether the facts that contradict his image of it were common and obvious at that time or are apparent only to the historian. If they were common and obvious at that time or if the available facts could have been interpreted in more than one way, then what does his erroneous perception of them tell us? If we use this method to study the radicals' propaganda directed to John Q. Worker in the 1890–1917 period, we find, in my opinion, that they perceived him falsely and that many facts from which a truer image could have been constructed were available to them, although beyond a certain level of generalization only later discoveries by historians and conceptual tools developed by social scientists could place these facts within a general theory.

Hence the comparison between the reality (so far as research can reconstruct it) and the radicals' perceptions, which forms the core of this book, proceeds on two levels: first, an examination of American society as seen by and knowable to people living at that time; and second, the formation of a set of hypotheses that include both the "reality" and the perceptions (a part of that reality) within a general theory. These considerations require that Section 2 focus on the rhetoric that the subjects used in their public agitation and propaganda and in their intra- and interorganizational debates.

Countless historians have reconstructed other people's perceptions of John Q. Worker—socialists', Wobblies', Communists', union organizers', religious missionaries', social workers', political ward leaders'. Yet few historians have tried to reconstruct *his* perceptions of *them*. The list itself provides a clue to the reason: John Q. Worker's perceptions of—or at least responses to—social workers and ward politicians have received some historiographical attention, and these are the sorts of outsiders (to John Q. Worker) with whom historians have tended to be least sympathetic. The more sympathetic a historian is to a certain such outsider, the less likely he is to try to see him through anyone else's eyes, for the more likely he is to find it natural to see that person's contemporaries through that person's eyes. But although it may be natural, this tendency creates a gap in the very knowledge that the historian is ostensibly seeking. John Q. Worker's perception of, say, the radical is an indispensable element in the reconstruction of that radical's ideology and perceptions. The historian, for example, may learn what that radical thought John Q. Worker believed concerning the radical and his message. But only the knowledge of John Q. Worker's thinking could tell the historian if the radical was right or mistaken and thus lead to inquiry into the sources of the belief. And not only that belief but also the radical's beliefs concerning why John Q. Worker thought as he did, what the chances were of converting him, and what role John Q. Worker's belief-system played in the functioning of the entire social order.

Chapter X is both an extended commentary on these attitudes and the beginning of an attempt to reconstruct John Q. Worker's perceptions of himself, the society, and the missionaries. It is offered only as a beginning, because social historians are still in the early stages of collecting and interpreting the sources on which the reconstruction will be based. It would be awkward to insert "perhaps," "I suspect that," "we may discover that," and other such qualifiers in every assertion I made beyond the available evidence in Chapter X. I therefore emphasize that those theses are largely suggestions for investigation, and their seemingly categorical form is made necessary only by considerations of style.

III

In this work the term *radical* will be used in its literal sense, to apply to those who would change society at its roots rather than reform it to make it conform more faithfully to its professed values and ideals—except insofar as every modern society professes to aim at universal happiness, brotherhood, material comfort, and so on. If used literally, therefore, the label *radical* should not be bestowed upon the Reconstruction Republicans, the Populists (other than that minority of them who worked to push Populism in a radical direction), or the left-wing New Dealers. The label would, however, be meaningless if it were withheld from movements that, although professing radical goals, had no effect or an antiradicalizing effect on their society—movements such as the Communist Party or the Weathermen—for by that criterion there has never been a radical movement in the United States since independence. To be useful, the term should be applied to those who wanted a basic change in the social order, regardless of what effect, if any, their efforts had and regardless of whether their tactics were mild or extreme.

Furthermore, the term will be applied only to those whose radicalism had to do with the political and economic structure of the society. This is not the only legitimate way it can be used. To a religious person, the change from private to public ownership of the means of production, or from absolute monarchy to republicanism might be merely a shift in the structure of worldly power relationships. A feminist may consider woman's status and the customs relating to sex to be the most basic criteria to distinguish one society from another; thus a basic change in these customs would be the one radical change possible. I shall use the relations-of-production and political-power criteria because the three organizations studied in this book used them. All three believed that if the forces of production became collectively owned, everything else of importance would change accordingly, to the extent that it had been infected by capitalism. Their criteria must be used if we are to see their society through their eyes and to study the consequences of this perception by comparing it with others. My use of the term *radical* is thus a mere convenience, implying no judgment as to what if anything is "really" basic.

Since this book focuses on attitudes and beliefs that were shared by three radical organizations—the Socialist Party, the Socialist Labor Party, and the Industrial Workers of the World (hereafter SP, SLP, and IWW)—and since it would be awkward to name all three whenever a common trait is referred to, I shall refer to them as "the radicals." There were other radicals, notably the anarchists and communitarians. They, along with the SP, SLP, and IWW, shared one more defining trait: they all mistook the birth pangs of large-scale industrial society for the death throes of the capitalist system.[5] Moreover, Americans at that time used the label *radical* loosely, often bestowing it upon Populists, Single-Taxers, and even Progressives, groups that were actually reformist, since they did not aim at a total reconstruction of society. For this reason socialists sometimes used *radical* in a pejorative sense, in contradistinction to *socialist*.[6] Hence it must be stated explicitly that the expression "the radicals" in the following pages will refer, solely for the sake of convenience, only to the articulate members of the SP and SLP and the radical core of the IWW.

Another term that will be used often is *John Q. Worker*. In some contexts it will be advisable to avoid the vague, collective designations *the working class* and *the workers* and to use a term that will suggest a real person with beliefs, hopes, fears, prejudices, problems, a family—a person who even in large groups never dreamed that he was part of a vast entity "destined by history to end the long ordeal of class society and effect the transition from prehistory to true freedom." There is a danger in the use of the term *John Q. Worker*, of course; it could gloss over the heterogeneity of American workers—their ethnic, racial, religious, sexual, political, ideological, and occupational distinctions; their membership in unions of various sorts or no unions at all; their distribution among geographical regions and neighborhoods; and the individual differences that were certainly as important as any of the others. It is hoped that the synecdoche, while reminding the reader that what is referred to is not an abstract collective entity, will not tempt him to ignore this variety. Whenever John Q. Worker is referred to, his composite nature should be kept in mind.

IV

A few dates and facts will be helpful, as a reminder of necessary background.[7] When Daniel De Leon joined the SLP in 1890 it was a mostly German-speaking sect with no impact on the American working class. He soon became editor of the party's paper, *The People*, and its chief ideologue, which he remained until his death. Failing to achieve the desired influence over the Knights of Labor and then the American Federation of Labor (hereafter AFL), the SLP wrote off the "reformist" unions and organized the Socialist Trades and Labor Alliance (hereafter STLA) in 1895. The STLA was to be the economic arm, and the SLP the political arm, of a single revolutionary movement. Some SLP members, however, opposed the dual-union policy of the STLA, and favored socialists' working within AFL unions. This basic tactical issue, and De Leon's personality, caused the split in the late 1890s that decimated the SLP.

In the same years, non-SLP socialists were trying out forms of organization and long-range programs. These included Eugene V. Debs, radicalized by the failure of the strike of the American Railway Union in 1894 and his imprisonment. One of the new organizations turned out to be permanent: the SP, founded in 1901 by former members of the SLP (most notably Morris Hillquit), former communitarians, Christian Socialists, Bellamy Nationalists, Populists, and Single-Taxers.[8] The core of the new party were the "Kangaroos," the SLP dissidents who favored "boring from within" the AFL because a dual union such as the STLA would alienate organized labor. Most SP members believed the unions should remain independent of the party and that party members should work within them to radicalize as many workers as they could, as well as try to induce the unions to adopt radical positions on political questions.

The boring-from-within tactic had limitations, however, in a period in which the unions comprised a small minority of the workers, and mainly the skilled ones at that. Some members of the SP were willing to try a new way of reaching the unorganized majority in the form of what became the IWW, founded in 1905. In addition to a few SP members (representing only themselves, not the party) at the IWW's first convention, there were anarchists, syndicalists, SLP members, and representatives of a few unions, the largest contingent representing the Western Federation of Miners (hereafter WFM). De Leon had a special interest in the new IWW, for the STLA had been stillborn; he hoped the IWW would provide the SLP with its desired link with a revolutionary union. The IWW was thus as varied in membership and doctrine as the SP. But unlike the SP, it soon discarded its right wing, some SP members who left within the first couple of years owing to the organization's hostility to the AFL and drift toward anarcho-syndicalism. The WFM soon withdrew also, convinced that there was an irreconcilable conflict between its own need to be a functioning union and the IWW's revolutionary aims and tactics. The IWW discarded its SLP-STLA wing in 1908 after a controversy over political action. Early in 1913 a referendum among SP members resulted in the recall, from the party's National Executive Committee, of William D. Haywood, a leading Wobbly. Most of those Wobblies who also belonged to the SP thereupon left the party. The three radical organizations were now clearly distinct from one another, each representing a version of radical theory, function, and tactics.

The SLP represented that version of Marxian orthodoxy that demanded centralized organization, doctrinal unanimity, and minimal participation in nonradical organizations or agitation for "immediate demands" short of the basic demand for revolution. The IWW focused on the economic organization of the unskilled workers on the theory that once they possessed the organization and the will to take over the economy, political change would follow, but that even massive voting for radical governmental officials would be fruitless so long as the capitalists wielded full control over industry. The SP remained heterogeneous in both membership and doctrine, but it mainly represented that version of socialism that placed greatest faith in individual socialists' agitation and propaganda in whatever organizations—unions, ethnic societies, etc.—the workers belonged to, along with the running of candidates for all governmental offices and propaganda on all issues including "immediate demands."

Each of the three organizations had a distinct membership base. The SLP's membership, tiny after the turn of the century, remained chiefly old socialists living mainly in the East—craftsmen, journalists, professionals. The IWW, because it was a union, attracted a large number of workers who drifted out as fast as they had drifted in. That fact and other evidence show that few of them ever believed in the IWW's revolutionary theory but had joined for the same reasons they and other workers joined other unions. The core, those who remained year after year, comprised mostly westerners, often anarcho-syndicalists without community roots or families or who had left their home communities and families to live as itinerant agitators among migratory lumber workers and newly arrived miners in the West. The SP's roots were in the old American radical tradition of the Midwest and West and in a few ethnic communities in the East and Midwest. The party included east European Jews and Finns who brought their radicalism along with them to America; former Populists disillusioned with their movement's tactics and limited demands: and professionals, clergymen, and other middle-class people who saw in the vast changes taking place the chance to build a just society for the first time in history and were appalled by the hideous conditions prevalent in the new factory towns and newly enlarged industries in the cities. None of the three organizations contained many women or blacks, although the IWW briefly organized with some success among both black and white workers in several communities in the South.

Owing to the differences among the three organizations in structure, theory, tactics, and membership base, it is possible to draw certain conclusions that could not be drawn from a study of any one of them alone.[9] The crucial fact is that all three failed miserably in their task of revolutionizing the United States. The SP, starting with 10,000 members in 1901, had 118,000 by 1912. It had elected about 1,200 government officials and was publishing more than 300 periodicals. Following several years of decline, its membership rose to 109,000 in 1919.[10] And as everyone knows, its candidate for President, Debs, received almost 900,000 votes in 1912. These figures, however, look impressive only from the customary perspective of radical failure. Debs's vote amounted to a mere 5.9 percent of the total cast, and the party never came near influencing, much less converting, the masses of workers it needed to convert if its predictions of the revolution were to come true. And its membership and electoral statistics made those of the SLP invisible. Although the IWW claimed more than 100,000 members in 1917, it never enrolled more than a tiny proportion of the American working class. In addition, whatever figures might be given for any one year are misleading, since the turnover of members was, as mentioned before, extremely high,[11] indicating that most recruits never subscribed to the official ideology.

V

At this point a few comments on fashions in the historiography of labor and radical movements are in order.

If any one of these organizations is studied in isolation, one could hypothesize that its tenets or its leadership or its tactics or governmental repression or something else peculiar to that organization was responsible for its failure. But the three organizations varied in all these respects and still met the same fate. Could it not be that there was something in the objective situation they all worked in that foredoomed them? I shall argue that there was.

Among the conditions necessary for revolution, one has received less attention than it warrants. In the United States any movement that was to succeed in leading the working class to power had to convert at least a large minority and win at least the passive acquiescence of most of the remainder. Whether it could have made the revolution, once it had acquired those two constituencies—the active and the passive—is a subject of disagreement. Radical historians sometimes argue that the workers' votes and freedom to unionize were mere tokens, allowed by the ruling class only so long as they did not threaten the latter's power. But even if true this is irrelevant to the situation that existed in the 1890–1917 period. Most workers seem to have believed that those two rights were real and acted accordingly. Never having decided, as a class, to use their votes to effect sweeping change, they never saw any reason to believe that they did not possess the power to do so if they chose. Their nonradicalism was thus, at bottom, the result of a choice they believed they had. They must have been aware of having the choice, since throughout this period the movements propagandized and agitated freely, suffering just enough repression to evoke sympathy from civil libertarians and to attract attention to their messages. The SP's more than three hundred periodicals, the SLP's and IWW's own periodicals, the influence that office-holding brings, and the socialists' indefatigable propagandizing in unions and neighborhoods and clubs all brought marvelous publicity and the opportunity for making converts.

Another historiographical fashion is to lay the blame for the radicals' failure on governmental repression. This explanation is, I believe, tautological. A radical movement is by definition a minority openly dedicated to the overthrow of those in power. Hence, opposition is implied in its very reason for being, and the movement's success can be defined, in its own terms, solely by its ability to overthrow that opposition. To say that the measures taken by those in power against their self-appointed destroyers explains the failure is equivalent to saying that the movement's reason for being is what defeated it, for the movement would not have existed if that power and its wielders had not existed. That is to say, since there is no radical movement in the absence of its power-wielding target, the movement's ability to prevail over its enemy's physical as well as ideological counterforce *is* the measure of its success, and to say that it would have succeeded had it not been for the counterforce is merely to say that it would have succeeded if only those in power had surrendered. Furthermore, governmental repression could not have been the reason for John Q. Worker's failure to convert to radicalism by the millions. Had he done so, he would not have permitted the repression, let alone have participated in it as he sometimes did. Hence we get back to the essential failure of the movements: to convert John Q. Worker.

To some radicals, of course, the movement's demands that were accepted and in some cases enacted into law comprised their "radicalism," but these successes were the successes of the discrete demands, not of the radical movement itself, whose belief-system was independent of any or all of such demands. In fact the acceptance of those demands meant the demise of the movement, which generally assumed that the various reforms could not be effected before the overthrow of the capitalist class. The reforms disproved this contention. The success of the movement itself should be measured by its own criterion, which was the accession of the movement to national power so that it could lead the working class in a fundamental alteration of the social order.

The failure of radicalism has often been attributed to the workers' preference for "Lockeian liberalism," the unofficial but all-pervasive American ideology, or to their having adopted petty-bourgeois aspirations once they had immigrated to the greener pastures of American industry. These arguments ignore John Q. Worker's own culture, the matrix of whatever ideology he subscribed to. They overestimate the one-to-one relation between economic and political institutions on one hand and individuals' thinking, feeling, and behavior on the other. They underestimate the importance to individuals of those social forms that mediate between the public sphere and the private sphere, those institutions and relationships such as the family, neighborhood, and club that keep the wielders of power at arm's length. John Q. Worker's nonradicalism does not imply that he approved of the capitalist class; it may, however, imply his acquiescence in a social order that allowed him that private space. Historians who ignore John Q. Worker's culture tend to assume that ideology is an either/or phenomenon: that he could believe only in either the capitalists' or the radicals' ideology, that his ideology had to "reflect" either the capitalists' or the workers' class interests (and that the radicals' ideology *was* the expression of the workers' class interests—a groundless assumption), and that it had to reflect either the current "System" of power relations or that of the socialist society to come. This is a hypothesis as worthy of testing as any other; but so is the hypothesis that there can be a third sort of belief-system, not so tightly connected with the "System" of power relations, if such a "System" in fact existed. It is, in short, possible that John Q. Worker, who in most cases was a recent immigrant, brought with him an inherited belief-system that he adapted to his new American circumstances and that his American-born children adapted further, and that this belief-system provided meaning to his experiences and circumstances. If it served this function adequately by proving flexible enough to accommodate new circumstances, no new belief-system offered him by Americanizers, radicals, religious missionaries, or any other proselytizers could succeed in making large numbers of converts—not because it did not also make sense of American life but simply because, unless a person's belief-system has disintegrated in the face of experiences that it cannot accommodate, his most deeply held beliefs are not open to challenge from any quarter.

The radical movements have been studied too much in isolation from the assortment of other proselytizing movements of the same period. From John Q. Worker's perspective, all those movements must have seemed less different from each other than they appeared to their own members. What he saw was a variety of people who wanted him to abandon some of his beliefs, associates, and daily activities in favor of new ones. Yet there were no masses of Jews and Catholics who converted to Protestantism; no masses of working-class immigrants who tried hard to forget their old languages and customs at the behest of the Americanizers; no rush of Germans to smash their beer gardens' fixtures or of Italians to dump their wine into the nearest sewer in response to the prohibitionists' urging—just as there was no stampede to radical ideologies. John Q. Worker learned English to get on in his job and to converse with his children; he joined unions when possible so as to earn more money in fewer hours; he adopted American customs and bought American-style commodities where they seemed superior or were more convenient. But no such act represented a wholesale change in his belief-system or more than an adaptation of his inherited culture.

The basic reason for the inability of the radical movements to effect mass conversions is, I believe, negative: the absence of fertile ground for their messages to grow in. The question is not whether an ideology was "true" or "false." [12] People do not change their basic beliefs and values simply because newly offered ones are "truer" than their old ones, since what is involved are their very identities and the structures of their universes. It is therefore irrelevant to say the radicals' explanations of American society were truer than those of, say, the religious missionaries in the ethnic communities (or vice versa); except for a minority, the proffered explanations never got the chance to be judged truer or less true, for John Q. Worker's own belief-system was psychologically true for him. Until it ceased to be so, the door to his innermost beliefs would not be open to alternatives offered by others.

What is said here concerning John Q. Worker applies as well to his would-be converters—radicals and others. So long as their ways of giving meaning to the reality they perceived "worked" for them, they too would be impervious to alternative gospels. That is why the radicals were convinced that, when John Q. Worker resisted conversion to their belief-system, he was being hoodwinked by the capitalists or priests. To them the radical ideology was self-evident to any sensible and honest person. And they were right, for it *was* self-evident, given *their* perception of society.

The radicals were even less successful in making conversions than their membership statistics imply. The reason is suggested by the well-known fact that radical and reformist fortunes tend to rise in the same periods and fall in the same periods. For instance, the Progressive era, during which millions of Americans supported reforms in all areas of American life, was the time when radicalisms enjoyed their greatest successes. The New Deal period, in which millions of the next generation supported reforms, was the period in which the Communist Party recruited more members than at any other time in its history. The pre–Civil War radical movements coincided in time with the victory of the first reform movement to win control of the government, the Jacksonian Democrats. [13] The most plausible explanation is that most adherents of both reform and radical movements wanted more or less the same changes but that some believed that those changes could not be effected without a basic alteration in the economic or social structure. What defined the radicals was not their opposition to an assortment of evils, since most of the same phenomena were defined as evils by many who were not radical. What distinguished the radicals from the reformers was neither courage, humanitarianism, nor activism, nor in many cases the particular foci of ameliorative effort, but a perception of the social context within which the evils existed. The radicals perceived these evils as existing within a "System" that inevitably caused them, and therefore they worked to abolish the System in order to abolish the evils. In time most of them learned that the desired changes could be or had been brought about without such drastic means, and from the standpoint of some other radicals they then drifted rightward, although in fact their values and objectives remained the same.

Many recruits to the SP, SLP, and IWW obviously fitted this description, for no one knew how flexible the social order would turn out to be and what alterations it could accommodate. For example, most of the Milwaukeeans who elected socialists to governmental office in 1910 did not consider themselves to be voting for socialism or their votes to be a step toward socialism; they were voting against a corrupt administration and for an agenda of social services. And most IWW members judged their officers on the basis of bread-and-butter issues regardless of political beliefs.[14]

In contrast to the members of the radical organizations for whom radicalism was a means to an end that turned out to be reformist, there were what might be called hardcore radicals. These were the people so alienated from their society that they remained radical even after it became clear that specific immediate demands could be satisfied within the current social order. When that happened, they shifted their attention to other grievances. For them the immediate demands were the propaganda and agitational means to the radical objective of revolution. In contrast to the temporary radicals, the hardcore radicals perceived a total society that was iniquitous regardless of the patching up it might be compelled to do. The animus of the temporary radicals was directed at particular injustices and hence at the System they thought responsible for them; the animus of the hardcore radicals was directed at the System and hence at any particular injustices they could find to blame it for. The SLP, which played down immediate demands, included few of the temporary radicals. The SP, which did work for immediate demands, included far more of them. In the IWW, which organized many workers in the hope of converting them later, the overwhelming majority of members were either temporary radicals or not radical at all.

This distinction between the two kinds of radicals should be kept in mind in view of the common assumption that the radicals were articulating John Q. Worker's inchoate beliefs and hopes. But the core of the membership that stayed through the organizations' vicissitudes and provided the leaders and spokesmen had little in common with John Q. Worker. This is especially the case with the SLP; because it insisted on ideological purity and unanimity on all important subjects, an individual had to know and accept the theory when he joined. When he did so, he was articulating not the workers' half-conscious beliefs but a deviant ideology.

If John Q. Worker's culture, rationality, and freedom to choose his leaders are acknowledged, certain explanations commonly offered for the radical movements' failure to convert him—those explanations that focus on the movements' errors—become much less persuasive. For example, it is pointless to say that the SLP failed to recruit millions of workers because De Leon imposed a sectarian line on it, or that the SP failed because it lacked the unity that a correct theory and a strong leadership might have given it, or that the IWW failed because it became identified in the public mind with violence and sabotage, or to offer any such explanation that implies that the organization would have succeeded had opposite conditions prevailed. Why did most party socialists between 1890 and 1899 accept De Leon as chief ideologue? Why did the main socialist party between 1901 and 1919 accept a catholic approach to leadership, tactics, and organization? Why did the revolutionary union engage in rhetoric and behavior that alienated the main body of workers and the public opinion it needed in that particular society? It makes no sense to blame De Leon for the impotence of the SLP after 1890, for its members were as free to repudiate him and his policies as they had been earlier to repudiate capitalism and its parties and leaders. It makes more sense to ask what it was about the socialists' self-image and the circumstances as they perceived them that elevated De Leon to intellectual leadership (he never occupied an official post in the SLP) and kept him there even after the bankruptcy of his and their policies had caused the secession of all the members except those who, for whatever reasons, were attracted to his personality, theories, and tactics. Likewise, in 1919 the vast majority of socialists were as free to choose between remaining in the SP and joining the new Communist Party as they had been in 1901 to choose between the SLP and the new SP, so it is illogical to blame the Communists for the SP's decline after the 1919 split. It is more logical to ask what the difference was between two types of people, equally dedicated to socialist revolution, the one remaining in the SP, the other switching to the CP and accepting all the well-known implications of commitment to a Leninist theory of the party in a western, industrialized, democratic nation.

The SLP membership between 1890 and 1899 did not produce De Leon; he was "there" to be chosen and followed or to be rejected and left isolated in his own imaginary world of perfect logic. Nor could he have imposed himself on the party against the will of most members, as the secessions of the late 1890s and his expulsion from the IWW in 1908 prove. Clearly, then, he satisfied certain needs of the SLP members during the period of his leadership, which ended only with his death in 1914—while as time went on some of them learned from experience, as they thought, and departed, leaving the remaining membership more and more composed of those who, with or without De Leon, saw reality through De Leonist lenses. Similarly, it is illogical—or rather, nearly tautological—to say that the CP could have been more successful if it had been more independent of Moscow; in a period in which several other radical parties existed, the CP was composed of those people who wanted to belong to the type of party that the CP in fact was. As to the IWW, although innumerable workers passed quickly through its ranks, the small core who believed in its revolutionary ideology perceived reality in such a way as to make them certain that the very rhetoric and behavior that isolated the organization and made public opinion indifferent to the government's and vigilantes' persecution after the war began were the means to its inevitable victory.

All the radical movements preached the message "Workers of the United States, unite against your united oppressors!" Yet the radicals themselves could not unite. One can imagine a sympathetic worker hearing the message, "Unite against your common enemy, and follow the vanguard that has the truth and the mission to help you free yourself!" and replying, "Yes, but which truth and which vanguard? I can either do as you say or do as you do; I can't do both." *In theory*, the radicals responded to what they perceived as a unitary reality—the System—by preaching the need for an integrated set of doctrines to explain it and guide those who would change it. *In practice*, they responded to its actual multifariousness by developing an astonishingly broad assortment of theories and tactics.

The interminable wranglings in the organizations' periodicals and conventions were more than the nit-picking of temperamental quarrelers. If the members had little in common but the perception of a System and the conviction that it must and would be overthrown, then the intramovement wranglings turn out to be vitally important. Anyone could say, "I hate capitalism" or "I am working for the proletariat's liberation"; but what lay behind his words? Since Samuel Gompers and other nonradicals used some of the same terms as the radicals, the latter had to add specific tenets to their general commitment and abstract theory. But whenever the question arose of which specific tenets should be added, disagreements ensued. If the radicals could not agree on what revolutionary theory and tactics meant, *i.e.*, what revolutionariness meant, then they did not really agree on what nonrevolutionariness meant either. All the disputes in all three organizations may be seen as attempts to define themselves, to locate the boundaries within which differences of opinion were acceptable and beyond which they were heresy and grounds for expulsion. Concerning specific tenets, the radical organizations' problem was the area of overlap between their beliefs and those of reformers: on any particular issue, did such an area of overlap represent a danger of betrayal of principle or an opportunity for needed contact with John Q. Worker—or both?

It was hard to know what theories and programs opposed capitalism when the capitalists and their ideologues sometimes called each other's theories and programs socialistic. It was hard to differentiate between labor leaders who were "really" agents of the capitalist class and those who were "really" furthering the workers' interests when, for example, some capitalists and some labor leaders opposed an unemployment-insurance law because each believed that its administration would be controlled by the other's agent in the government.[15] The same problem existed within the radicals' own ranks. For example, some advocated an enormous expansion of the government's power to control economic activities; others dreaded what they called "state capitalism" but some of their comrades called "state socialism." On many other questions too, the society's own boundaries between acceptable and unacceptable theories were so blurred as to make it difficult for radicals to locate their own beliefs with reference to them, even though their very mission was defined by opposition to capitalism.

The ensuing chapters will pay little attention to the inter- and intraorganizational disputes except as they relate to the encounter between the radical and John Q. Worker. The latter could not have been much aware of or interested in the factionalism and disputes that used up so much of the organizations' energies. A worker with a taste for doctrinal and organizational wrangling could engage in it to his heart's content in an ethnic society; consequently, even though the radical organizations may have attracted the sort of person who enjoyed such activities, this could not have been his only motive for joining. The fact that ethnic societies were available suggests that—except for the Finns, Jews, and Franco-Belgians, all of which groups contained large radical elements— the working-class converts to radicalism were mavericks who were alienated from their own communities, and that the radical movements were, in part, havens for individual defectors from their cultural communities.[16] With the aforementioned exceptions, American radical organizations have always been groupings of *individuals*, held together either by an iron dogma or by an iron personality or discipline, or not at all; none has been generated by the working class or any sizable portion of it.

Apart from the exceptional ethnic groups mentioned above, the true converts that the radical movements garnered were people whose inherited belief-systems had lost meaning for them as individuals.[17] They, however, expected the working class to follow their lead, and soon. What in this chapter has been referred to as "conversion" they called "awakening." The difference between their thinking and that of the nonradical workers was not, to them, a difference between belief-systems; it was a difference between levels of consciousness along a single continuum analogous to the single continuum of "progress" we find in radical historiography. That is why radical historians have seen

John Q. Worker pretty much as past radicals saw him—and an excellent reason why we should not.

We do not yet have a systematic investigation of how John Q. Worker perceived the radicals as they offered him their alternatives to his beliefs. A beginning has been made in those few studies of ethnic groups that attend to the relationships of radicals to their coethnics.[18] But even the best of these studies pay little attention to John Q. Worker's perception of the radicals. Perhaps the data do not exist. Consequently, that perception can be only guessed at on the basis of indirect evidence, and hypotheses must be offered tentatively.

One thing we cannot assume is that he could have been converted in the same way as the radical missionary had been. The radical did assume this and presented John Q. Worker with the arguments that he thought had been most persuasive at the time he himself had seen the light. (We are, of course, not obliged to believe he understood the process of his own conversion.) He had been converted when the radical organization had offered him what he needed, but there is no reason to assume that John Q. Worker needed it too. The radical's conversion could just as well have manifested his difference from John Q. Worker. The same observation applies to the later radical historians who assume that John Q. Worker really wanted what the radical offered him and would have accepted it if only the right tactics had been used. Such historians are universalizing what they believe to have been their own experience.[19] There is no historical support whatever for the assumption that radicalism is "naturally" appealing to workers or any other category of the population.[20] A movement attracts people who feel the need for what they believe it offers. Most workers in the period 1890–1917 had other needs, needs that were satisfied in terms of the world views *from* which the radical movements were trying to convert them. The reason the radical could not understand how such self-evident arguments as he presented in his propaganda could be rejected is the same as the reason John Q. Worker doubtless could not understand how the radical could reject *his* beliefs. That worker whose world view continued to be functional was not a dupe of bourgeois propaganda; radical periodicals themselves have always joyfully played up evidence that he did not necessarily believe what the capitalists told him or vote as the capitalists bade him to. "Bourgeois" as well as radical beliefs and values need fer-

tile soil or they cannot take root, and, as noted before, a nonradical belief is not *ipso facto* "bourgeois." [21]

VI

On the basis of their perceptions and the general theories that incorporated them, the radicals invented an assortment of organizational structures, secondary theories, and tactics, which they used in various
combinations. Over the years the organizations encountered a variety of
responses from nonradicals and the government ranging all the way
from sympathy to repression. They worked in prosperous times and in
depressions, among native-born Americans and among immigrants, in
extractive and in manufacturing industries, among skilled and unskilled
workers. Yet despite the variety of means they adopted to achieve the
goal that their perceptions and theories told them they would soon
achieve, their predictions never came true. If John Q. Worker had fitted
their image of him, the difficulties they met with in elaborating their
theories and implementing their tactics would have been mere problems. But since those perceptions were inaccurate, those difficulties
were actually dilemmas—that is, they were insoluble.

The radicals did not, of course, perceive their tough choices as dilemmas; if they had they could not have remained radicals. On the one
hand they had to propagate the true doctrine, but on the other they had
to win the confidence and assent of people who disagreed with them.
The vanguard must remain in advance of the army, but not so far in advance as to antagonize or lose contact with it. Should it restrict its message to the milk fit for babes or offer the workers the meat that adults
must have? How much compromise for the sake of gaining a hearing
and adding some recruits would be permissible, and at what point
would it betray principle? Do immediate demands prepare the workers
step by step to demand more and then more, until they are ready to
demand power itself? Or do immediate demands lull them into complacency, leaving them satisfied to accept the half loaf that is better than
none? Does the forcing of a concession weaken the capitalist and
strengthen the workers by eroding the former's power base and giving
the latter a taste of power, or does it strengthen the capitalist by improving his image and weaken the workers by giving them illusions about
their power within the System? Does the election of a radical congress-

man, giving the workers a highly visible spokesman, do more good than the harm it does by making the movement a participant in the System?

These and a host of other choices all involved the question of the effects that the movements' policies would have on John Q. Worker, who must be converted by the millions. The radicals never doubted that the answers were "there" to be discovered and that the implementation of the right policy would bring millions of recruits and then power. From one point of view, the several radical organizations can be regarded as embodiments of the several alternatives. And the fate of each elucidates the consequences of the rejection of the alternative it rejected. For example, on the first question asked above, the SLP chose the "left" horn and the SP the "right" horn of the dilemma of purity versus popularity and meat versus milk. Other alternatives were exemplified in other combinations in the three movements under study.[22] The thesis offered here is that there was no "right" policy, the adoption of which would have spelled success—or rather that in several cases both alternatives were "right" and yet mutually exclusive.

Some radical movements switched their choices in different periods. Others remained impaled on one or the other horn of one or more dilemmas; all together they provide evidence that this sort of predicament was unavoidable regardless of how astute their leaders were, how "correct" their tactics were, and how tolerant the society and government were.[23] If one sets oneself an impossible task and then encounters problems in the attempt to accomplish it, one will not see those problems as evidence of the incorrectness of one's starting assumptions unless one is willing to give them up. The more important the assumptions are to one's self-identification, the more likely one is to assume that the defeats are temporary and due to corrigible errors or adventitious causes. The radicals' contentiousness within their own organizations was due in part to their putting some of the blame for their defeats on their own tactics. Ironically, they were in this respect too self-critical, or, more often, too critical of other radicals, for many of those tactics had been well chosen—*in the light of their devisers' perceptions of John Q. Worker.*

The radical organizations each had two self-imposed functions that canceled each other out so long as John Q. Worker retained his nonradical belief-system. The IWW was a union, but also a revolutionary organization. The SLP and SP were political parties, but also revolutionary organizations. John Q. Worker was happy to accept Wobbly leadership in a strike and even to belong to the IWW during and for a time after the strike, but he quit when the second function impaired the first. He was willing to vote for a revolutionary party when he thought it could get him a spokesman in government or a municipal administration that provided more social services, but not when he thought he had a better chance to get them by voting for another party. In other words, the apparent successes that the radical organizations enjoyed occurred only where the goals of both John Q. Worker and the radicals happened to require the same means. To the radicals their organizations' functions were not just to win the aforementioned improvements but also to radicalize their own members and constituents and eventually demonstrate how limited in value those improvements were. But this conversion was merely a means to their long-range function of revolutionizing American society.

One category of dilemmas pertained to the organizations' functions. If the IWW was to be a functioning labor union, it had to recruit mostly nonradical workers who would join for the same reasons they would join any union: to obtain higher wages, better working conditions, and shorter hours. Yet the IWW's long-range revolutionary objective repeatedly hampered the realization of the short-range goals. Although it could sometimes lead successful strikes, it could be a revolutionary organization or a union, but not both. And in the long run it could not succeed in being either, so long as it tried to be both. If the SLP or SP was to be a functioning political party, it had to give the voters reason to vote for it, and that meant it had to participate in the American political system and be attractive to far more voters than it could recruit as committed radicals. Yet its long-range revolutionary objective conflicted with the grounds on which its electoral popularity must be based. Although it might win offices here and there, it could be a revolutionary organization or a functioning component of the American party system, but not both. And in the long run it could not succeed in being either, so long as it tried to be both. These dilemmas found expression in theory, or, to be more precise, in attempts to elaborate the basic revolutionary doctrines, to justify whichever horn of the functional dilemma an organization chose at a given time and to demonstrate in theory that the decision would help the organization to attain its ultimate goal.

A second category of dilemmas pertained to tactics. A peculiarity of this category is that the organizations' ultimate failure was due not to the failure of any particular tactic but in part to its success, for the successful implementation of one tactic was the rejection of its opposite in a situation that required the successful implementation of both. For example, a radical organization had to be faithful to its basic theory and at the same time get recruits en masse; its theory included the reasons why it needed the millions of recruits, but the same theory proved unappealing to them. The organization could succeed in being either pure or popular, but it had to be both pure and popular. Similarly with other tactical choices, such as (for the SP and SLP) the question whether to bore from within the existing unions or to found competing unions that accepted radical doctrine. It could play up "immediate demands"—mostly demands made by reformers—in the hope of teaching people attracted by them that such demands could not be met without revolution (thus predicting the failure of their own efforts to win the demands), or it could concentrate on the ultimate demand for socialism. The organization could, by its indictment of capitalism for creating injustices so sweeping that they corrupted even the most intimate aspects of workers' lives, imply that socialism would change even those aspects—the "private sphere." Or it could assure potential converts that socialism would change only the "public sphere"—economic and political relations. The former tactic would arouse apprehension; the latter would contradict the movement's sweeping indictment of capitalism. Each of these tactical choices (and many others) reflected the radical leaders' temperaments, but each was given legitimacy by theories that attempted to show how it derived necessarily from the fundamental tenets on the one hand and the need to win millions of recruits on the other.

Let us examine a brief sample of these dilemmas in action.

First, consider the Wobblies' refusal to sign contracts with employers. This was not a tactic but a principle derived from the organization's function. It is significant that this most purely negative of all the IWW's tenets was also one of the few on which Wobblies agreed.[24] Their bond seems to have been purely negative, an overwhelming hostility to the System and to unions that played by its rules.[25] As "Big Bill" Haywood put it:

Agreements with capitalists are the death warrants of labor. . . . An agreement between the capitalist class and the working class is an unholy alliance, and when entered into by any body of workingmen it removes them from their class and the class struggle and makes them auxiliaries of the enemy of labor. When the soldier enlists he enters into an agreement to fight the battles of the capitalist class and shoot down his fellow workers. When the trade unionists sign an agreement with the capitalist class, they likewise enlist to furnish the soldiers with guns, with food and with clothing. They are the enlisted men behind the man behind the gun.[26]

Haywood's military metaphor shows that the basic function of the IWW was the permanent mobilization of the workers to wage the class war. But most workers had no intention of enlisting in a permanent confrontation with their bosses; they wanted what contracts could obtain. They joined IWW unions or called in Wobbly organizers when they thought that by so doing they could win those objectives. Their goals and those of the IWW were worlds apart. The Wobblies' few successes occurred in two situations: where the divergent goals temporarily required the same means, and where the Wobblies acted like ordinary union organizers (as in the Agricultural Workers' Organization, which dealt with conditions far different from those in other industries[27]). If those successes were to be made permanent, however, workers by the millions would have had to abandon their goals and adopt the Wobblies'. But regardless of how the workers might have altered their beliefs or aspirations in the course of IWW-led strikes, their enlistment in permanent class warfare was a statistical impossibility. The people who are willing to so enlist are a small minority in any society.

Edwin Fenton's lucid description of the rise and fall of the IWW's prestige among Italian workers in the Northeast makes it clear that the revolutionary function of the IWW clashed with the prerequisites for long-term leadership of the workers whom the AFL had ignored. Between 1910 and 1913, Italian Wobblies undertook a large number of organizing campaigns, all of which collapsed after some initial successes. By the start of 1914, the IWW "was no longer a force to be reckoned with among the Italians in the United States." Fenton's mention of that year shows that wartime repression did not destroy the Wobblies among the Italian-Americans or, presumably, among other groups; the organization's prior decline had already isolated it and made it vulnerable to persecution.[28]

The conflict of functional principle with the conditions for success was especially glaring in a barbers' strike in New York City in 1913. The employers' association in Brooklyn agreed to the demands of the IWW-led union. When the Wobbly leader, Leonardo Frisina, signed the contract, he was suspended by the IWW's national officials in Chicago. They appointed others to continue leading the strikers, and these new leaders decided to stay out. The rank and file refused, and Frisina withdrew his local from the IWW. The parent organization's subsequent tactics among the New York barbers soon discredited it entirely.[29] This result was not due to dogmatism or stupidity on the part of the national leaders. Given the IWW's very reason for being, they were perfectly right in suspending Frisina, for the only alternative was to do what he in fact did—obey his constituents' wishes and thus transform the union into one that was conventional in function but contained radicals.[30]

Wobblies argued that when workers signed a contract they were not really free agents; economic need coerced them. Consequently the contract was not binding and they were free to break it whenever they chose. The working class must organize, as the capitalist class was organized. "Why tinker and hesitate and compromise," asked *Solidarity*, "when all we need to put complete power in our hands is organization? . . . Why make contracts with bosses when industrial organization will enable us to dictate terms?"[31] Perhaps so, but as several historians have shown and as many contemporaries knew well, in most localities it was difficult or impossible to organize unskilled workers under the circumstances then prevailing. The AFL certainly neglected many organizable workers, but the Wobblies' ephemeral successes prove only the workers' desire to organize, not their ability to do so in the absence of financial resources and government support. The exertion of working-class power en masse would indeed depend on organization, but that organization in turn must follow a period of contract-signing, union recognition, and the regularization of labor relations. The no-contract principle thus conflicted with John Q. Worker's needs at the time. It was appropriate only to a revolutionary situation, a war in which all was fair because power alone counted. Wobbly theory in effect required the workers to wield power before they possessed it.[32]

Corresponding to the IWW's dilemma growing out of the no-contract principle was the socialist parties' dilemma growing out of their having to win political victories without at the same time legitimizing the "capitalists' government." The SLP evaded this dilemma by adopting policies that insured that its candidates would never get elected. The SP took the opposite path from the IWW and SLP, freely entering into the sort of relations with the enemy that were the political analogue of union contracts. The result was that, just as the Wobblies' no-contract principle exposed the revolutionary horn of the functional dilemma, the SP's acceptance of political office exposed the antirevolutionary horn. The municipal administrations of socialists in Milwaukee and elsewhere were indistinguishable from those of reformers; what else could they have been? The socialists never intended to demonstrate that the "bourgeois state" could be administered more efficiently and honestly than the "bourgeois parties" had been administering it. An analogous fate would have befallen the Wobblies if they had dropped their no-contract principle. In fact it did in those few situations where the IWW signed contracts and behaved like a regular, nonrevolutionary union (the only alternative), thereby showing that the only thing that functionally distinguished it from nonrevolutionary industrial unions was the no-contract principle, which by no coincidence was the one item in the IWW's practical program that John Q. Worker rejected.

On the level of specific tactics the chief dilemma that the two socialist parties encountered—although they assumed it to be a soluble problem—pertained to their proper attitude toward the unions. The SLP chose the left and the SP the right horn of this dilemma. The SLP contended that the revolutionary party and the unions were the two arms of a single working-class movement and should be organically related, whereas the SP adopted a neutral policy toward the unions, its individual members working within them to radicalize their members and influence leaders' policies. Since this topic has been discussed at length by historians, it may be omitted here in favor of one that has not received as much attention: the dilemma resulting from the party's choice whether to attract as many recruits and votes as possible or to remain as doctrinally pure and "correct" as possible, and whether to agitate for immediate demands. To represent John Q. Worker's beliefs and aspirations and at the same time function as his advance guard, the party would have to convert him. But how should it function before mass conversions had taken place? Like the IWW, the SP encountered its functional dilemma as a result not of its failures but of its successes. And like the IWW's, the SP's functional dilemma was due fundamentally to John Q. Worker's insistence on choosing his own means to his own goals. His means, but not his goals, sometimes overlapped the SP's, and he helped elect over a thousand socialists to office in municipalities and state legislatures. If the SP or SLP had implemented a policy corresponding to the IWW's no-contract policy, it would not have run any candidates for office, because in doing so it was taking risks that the Wobblies usually spared themselves: not only the risk of "corrupting" their own members but also that of giving a false message to John Q. Worker—that the "bourgeois state" was legitimate. The SLP's electoral campaigns were largely educational; it was the SP, which won so many offices, that had to face the issue.

To engage in reformist propaganda so as to win votes was to create a danger to the organization: the more such propaganda attracted sympathy for the party, the more recruits it would receive who were not really socialists, and the more these members would push the party in a reformist direction. Advocacy of reform proposals and efforts to win public office created a theoretical problem as well. The SP's theory postulated that political power was indivisible because it was merely the economic power of the capitalist class expressed politically. Yet the SP's activities as a bona fide political party implied the opposite. This contradiction became glaring when party members became mayors and city councilors, for the excellent administrations they ran disproved their own theory and they instituted, within the capitalist System, important reforms that party ideologists contended were impossible. They could, of course, argue that the all-powerful capitalists permitted such changes because they were unimportant. Yet the advocacy of such "unimportant" reforms was what had brought the votes—the votes of people to whom the reforms were important. If the radicals had told John Q. Worker, "The capitalists allow reforms that not only leave their System intact but also cement your loyalty to it," he could have replied, "Then so be it; I *am* loyal to it, because those reforms—not socialism—are what

I'm after." He might, in turn, have asked them, "If these reforms are so unimportant, why have so many capitalists and their supporters opposed them instead of leading the fight for them? Does 'the System' have a mind, conscious of 'its' interests, separate from the minds of flesh-and-blood people?"

But could not the socialists have agitated for immediate demands that could not be satisfied within the System and thus helped teach John Q. Worker that the attainment of his goals required a revolution? The answer is given in the fact that the immediate demands in the SLP's "municipal programs," even after the national party dropped them from its platform, were similar to those of the Milwaukee Social Democratic Party when it won power.[33] If there had been immediate demands that were impossible for the System to concede, De Leon would have found them. He thought he had; neither he nor most other socialists believed many of them could be met by the System. Yet, as was pointed out before, the defining tenets of the radicals, those that distinguished them from all reformers, did not include specific reforms; what defined the radicals was their certainty that no substantial improvements in the workers' conditions could occur within the capitalist System. The SLP's decision not to press for them, however, suggests it was not so sure after all. At any rate, immediate demands were by definition those that non-radical workers would support. Supposedly those workers would learn, in the course of struggling for them, to demand what the System could not yield. Radical parties are still assuring themselves that this is so.

The SLP demonstrated the inevitable consequence of the alternative policy. Expecting objective circumstances to bring the recruits in droves, it endeavored to be the sort of revolutionary vanguard that could then lead them in the fulfillment of their historic mission. It made certain that its differences from "bourgeois" parties remained sharp and its theory far "in advance" of John Q. Worker's beliefs. It alone of the three organizations escaped the functional and hence tactical dilemmas created by contact with the unconverted workers and by the choice of "popularity" over "purity."[34] In other words, its theory rarely crashed against the consequences of practice.

Some historians have argued that the SP succeeded since almost all its immediate demands have been enacted or have been met in other ways. These historians are mistaking tactics for ultimate goals. On the contrary, the "success" of the SP as a political party—if we can assume that its agitation and propaganda contributed to it—was its failure as a revolutionary organization. And the SLP's success in remaining a consistently pure revolutionary organization was its failure as a political party.

In short, the IWW could have been an effective union or a consistently revolutionary organization, although to achieve its goal it had to be both; and the socialist parties could have been effective political parties or consistently revolutionary organizations, although to achieve their goal they had to be both. The irony is not merely that their double function caused their double failure but that any success they had in fulfilling one function defeated their efforts to fulfill the other. These facts are essential to an evaluation of the revolutionary theories that the radicals were convinced were scientific, theories that assigned them their historic role of the workers' vanguard and that gave them the ability (they thought) to predict the future of their society. All these aspects of their theories—scientism, vanguardism, and the ability to predict[35]—included theories about John Q. Worker and required an accurate perception of his thinking. Yet they had been formulated aprioristically, without reference to the real John Q. Worker, and it was the gap between the abstraction they called The Worker and the real John Q. Worker that, in the final analysis, defeated them.

Section 1

Approaches to the Study of American Radicalism

Celui qui fait au peuple de fausses légendes révolutionnaires, celui qui l'amuse d'histoires chantantes, est aussi criminel que le géographe qui dresserait des cartes menteuses pour les navigateurs.

Prosper Olivier Lissagaray, *Histoire de la commune de 1871* (1876)

II The Ghost of Werner Sombart

If a fortune-teller had told Werner Sombart in 1905 that seventy-odd years later historians would still be asking his question—*Why Is There No Socialism in the United States?*—he would have snorted in disbelief, not merely because he probably did not believe in fortune-telling but because he expected the question to become obsolete within a generation.[1] Yet in 1971 a historian reviewing the literature on American socialism felt obliged to refer to "this now perennial question."[2]

Sombart's own answers were the American worker's high standard of living and the freedom and equality of American society. Later writers, sometimes referring to Sombart and sometimes not, have added other "causes" for the American worker's nonconversion to socialism. Writing in 1952, Communist leader William Z. Foster listed the absence of a feudal tradition; the ethnic, cultural, and religious heterogeneity of the working class; the frontier safety-valve; the upward mobility of some workers and middle-class aspirations of many others; the shortage of labor throughout most of the country's history; and the existence of a labor aristocracy. Marc Karson in 1958 added the influence of the Roman Catholic Church.[3] Twelve years later a scholarly summary of the arguments listed fifteen factors.[4]

Even before Sombart published his essay a prominent American socialist, Ernest Untermann, cited the factors that were to become the standard "obstacles" to the radicalization of the American working class, but he used them to predict that the United States would soon lead the world in overthrowing capitalism. American workers are, he wrote, "unencumbered by any fossil remains of feudal superstitions," whereas in England "the grand advance of the proletariat . . . meets obstacles unknown in the United States. The time-hallowed traditions of the nobility and the Grace-of-God kingdom, the emigration of the independent and aggressive workers, the absence of universal suffrage" were among the reasons why "it is safe to predict . . . that socialism in the United States, though at present considerably behind the march of industrial evolution, will shortly out-distance the proletarian movement of all other countries." He even anticipated, while reversing, the by-now customary inclusion of ethnic heterogeneity among the critical factors: "While much more heterogeneous elements are peacefully co-operating in the United States, under the leadership of the Anglo-Saxon race, they are fighting each other tooth and nail in the Austrian Reichstag, and all of them fight the luckless Jews. The socialists are the only ones who successfully unite all the different races in one political party."[5]

The *International Socialist Review*, which published Untermann's essay, delightedly printed Sombart's first chapters in English translation a few years later. But when the editor realized that Sombart was emphasizing the Americans' high standard of living, he refused to print the remaining installments. Sombart himself, wrote editor Algie M. Simons, had pointed out that even in prosperous times not fewer than ten million people in the United States lived below the poverty line, at least four million of them on public assistance, yet Sombart did not even try to reconcile these facts with his statement that "on roast-beef and apple-pie were all Socialistic Utopias ruined."[6]

Both in Untermann's time and later, speculations about the relations of socialism to poverty, mobility, ethnic heterogeneity, broad suffrage, and so on have included mutually exclusive theories. Extreme poverty deadens hope or it makes workers desperate enough to revolt; upward mobility creates rising expectations unfulfillable within capitalism or it fosters petty-bourgeois values; ethnic cohesiveness divides the working class or it creates a supportive milieu for militancy; broad suffrage engenders illusions about the popular base of government in a capitalist country or its fruitlessness tears away the last illusion; and so on through the entire list of "factors" allegedly accounting for the non-radicalism of the American working class. The literature on this subject illustrates the *post hoc ergo propter hoc* fallacy: the American working class is not radical; certain characteristics prevail among the American working class; ergo, those characteristics, whatever they are, account for its nonradicalism.

At issue here is not the adequacy of these answers to Sombart's question but the implications of the question. If a question has been asked repeatedly for over seventy years without evoking answers that satisfy historians specializing in the field—if they did the question would not keep being re-asked—it is reasonable to wonder if something is wrong with the question itself. True, philosophers have been asking, for a good deal longer than seventy years, about the existence of God and salvation, and about free will versus determinism. But the former question is by nature unanswerable by means of logic and evidence, and the latter is a true antinomy. Sombart's is, in form, an empirical question ostensibly answerable by means of evidence concerning the American workers' belief-systems. It is all the more remarkable, therefore, that, as John Laslett has pointed out, not much basic research on the workers' attitudes toward socialism has yet been done.[7]

The following discussion will argue that the Sombartian approach (a shorthand expression that should not be construed as applying only to those writers who refer to Sombart) is, first, counterfactual and tautological; second, a hindrance to inquiry into the etiology of socialists' belief in socialism; third, teleological; fourth, antihistorical; and fifth, reductionist. I do not contend that these implications of the Sombartian approach are logically entailed by it; rather, a survey of the literature suggests that they are tendencies more or less common among writers in this tradition. These tendencies are most apparent in writers on the left, but some nonradical historians too have addressed the problem of American workers' nonradicalism in these terms.[8] Those who regard the Sombartian "factors" merely as helping to create a situation in which American workers had no positive reason to be dissatisfied with their belief-systems (a different thing from having no reason to be dissatisfied with their circumstances) do not display the tendencies enumerated; in their explanations those "factors" play the negative role of preventing a situation from arising in which people's world views are felt to contradict experience. The various elements in the workers' cultures and world views that commonly appear as Sombartian factors hindering radicalization can be seen in this way only in the sense that they were also obstacles to an indefinite number of other alternatives to these workers' belief-systems.

The first and most obvious assumption in the Sombartian approach is that if the workers' standard of living had been lower, if the working class had been more homogeneous, if one or more of the other suggested "obstacles" to socialist conviction had been absent, the American workers would have become socialists in large numbers, as European workers supposedly have done.[9] This assumption is contrary to historians' mode of understanding the past on both the methodological and empirical levels. The methodological error can be seen in pure form in the charmingly naïve statement by an undergraduate in a term paper written in 1975 at Boston University: "Ideally, it [the advent of socialism] should have happened and America should be a Socialist nation today," if it had not been for an assortment of "obstacles" listed by historians. Here we find in blatant form what is generally obscured by abstruse reasoning, wage-movement indexes, labor-union-structural analyses, and other complications: the interpretation of historical change in terms of its conformity with or deviation from an ideal in the minds of a small minority, including some historians who do not consider themselves socialists yet regard socialism as the natural belief-system for workers in advanced capitalist societies.

The *reductio ad absurdum* of this contrary-to-fact-conditional proposition is implied in a recent survey, by a political scientist, of the "obstacles," a survey that by its very completeness suggests the flaw in the whole approach. The article lists *twenty-eight* such obstacles and implies there are even more.[10] They very nearly amount to the statement that, given sufficient reasons to believe in socialism, people will believe in socialism. For if more than twenty-eight factors (the opposite of the more than twenty-eight obstacles) must be present for socialism to spread among the working class, then what can the socialist ideology be but the ideology that might be prevalent among the working class if those more than twenty-eight factors were present? But then what sense does it make to ask why the American workers have not turned to socialism, as though such conversion were the normal and expectable thing? How could it be the normal and expectable ideology of the working class in advanced capitalist society if more than a score of factors *in addition to* that class's proletarian status must be present for the mass conversion to take place? Socialists have never said, "Socialism will win over the working class provided *x* number of factors are present." They have always said, "Socialism will win over the working class owing to the development of capitalism and its inherent contradictions." These two statements can be reconciled only by a third, such as: "The development of capitalism and its inherent contradictions will eliminate all the obstacles to and create all the conditions for the conversion of the working class." Obviously, any solution of the problem must be put in the future tense, resorting to prophecy on the basis of a priori assumptions. It cannot avoid making all the aspects of social life and thought, which form the content of the "obstacles," mere epiphenomena of the economic structure of society—or, to use the Marxist term, superstructural—having only limited and temporary autonomy. Long-range prophecy and reductionism often go together.

The Sombartian approach seems best suited to an ideal world uncontaminated by real life, a world in which workers define themselves solely by their economic relation to the means of production and waste no time with such nonsense as religion, ethnicity, family, and community; in which the capitalist class is a monolithic, rational exploiting machine; and in which there is no middle class or tradition or history. Perhaps in such a society the working class would be solidly socialist—or perhaps not: Plato for one, portrayed the heaven of archetypes in other terms.[11] If roast beef and apple pie, the frontier, ethnic variety, mobility, the absence of a feudal heritage, and other "obstacles" to the acceptance of socialist theory do exist and have a degree of autonomy, despite that theory's inability to accommodate them, then perhaps the simplest comment that can be made is that that theory cannot accommodate reality. Socialist theory, however, not only purports to explain social phenomena but also predicts its own acceptance by the "masses." Hence the way out of the tautology is via prophecy of the future radicalization of the American working class, for the future is a secular philosopher's alternative to the heaven of archetypes.

Sombart in 1905, William Z. Foster in 1952, and others on the left who have speculated on why the American working class had not (yet) become radicalized generally predicted it would be very soon. Since they were wrong, perhaps they also misinterpreted those "obstacles" to socialist consciousness that they perceived in their own day. Their approach implies that the reasons why socialism has not yet arrived are less "real" than the reasons why it "should have" arrived. Suppose a movement has for the past century preached that it was inevitable that the great mass of people would come to see the truth of numerology and that some historians have written the history of the United States in terms of the question, "Why have the mass of Americans not come to believe in numerology?" The reader would see at once that something is wrong with the question, for the questioner assumes that the reasons he offers, why most Americans have not accepted numerology, treat Americans' actual beliefs only within that frame of reference and thereby place elements of culture, belief, and institutions in counterfactual relations with one another. The analogy does not suggest that the reason most American workers have not converted to socialism or numerology is that either is wrong; after all, all people in all periods have sometimes held erroneous beliefs. It is meant to call attention to hidden assumptions in the mind of the inquirer about people's beliefs.

If a historian takes for granted that an unsuccessful radical movement was a true vanguard—a partial embodiment of the future and a pointer of the way to it—then he is apt to study its ideology and tactics with reference to the "obstacles" to its success, and to see those obstacles as bad or based on false ideology to the same degree as the radical objective and ideology are good and true. But this approach is an obstacle to the accurate perception of what is thus defined. That historian's ideological bent encourages him to measure reality against a theoretical yardstick that, although relevant to him, was irrelevant to or nonexistent among his subjects. If one asked that historian why his conceptual framework is better than any other, he would likely reply in terms of his own values: that all historians select their subjects and their data from the unmanageably large mass available, that his selection is no less true than that of another historian, and that his partial selection is the one that serves "some present human need" and helps to show "what we must do to attain [sic] it."[12] But insofar as he substitutes the meanings that are important to him and his interests for those that were important to his subjects and their interests, his portrayal of the latter is false and ahistorical. As to the efficacy of a picture of the past in inspiring or mobilizing radical behavior in the present, myths perform this function effectively. If, alternatively, one evaluates historical hypotheses according to their explanatory power and frames questions in such a way as to help him discover his subjects' meanings, there is less danger that the questions will contain built-in assumptions that will distort the meaning of the data.

The biasing assumption in the present instance is that socialist belief is the norm for workers in advanced capitalist countries. (This proposition is sometimes accompanied by the proviso that a Marxist party be present to disseminate it.) It is stated frankly by William Z. Foster, who with a naïveté matching that of the aforementioned undergraduate, entitled his list of answers to Sombart's question (although he does not mention Sombart) "Factors Retarding the Ideological Development of the Workers."[13] The workers, in other words, have not had true ideologies different from that of the socialists. What is necessary is not that they change their minds but that they be "developed."

If the workers' beliefs and values are essentially negative—if the workers are either asleep or infected by bourgeois ideology—it is not surprising to discover that each of the "obstacles" is really the reverse of some element in the writer's own ideal paradigm of industrial capitalism. Upward mobility, for example, is the opposite of the tenet that the proletariat is fixed in its propertyless status, living only to produce surplus value for the bourgeoisie; ethnic heterogeneity is the reverse of the ideal depiction of the working class as having no country and self-defined by its economic status; and so on. Not one of the "obstacles" is the result of research into the actual process of attitude- and belief-formation and change. Every one of them has come out of the writers' own assumptions as to what should cause a worker to become a socialist.

The metaphor of "awakening"—the assumption that socialist belief is the norm and the workers' actual beliefs and values are exceptions or abnormal or inferior—points to a second characteristic of writings in this tradition: they never study the etiology of socialists' belief in socialism. Logic, at least, is on the side of these writers. If socialism is what a worker should believe in, if workers who believe otherwise are asleep or ideologically undeveloped, not only is there no point in accounting for a socialist's belief in socialism, but an investigation into its origin must be morally suspect, implying that the belief had causes and motives other than possession of the facts and a devotion to the people's interests.

This attitude was exemplifed innumerable times during the heyday of the New Left, when attempts to account for the sudden upsurge of radicalism among young people so often met with the impatient response that the Vietnam war, poverty, and oppression were its only causes—as though no one but radicals opposed war, poverty, and oppression or worked to end them to the extent possible. Those who answered in this way were in effect likening the mind to a window that is either clear or obstructed by ideological dirt; if it is clear, then the obvious facts and correct values shine through, unconditioned by culture and personality structure. The connection between this assumption and some historians' denigration of past workers' ethnicity, religion, and culture as "obstacles" to their radicalization is obvious. The alternative is not necessarily cultural relativism but can merely include the insistence that all belief, true and false, is conditioned by culture and personality structure. In sum, a fallacy implicit in the Sombartian approach is the image of the mind as a tabula rasa, the ignoring of the cultural matrix of all beliefs and values, including those of radicals.

Of the many similarities between radical and Progressive historiography, one is germane here: Robert Skotheim has noted that the Progressive historians never investigated the etiology of those events and situations in American history that they approved of, but probed the sources of only those they disapproved of. To Vernon L. Parrington, liberal ideas were currents, whereas illiberal ideas were barriers, reefs, chill winds.[14] The Sombartian approach to American working-class history epitomizes this attitude. Historians in that tradition never ask, "Why did the socialists believe in socialism?" but always ask, "Why did the workers *not* believe in socialism?" The attitude that prevents the asking of the first question sets the terms in which the answers to the second are sought.

For example, one sophisticated radical counterpart of Parrington is Melvyn Dubofsky, who, in trying to refute Vernon Jensen's accusation that his study of the IWW, *We Shall Be All*, is teleological, in fact confirms it. He attempted to show, he writes, "how class lines were blurred by ethnicity and by certain pre-industrial community values. The book is in fact an account of why recurrent conflict failed to result in what, for want of a better term, can be labelled Marxian class consciousness. Never do I portray American workers as ripe for revolution; indeed I do quite the reverse. I indicate how the explosive situation which might have resulted from working-class consciousness was defused by employers and public officials. *We Shall Be All* is a history of radicalism domesticated and occasionally repressed." [15] It will be noted that ethnicity blunted class consciousness, not that class consciousness blunted ethnicity (in fact, both statements have at times been true); class is the norm, ethnicity the obstacle, along with ruling-class repression. Further, class consciousness is explicitly equated with radicalism, notwithstanding the hardly obscure refutation of this equation in the person of Samuel Gompers as well as other labor leaders who figure largely in the history books and were strongly class conscious but not socialists. Jensen's point is sufficiently proven by the contrary-to-fact formulations "failed to result" and "might have resulted" in Dubofsky's reply, for its context shows he does not consider the other possible results.

The third implication of the Sombartian approach can be seen if we relocate the little word *not* in the two questions asked above: suppose one asks, "Why did John Q. Worker believe in his belief-system?" and "Why did those socialists who had grown up within John Q. Worker's milieu *not* believe as John Q. Worker did?" I am not advocating the Sombartian approach with the terms reversed, the positing of John Q. Worker's belief-system as the norm by which the socialist's must be measured and in terms of which it must be accounted for, or a preference of one over the other as truer. Rather I suggest that a historian who brackets his own beliefs and who approaches both John Q. Worker's and the radical's world views as clusters of attitudes, beliefs, and values that were meaningful to real people in real situation is far more likely to ask questions that can be answered, as Sombart's question cannot, and in so doing discover new truths about American history, as Sombartianism cannot.

One reason it cannot is that it substitutes teleology for historiography. In the Sombartian frame of reference, John Q. Worker's world view occupies a status somewhat like that of evil in orthodox Christian theology—a relative subtraction from the Good and never, on pain of excommunication, to be regarded as ontologically real. The socialist was John Q. Worker as he would be in the future. The socialist himself perceived

John Q. Worker in that light, and the Sombartian historian tends to perceive the John Q. Worker of a past generation through the eyes of the socialists living at the same time. His religion and culture; his beliefs about society, the state, and his job; and his attitudes toward family, sex, and authority can be studied in terms of their meanings to John Q. Worker or ignored as so many obstacles to his awakening by the socialist missionary. In fact the more fully a historian looks at the past through Sombartian eyes, the less attention he gives to such beliefs and attitudes. Old Left historians, for example, never attend to them at all; immigration, religion, family structure, recreational activities, and the like are mentioned, if at all, either as irrational holdovers from the prebourgeois past or as blinders imposed by the capitalists and their agents. The holdovers will wither away or be transformed appropriately, because in the long run consciousness reflects being; the blinders will be torn off by the propaganda and agitation of the vanguard. If that vanguard in the past had no need to study those constituents of John Q. Worker's belief-systems *and their meaning to John Q. Worker*, neither does the Sombartian historian today.

Here is a statement written in 1913 by a leader of the IWW, atypical only in its explicitness: "What still remains in the minds of mankind, as a force for separate nationalities," wrote William E. Trautmann, "is merely imaginary. A heavy load of traditional falsehoods, holding living human beings in a bondage of ignominious, deep-rooted, and ingeniously fostered intellectual, and hence also in industrial, serfdom, must disappear; national separation must be swept aside by the advancing forces of international co-operation." [16] Ethnicity is thus not natural but is ingeniously fostered by clever exploiters among (obviously) passively receptive workers. If the former did not foster it, it would go away by itself, with a little help from socialists and Wobblies. Almost forty years later William Z. Foster listed the "Factors Making for Class Consciousness," which warranted his declaration that "today . . . the foregoing factors, hindering the development of class-consciousness and a Socialist perspective among the workers, have either wholly disappeared or are on the eve of so doing." The second of his five factors was that "the working class is swiftly becoming more homogeneous. The immigrant masses have largely learned the English language and domestic customs; the second and third generations of their descendants, while not ignoring their national backgrounds, are quite American; and the Negro and white workers are developing a real solidarity in organizations and action."[17] The expression "while not ignoring their national backgrounds" seems to be purely formal, for homogeneity is clearly Foster's ideal; presumably the respect paid to national background will consist of cuisine, folk dances, and the commemoration of proletarian heroes in the Old Country.

What is true and important, for both Trautmann and Foster, is not what was but what is to be; whatever is to be swept into the dustbin of history need not be studied. Since ethnicity and religion are doomed to disappear, such histories contain no statistics about membership in ethnic societies and in churches but pay minute attention to the numbers of those who voted for radical candidates or belonged to radical organizations. For example, the 760,000 subscribers to the socialist *Appeal to Reason* in 1913 are accorded great significance whereas the million subscribers to the anti-Catholic *Menace* in 1914 are ignored, presumably because they represented an ephemeral phenomenon.[18] Even if the *Appeal to Reason*'s brand of socialism had not been an ephemeral phenomenon, the fact remains that the juxtaposition of these contemporaneous statistics evokes more significant questions about the state of American society just before World War I than either of them alone. A historian must limit his scope if he is to write a book at all, but the facts omitted must not be of the sort that the omission of them distorts the meaning of those that are included.

Hidden within the teleological style of historiography is a perception of society as an organism developing or evolving according to "laws" that work more or less like a genetic program. It is not teleological to predict that an acorn will at length produce an oak rather than a tulip. But there are two reasons why it is teleological to say, as some historians do, that the expectable or natural consequence of nonrevolutionary strikes is their participants' radicalization or to make any of the other predictions common in the Sombartian tradition. The first reason is statistical: the simple mass of historical data about strikes and the consensus of scholarly study of the causes of mass radicalization where it has occurred. The second reason is that the organic metaphor for society has never been successfully sustained despite centuries of effort to liken society to a human being who is born, matures, and dies in accordance with his innate nature. The ultimate test of such a theory is its power to predict, and the fate of the many predictions made by Marxists and non-Marxist radicals has been discussed too frequently to require repetition here. It will suffice to note that teleology discourages a study of the specific historical circumstances that gave rise to the specific ebbs and flows of radicalism in the course of American history.[19]

The fourth implication of the Sombartian approach is a corollary of the third: if John Q. Worker's beliefs, values, and relationships have meaning only as evidence of his unenlightenment, their meaning to him is irrelevant and can be ignored. Hence, in this genre of historiography, we never find investigations of the *relationships among* these things, for that is where their meaning is to be found. Consider Foster's list of retarding "factors": each is given a numbered paragraph, and the entire section is followed by another, entitled "Factors Making for Class Consciousness," in which each numbered factor is disposed of in a sentence showing it is withering away "today" (1952). In neither section are the factors—the workers' religion, aspirations, cultural heritage, and so on—related to one another. In short, their meaning in Foster's teleological frame of reference is substituted for their meaning in John Q. Worker's mind. One is therefore not startled to discover, in this type of history, that the motives attributed to John Q. Worker are sorted into two categories: when he fights his boss he is acting autonomously and starting to wake up, but when he goes to church, dominates his wife, joins an ethnic choral society, refuses to work alongside a black, and votes for Bryan, he is not only responding to the influence of the capitalists and their agents but doing so discretely in each instance. His churchgoing is due to the delusory authority of his priest; his vote for Bryan is due to illusions about the two-party system; his racism is due to divide-and-conquer propaganda by the capitalists; his sexism is due to cultural lag; and so on. The elements do not give meaning to one another, do not add up to a world view. Documents surviving from past radical movements contain innumerable evidences that one source of the socialist's feeling of superiority is his conviction that his theory not only explains every thing but also explains how everything is related to everything else. The socialist believes that John Q. Worker's conversion is inevitable because it can offer him what he needs but lacks, an understanding of how everything is connected up in a system.

The fifth implication of the Sombartian approach—reductionism—pervades all Old Left and much New Left historiography. Only in recent years have some independent radical historians urged their colleagues to pay more attention to culture and ideology as semi-autonomous forces and to become more aware that workers' on-the-job behavior cannot be understood if their off-the-job lives are ignored. Consider the way some New Left historians have reacted against Old Left "elitism." Rejecting the Old Left habit of equating labor history with union history and of exaggerating the influence of labor leaders on the rank and file, they have called for what Jesse Lemisch terms "history from the bottom up." Yet the resulting accounts amount to little more than the alleged discovery that John Q. Worker's autonomous behavior was essentially spontaneous struggle against the ruling class. Lemisch, for one, seems to assume that the more the late-eighteenth-century worker behaved rationally and perceived his society accurately, the more he behaved and perceived as Lemisch believes he himself would have if he had lived then. The implicit anachronism in this assumption has been pointed out by James H. Hutson. The late-eighteenth-century Philadelphia worker's realism, rationality, and autonomy cannot be measured by the degree to which he opposed the Tories, any more than the late-nineteenth-century worker's realism, rationality, and autonomy can be measured, as Philip Foner measures them, by the degree to which he opposed Samuel Gompers and craft unionism.[20]

Another New Left historian, Jeremy Brecher, wrote his book *Strike!* to disprove the conventional picture of American history as a success story and present "The True History of Mass Insurgence in America from 1877 to the Present—as authentic revolutionary movements against the establishments of state, capital and trade unionism" (the book's subtitle and cover copy). Brecher has demonstrated anew what has been known for a long time: that the American working class has been among the most militant in the world, sometimes much more militant than its union leaders. This is the same working class about which the Sombart-type essays have been written to account for its nonradicalism. Only wishful thinking would see a contradiction here. Because the workers' struggle was really a challenge to the power and authority of the rulers, says Brecher, "and because carried to its logical conclusion it would have to replace them, the mass strike can be considered in essence a revolutionary process." Brecher thus justifies his disparagement of the strikers' own motives by substituting logic for history and essences for facts.[21]

Brecher and Lemisch have turned Old Left "elitism" on its head. John Q. Worker is no longer clay in the hands of his union officials or other misleaders, or the passive beneficiary of radical agitators' superior understanding. His militance is now autochthonous and implicitly radical although he does not consciously know it. In other words, John Q. Worker was and is either radical (actually or incipiently) or passive; this is an inescapable corollary of an approach that evaluates all his behavior along a single scale with conscious radicalism at the top. According to Brecher, "Most people in their work life and community life are passive—submitting to control from above. They are also atomized—separated from each other. What we see in mass strikes is the beginning of a transformation of people and their relationships from passivity and isolation to collective action." He evidently cannot conceive of initiative as being other than radical or of social bonds in any other context than the economic. Another example of the assumption that nonradical workers must have been passive is in Dubofsky's *We Shall Be All*: the Wobblies' free-speech fight in Fresno "demonstrated once again that the most exploited and dependent groups in American society could act for themselves." This can mean only that those millions of the most exploited and dependent workers who did not engage in this sort of activity were not acting for themselves.[22]

A similar view is expressed in a recent book on labor and socialism:

In their attempt to carry the trade unions, the Socialist Party ultimately failed, and in this failure probably lies the fundamental reason for the failure of socialism in the United States. Many reasons have been given: lack of class feeling, social mobility, political ties. These explanations assume an active body of trade unionists, consciously rejecting even revisionist socialism as foreign and irrelevant to their situation, and equally consciously adopting the "American way." However, it makes as much sense to argue that trade unionists were essentially passive in outlook, while being continually bombarded with antisocialist propaganda from their newspapers.[23]

It would make even more sense to argue that they were neither radical nor passive but interested in other things that the Socialist Party could not, in their opinion, promise them.

The Sombartian approach to John Q. Worker is incompatible with an approach to him "on the cultural level—the level of meaning," an approach that "takes into account . . . man's need to live in a world to which he can attribute some significance, whose essential import he feels he can grasp." [24] Sombartianism rests ultimately on the assumption that culture is epiphenomenal to social structure; hence it is determinist, notwithstanding the disclaimers that one finds in much radical historiography.

Denying the relative independence of culture and social structure, Sombartian historians cannot see how the two affect each other. John Q. Worker becomes Economic Man, who barely existed outside working hours. The temptation is then virtually irresistible to account for things he did off the job solely in terms of his identity as a worker, regardless of how he identified himself. (If he identified himself some other way, *e.g.*, if he put his religious or ethnic identity at the core of his feeling of self-hood, he was a victim of false consciousness.) This historiographical bias had its counterpart in the bias of John Q. Worker's radical contemporaries. To many of the radicals of the pre–World War I generation, John Q. Worker was an abstraction, produced by the same ideology embodied in the propaganda aimed at him. Nevertheless, he was not, as Mao Tse-tung said of the Chinese peasant, "blank," "a clean sheet of paper" waiting for the revolutionary to write beautiful words on it, or a semiconscious vessel half full of obsolete beliefs and bourgeois-induced illusions, or an instinctive freedom-fighter personifying and ratifying the ideology of a modern historian. The worker had a culture, in terms of which he interpreted his experience, and hence did not necessarily construe what the socialist missionary said to him as the latter construed it, any more than the socialist necessarily understood John Q. Worker's rational adjustment of means to his own ends as John Q. Worker understood it.

One condition for John Q. Worker's understanding of the radical's message in the latter's terms would have been that he perceive the capitalist System as the radical perceived it—as a System in the strict sense of the word, in which the economy, government, and all important institutions were tightly integrated and ruled by a single class in accordance with its needs. If that perception were a given, it would make sense to argue that one who did not reject the System accepted it, or that John

Q. Worker, in rejecting socialist values, accepted bourgeois values. But this is an instance of how a question that contains unacknowledged assumptions can bias a historian's search for answers, for the capitalist System as an integrated whole with all parts working together is not a datum of perception but a theoretical construct. For John Q. Worker the question of these two alternatives generally did not arise, even though he must have been aware that different societies were organized differently. Only if a historian assumes that the society appears the same to all clear-eyed perceivers—which is to say, the same as it looks to him now as he reads the historical sources—will he assume that the workers who did not fight against the System were *ipso facto* passive and submissive.

A related assumption commonly encountered is that class consciousness equals radicalism, that a worker who knows himself to be part of the working class almost inevitably comes to oppose capitalism. This assumption is basic to the Sombartian approach, for, starting out from the unarguable fact that there is a working class, it proceeds to an arguable decree that the working class should have a single world view and defines what that world view should be. Consider just one example of this apriorism: the argument about ethnic heterogeneity. Ethnic solidarity sometimes hindered working-class solidarity and sometimes fostered it, and there is no empirical ground for predicting a radical outcome in either case. In some cases it proved inconsistent with radical beliefs and in other cases, notably among a large minority of the Finnish and East European Jewish immigrants, it proved consistent with it.[25] Most radical historians have, however, made the assumption that socialist conviction must follow the erosion of ethnicity, and that it occurs when workers come to identify themselves primarily as workers and only secondarily, if at all, as members of ethnic groups. But if we are to indulge in prophecy at all, we could just as well predict that such "massification" would engender susceptibility to some form of totalitarian ideology rather than the hope for a "democratic socialist" society (assuming, for the sake of argument, that the latter is not an oxymoron). If John Q. Worker had become alienated from his various social bonds, or if they had decayed or been destroyed and his world view had become unable to cope with his experiences, he might have replaced them with a radical group and ideology. But he might have replaced those bonds with a criminal subculture, a professional subculture, or a religious community, any of which could satisfy the same need to identify with a group having a common bond, smaller than the nation but bigger than the family, and providing meaning to his life. Alienating work does not produce alienated people if workers' off-the-job social bonds retain their vitality.

In all the discussions of John Q. Worker's backwardness or dim consciousness, there is one idea that never appears even as an object of refutation, and that is the idea that John Q. Worker had plausible reasons for disagreeing with the radicals. The capitalists' disagreement is brushed off as self-serving, the labor leaders' as sycophantic, but John Q. Worker's is viewed as a sign that he was asleep. Sometimes his somnolence is due to cowardice or to a hope of rising into the middle class, but most often he is just asleep, waiting to be awakened by the radicals' call to revolution. But what of the worker who found value in life as it was, in work, church, family, and who in pursuit of his goals used those means over which he had control? His behavior was rational in the only sense of the word that has real meaning. His ideology included large elements of meanness, sexism, racism, and superstition. Such things are beside the point, which is that the ideological and characterological differences between him and the radicals were not differences in degrees of wakefulness; they were differences of opinion and sometimes of values, differing solutions to the problems that difficult life situations posed. Some radical historians' inability to consider such an explanation parallels past radicals' inability to acknowledge John Q. Worker as both awake and courageous. This description refers not to the demoralized victims of industrialization and deracination who retreated into drunkenness, crime, or apathy, but to the millions of anonymous John Q. Workers who went to work every day and went home to their families every night and could never see the radicals' ideology as a better explanation for their lives than the ones that they subscribed to and that made their experiences meaningful to them.

To sum up, instead of assuming that in failing to convert to radicalism John Q. Worker was irrational or passive, a cork bobbing on the sea of sociological determinants and delusory ideological influences, it would be fruitful to start with the assumption that he assessed the situation he was in, chose his objectives in terms of them, and adjusted means to ends in the light of his perceptions of the relevant conditions, perceptions that were shaped by both a culture and a personal history. The contrary assumption is based not on what he did and thought, but on assumptions concerning what he should have done and thought, in the light of what those making the assumptions postulate as the "essence" or "logical outcome" of his behavior. But if anthropologists are right in seeing culture as providing the forms through which people perceive the world and behave rationally rather than as an obstacle to clear perception of the world and an impediment to rational behavior, a judgment of John Q. Worker's responses to the radicals' message should start with an effort to discover what his mental universe was like. There are, I believe, enough indications that within that universe he made free choices of ends and means, to warrant the presumption that he knew what he was doing.

Moreover the assumption that John Q. Worker's cultural forms were obstacles to clear perception of reality takes for granted that the radicals' perceptions were those that anyone would have had if the cultural forms had been peeled away, or, to change the metaphor, that those forms were like dirt on a window, which needed merely to be cleaned to permit the direct perception of reality. It assumes that the radicals' perceptions were unconditioned by culture and ideology. Such an assumption cannot, of course, be refuted any more than it can be proven, for it is one of that class of circular propositions of which the premises cannot be known to be true unless the conclusion were first known to be true. I can merely state my belief that anthropologists and social psychologists are right when they insist that there is no such thing as a perception of raw reality unmediated and unorganized by culture.

What I propose as a way of getting closer to the reality of the encounter between the radical and John Q. Worker is an effort of the historical imagination not to judge the rationality of either by the other's criteria. This approach requires us to see how each party to the encounter did in fact judge the other to be wrong, and to understand the grounds for both parties' judgments—in other words, that both be viewed with both empathy and detachment.

III · System or Society?

I

Several years ago a book reviewer noted that each historian writing about the decay of institutions and order in a particular period discovers it to have occurred in the period just before the one he specializes in. By now every generation between 1650 and 1890 has been called the transition between order and disorder, deference and egalitarianism, premodernization and modernization, or psychological security and pervasive rootlessness. As characterizations of objective fact these theses cannot all be right, but in another sense they all point to something true and important about all of American history. It has often been noted that the United States telescoped into a mere two and a half centuries changes that west European countries took far longer to experience. By European standards all of American history has been "disorderly," with relatively stable and relatively chaotic periods—what I shall call "shake-up periods"—within it. Change has been so chronic that social institutions and norms, economic institutions and norms, and political institutions and norms have never had as much time as they have had in Europe to become relatively consistent with each other. At the same time, several values and institutions have persisted or changed only slowly. Even in Europe, however, it would be erroneous to refer to "the System," *i.e.*, a social order in which the political, economic, and social spheres were tightly integrated and mutually consistent in their values. The term is even less appropriate to the United States.

For example, far from being a microcosm of society, the American family in the nineteenth century was partly a negative mirror image of it, fostering several values and norms at odds with those that young men had to accommodate to when they passed from the family into the larger society.[1] It is in this sense that each of the aforementioned historians could be right: if each of those periods cannot have been the Golden Age of Stability in reality, it could have been that in people's minds. Alexander Saxton describes the appeal of a false Old South image to urban northerners who had never lived in a rural milieu but felt nostalgia for a "place where simplicity, happiness, all the things we have left behind, exist out of time," and he suggests that "what has been left behind collectively may be a rural past, but individually it is childhood."[2] One of the constants in human nature is a need for emotional landmarks in a social order in which people act in predictable ways. Adult Americans have more often than not lived in a social order in which this need has been satisfied precariously and in limited milieux. The primary sources on which historians base their hypotheses that massive disruption of the social order began shortly before the authors of those documents wrote them, could be interpreted as expressing nostalgia for a wishfully remembered tradition and stability that seemed to have broken down some time in their childhood. In a hierarchical-organic-traditional society, the child passes from the institutional order of the family to that of the society without the wrench of deracination, because the family is a microcosm of the social order and shares its features. The American passes, however, from the "social order" of the family into an individualistic and rootless larger society, so that the need for roots and order is often felt as memory as well as regret. But the common human tendency to legitimate what exists has ratified constant change by calling it "progress," and most Americans, while remembering the orderliness of "society" in their youth, also project their need for order into the future, as hope for material security obtained by ever-increasing income, and emotional security made possible thereby in family and other private association.

In transferring this need for order, from memory to hope, they are not merely justifying what exists or rationalizing materialistic striving. They are also expressing ambivalence about the security that a highly structured environment—whether familial or social—provides, for security and structure can be stifling and boring. What some people feel as loss others feel as liberation. Nostalgia and hope not only can help to make the present tolerable, but can also justify the exclusion from the present of what is remembered or hoped for.[3]

But not complete exclusion. The statement that the American passes from the "social order" of the family into an individualistic and rootless larger society should be amended to take account of the rich associational life that has made Americans "a nation of joiners."[4] Voluntary organizations possess characteristics of both the family and the society. The hierarchy, elaborate rituals, and titles in some associations, on the one hand, reproduce the form of the lost world of comfortable authority which in the United States exists only in those institutions that bring different generations together for the purpose of protecting and socializing the young—and is now weakening even there. Their content, on the other hand, is that of the democratic government. In this way they help to mediate between the hierarchical family and the egalitarian society.[5] Yet egalitarianism is a self-perpetuating value. We are told that the unease engendered, in the twentieth century, by the erosion of the authority of family, religion, and community is to be cured by its further erosion; authority that has been delegitimated is felt as more oppressive than legitimate authority, and its cure is, allegedly, further delegitimization. Hence to the statement that "what some people feel as loss others feel as liberation" should be added another; both feelings often occur simultaneously in the same people.

The dual pull of nostalgia and future-orientedness, and the consequent assumption by Americans, noticed by so many foreign visitors, that social formations intermediate between the family and the state are only temporary here, might not have been so great if the larger society had had a legitimate authority—a traditional ruling class—to play the role that parents play within the family. But, as those same visitors have also noted from Tocqueville on, it has not. By sanctifying public opinion it has made the authority of "ruling" classes merely a functional authority. It lovingly commemorates the Founding Fathers while taking comfort in the fact that they are safely dead, and it denies parental authority to any group in the present, for the sons are all equal and their will is to be determined by majority vote. All leadership is suspect,[6] as a potential arrogation of the role that only the dead Fathers could play; since leadership is necessary in every institution, it is legitimated as that of the first among equals.

But this situation poses a problem: in the absence of a legitimate elite to announce alterations in ideals and norms, how are they to be proposed and evaluated in new circumstances? Anyone arrogating the Fathers' function of announcing what is right or wrong, true or false is denying the equality of the heirs to the Fathers' mantle. No one class or individual has had a presumptive right to play that role. On the contrary, democratic egalitarianism prescribes that the electorate or "public opinion" must promulgate the standards by which the behavior of all classes and groups is judged. This belief is a "self-fulfilling prophecy," to use Robert K. Merton's phrase. The source of new norms must be John Q. Citizen multiplied by millions, and he has jealously guarded that right even to the point of suspecting expertise in any area except science. But how is he to decide when new norms are right and good, since the very act of dissenting from the majority's view, when it involves a basic tenet, is not just disagreement with a particular tenet but a sacrilegious challenge to the only legitimate *process* of discovering truth and right? Any attempt to answer this question would have to be a hypothesis concerning the structure of American society, its ways of adjusting to economic change, and the nature of reform and radical movements within it.

II

Many hypotheses have been devised to account for the structure of American society and the changes that have taken place over the past century and a half. For present purposes three approaches may represent all those that begin by postulating that American society is and has been a System in contradistinction to a Society. By *System* I mean the holistic model referred to at the beginning of this chapter; *Society* will refer to a model of American society as more loosely structured, its sectors and institutions semiautonomous. (For the sake of convenience I shall use the capital *S* when referring to these models and the lowercase *s* when *system* and *society* are used in the conventional ways and when *system* refers to the political or economic system—that is, to a system-type sector of the larger society.) The first of the three approaches is what might be called the vulgar-Marxist. The second is the sophisticated

Marxism that emphasizes the ideological hegemony of the ruling class. The third is the psychological-political model of Sebastian de Grazia. To do justice to these three models would require three books; the purpose of the following discussion is merely to glance at those of their features that, in my opinion, make it advisable to seek another model.

The first System approach is never backed by arguments but is simply stated as self-evident or else unstated but taken for granted. It is found in such statements as that by New Left historian Jeremy Brecher in his book *Strike!*: "In the final analysis, state authority and industrial authority function as parts of a unified system."[7] That assertion combines the political and economic sectors into a System; others by many modern radical writers include various social institutions, ideology, and culture as well. Particularly interesting assertions of the subservience of the "superstructure" to the interests of the System's rulers can be found in the writings of Old Left authors. Communist Party chairman William Z. Foster wrote in 1952 that pragmatism is "the hard-boiled philosophy which says that whatever the capitalists are and do is right."[8] Foster may never have read the writings of James and Dewey, but he had no need to, for, as he wrote in another book, "The United States has the form of a democracy, but through their ownership and control of the industries, the press, the schools, the armed forces, the churches, and all other key institutions, the capitalists are able in election after election to fill up the national, state, and local governments with their agents."[9] Writers like Foster need not study philosophy or any other part of the "superstructure," for all they need to know can be learned from the economic sector. What is true of the pragmatist philosophers must also be true of historians, for, as Herbert Aptheker has written, "With current American reality being the domination of the Government by monopolists, and therefore a sharply reactionary orientation internally and externally, the ruling tendency in historical writing [on the Civil War] is pro-Confederate, just as for World War II it is anti-Soviet."[10] "Current American reality" is not merely dominated by the monopolists' domination of the government; it *is* that domination. And historians, like other intellectuals and producers of superstructural elements of the society, have no independence whatever, for all elements of the System are totally functional within it, where they are not "contradictions" auguring its overthrow.

Sooner or later Old Left simplism had to exasperate radicals who were sensitive to the complexity of American society yet wanted to retain the System concept and the Marxist emphasis on class. The reintegration of culture into a radical model derived from two sources: the discovery of Antonio Gramsci and the youth culture of the 1960s. As part of the generation that produced hippie experimentation with new cultural forms, some New Left historians took a new look at workers' actual lives and set themselves the task of writing working-class history with full appreciation of off-the-job activities and relationships, including the family.

Some of these historians, writing mostly in *Radical America* and *Radical History Review*, cogently criticize CP historians for focusing exclusively on the workplace and union, as though workers had no existence in other milieux. But the reason they themselves are curious about workers' beliefs and activities in the home, the neighborhood, the saloon, the church, and the club is that—as they willingly admit—they see such milieux as arenas of struggle against capitalism, actually or potentially. Consider one such article, a survey of working-class historiography up to 1969, by Paul Faler, which epitomizes the best in the New Left's approach. He argues:

Anyone who views class as a social term, discernible in patterns of relationships and distinctive institutions, must be able to show that workingmen are distinguishable by some feature other than the functional one of their economic role. It is not enough to assume that the economic experience of working people spontaneously generates an army of institutions as peculiar to the needs of workingmen as is the trade union. The union is often merely an instrument for protecting and improving the material condition of working people. It may be a weapon against economic exploitation. But capitalism is more than an economic system. It is an entire cultural apparatus with peculiar ideas about the nature of man, the proper distribution of political power, and a desirable social structure. Its values permeate an entire society and appear in social attitudes toward recreation, child-rearing, education, and sexual codes.[11]

Despite the present tense, Faler makes it clear that he sees past working-class life in the same way. He asks all the right questions. Yet, although he states that we do not yet know enough to answer them, it is apparent throughout the article that he sees cultural forms principally in terms of their functioning as vehicles for and shapers of the struggle against capitalism. For example, he recounts an incident in 1851 in Massachusetts that shows the capitalists' lack of cultural hegemony over the workers, but then comments that "townspeople were resisting a basic tenet of capitalism: that ownership conferred rights that were superior to the rights of the propertyless." In this case it was the right to abolish a traditional lunch break in midmorning. "If the strike," he continues, "did not produce demands for expropriation, it was nonetheless radical in that it challenged the fundamental basis of capitalism."[12] But this substitutes theory and logic for history. By the same reasoning even government regulatory legislation and every union victory are "radical." In practice there was nothing radical about the demand; the controversy he describes was an incident in a long process of mutual adjustment of claims and resistances on both sides, neither party knowing what intermediate position would eventually be settled upon.

It is one thing to say that capitalist economic imperatives forced certain changes in life-style, beliefs, and values in the workers' off-the-job milieux, and that one cannot understand the economic and political without understanding the cultural, and vice versa. But it is quite another thing to assume that the chief significance of John Q. Worker's noneconomic institutions and associations is their use as vehicles either for resistance to capitalism or for reinforcing the hegemony of the capitalists. What such historians will not entertain is the possibility that John Q. Worker valued his church and recreational club and saloon and kinship network not only independently of their ability to support his economic/political struggle but also because they could be made to have little to do with it, and that American society was sufficiently "open" to permit "social space" in which these institutions and activities could flourish with little reference one way or the other to the economic sphere, that is, without obeying some inner logic of historical development contrary to the participants' intentions. In sum, some New Left historians have gone to the opposite extreme from the CP historians whom they have criticized and corrected. Whereas the latter ignore culture and exclude the off-the-job milieux from their purview, the former have rediscovered their importance but then integrated them tightly within the class-defined System.[13]

Some of the New Left historians' articles manifest a trait that to the

CP historians should be as heretical as "revisionism," and that is curiosity about the past. If it is true that "where there is life there is hope," then where there is curiosity there is hope of enlightening discoveries, for curiosity is the life of scholarship. To date, however, article after article by these young scholars have stopped just short of treating the evidence concerning John Q. Worker's off-the-job life on its own terms and instead have ended up incorporating it into a paradigm in which history becomes a tour of the battlefields of the class war. Whereas CP historiography focuses on the front lines, New Leftists include the home front, as is appropriate nowadays considering the changed conduct of real warfare. The motive for this orientation, explicitly acknowledged, is "relevance," the use that history might be put to in current and future struggles, but its implicit theoretical warrant is the System model.

Gramsci called that home front "civil society," and the vehicle for the capitalists' domination of it is ideological hegemony. The thinking of the Italian Communist leader is best explicated in the fine biography of him by John Cammett, and a version of it applied to the United States has been offered by Eugene D. Genovese.[14] Cammett writes, "In its general sense, hegemony refers to the 'spontaneous' loyalty that any dominant social group obtains from the masses by virtue of its social and intellectual prestige and its supposedly superior function in the world of production." In an attempt (which I now reject) to apply Gramsci's theory to American history several years ago, I argued as follows:

Universal suffrage, social mobility, the absence of a true conservative tradition, and other facts of American life have worked powerfully to maintain the illusion that there is no ruling class in this country, even in the face of enormous differences in wealth and status. The perpetuation of this myth requires that the mechanisms of ideological hegemony be disguised as their diametric opposites. The population at large must be seen as wielding the powers that in overtly class societies are wielded by the acknowledged ruling class. And that means that threats to the ideological hegemony of the ruling class must always be regarded as threats to the power of the population at large. A radical movement must thus seem to be an attack on democracy itself. . . . Hence the peculiar epithet "unAmerican" applied to a movement that attacks the hegemony of the ruling tenth of American society; the movement is seen as an attack not merely on the workers' interest . . . but also on the workers' power. The illusion of that power is strengthened by the partial reality of that interest. If it were a total fraud the fraud could not have lasted as long as it has. . . . [Most Americans are better off and freer than people in other countries, so that] it is easy to see why the average American worker is convinced the system works in his interest. . . . [Hence,] threats to the ideological hegemony of the ruling class have sometimes been countered by popular movements, and . . . occasionally sections of the ruling class have proved more tolerant of dissent than have large sections of the working class.[15]

The above hypothesis is clearly preferable to that of the vulgar-Marxists in that it recognizes the contribution of the ruled as well as the rulers to the formulation of the hegemonic ideology. In so doing it avoids a contradiction endemic in non-Gramscian Marxian theory: on the one hand the working class is the passive recipient of ruling-class ideology (see Foster's statement quoted above, to the effect that by virtue of the capitalists' "ownership and control" of just about everything, they get their agents elected year after year), but on the other hand American history is the history of the workers' continual struggles for freedom (see almost every book written by Herbert Aptheker and Philip Foner). Yet it is just as deductive. So far as pre–World War I American society is concerned, the contention that freedom, mobility, education, etc., served the System, ultimately against the interests of the majority, is tenable only if the System is postulated to begin with. One could reasonably hypothesize that that majority accepted the *economic* hegemony of the owners of capital as the price for that freedom and the other good things. The problematic word in the foregoing quotation is "partial"— the partial reality of the worker's interest in maintaining the social order against radicals' demands that it be replaced. Where is the line separating partial reality from reality? How disguised can a class's rule throughout the society be and still be that class's rule throughout the society? Howard Brotz suggests the answer in his remark that "if power . . . is ashamed to become visible, it cannot exert moral authority."[16]

Furthermore, the ideological hegemony of the bourgeoisie, owing to its presumed leading role in production, could exist (if at all) only in a comparatively settled period. There would have to have been time enough not only for other classes to accept that leading role as legitimate and not only for the capitalists' influence (as distinguished from their power) to have spread to noneconomic spheres, but also for the capitalists themselves (with the help of the workers) to have developed an appropriate world view acceptable to all classes. Even if one accepted the Marxist theory that the mode of production is *"ultimately"* the source of ideas and values, that word, quoted from Engels' letter to Bloch, September 21, 1890 (italics Engels'), constitutes an admission that some time must elapse between the inception of the new forms of power and their ideological "reflection." Engels of course had *logical* ultimateness in mind, but the inference is nevertheless inescapable.

In a "shake-up period" the ruling class's ideas cannot be the ruling ideas of the society[17] because it is not yet clear whose rule is legitimate and what the most powerful class's ideas are. What Michael Walzer writes about the Puritan Revolution is true (although to a lesser extent) of the United States in the pre–World War I generation: "Ideology cannot be consistently linked with class experiences because those experiences no longer take place in a regular and predictable order."[18] In the 1890–1917 period, American capitalists were as confused on this score as everyone else—including the radicals, who might have been expected to possess a clear-cut ideology but did not. The various radical and reform movements that proliferated in that period were hence not challenges to a hegemonic *capitalist* ideology; in that period there was none, although there were consensual values. To say that a world view that legitimates a System in which one class is the most powerful and wealthy is that class's hegemonic ideology, even though no one is conscious of it, is no solution to the problem; or rather, it is solution by definition. It begs the question of whether the society is a System in which all important parts are integrated and dominated by the ruling class.

In fact, the assumption is made explicit in a statement that Cammett quotes from a modern exegesis of Gramsci's theory: hegemony is "an order in which a certain way of life and thought is dominant, in which one concept of reality is diffused throughout society in all its institutional and private manifestations, informing with its spirit all taste, morality, customs, religious and political principles, and all social relations, particularly in their intellectual and moral connections."[19] This description may have fitted Gramsci's Italy and the American Slave South, but only a reversal of every element in it could yield a description of the United States in the turn-of-the-century generation. And it was, by no coincidence, in that generation that radical movements achieved their greatest, albeit very limited, successes.

Despite the variation in sophistication discernible in these New Left and Gramscian approaches, their System paradigm pulls them in the same direction—that of studying noneconomic aspects of American society only with reference to the assumed domination by the ruling class of all those aspects, directly or indirectly. Foster simply assumes both the workers' passive acceptance of ruling-class ideology and their relentless struggle against the System. The New Left and Gramscians study culture and ideology, as Foster and his comrades do not, but never on their own terms to construct a historical situation from the documents by means of a procedure that admits the possibility that workers' culture and ideologies "worked" to some degree without reference to a System.

This point may be illustrated with a statement by Gramsci: "Men, when they feel their strength and are conscious of their responsibility and their value, do not want another man to impose his will on theirs and undertake to control their thoughts and actions."[20] As a general observation about human nature, this is self-evident. But one who posits System assumes that industrial workers in a capitalist country are thus imposed upon even though they may not know it, and if they do not know it, that just shows how imposed upon they are. That is the logic of the type of psychoanalyst who, if his patient agrees with an interpretation of his symptoms, says he is making progress and, if the patient disagrees, concludes that he is resisting. The patient cannot be right. But for the same reason the analyst's interpretation cannot be tested. In a given case it may be right, but the proof must come from evidence interpreted in a theoretical framework that permits disproof as well as proof of a particular hypothesis. All theories that I know of that regard American workers' nonradicalism as false consciousness manifest this circularity.[21] The starting assumption, which is not subject to empirical testing by means of a falsifiable hypothesis, rules out any possibility that the workers' nonradical ideology was a "true" consciousness, and that, having a culture that satisfied their emotional needs, the workers chose not to grasp for full control over the economy and state, with the unremitting activism in political and economic life that that would entail, to say nothing of the sacrifices required during the revolutionary struggle.

Genovese says that the franchise and bourgeois democracy "drew the revolutionary teeth of the proletariat and helped extend over it the hegemony of the bourgeoisie."[22] There is no evidence that there were ever any revolutionary teeth to draw. If political democracy prevented them from growing, the question that should be asked is whether the workers erred, in the light of their own interests, in accepting it. It does not help to say that if a ruling class had somehow managed to disfranchise the workers they would have rebelled. Of course they would, doubtless to establish "bourgeois democracy." But that begs the question in the same way as the statement that if someone were deprived of something he wants he would try to get it. That the American workers gladly accepted the political democracy that they helped to create does not mean they subsequently accepted the ideological hegemony of the bourgeoisie in all other areas of their lives, or even in the political. Genovese's comment that for an American socialism this bourgeois-democratic political process "ushered in a debacle" is, I believe, a tautology: health ushers in a debacle for disease, and disease does the same for health. The American working class has not (yet?) decided that the bourgeois-democratic political process is an inadequate compensation for the complete state power and ownership of the means of production that it "ought" to have.

To Genovese's statement that "in bourgeois-democratic society the hegemony of the bourgeoisie masks its dictatorship,"[23] one may respond that a masked dictatorship in a country where the masks include broad suffrage, frequent elections, a checked-and-balanced government, strong unions since the 1930s, abhorrence of the very idea of an officially enforced ideology, and—most important—strong intermediate institutions is a very limited dictatorship. Where is the line separating a limited dictatorship from something less than a dictatorship? The obvious answer from the System standpoint is that any idea or value, accepted or approved by workers, if it is compatible with the continued existence of the social order, serves the interests of the ruling class. Two responses can be made to this contention, the first pertaining to its cognitive content and the second pertaining to its influence on the thinking of those who make it. First, the contention may be true, but it does not follow that the social order is a System or that the interest of the economic ruling class is contrary to the interests of the other classes in the economic or any other sphere, or that specific cases of oppression or injustice are due to the System. Second, that approach discourages study of the intrinsic truth or appeal of the idea in question. The most notorious example of this bias is the Old Left's treatment of religion, which appears as either a ruling-class trick or a half-articulated revolutionary philosophy, but never . . . religion. Another example is ethnicity, which on the rare occasions when it is mentioned is treated in the same way. Other radical historians in recent years have begun to correct this bias; it remains to be seen how far they will go toward perceiving these phenomena through John Q. Worker's eyes and still be able to retain the System model, for the two perceptions are inherently contradictory.

Of the approaches discussed so far, the vulgar-Marxist is by far the safest. By simply excluding or ignoring data that cannot fit, it can be adhered to for a lifetime. (That procedure is, incidentally, perfectly consistent with total sincerity; it is the model, not the motive, that slights the data.) It is to the Gramscian version what the Aristotelian is to the Ptolemaic model of the solar system. A historian who reads the documents in the light of questions that leave open the possibility of non-System relationships is risking discoveries that may induce him to wonder how many more epicycles can be added to a perfectly circular orbit before the basic paradigm should be challenged. So far as American history is concerned, ideological hegemony, like an epicycle, is needed more to support the paradigm than to explain the data.[24] The paradigm is the conception of System, but the data do not need that theory, for they can be adequately accounted for without it, and those who tack it onto them create conceptual problems with no relevance to the data. If Gramsci's theory is restricted to the economic system, it has a large measure of truth, but that would be unacceptable to its advocates, for whom it is a way of integrating phenomena in all parts of a society and explaining, as other versions of Marxism have been unable to do, the working class's failure to become revolutionary when and as Marx and Engels predicted it would.

But although it explains the failure of the working class to become revolutionary in the past, it runs into a difficulty of equal magnitude in its prediction of how this change is to occur in the future. Leninism solved the problem by frankly admitting that the working class cannot spontaneously awaken to socialist truth; the vanguard party would impose true theory on the trade-union movement "from without" (Lenin, *What Is To Be Done?*). This has never troubled Marxist-Leninist historians in the United States, whose works portray precisely that spontaneous understanding that their own party's theory denies is possible. Their conception of struggling workers throughout American history, of course, requires a conception of fully conscious (in the Marxist sense) capitalists conspiring to hoodwink the workers into believing in an ideology they themselves do not take seriously. Gramscian theory dispenses with such fictions. It acknowledges that the capitalists could be shortsighted as well as sincere believers in the values and doctrines that support their domination. But it produces a new mystery—how both exploiters and exploited could voluntarily believe in a world view that serves the interests of the one and violates those of the other. In a society in which the political and social spheres were clearly dominated by the class that dominated the economy this might not be a mystery. But this is not so with respect to the United States in the late nineteenth and early twentieth centuries. It may be replied that ultimately the rulers could resort to force, the true ground of their power that is always in the background. This argument is contradicted by a fact that is generally mentioned among the evidences for ideological hegemony: that most Americans believe their votes count, in the long run, and that a majority for just about anything would prevail. There is, however, no evidence that large sections of the working class have ever refrained from voting for radicals on the ground that a majority vote for them, amounting to a mandate for radical change, would be met by forcible perpetuation of capitalist rule.[25]

The Gramscian alternative to Leninist elitism is essentialism. Rather than contending that Marxism must be brought into the working class from without, it postulates that it is essentially or potentially within the working-class movement, and that the task of the vanguard party is to work within the workers' civil-society institutions to develop the embryonic hegemonic culture and ideology. As one scholar puts it, according to this theory "revolutionary consciousness is not something that is externally transmitted to workers; instead, it is already implicit in their activity."[26] Gramsci, however, always considered himself a Leninist. Leninist elitism and Gramscian essentialism meet in their common denial of John Q. Worker's full consciousness of what he is doing. In the end Gramsci needs the radicalization of an elite (bourgeois intellectuals) as much as Lenin does and has as much trouble explaining their conversion so that they may—for Lenin—bring the workers the truth or—

for Gramsci—clarify the workers' nascent radical beliefs and provide leadership in their struggle for the new society.[27]

The third approach to be discussed, Sebastian de Grazia's psychological-political theory,[28] differs widely from Gramsci's class theory. Yet they share two important features. First, they both rely on the concept of System, with one ruling class directly or indirectly dominating all important institutions and accepted by other classes as the authoritative arbiter between right and wrong and true and false. Second, both models apply better to preindustrialized class societies and, up to a point, to those modern democratic societies that retain premodern attitudes toward class hierarchy, than to the United States.

In de Grazia's theory, System is a universal psychological need, so that if one part of it, the economic, conflicts with the political and social, pervasive anomie inevitably results. The political sphere is the family writ large,[29] and a society's ruling class is to adults what parents are to their children. The System is upset when the ruling class ceases to play its parental role. But the two examples he cites reveal what is wrong with the theory.

De Grazia describes the medieval Polish nobility, who perpetrated all manner of outrages on the peasants. The latter did not, however, rebel so long as their rulers spoke the same language, ate the same kind of food, dressed the same way, and so on. When the nobles adopted the French language and life-style, the peasants revolted periodically even though they were now treated more humanely and enjoyed a higher standard of living. According to de Grazia, the peasants had become convinced that "the lord to whom they paid homage no longer made their commonweal his primary concern . . . and that they could no longer rely on him to protect them from enemies, defend their faith, and represent them to God."[30] His second example is from the American Gilded Age, when nouveaux riches flaunted their wealth and bought foreign, titled sons-in-law. The sequel was similar to that in Poland, except that instead of peasant revolts the United States experienced mass strikes, the muckraking and antitrust movements, and political victories by Progressives. "Now ordinarily," says de Grazia,

in well-knit political communities people like to believe the *ruler* [a term he uses to designate either an individual or a class that performs this social-paternal function] lives richly and gives generously—so long as he remains one of them, so long as he is *their ruler*. Even if they are themselves living on a bare subsistence level, they will see that he gets the lion's share. But in this period the captains of industry unwittingly separated themselves from the community at a time when they should have been reaffirming mutual ties. . . . By importing alien cultivation, accents, clothes, and manners, they repudiated their leadership of a community which had believed in them and banked on their support.

The growing support of third parties and reform and radical movements "indicated that people felt leaderless and protectionless, without a system of beliefs to guide them in their troubles. In a word—anomic." [31]

To juxtapose these two episodes is to reveal the flaw in the second: the American industrialists had never played the role in their society that the Polish nobles had in theirs. The public outrage was evoked not by their ceasing to behave like a true ruling class but by their aristocratic pretensions; even if the owners of the new, big industrial enterprises had behaved as the Polish nobility had before the latter departed from the old traditions, they would have evoked the same outrage. The common feature of the two classes' behavior—their aping a foreign aristocracy—has misled de Grazia into ignoring the opposite historical contexts in which it took place. One accepted caste and all its implications, and the other explicitly rejected it for whites. One of those implications, for Poland, was the ruling class's legitimate domination in the social, political, economic, and religious spheres. Another was the acceptance by the serfs of the ruling class's right to leisure while they themselves worked. In the United States, on the contrary, those four spheres, though connected by many crisscrossing influences, had since at least the early nineteenth century been only loosely connected, with no single group exercising hegemony over all of them, despite efforts by powerful classes to exert it. As to leisure, it suffices to recall the perplexity of many European visitors who could not understand why rich Americans worked as many hours a day as their poor compatriots did, and throughout their lives. The traditional American distinction between "producers" and "parasites" is alone sufficient to undermine the parallel between the two countries.

There is still another feature common to de Grazia's and Gramsci's theories, which they share with all theories that postulate System: they cannot adequately account for social change. The more integrated the System, the more "functional" all its key parts must be to its essential structure and the interest of its rulers. Indeed, the similarities between sociological functionalism and Marxism have often been noted. If one sees System rather than Society, one must see incompatibilities of ideology, behavior, values, etc., as contradictions that threaten the System's existence and that must be resolved one way or the other. One must explain them away or discover invisible connections between them and the System; or else one must assume they are "contradictions" that augur the System's destruction. None of this theoretical elaboration would be necessary if the System model were discarded, for all such elaborations are needed to account for difficulties that the model itself creates in trying to accommodate the empirical data. It is time now to explore what happens when we discard the System model and postulate Society instead.[32]

III

The first step requires recognition of one enduring American attitude that is often overlooked, the attitude toward power. Americans have never feared to deposit great power in the hands of appropriately chosen men. What they have feared has been arbitrary power, guided by no checks and balances, no rules. This distinction is essential to an understanding, for example, of why, by 1860, the northern public had become convinced that the slaveholders wielded dangerously arbitrary power, while the abolitionists failed utterly to convert it to antiracism. It also helps us understand what happened when a new and unprecedented power appeared after the Civil War, the power of the owners and financiers of industrial concerns organized on such a scale that customary norms governing industrial relations could no longer apply, and, what was equally unsettling, that power infected government at all levels.

The mere existence of a gap between ideals and reality cannot account for the malaise of the period. There had always been a gap between the ideal of democratic distribution of economic opportunity and political power and the reality. It can even be argued that such a gap, in a society pervaded by the values of progress and achievement, is a stabilizing force so long as most people believe they have the power to alter reality in the direction of the ideal. One perceptive student suggests that

the gap between the prevailing ideology and values and the social and economic reality contributed to the maintenance, rather than caused the disintegration, of the social order. It may be that the affirmation of cultural traditions functioned as a gyroscopic force in a society which was undergoing rapid economic and social change. Although many different cultural traditions were invoked by both native and immigrant Americans in response to social changes, they may have had something in common insofar as all of them provided Americans with a qualitative, as opposed to quantitative, means of identifying themselves. The traditional moral and religious values may also have acted as a compensatory ideology in an age in which individualism, competition, and achievement were glorified.[33]

Americans' confidence in their ability to alter reality is shown as much by their retention of the ideal as by their attitude toward reality as improvable. The question in the late nineteenth century was whether this was still the case. Reformers insisted it was: that the ideals of equality, achievement, and popular sovereignty—as well as those specific to the different subcultures—were still valid but needed new rules to make continued striving toward them realistic. Radicals said no: not new rules but a new social order was needed, for the power of the new industrial capitalists was too great to trammel by rules. Radicals and reformers, it will be noticed, agreed on the ideals.

Before starting to answer the questions asked at the beginning of this chapter—about how, in a society lacking an official value-giving class and in which "public opinion" had to sift the assortment of reform and radical proposals to decide which were good and true, and how that sifting was done—we must note certain features of the situation that the public saw confronting it at the beginning of the shake-up period of the late nineteenth and early twentieth centuries. Here I must repeat what was said earlier: the shake-up of certain customary norms was only relative, for it had been endemic in American society for at least two generations. This was not a "settled status" society that suddenly exploded with the advent of large-scale industrialization. By the 1880s, however, the changes had progressed so far and their magnitude had finally become apparent to so many people, that the need to explain them produced an ideological shake-up. One of the most disturbing aspects of the situation was that the capitalists' enormous power, although built on industrial innovation, threatened to end the particular form of economic mobility that had become an ideal among native-born Americans (many immigrants did not share it): the rise to self-employment traditionally considered the prerequisite of political and social independence.

Two consequences of the birth of big industry warrant particular attention owing to their widening that gap between customary norms and practice: first, the enormous increase in the economic and political power, though not the legitimate authority, of industrial and finance capitalists; and second, the attraction to the new industrial sites of only partly "modernized" employees from Europe and the American countryside.

Modernization [34] had begun much earlier; Richard D. Brown has persuasively argued that American society was substantially modernized by the time of the Civil War, although the process has continued to the present.[35] When a Socialist Laborite wrote in 1896, "A crisis, a social shake-up is approaching," [36] he was obviously referring to a phenomenon within that larger process. By the late nineteenth century the assortment of personality traits appropriate to life in an industrialized society had won widespread approval: punctuality, time-orientedness, ambition, and so on.[37] The shake-up was not in that area or in the area of basic American values, but in that of leadership and authority in the economic sphere, and the norms and values related to them.[38] It might be seen as similar to the chaos that attends the construction of a new community—in this case an economic structure—when individuals compete for leadership and status before "the group has shaken down and the members have come to know the virtues and deficiencies of their fellows more thoroughly." [39] Industrialists themselves did not yet know which of them and their corporations would or should lead their "community." The chaos resulting is not reducible to the economic cannibalism of the Rockefellers and Harrimans; it should be seen as a variant of the competition that every new social institution or community experiences before an accepted rank order has evolved.

In fact, the persistence of the old ideals into a period characterized by an unprecedented increase in the economic power of one class gave many on the right, left, and center a standpoint for moral judgment. This is one reason why American society in that period should not, in my opinion, be perceived as anomic or "massified." Leadership and authority patterns in family, community, religious, and associational relationships suffered less massive and rapid obsolescence than did those in the economic sphere. John Q. Worker behaved in a "modern" manner chiefly on the job; it took a long time for the "modern" traits to infiltrate his "private sphere," and that process is still not complete and may never be.[40] On the contrary, the vitality of those patterns in the private sphere made the new raw power of industrial capitalists all the more incongruous. When some factory owners installed paternalistic welfare schemes to win their employees' loyalty, they forgot that adult Americans are wary of a claim to paternal authority by anyone outside the family. The rules that had to be formulated to legitimate the authority of the industrial capitalists in their enterprises had to regulate relations among ostensible equals, which is why their legitimacy and that of mass unions evolved at more or less the same time. Employees accepted the benefits of the companies' welfare schemes, of course, but their increased loyalty to their bosses seems to have been based on the same mixture of calculation and conventional norms of fairness as were the motives of some bosses.

A minority blamed the grievances resulting from the capitalists' increased power on something they called "the system." But the majority personified the grievances, judging the behavior of all parties to the disputes by ideals and values they all accepted and condemning that of the rich as subversive of them. That is, there seems to have been a widespread conviction on the part of workers and the middle class that the capitalists performed at least some useful economic functions—gathering capital, supervising, organizing; rather, they were criticized for performing them unjustly and for illegitimately using their wealth to influence the noneconomic spheres. This is very far from a demand that the workers themselves own and run the factories. Radical propaganda at that time was, on the contrary, filled with references to the uselessness of the capitalist, his not performing any functions in return for his profits. Hence the radicals did not demand that he play fair; they wanted him out of the game entirely. The modern reader is, of course, free to believe that the radicals' doctrine represented the interests of John Q. Worker; it did not represent his thinking.[41]

In one crucial respect the radicals were wrong. Their concept of System implied two characteristics of the social order that were spectacularly lacking: the synergistic functioning of the economic, governmental, and social realms in the interests of the ruling class, and a clear understanding on the part of the ruling class of what its interests required. Many data reveal the confusion that was so prevalent during the late nineteenth century in part because the capitalists did not know what policies were in their best interests and sometimes were surprisingly apprehensive about the viability of their own "system." (See Supplement.) "In this period," writes Herbert G. Gutman, "industrial capitalism was relatively new as a total way of life and therefore was not fully institutionalized. Much of the history of industrialism at that time is the story of the painful process by which an old way of life was discarded for a new one. The central issue was the rejection or modification of an old set of 'rules' and 'commands' which no longer fit the new industrial context."[42]

The same process that brought such power to the capitalists convinced most Americans that for the first time material security and increased affluence were possible for all. At the same time, however, it was becoming harder for an individual to become self-employed, owing to the rise of the large corporation and the high cost of machinery. As time passed, mobility became the promotion of employees within their companies, as mechanization simplified industrial tasks and in the process created many new rungs on the occupational ladder, close together, that workers could climb, and service and white-collar jobs became proportionately more numerous. But the old American tradition of rags to riches and the belief that a high standard of living was now possible for all Americans clashed head-on with the evidence that industrialists were taking too big a share of the new surplus and using technological innovations to create not only abundance but also unemployment and insecurity.[43]

Far from being credited with the new possibility of increased material comfort for all, the new factory owners were often seen as obstacles to its realization. As Gutman shows, they were also perceived as disturbing elements in some of the towns and small cities in which they built their new enterprises. He dissents strongly from "the widely held view that from the start, industrialists had the social and political power and prestige to match their economic force, and that they controlled the towns." On the contrary: "Through its early years, for at least a generation, the factory and its disciplines, the large impersonal corporation, and the propertyless wage-earner remained unusual and even alien elements in the industrial town. They disrupted tradition, competed against an established social structure and status hierarchy, and challenged traditional modes of thought. In these years, therefore, the factory owner symbolized innovation and a radical departure from an older way of life. His power was not yet legitimized and 'taken for granted.'"[44]

The second consequence of the birth of big industry that warrants special attention is the massive redistribution of people in response to its needs.

The immense transfer of population called the "new immigration" is well known, but that of native-born Americans was also significant. An editorialist in a Wobbly paper, describing Akron's rubber workers in 1913, observed that seventy percent were native-born and had been drawn by advertisements from rural districts at such a rate that "Akron has become a city 'of furnished rooms,' the workers being mostly young men and women. Family life has become impossible, and the boasted 'city of opportunity' a veritable 'spider's parlor' in which to lure 'flies' to their undoing. The process is identical with that at Lawrence [Massachusetts]. The only difference is that in the textile center, the mill owners' agents with their glowing advertisements scoured foreign countries and brought 'flies' to their 'parlor' from the four corners of the earth."[45] Even though the industrial working class was by then overwhelmingly foreign-born, this radical journalist, in linking Lawrence and Akron, was far more perceptive than the nativists who blamed a large part of the shake-up on the threat that the strange cultures posed to American homogeneity.[46]

The cultural perspective, however, permits an insight that the class perspective obscures. It can be inferred from John Higham's description of the late nineteenth century as "a time of mass strikes, widening social chasms, unstable prices, and a degree of economic hardship unfamiliar in earlier American history."[47] That "widening" and "unfamiliarity" assume a standard of comparison that the immigrant could not have had. To him the social chasm and degree of economic hardship he encountered were givens. In fact, both were smaller than those he had known in the country he had left to take advantage of American opportunity—opportunity made known to him, incidentally, not only by employers' agents but more importantly and accurately by letters from friends and relatives in America. American workers migrated *within* a culture, or the industrial enterprises they went to work in had migrated into the workers' hometowns;[48] the immigrant found greater economic opportunity and entered a foreign culture in the same act of migration. This contrast should be kept in mind in any attempt to account for the fact that, although only a small minority of native- or foreign-born workers became radical, the proportion was greater among the natives (most radical immigrants were already radicals or on the way to becoming radicals before immigrating). The immigrant had an advantage over the native, ironically, by virtue of his very foreignness. As one scholar expresses it, even though he entered an unfamiliar society that was changing rapidly, his disorientation was "partially cushioned by the support of his ethnic group." Membership from birth in an ascribed group has "the advantage of relative permanence in an unstable cultural situation, provided that it remains meaningful to the individual concerned."[49]

Although psychologically beneficial to the immigrants, however, the increased cultural heterogeneity ran counter to the modernization process and to industry's need for interchangeable workers. The radical movements can be seen, from this standpoint, as modernizing movements in that they proclaimed that the uniform working-class identity of all workers was the sole important measure of a white man—and eventually of a black and of a woman too—and that ethnic differences were unimportant. Repeatedly they told the worker: "The bosses care nothing for your nationality except to divide you, and neither should you, so that you may unite." In effect they were saying that the nature of the job should determine the nature of personal relations, on and off the job, until after the revolution.[50] The immigrant worker, on the contrary, although willing, because obliged, to acquire the various personality traits associated with "modernity," combined them with inherited cultural traits and customs in a new ethnic identity only partly shaped by the imperatives of the miscellaneous jobs and middle-class occupations that divided his coethnics.[51]

What must be stressed, however, is that to the immigrant everything in the United States was new except some aspects of the culture of the immigrant enclave he either lived in or visited frequently for worship, social contacts, and shopping. But because everything American was new, from his standpoint everything American that he perceived could have been the way things had always been in America. What to the native-born worker was unprecedented and illegitimate may to the immigrant have borne the presumption of tradition and legitimacy. At the same time there was nothing about the class relations, the polity, and other aspects of American life that was legitimate *to him*, in the sense of their being taken for granted as part of his culture. They would all therefore have appeared to him in the light of expediency and power—as things that required or did not require his accommodation. What he did take for granted was the purpose of his immigrating—the welfare of his family and the values he intended to continue to live by. That is why he subjected himself to the onerous and dangerous conditions of his job. It seems a plausible inference, therefore, that he made a mental separation between those goals and the economic and political means to achieve them, especially if his job was unskilled or semiskilled, affording little satisfaction in itself.

If this inference is correct, the immigrant workers, despite the premodern traits that many brought with them to America, were conforming to a crucial trend in modern industrial society: the privatization of the family and the segmentation of social life in general.[52] At the same time as capitalism tended to rationalize all human relations, it also permitted newly freed individuals to mark off the private sphere as the realm in which their nonrationalized and nonbureaucratized relations could be acted out. As Tamara Hareven summarizes the interpretation now emerging from social historians' study of ethnic and family history:

Migration is now being interpreted as a continuous process of the transmission of culture, rather than as a course of disintegration. Modernization ceases to be seen as a linear process by which immigrant peasants, pushed through a tube, emerge as "modern" individuals on the other end. It becomes, instead, a process of interaction by which pre-industrial people bring their own cultural traditions to bear upon the system which "modernizes" them.

This new historical outlook presents workers and immigrants as active agents, who despite the presence of powerful and economic institutions exercised controls over the forces that tended to regiment them. Instead of being submerged and absorbed, newcomers to industrial society tended to shape the system to fit their wants and traditions.[53]

IV

If all the foregoing facts are brought together, they add up to an inherently unstable mixture of volatile elements. First, the traditional American disapproval of "nonproducers" and "parasites" who dealt in negotiable paper rather than producing tangible goods, created an audience for those reformers and radicals who depicted a financial octopus reaching from Wall Street into all corners of the land. Second, the atrocious conditions in factories and mines, which employed large numbers of workers who had less power to set their own terms of employment than ever before, conflicted with the traditional picture of the independent American, the reality of which caused discomfort to European visitors accustomed to deferential behavior by the lower orders. Third, the lack of rules and norms in big industry, along with the enormously increased power of its owners, gave freer rein to cruel or amoral employers who, although perhaps atypical, proved the need for new rules and norms. Fourth, the lavish living and aristocratic pretensions of many nouveaux riches and their frequent buying of titled sons-in-law (played up in the radical press[54]) violated traditional patriotic and egalitarian ideals. Fifth, their use of government—e.g., the employment of troops to break strikes, the purchase of legislators, and the nonenforcement of labor laws—offended traditional political norms including the separation of economic from political power. All these things had existed before on a smaller scale; their greater significance during the generation starting about 1880 is epitomized in a phrase used earlier in this chapter—"raw power." It is time now to examine its implications.

In the absence of rules and norms, only force can decide a dispute, and, as has been noted by many observers then and since, labor disputes were particularly violent in the United States in that generation. The contrast with an equally industrialized country that had traditional norms for interclass relations adaptable to the new situation was well expressed in a leaflet published by English radicals: "It is hard for the

British worker, who is used to some pretense of justice, to understand the conditions in the U.S. There, the class war is fought nakedly and with brutal ferocity; trustified capital uses ALL means and methods, legal or illegal, to prevent the workers from organizing and so gaining power."[55] Since the last four words expressed the authors' wishful thinking, the admission in the rest of the statement is all the more significant, for it points to the double meaning of raw power. The new industrialists' power over their employees was naked in two senses: unclothed by customary rules and norms, and unmediated by a middle class and a developed community structure. In the first sense it pertains to class relations within industry; in the second, to the relations between industry and American society. Each of the three entities involved—the industrialists, "public opinion," and the workers—had its own reasons for wanting raw power to be replaced by rules and norms; we shall examine briefly each of the entities in turn.

The long-term trend in the North among nonworkers, as a recent article points out, had been "away from violence, away from duelling and public hanging, blood sports and the corporal punishment of children, wife-beating and the use of the lash on servants. Violence was increasingly a sign of being undisciplined and an attribute of the lower class."[56] That the great entrepreneurs of the shake-up period were sometimes called robber barons and industrial buccaneers shows that they evoked images that were anachronistic and horrifying as well as romantic. Their exercise of raw power was not only illegitimate but made necessary by their lack of ideological hegemony. If manufacturers had dominated public opinion they would not have had to hire private armies or call for government troops to prevail over their striking employees.[57] They could get away with such actions because of the sheer economic power at their command, and many wielded it with little restraint, breaking the old craft unions, preventing the organization of the unskilled, and judiciously using welfare schemes to buy the workers' loyalty and public opinion's acquiescence.[58]

It would be a mistake, however, to assume that all industrialists wanted nothing more than unfettered power. Many wanted the legitimation of rules and procedures not only for the sake of industrial peace and efficiency but also for the sake of a clear conscience and the approval of public opinion. Vanderbilt's "the public be damned" has been quoted so often that it is easy to assume he spoke for his entire class. But the evidence of contrary sentiments ought to receive its due attention too.[59] The capitalists were, after all, products of the common heritage of values and ideals, including that of the supremacy of public opinion, and many of them, like everyone else, needed an ideology they sincerely believed in to be assured that their way of life was in the best interest of all.[60] The ingrained American deference to public opinion made it hard for the employers to perceive their power as real unless public opinion ratified it, and public opinion had never ratified untrammeled power. Hence we should not be surprised to find many expressions, by capitalists and their allies, of fear of radical conspiracies and of apprehension that the economic system was too fragile to last. This lack of confidence was expressed in their unusual openness to proposals for drastic change offered by reform and radical movements. The same combination of fear of conspiracy and openness to criticism had existed in the earlier shake-up period of the 1820s and 1830s.[61]

This brings us to the second entity involved—the "public." Its status is suggested in a recent study of plans offered at the close of World War I, aimed at "enfranchising" public opinion and giving it an important role in settling industrial disputes.[62] One such plan was modeled after the federal government's structure; it proposed a senate, a house of representatives, and a cabinet, in effect proclaiming not only the illegitimacy of the raw-power methods then prevailing but the consensual legitimacy of the existing ways in which the government ascertained and acquiesced in the decisions of public opinion. The plan was not just evidence of the political system's legitimacy; it was an effort to cure a problem, created by the lack of legitimate authority in industry, by borrowing some of the political system's aura of legitimacy. Another plan called for employee representation in shop committees—again reflecting the government's structure and the egalitarian ideal. All such plans that appealed to "outside" forces, including one for boards of arbitration with "public" representatives, can be interpreted as signifying that adequate norms had not yet developed *within* industry. The recourse to public opinion thus suggests the illegitimacy of both sides' naked interests in contradistinction to those of the "public," which would have to decide each dispute on its merits.

An even better indication of the legitimacy of public opinion is what happened where there was none, as was the case in mining settlements and in new industrial towns in the West. In neither type of town was there a preexisting social structure to limit the arbitrary power of the owners of mines and factories.[63] Tradesmen and professionals in recently settled towns in the West were as new to the localities as everyone else and usually possessed no independent class identity distinct from those of bosses and employees. The consequences of the absence of social structure were so obvious that even a few radicals at the time recognized them, despite their conviction that oppressive conditions were inherent in capitalism in all its forms and stages. One thoughtful socialist (an ex-Wobbly) wrote that the Ludlow massacre of 1914 could not have happened in Wisconsin or Ohio, not because the capitalists there were better than those who owned the Colorado mines, but because the middle class and public opinion were strong in the older parts of the country.[64]

Yet another sort of evidence of the supremacy of public opinion was industrialists' use of *agents provocateurs*; according to Robert Hunter, writing in 1914, they were used in every major strike in that period.[65] Apparently employers needed to win not only the strikes but also public approval, and knew they could not unless they showed the strikers to be led by violence-prone anarchists. In short, they were appealing to public opinion's fear of the one form of social disorder it would not tolerate—violence.

This point reminds us that often it was not only the industrialists who were alien elements in those communities (other than large cities) that did have a preexisting social structure; so were the newly arrived, unskilled workers. Industrial unions, even if they had been possible on a mass scale at that time, might have been condemned as ratifying a caste system in which an oppressed mass struggled continuously against an exploiting plutocracy. When those older communities supported unskilled strikers by extending credit, donating goods and money, and so on,[66] they were not showing approval of mass unions, but were expressing the old-fashioned values of fairness, belief in the independence and dignity of labor, and disapproval of the capitalists' arbitrary power. It is likely that the "public opinion" in such situations was siding not with workers as such but with *people* (preferably white Americans).[67] What was illegitimate, fundamentally, was the class relationship of untrammeled power on the one side and helplessness on the other, and when one party to that relationship attained respectability by submitting to rules, so did the other by helping through unions to administer them.[68] This outcome was signaled on a nationwide scale when the federal government finally legitimated mass unionism in basic industries during the New Deal.

The interest of the third entity involved—the workers—in trammeling the bosses' raw power is suggested by their reaction to the IWW's principled opposition to time contracts. The Wobblies had a point: contracts legitimated the capitalist-worker relationship, and they prevented workers from striking spontaneously whenever a grievance occurred. Yet this principle was irrelevant to the needs of the unskilled workers. Their most serious problem was not low wages, long hours, or bad working conditions, but insecurity of employment. Many managed not only to live on what they received but to save a little and send money to relatives in the Old Country. When conditions became intolerable they had little choice but to submit or move away, for unskilled strikers could succeed only if they controlled the entire pool of unskilled labor that might be used to replace them or if they had the support of well-organized, skilled workers with bargaining power. (But where an old skill was becoming obsolete, the latter too lost their bargaining power.)[69] Or the unskilled could explode in blind savagery, as the Slavic miners in Pennsylvania did several times in the 1890s,[70] or in strikes that sometimes manifested the workers' sheer outrage rather than their calculated decisions as to their chances for success. What they needed most was a way of ending the capricious treatment accorded them by bosses and foremen, a weapon they could wield in their own defense—in short, a union that could force a contractual relationship on the bosses. The Wobblies' no-contract principle, if widely accepted, would have multiplied the unpredictable confrontation of power against disastrously inferior power that Americans and immigrants alike wanted to avoid. During the IWW's heyday it received support only where the raw power of the employers had such completely free rein that the labor movement was nonexistent or shattered, and where the all-or-nothing mentality could therefore flourish.[71] The AFL's occasional success in getting contracts was due not to a sellout of workers' demands for power but to the success of struggles for the regularization of relations with employers. A reason for that success, intermittent though it was before the Great Depression, was that it coincided with many people's felt need for new rules and norms and the bureaucratization of the new power relationships created by industrialization.[72]

The workers' problems not only were organizational and economic but also had a psychological dimension. A dependable tyranny is psychologically more tolerable than a capricious one. That is why aggrieved peasants, unable to conceive of social revolution, sometimes petitioned their innovating rulers to return to the ancient ways. In the American situation there were, of course, no ancient ways to return to, or anything like the lord-peasant relationship; the need for predictability was manifested in other ways. When a superordinate behaves in unpredictable ways, legitimate authority degenerates into illegitimate authoritarianism. The subordinate cannot orient himself confidently but must respond to each act separately without the guidance of customary rules; and what might be a relationship (albeit unequal) with reciprocal obligations and rights becomes a repeated demonstration of power versus powerlessness. In a traditional society, both subordinate and superordinate implicitly are subject to an ancient code of rules and norms, and in a modern democratic society they abide by rules and norms that both participated in developing. In both types of society the superordinate's behavior gains legitimacy partly from its predictability, and the subordinate can feel his experience is to some extent the result of his own autonomous decisions.[73]

These facts help to explain an apparent paradox: the foreign-born majority of American industrial workers in the shake-up period, often treated arbitrarily by foremen and subject to barely limited power by bosses, clearly wanted to be treated according to "modern" norms—impersonally and therefore equally, according to the job and not religious or national stereotypes. They wanted to be treated according to criteria for hiring, performance, and promotion that were known in advance and equitably applied. That they often were not treated in this way was due not just to prejudice or divide-and-conquer tactics but more basically to the still unsystematic management practices in big industry. Yet the need for predictability remained, and so John Q. Worker sought and found it in one of the least modernized corners of American society, the immigrant community—with far-reaching consequences for the subsequent cultural history of the United States and for the fate of radical movements in the shake-up period. He was able to do so, however, because the characteristically modern compartmentalization of social roles and institutions had proceeded far enough to afford him "social space" to live his own way in a private realm remote psychologically and ideologically as well as physically from his boss's influence.

IV   The Place of Radical Movements in American Society

The compartmentalization of social roles and institutions referred to at the end of the previous chapter could not have been complete, or a functioning society would have been impossible. Nor does rejection of the System model entail adoption of its negative mirror image, *i.e.*, a "society" made up of totally independent social forms. The discussion up to this point has alternated between the nature of American society in the shake-up period and a style of thinking about it. It is time now to examine first, the relationship between those two topics; second, the way in which nonradicals' perception of the radicals at that time reveals important tensions in their society; and third, the ways in which the radical movements both reflected a minority's response to the shake-up and helped the majority to relocate the boundaries that separated acceptable from deviant beliefs and behavior.

I

As Stephen Toulmin argues in his book *Human Understanding*, if System is postulated in the history of science (including the social sciences and history) and in the history of societies, then change in either sphere can be accounted for only with reference to its effects upon and its generation by the System. Thus, according to Thomas Kuhn's theory of scientific revolutions, so long as a certain paradigm rules, scientific change either serves the paradigm, by solving problems the paradigm itself defines and for which it provides the conceptual tools, or subverts it, by accumulating "anomalies" that eventuate in the abandonment of the paradigm in favor of one that better accommodates the by-then sizable heap of conflicting facts and hypotheses. This constitutes a "scientific revolution." With respect to bourgeois society, the same way of thinking assumes that important social change either subserves or subverts the System, until the "contradictions" reach the point where, to use Marx's phrase, their capitalist integument is burst asunder. Kuhn's famous portrayal of the structure of science thus bears a striking resemblance to the portrayal of American society as a System in the writings of some historians and sociological functionalists. "The assumption of 'systematicity,'" writes Toulmin, makes "the explanation of social change as hard as the explanation of conceptual change has been for 'systematic' philosophies of science. For how could the balance between institutions then be altered, except by 'dysfunctional' changes?"

Toulmin goes on to liken those "social physiologists" to pre-Darwinian thinkers such as Herbert Spencer.

Neither side, indeed, shows any sign of having learned the general historiographical lesson of Darwinism: that, in the development of historical entities or populations, it is not the *current* structure and relationships within that population which require to be explained as "functional," but rather the *changes* taking place in them which require to be explained as "adaptive." Each of the coexisting institutions and customs making up a society or a culture will possess, at any particular time, its own internal forms and structures, which serve—in a quasi-physiological sense—to define the normal "functioning" of each separate element. The relations between these different institutions or customs, on the other hand, will be—in this sense—neither "functional" nor "dysfunctional." Each individual element in the society or culture will normally have come into existence at a different point in history, to meet some particular set of needs, problems, or "demands." And, just as we can legitimately raise questions about the "functional" adaptedness or "effectiveness" of a science, only when we are considering how changes in the relevant concepts serve as responses to the current pattern of "intellectual demands," so too with the institutions of a society and the customs of a culture.[1]

In the face of dissent, American society was neither so strong nor so weak as the radicals perceived it to be; it lacked both the impregnability of a System in which each part reinforced the others, and the vulnerability of a System in which disease in one part must infect the others. In terms of a Darwinian "populational schema," Toulmin suggests that "the balance between variation and selection within a population of constituent elements is, evidently, one of the possible processes by which historical entities preserve their transient identity." To which we may add, for present purposes, that instead of identifying the "essential" meaning of, say, a strike regardless of its actual intent and effects, or seeking an invisible coordination of all parts of a society in the interest of one class, it would be more productive to begin with a picture of social institutions as both interdependent and partly isolated, as biological species are. Instead of studying past society and its radical movements in terms of an assumed telos, it would be preferable to be as neutral as Darwin was "about any supposed overall direction of historical development."[2]

In Toulmin's terms, certain radical or reform doctrines in the shake-up period might be analogous to mutations that succeeded in altering the constitution of a variety of voluntary groups within American society that in turn endeavored to compete with other "populations" in affecting the entire ecological pattern. It is possible, however, to carry the biological metaphor too far and to assume that the ultimate success or failure of a "mutation" was due to an automatic or mindless process. The fates of the various reform and radical movements were results of conscious choices, and those movements helped to define the situations in which the choices were made. They did this in various ways: obviously by directing public attention to "problems" needing solutions and less obviously by developing symbols for public discourse that, to a large minority of Americans, drew together an assortment of ideas, images, feelings, and aspirations. Any usefully simple metaphor would present the temptation to oversimplify, but with this warning in mind I suggest that the reform and radical movements in the shake-up period were like items on a menu from which a society hungry for adaptive changes could choose. It is true that an injudicious selection could give a *System* indigestion, or worse. But experience has shown again and again that menu choices that radicals assumed would have revolutionizing effects, owing to the interdependence of all important elements in the System, have had no such consequences.

Their error lay in their assumption that certain proposals expressing the core of their ideologies would also touch the core of the System. That is, when they appraised various components of American society, some appeared to be "core" and others "peripheral," according to whether the System could or could not survive if they were changed. The elements in the radicals' ideologies that pertained to those components were correspondingly core or peripheral elements in those ideologies.

For instance, to the IWW, industrial unionism was a core tenet, whereas to most members of the SP, it was a peripheral tenet; the Wobblies believed that mass organization of the workers into industrial unions would lead quickly to the abolition of capitalism, whereas those SP members considered craft and industrial unions appropriate to different situations and equal in their potential usefulness for radical or procapitalist tacticians. This point must be stressed because the assortment of core and peripheral tenets has changed over the years, and historians tend to read current radicals' clustering of tenets back into earlier periods. But in fact, in the shake-up period, the various radical movements' ideologies were assortments of "menu" items, reflecting the circumstances of their time, just as is true today. We can best understand the relationships between the radical movements and their society if we include them among those social groups that cooked up menu items, some of which were eventually selected. If American society had been a System, with a ruling class or caste whose belief-system carried the presumption of rightness, the assortment of radical and reform movements in the antebellum generation and then in the turn-of-the-century generation would have had only the minor adjustive function of coordinating the System in the capitalists' interests. But, as was argued earlier, the capitalist class was itself subjected, in both periods, to criticism by the criteria of various "higher laws" that were explicitly disassociated from any particular class or group except some vague entity called "the productive classes." Because the society's "core" values changed much more slowly than the economy, they provided a standpoint for reformers who denounced the capitalists and their raw power.

These remarks help explain why certain menu items were accepted and others rejected. If the society had been a System, the System's needs would have determined the selection. It is hard to see how one could accept this concept without committing the twin fallacies of teleologism and reification. If, on the contrary, the society was a Society, the explanation for the selection must start at the other end, the felt needs and the beliefs of the people affected. Of course they were unequal in power and influence, and sophisticated Marxists do take into account the contributions made to the "hegemonic ideology" by the less influential and less powerful people. However, they see such contributions as shaping the form but not the content, which had to be the interest of the ruling class, fundamentally the same regardless of the stages and differing national forms of capitalism. To these Marxists that was the price the bourgeoisie had to pay for its hegemony. But if the United States was a Society, in which the parts were connected only loosely, the economic ruling class's partial hegemony in the economic sphere can be considered just as plausibly the price John Q. Worker willingly paid for his semiautonomy in the private sphere. The menu choices were made on the basis of more "local" felt needs and wishes, and there is no compelling reason to assume they all ultimately worked together in the interest of an all-encompassing System. Instead, the Society itself *was* the sum total of the groups and the consequences of the choices made at each juncture.[3]

This is true for another reason as well: if the society had been a System, all menu choices that pertained to important subjects would have required the System to be redefined at every junction point, so that the more variation we find between different stages of the System and between different national versions of it, the more "underlying" its basic structure would have to have been, to remain essentially the same at all stages and in all capitalist countries. Hence, the further removed its basic structure would have become from empirical reality and from all those components of the System that it supposedly determined. In addition, it would correspondingly become more and more likely that a historian's retention of the concept was traceable to something other than the need to explain the evidence.

The assortment of menu items offered in the shake-up period was not random, as the "mutation" metaphor might imply. Most of the items dealt in one way or another with the question of power and authority—political, economic, or social. In the economic movements this is obvious, but it is true as well in such movements as the city-manager, feminist, antiobscenity, prohibitionist, immigration-restriction, racial-equality, Populist, and other movements. Since it was the legitimacy of authority that was controverted, many movements talked not about authority but about power, the unjust power that one group or person exerted over others. Even the resurgence of Fundamentalism, as well as the other religious movements of the period, can be seen partly in this light. To a System-thinker, this fact proves his contention by revealing the "real meaning" of all the programs and demands: widespread resistance to the economic power of the bourgeoisie, split into many forms because nobody but the radicals understood its basic cause. The evidence suggests rather that the revolt against the decay of the legitimacy of various forms of authority *included* the economic. Any hypothesis that interpreted both the Fundamentalist and Ethical Culture movements, both the feminist and the Comstock movements, both the Niagara and the antiblack movements in terms of a response to the hegemony of the big bourgeoisie would, I think, be self-refuting. That the raw power of that class played a crucial part in the process is unquestionable, but it played a part in a larger process and was not the process of which the other responses were parts. The evolution of the economic system furthered the erosion of authority systems that had been going on for several generations. That process began with the denial of authority to the state, during the Revolution; it went further with the denial of authority in the economic sphere; in time it has penetrated closer and closer to the individual, in the sphere of family relations, with first women and eventually children declaring their independence of paterfamilias.

The process received a setback when the new-immigrant workers arrived. For them, that erosion had barely begun, and they introduced a new, group-centered force into the society—the ethnic group—which evoked a shocked response from some Americans whose individuation had proceeded much further. Herbert G. Gutman suggests that this "continued infusion of prefactory people into an increasingly industrialized society" may help "explain why movements to legislate morality and to alter habits have lasted much longer in the United States than in most other industrial countries."[4] In shake-up periods political discourse tends to be more moralistic than usual. Political alternatives tend at such times to be seen as choices between right and wrong and hence in more religious terms than in periods when values and practice are more clearly consistent with each other. The moral principles applied in shake-up periods reveal what remains unquestioned. People appeal to transcendent principles when more pragmatic criteria seem inadequate, not only because they need a standpoint for judgment but also out of the need for permanence in the midst of change. When a debater on the currency question proclaims that gold is God's currency and is answered by the cry that gold is the cross on which The People are crucified, money is obviously not all that is at stake.

The transcendent criteria applied most frequently by Americans in the turn-of-the-century shake-up period were the traditional values of Protestant individualism, outraged by the fruits of the equally traditional custom of according status to white men according to quantitative criteria. Such fruits were the appearance of bigness in industry, in urban settlement, in business organization—big institutions getting bigger and less controllable by a society of individuals. In such a situation the sudden proliferation of new voluntary groups, including reform and radical organizations, can be seen as an effort at reintegration. Some menu items, in other words, were suggestions for reconstituting social groups in a society in which the all-powerful individual had turned into the powerless prey of economic overlords. In the light of the widespread efforts to organize separate interest groups rather than the entire population,[5] even the formation of the strange new ethnic groups began to seem a legitimate correlate to what native-born Americans were doing. In time the ethnics too were accepted in the new pluralism, on the condition that they divested themselves of what some perceived as their ideological—i.e., radical—foreignness. A "good" ethnic in time became as acceptable as Theodore Roosevelt's "good" trusts.

In a democratic-pluralist society in which individualism is a cherished value, part of its tradition—what some would pejoratively call a "myth," meaning delusion—is that power is diffused in the electorate. In a nation in which the majority believes that each vote counts, that government officials are the servants of their constituents, and that each man is responsible for his economic success or failure, individuals who are very dissatisfied with some institution or public practice will consider it their right and duty to organize to change it. In the aristocratic-hierarchical society from which the earliest settlers came, such behavior was regarded as conspiratorial or seditious. They went ahead anyway, and bit by bit the definitions of conspiracy and sedition narrowed: first political organizing and criticism of the government became legitimate, and later unionizing did too. Ordinary Americans' belief in the "myths" of their own power and responsibility for the public weal caused them to defy prosecutions and court decisions, and it was the "myths" that finally prevailed. So long as such beliefs retain their vitality, any shake-up period will produce a new crop of voluntary associations to take their places with those that exist at all times in such a society.

Since the 1820s, the institutional diversity of the American social order has permitted independent activity to radicals and reformers, who are as much legitimate precipitants of the culture at any moment as are the standpatters or indifferent people. This is so not only because there is always a gap between ideals and reality that offends people of tender conscience, but also because a few general ideals are as necessary to the social order as are its business-sphere values. A society characterized by extreme division of labor, mental as well as physical, requires separate groups to be the custodians of values—and they include those radicals who believe their values are alien to the American social order. Hence, minority movements of dissenters perform, in our society, one of the functions of a ruling elite in an officially hierarchical society. Whereas certain values are assigned to the home for nurturing, others to the business arena, and others to the churches, changes in those values or in their institutional embodiments are the job of certain types of voluntary movements.

Just as the federal structure of the government permits one state to try out legislative novelties, with no great loss if they fail in that limited area, dissenting movements try out this and that solution to social problems on a small scale and in the realm of thought, advancing with a few followers along a variety of possible paths to the future and sending back reports about what it may be like, so that the rest of the society can then choose which path it prefers. (Needless to say, the process is not that conscious or deliberate.)

Another difference between a democratic-pluralist and an aristocratic society is suggested by this assignment of different values and ideals to specific spheres. Where an authoritative ruling elite makes the menu choices, public opinion has a correspondingly minor role in ratifying them. In the United States, where an undifferentiated public opinion must ratify those choices that affect the entire society, the walls surrounding each semi-independent sphere are somewhat lower, and each citizen considers himself correspondingly more competent to cast his "vote" on the choices—in every sphere besides science, the arcane vocabulary of which has kept its walls high.

A comparison between British and American abolitionists can elucidate this difference. In Britain the abolitionist leaders were highly respectable: peers, MPs, rich merchants. Many were Quakers, that is, members of a "deviant" sect. But their Quakerism and their espousal of abolitionism had no effect on their respectability and elite status, for these were defined independently of their beliefs, as well as because abolitionism was a peripheral issue to the conventional belief-system and ruling-class interests. For all these reasons these people wielded great influence on the public opinion that counted in the circumstances; it did not matter what John Q. Worker thought. In short, abolitionism in Britain represented, in part, a change in an important principle, handed down by a hegemonic group and accepted by the rest of the population. In the United States it represented, in part, a criticism of a regional ruling class by ordinary citizens who tried, by means of democratic propaganda, to mobilize public opinion to effect the change from below. Later in the century other ordinary citizens repeated the process, an important part of which was the proffering of new menu items that were seen as "deviant."

The sociological literature on deviance has focused mainly on its function of creating solidarity and a feeling of identity among the majority. It therefore deals mostly with those forms of deviance that are defined as criminal and insane. But it is at least as important to take note of ideological deviance, not only insofar as it sharpens a society's awareness of the extent of acceptable belief and behavior but also as it enables a society to discover what beliefs and behavior it will choose to endorse or tolerate.[6] Although this process operates continuously in an egalitarian-democratic society, it is especially important during a shakeup period, when there is widespread uncertainty about some contents of the approved belief-system and the location of the boundary separating the acceptable from the deviant. The demands made by the unusually conspicuous dissenting movements are scattered at all points on the hither and far sides of the old boundary, and in choosing among them the society eventually relocates the boundary by defining some as newly acceptable and others as deviant. Hence, the radical movements in that period can best be understood as "limiting cases" of the ap-

proved beliefs and values. That is, people used them not just to rein-
force the existing boundaries but also to discover where the new ones
should be, and until they did, no one could be sure which dissenters or
which parts of their programs would fall outside. Or, to put the point a
bit differently, since "it was necessary to discover an enemy by distinguishing subversion from simple diversity,"[7] to a society that considered pluralism a good, a shake-up period posed a special problem: the
menu of new beliefs and norms proffered by radical and reform groups
represented both the fearful threat of disintegration and the provider of
the solution to the problem. How could one tell which alternative a
movement represented if it seemed very close to the boundary? Which
were the permissible variations of the necessarily abstract and vague
values that a pluralistic society must agree on if it was to cohere, and
which were alternatives to them?

   With respect to the central problem of the 1890–1917 shake-up period—the capitalists' raw power—the radicals' contention that the only
cure was the abolition of the capitalist class ran head-on into the ingrained belief in the power of public opinion. In fact, if that contention
had been accepted, the public whose opinion it was would have been
relinquishing the very power by which it had traditionally limited that
of the most powerful groups. Hence the radicals' most basic demand
was clearly outside the boundary from the start. Yet every other proposal they made received widespread support. No one knew, however,
which of them, if any, entailed the abolition of capitalism and which
could be put into effect without such drastic consequences. The supposedly all-powerful and all-influential capitalist class did not hand
down the answer; it was the defendant in the proceedings.[8] In effect the
verdict was that it would be permitted to continue running the economy
but on the condition that the boundary around its acceptable behavior
be redrawn more narrowly. In time a quid pro quo took place: the politically active part of the population agreed to put certain of the radicals'
demands outside the boundary and at the same time placed limits on
the capitalists' behavior inside it. We shall, they said, define a working-
class political party and a revolutionary union as deviant, and you will
agree to behave in such a way as to make them unnecessary.[9] This agreement turned out to be self-validating, since the power of noncapitalists
to force it made the radicals' theories less credible. The outcome of the

shake-up period seemed to Americans to show that their society's boundaries enclosing acceptable belief and behavior were in fact drawn in part by public opinion and not totally by the wielders of economic power; that economic, political, and ideological powers were not coterminous; and that the economic power of the capitalists was wielded on the sufferance of the whole society.

As the boundary metaphor suggests, the choices that were made from the array of proposals for change did not require positive consensus on all important norms, values, and beliefs within the boundary. Within the assortment of semiautonomous and partly conflicting groups, a range of belief and behavior could be tolerated. Within some of those groups, a rigid consensus was indeed required, on pain of expulsion. Yet even some of those groups experienced their own shake-ups before locating their own boundaries. The histories of the SLP, SP, and IWW exemplify this process.

II

Insofar as the radicals of the 1890–1917 shake-up period are concerned, the rhetoric that they and their adversaries hurled at each other reveals not only what they disagreed on but also what they shared, the symbols and cultural categories brought to the surface by the shake-up in economic power relations, and the ways in which both sides were, unwittingly, collaborating in defining their society. Thus, the very misunderstandings, both sides' inaccurate images of each other, become revealing data.[10]

For example, consider the popular image of the Wobblies as bent on wholesale violence. Melvyn Dubofsky and Joseph Robert Conlin have proven the falsity of that image.[11] Conlin especially tries hard to show how very conventional the Wobblies were. "The image of the Wobblies," he explains, "as contemptuous of conventional society ignores the IWW's frequent solicitude of public favor. The union was vividly aware of the value of a favorable public opinion. An outraged citizenry had played a crucial role in the Wobbly victories in Spokane in 1909 and in a textile workers' strike in Lawrence, Massachusetts, in 1912. More often, as the union was also aware, a newspaper-molded public opinion was hostile to its purposes." Wobblies even gave "tacit support" to the prohibitionist movement. "The idea of roughhewn Wobblies pulling alongside blue-stockinged Republican dowagers and clerical conservatives seems preposterous if one persists in envisioning the Wobblies as nothing more than erratic Reds." [12]

Yet the best explanation he can suggest for the inaccurate portrayal of the Wobblies is that Americans tend to dismiss revolutionaries "as bizarre by definition," and that historians assume that the IWW was a revolutionary movement instead of just a union. "In fact," adds Conlin, "if the revolutionary rhetoric is momentarily set aside, it is clear that the IWW conducted its major eastern strikes . . . for the same pragmatic ends for which the AFL conducted its many strikes during the same period." [13] Even if this were so, is nothing crucial to be learned from that rhetoric, from asking why a presumably conventional union chose to use it, and from the fact that the public took the rhetoric more seriously than the behavior? On the contrary, the more conclusive the evidence for the Wobblies' conventionality, the more the public's attention to the violent rhetoric cries out for explanation. The question of violence was of utmost symbolic as well as literal importance during the shake-up period and warrants a closer look. This requires examination of the American public's image of those two groups that they equated with violence: the terrorist wing of the anarchist movement and the Wobblies.

Conlin portrays the Wobblies as so conventional that the reader may wonder what the to-do was all about. He states that no Wobblies were ever caught committing violence or sabotage. He blames their "bloody reputation" on their enemies: employers, city authorities, AFL union rivals, antiunion politicians, and reformist SP members. [14] No doubt these were partly responsible. But why did the public believe them rather than the evidence of the Wobblies' own behavior? John Q. Worker did not automatically believe everything the "influentials" told him; he had his own reasons for believing one thing and disbelieving another. It is, moreover, likely that if the authorities had not suppressed those who violated conventions of law and order, the majority of politically active people, including workers, would have punished such officials at the next election. [15]

As to the anarchists, we may take for our text "The Anarchist Scare of 1908," by Robert J. Goldstein. The scare was touched off by an anarchist's murder of a Denver priest and by two assassination attempts, in Chicago and New York City, in the next two weeks. "It is difficult," says the author, "to understand how the anarchist scare of 1908 could have developed if the standard historical interpretation of the early years of the Progressive Era is accepted," an interpretation emphasizing "buoyant optimism," "unity," and "confidence." Beneath the good feelings lay tensions and fears stemming from recollections of the Paris Commune, the spread of radicalism in the years just before 1908, and concern about social stability after the 1907 depression.[16]

Goldstein amply documents the widespread fear of anarchism[17] and the desire to preserve law and order. He quotes several public figures, especially Theodore Roosevelt, and a few newspapers as equating all socialists and other radicals with anarchists. The police often ignored the difference between violent and nonviolent radicals. Yet Goldstein's data suggest that many, perhaps most, officials and journals made precisely that distinction. He quotes six newspapers denouncing anarchist sentiments, and adds, "A handful of papers maintained a sense of perspective . . . and opposed the use of repressive measures," quoting four examples. It is not clear how representative each batch was of American journalism. The same problem of typicality arises several pages later in another press survey, this time on reactions to a police attack on a demonstration by unemployed workers in New York's Union Square. "Many newspapers" called for repression of anarchy, some blaming socialists for instigating the discontent from which anarchists benefited. But many others, as Goldstein honestly points out, applied the anarchist label to the authorities who showed contempt for the law.[18] What is clear is that many, perhaps most, of those who called for repression of the socialists did so out of fear of "anarchist" violence and not out of a desire to suppress radical propaganda per se. Or, in other words, many of the writers and officials whom Goldstein cites as opposing violence because they equated it with socialism seem rather to have opposed socialism because they equated it with violence.

This supposition gains added plausibility from several details that he does not analyze. For one thing, he states that the Western Federation of Miners "announced that it was dispensing with the services of William Haywood, apparently because his radical utterances were regarded as not very politic given the general state of public opinion."[19] The implication of dishonest opportunism is misleading. What of the "public opin-

ion" among the union's own rank and file? By the end of the Moyer-
Haywood-Pettibone trial, most of the leaders and members evidently
agreed with the public opinion outside the union that Haywood's increasingly impolitic language would do labor more harm than good.[20]
For another thing, referring to a new law barring incitements to arson,
murder, or assassination from the mails, Goldstein comments that for
the first time "political criteria were established";[21] yet these were criminal, not political, criteria. Third, his comment that the post office excluded the anarchist *La Question sociale* from the mails "on the technical
ground that it was not a newspaper or other periodical within the meaning of the law, apparently because there were no other legal grounds for
acting against it,"[22] ignores the fact that during the same era the periodicals of the SP, SLP, and IWW retained their mailing privileges.[23] (The Socialist New York *Call* was denied mailing privileges briefly in 1912, for
publishing articles on birth control, not socialism.) The respectability of
socialism is in fact shown by Goldstein's quotation from a New Haven
paper, which referred to crimes "committed under the protection and
guise of socialism,"[24] although other papers assumed that socialism
meant violence; in other words, it was violence they feared.

I should like to propose that, in the absence of evidence to the contrary, when a person says he is for law and order we assume he is for
law and order, and when he advocates sanctions against violence it is
because he wants to suppress violence and not necessarily radicalism
(although he may also *oppose* radicalism). On these assumptions, it is
not difficult to account for the anarchist scare of 1908 and at the same
time accept the conventional view of the Progressive era, for the scare
was due to certain anarchists' violent acts, just as most people at the
time thought it was.

This does not mean that other tensions and fears were absent. Attention to the rhetoric that such episodes produced enables us to understand what the adversaries were disagreeing about and what they were
not disagreeing about. Thus, Robert Hunter of the SP's right wing revealed more than he knew when he called the big capitalists, with their
private armies, "the oldest anarchists."[25] The same is true of De Leon's
Daily People which, according to Goldstein, approved of President Roosevelt's barring an anarchist paper from the mails and advised workers

not to heed calls for physical force.[26] Again and again the SLP and the SP denounced capitalist "chaos," "anarchy," and "disorder," and proclaimed themselves the herald of the restoration of order.

At times, some Wobblies seemed intent on doing all they could to prove their enemies right. Elizabeth Gurley Flynn recalled a spat she had with Haywood shortly after the United States entered the war. She asked him to remove certain inflammatory pamphlets from circulation, including one she herself had written on sabotage. The IWW's new orientation "toward job organization and mass action and away from individual action, like sabotage, I felt was correct." But Haywood asked, "'What's the matter, Gurley? Are you losing your nerve?' He ordered a new edition printed with a lurid cover, designed by Ralph Chaplin, of black cats and wooden shoes [symbols of sabotage]. But the executive board stepped in and ordered that it should not be published."[27] And a 1911 pamphlet coauthored by William Z. Foster—then still a member of the IWW—announced, "The syndicalist is as 'unscrupulous' in his choice of weapons to fight his every-day battles as for his final struggle with capitalism. He allows no considerations of 'legality,' religion, patriotism, 'honor,' 'duty,' etc., to stand in the way of his adoption of effective tactics. . . . With him the end justifies the means."[28] It is not so hard to see why people who read and heard such declarations, in a period of great uncertainty over industrial relations, feared that those who made them would act on them.

That some public authorities were both able and willing to distinguish between that sort of thing and peaceful advocacy of socialism is shown by another incident recounted by Elizabeth Gurley Flynn, this one in the summer of 1917. Arriving in Duluth to speak at the Finnish socialists' annual picnic, she went to the IWW hall where she was told that, owing to the war hysteria against the IWW, she should say, if asked, that she had "come for the Socialist picnic which had been a respected annual event there for many years."[29] It will be noted that this took place shortly after the convention at which the SP publicly opposed the war. The authorities made the same distinction in 1913 when some sailors demolished both the SP and IWW headquarters in Seattle. The ensuing statements by public officials and newspapers repeatedly used the phrase "the IWW and those socialists who are friendly to them," or words to that effect, implying that other socialists were innocent of the unpatriotic behavior that had enraged the sailors.[30]

For a time, public opinion placed the labor movement athwart the boundary between peaceful advocacy of radical change and sabotage. The IWW inadvertently proved helpful in placing the other unions on the peaceful side, and it did so, ironically, in the course of trying to locate its own boundary between correct and incorrect methods of agitation. Conlin mentions that the organization suspended the weekly *Industrial Worker* for publishing an article, in December, 1912, that obliquely advised lumber workers to drive spikes into logs bound for sawmills. He quotes a lawyer, a priest, and an editor who urged that Wobblies and strikers be shot so as to discourage such sabotage. But the historians who perpetuate the violent image of the Wobblies, Conlin complains, do not portray lawyers, priests, and editors as violent: "Historians today would not as a rule react adversely to the idea of labor unionism. But to regard the IWW as a force for violence in American industrial history is to be shackled by the antiunionist encumbrances of the past. The contemporaries of the Wobblies who affixed the reputation for violence to the IWW knew that it was a labor union which they were attacking. If labor historians realize the same, the Wobblies can be studied for what they were, rather than for what their enemies maintained they were."[31] Certainly those who overreacted to the articles—there were many helpful hints for would-be saboteurs in the *Industrial Worker* and *Solidarity*—should be portrayed accurately. But Conlin's erasure of the difference between the AFL and the IWW distorts the picture more than does some historians' tendency to ignore the fact that the IWW was indeed a union. That it tried to be both a union and a revolutionary organization is precisely what makes it and its public image so valuable in our effort to reconstruct the process of boundary-drawing between deviant and acceptable belief and behavior. It explains why the IWW withered and the AFL survived and in time grew powerful.[32] Opposition to violence, sabotage, or even peaceful revolution is not the same as opposition to unionism. More to the point, contemporaries of the IWW in the shake-up period were beginning to put unionism within the boundary, but only on the condition (among others) that it eschew violence and sabotage. Or, to put the point another way, the AFL ended up nondeviant by virtue of the same tacit quid pro quo that made the IWW the model of what a union must not be.

When the SP recalled Haywood from its National Executive Committee early in 1913, the press across the nation evidently understood that the party's repudiation of violence was sincere. The *Literary Digest* commented that "most outside observers of the Socialist party view the recall . . . as a condemnation of violence or 'direct action,' as a means of overthrowing capitalism." [33] Wobbly writers on occasion disavowed anarchist tendencies. When the SP made such disclaimers, some historians say it was currying the favor of middle-class public opinion, but when Wobblies did, historians say they were counteracting false images in the public mind. A historian with no ideological ax to grind will ask why both organizations felt impelled to make the same disclaimers. One answer is obvious: *violent* and *anarchist* were labels guaranteed to ostracize any person or group wearing them.

Attention to the rhetoric impels us to ask why even those whose motive was clearly to suppress peaceful advocacy of socialism had to say they were merely advocating suppression of violence and sabotage. Part of the answer involves the tradition, discussed earlier, of grass-roots initiative in choosing the direction of change and of ordinary citizens' feeling of responsibility for the choices that were made and their consequent need for free public debate. This meant not only that peaceful advocacy had to be protected but also that violence, which impeded purely verbal conflict, had to be regarded as evil to the same degree as freedom of advocacy was considered good. But violence represented something more: most often the supposedly violence-prone radicals were feared and denounced not because—or not solely because—of the nature of the future society they were working to create but because of their alleged propensity to commit violent acts in the present. Persuasion left the decision on the issue up to the individual, but violence could affect anyone, at any time, unexpectedly; it represented an extreme form of "raw power," of behavior without rules, the extreme denial of that individual autonomy that was a traditional American value and the decay of which at that time was a principal grievance of all radicals. [34] We may here recall Robert Hunter's hurling of the epithet *anarchist* back at the capitalists: one of the chief causes of much of that period's reformism and radicalism was outrage at the rulelessness, the disorder, and the violence suffered by workers—to which radicals added their own theory that the only antidote was the abolition of the class responsible for them. Hunter, and many other radicals who used this argument, were denouncing violence not to mollify public opinion so that it would listen to radical propaganda on other matters; they were trying to tell nonradicals who also feared violence that their proposals concerning those other matters would restore order, predictability, and individual security.

Moreover, this was widely understood. Most of the many magazine articles published in this period commenting on the rise in the SP's popularity were calm and confident, implicitly assuming or explicitly predicting that the socialists would continue to rely on persuasion and that the American working class, free to choose between socialism and the current social order, would choose the latter. Even those writers who considered the advent of socialism a real possibility were unfrightened by it, believing that it would come, if at all, gradually and peacefully in the form of the orderly increase in economic democracy and popular control of industries affected with a public interest.[35] When the socialists won control of Milwaukee in 1910, according to one scholar, "the United States remained remarkably calm in the face of a socialist victory in its fourteenth largest city."[36] Again, the boundary between confidence and fear was drawn partly by the advocacy of violence or sabotage, and although IWW leaders and journalists loudly and sincerely disclaimed approval of violence, many of their speeches and articles as well as the SP's disavowal of Haywoodism put the IWW on the far side of the boundary, so far as public opinion was concerned.

Although government repression of violence has sometimes been a mere cover for repression of radical doctrines, it could not have succeeded unless there had been widespread fear of and opposition to violence. The propensity to dismiss as imaginary the ordinary citizen's abhorrence of violence would be puzzling if it were not for the fact that acknowledgment of its existence would entail recognition of the toleration accorded peaceful advocacy of radicalism in most periods of American history, including the 1890–1917 shake-up period when the radical minority was larger, proportionately and absolutely, than ever before or since. And that recognition in turn would contradict certain assumptions integral to most radical historians' version of past American radical history, among which is the assumption that John Q. Worker has been far more receptive to peacefully propagated radical doctrines than he has ever been in fact. The implications of this and related assumptions are important enough to warrant some scrutiny at this point.

Historians on the left possess an image of the relationship among John Q. Worker, the government, and the radicals throughout American history that is held with a conviction as complete as the lack of documentary evidence to support it. That image is of a government at all levels continually silencing and sometimes committing violence against radicals and thereby suppressing the people's "natural" inclination to support them. To challenge this image is to evoke the inevitable objection: "But what about Haymarket? And the Panthers? And the Palmer Raids and the Smith Act trials and Kent State?" I would reply that all such episodes combined not only do not add up to the aforementioned pattern, but are far outnumbered by instances of government toleration of or indifference to radical activities. There were the labor radicals of the 1820s through 1840s; Fanny Wright and Robert Dale Owen, who lectured and published with little interference; the organization and agitation of a series of socialist parties from the 1870s on; the widespread discussion of socialism during the Progressive period; the generally unmolested activities of the Socialist, Communist, Socialist Workers, and Socialist Labor parties from the 1920s on; SDS and Progressive Labor activities during the 1960s and early 1970s; and the unchallenged advocacy of socialism by some state legislators and free publication of many scholarly books and articles expressing a radical philosophy by academics up to the present time. Toleration and indifference are less conspicuous than incidents of repression; they do not liven up the historical record and catch the researcher's eye. Their significance is likely to be noted only by historians who are looking at the larger pattern and are willing to consider that the repressive episodes might be exceptional.

Moreover, the exceptions should be separated into two categories. Some episodes, such as Haymarket and the Palmer Raids, were all that they are generally held to be: hysterical reactions to imaginary threats and gross miscarriages of justice. Others, however, were defenses of the society or segments of it against violence; these include raids on members of groups that preached violence and were found to possess arsenals or that committed acts of violence. The difference between these two categories is not that between threats and nonthreats to the "System." It is the threat or nonthreat of violent acts that marks the difference.

Radicals, confronted with such evidence of toleration or indifference, reverse their argument and contend that the government has been willing to allow free speech to radicals so long as they did not threaten the "System." The implication is that the government has been hypocritical and that the freedom it accords to radicals has been meaningless because harmless. Yet their hope for success depends on their using that freedom to speak and publish, to convert millions to their philosophy. The only threat they can pose to the social order—in contradistinction to the threat, by small groups, of violence against individuals and property—would be their success in making millions of converts by the use of press and platform. Hence, radicals' freedom to propagate their views without threatening the "System" (because too few people agree with them) not only is not a meaningless freedom but is meaningful in the only circumstances in which it can be meaningful, for it is exercised during the period in which their doctrines are afforded the freedom to meet the only test that counts in practice: their persuasiveness to the majority of the people when the latter are free to accept or reject them.

Why have radicals, enjoying this freedom of advocacy in a democratic country, proclaimed via platform, lectern, and the press that they are exercising a meaningless freedom (presumably hoping by that very act to persuade people not only that their doctrines are right but also that what they are doing is pointless)? The answer seems to lie in the fact that they have failed, generation after generation, to convert enough people to their side to constitute a threat to the continuation of the "System." Since their own doctrine states that the people must freely discover that the radicals are right, the failure must be due to the people's somehow being prevented from receiving the truth. They are prevented by the very fact that the radicals are given this freedom; this deludes people into thinking that they live in a free society. Freedom is evidence of unfreedom. Alternately, they say the radicals have been silenced by repression or the threat of it; that too is evidence of unfreedom.

The fallacies of overgeneralization and apriorism, and the construction of a "tradition" by the selection of certain incidents and ignoring of the many contrary ones over a long period, are overlooked because of the two axioms mentioned earlier: that radicals have been the tribunes of the people whom the people would have supported but for government intimidation, and that the government has been a hostile power set over the majority. Without those two undocumentable assumptions—which moreover imply the people's passivity and gullibility—the entire tableau falls apart. In short, the argument is unempirical and its documentary foundation highly selective. The American people never seem to have perceived the three-way relationship among themselves, radicals, and the government as radicals have, although they have heard that message for over a century. They have considered the government their government (although this has recently become less true, to the same degree as the growth of the social-engineering state), and seem to have regarded the government's persecution of certain radical groups as protections of democracy in certain situations in which they thought (mistakenly) that democracy was threatened.

III

Radical historians tend to see radical movements as central to American history; many nonradical historians see them as peripheral (whether "good" or "bad"). Both those contentions are true of rare movements here and there, but both are one-sided as general propositions. A phrase used earlier in this chapter—that radical movements might be seen as "limiting cases" of acceptable belief and behavior—can, I believe, retain the elements of truth in both. Radical movements have been central in that they have cathected central problems and tensions in their generations and helped their compatriots to relocate the boundaries between acceptable and deviant beliefs; and they have been peripheral in that they have invariably failed in their main self-appointed task of radicalizing the society and have never comprised more than a small minority of any class. Three examples can illustrate how by their very failure in the shake-up period they functioned as "limiting cases."

The first is the campaign for the woman suffrage amendment to the New York State constitution. The SP saw an opportunity to get it passed when Morris Hillquit ran for mayor of New York City in 1917. As he recalled in his autobiography, his three opponents would have preferred to say nothing on the issue because the voters were split, but they feared that all the prosuffrage votes would go to Hillquit. Therefore they endorsed the amendment and it passed.[37] This episode showed that the boundary between an acceptable and a deviant attitude toward women's participating in politics had shifted since 1915, when the amendment was defeated. But only a party with nothing to lose by taking a stand on the issue could be the means whereby the necessarily more cautious major parties discovered the shift. No doubt the SP had helped to increase the prosuffrage sentiment somewhat in New York City. But its main contribution lay in its forcing the politicians of the major parties to catch up with their constituents' beliefs, which had changed mostly in response to the strong campaign waged for many years by the nonsocialist suffragist movement.

The second illustration shows a radical movement working as a "limiting case" of acceptable beliefs in a negative way. In the July 19, 1913, issue of the IWW's eastern weekly *Solidarity*, an editorial on the "Significance of the Eight-Hour Movement" described the atrocious conditions prevalent in industry. "These conditions," it observed, "are steadily growing worse under capitalist pressure. We also find the workers everywhere breaking out in revolt against them. Their instinct of self-preservation, coupled with the agitation of the I. W. W., drives them to resist. . . . By actually improving their material conditions, even if for the time being only, they are gaining a toe-hold for future improvements and struggles, all tending in the direction of the goal of emancipation." Every statement in the editorial is correct except for the "even if for the time being only" and the last clause in the quotation. What the writer's ideology could not allow for was that the gains or losses in the workers' struggles would help to create the rules by which future struggles within the capitalist framework would be waged. The IWW doubtless contributed to the struggles and some gains that resulted from them, but it contributed negatively to the ultimate formulation of the new rules. Wherever the IWW led a strike, the workers themselves discovered where the boundary of acceptability lay between very militant tactics, on the one hand, and the IWW's repudiation of rules and contracts and its assumption that the strike's significance was "the goal of emancipation," on the other. The Wobblies' devoted work, wherever strikers asked them to lead, doubtless helped to push the boundary of acceptable militancy to its furthest limit by testing the limit at several points and sometimes crossing over into sabotage and violence. But whenever that happened the workers' cause suffered.[38] The IWW did help the workers to gain that toehold and the future improvements, but it helped them win more improvements than the Wobblies thought possible without a revolution. At the same time it showed that revolution was not a prerequisite for those gains that the workers wanted.

A third way in which the radical movements worked as "limiting cases" pertained to the SP's demand that the government's scope be enormously enlarged, which it would have to be if the principal means of production were nationalized. Most socialists viewed lesser enlargements of the government's powers in the workers' interest as temporary steps toward the wholesale take-over, because welfare laws strengthened the workers physically and increased their ability to fight for more, and because they helped to break down the traditional hostility to collective responsibility for social welfare. In the fight for the woman suffrage amendment in New York, the SP acted as the left wing of the Progressive movement; in the industrial struggles the IWW was a negative reference group; in this third instance the SP worked as a limiting case in the sense that it was a true vanguard (though not of the proletariat), a herald of the welfare state.

At issue in the shake-up period was not only the contents of specific laws but also the propriety of governmental action in those areas. That is, a person might oppose a certain reform bill because he opposed the reform, however effected, or because he opposed legislation in the social-welfare field even though he favored the reform if effected by nongovernmental means. The boundaries of acceptable belief were expanding with respect to both those subjects, and the radical movements helped to relocate both of them.[39] The socialist administrations in several towns and cities that inaugurated "gas-and-water socialism" showed that radicalism flourished only where and when Progressivism did. What made the SP flourish was the same outrage at corporate arrogance and power that put Progressives in power, and as David Thelen shows,[40] such demands appealed to people in all classes.[41] It is for this reason that they are "limiting cases."

Here is how a political scientist formulates the thesis that American social movements have acted as limiting cases: "Often such movements erupt along the margins of the political system, and they sometimes serve the purpose of encouraging political and social mobilization, of widening the boundaries of the polity. . . . By confronting the political authorities, or by locking themselves in peaceful—or violent—conflict with some other element of the society, social movements provoke trials of strength between contending forces or ideas. . . . Through such trials . . . the agenda of controversy, the list of acceptable, 'key' issues may be changed." In short, social movements work "to break society's log jams, to prevent ossification in the political system, to prompt and justify major innovations in social policy and economic organization."[42] It follows, I believe, that the explanation of the relative success of the radical movements in the shake-up period is the same as the explanation of their absolute failure then and at all other times.

This is equally true of certain deviant-type reforms by capitalists, especially the Pullman, Illinois, experiment in an all-encompassing benevolent autocracy.[43] This was a limiting case at the other end, so to speak. Once the truth about Pullman became well known, it was seen as a violation of the American ideal of individual autonomy and equated in that respect with the closed shop, the legitimacy of which was still more than a generation away. The boundary with reference to such experiments as Pullman had to be drawn to enclose the ideal of individual freedom, and when enough people came to believe that the power of big business made that freedom depend on strong unions, strong unions fell inside the boundary, which therefore legitimated not class solidarity looking toward eventual working-class hegemony, but individual autonomy guaranteed by institutional protection against the would-be Pullmans. Class-based action was legitimate insofar as it was necessary to make individual achievement possible. The company town violated this ideal in another way too: it represented the power of men over other men, in contrast to the power of norms and rules over all men. It appeared in the shake-up period because the new economic power of big economic enterprises of the sort that Pullman represented was too new for norms and rules to have evolved to regulate their relations with the employees and the townspeople in their regions. This does not mean that when the workers organized unions and fought the bosses' power they were trying to develop such rules and norms. They were trying to get higher pay and better conditions and some freedom for themselves off the job. But the upshot of those struggles was what neither adversary could have foreseen: a new set of rules and norms that, after many trials and errors and much bloodshed and hardship, drew a series of lines between acceptable and unacceptable actions on the part of all concerned.

In so doing they loosely rewove the vertical ties between classes that had become frayed at the start of the shake-up period. When leadership and authority in the economic and political spheres became legitimated to end the shake-up period, the principles ratifying them were not quite the same as before. True, they were still merely instrumental, permitting leaders to exercise authority on the condition that they deliver the economic and political goods and preserve order. But a new pluralism had gradually formed, legitimating the heterogeneity of American society. The shake-up in the craft and industrial structure that had produced the incredible complexity of overlapping jurisdictions of AFL unions around the turn of the century gave way to a more systematic organization. Immigrants became ethnics, their churches and communities became recognized segments of the Society, and each such segment had its own vertical bonds between leaders and led. The Progressives' enlargement of governmental functions gave the various communities and interest organizations a focus for separate collective action and at the same time a common bond. In all these and other ways, multiple bonds between leaders and rank and file re-formed, and in the process the reform and radical movements returned to the minor niches they had occupied in the Society at the start of that generation.

Historians who postulate System, and who therefore search the past for movements to link up into a radical heritage, interpret this subsidence as a temporary interruption of "progress." For them the task of the radical is to awaken John Q. Worker to the existence of the System, essentially the same since the birth of capitalism. One who postulates Society, however, perceives an *encounter between* the radical and John Q. Worker, one among many intergroup encounters that shaped the rules and norms by which Americans dealt with each other in the interstices between the many constituent elements that made up their Society.

Section 2

Studies in the Rhetoric of American Radicalism, 1890–1917

"When I make a word do a lot of work like that," said Humpty-Dumpty, "I always pay it extra."

V   The Radicals' Perceptions of John Q. Worker

As W. I. Thomas pointed out, if a situation is defined as real it is real in its consequences. Hence, if we are to understand the meaning of the policies that the radicals adopted, we should ask how they perceived their situation. The next five chapters will examine their rhetoric as it reveals their perceptions of John Q. Worker (both directly, and indirectly via their attitudes toward nonwhite and women workers), of the capitalist class, of American society, and of themselves.

I

The radicals' perceptions of themselves were inextricably bound up with their perceptions of John Q. Worker, as are the perceptions of actor and that which is acted upon. Their perceptions of themselves as the possessors of the truth about American society implied a dual perception of John Q. Worker as both inert and heroic and also a perception of the capitalist class as their own main adversary in a titanic struggle for the worker's mind.

As "teachers" of John Q. Worker, the radicals were in a sense "intellectuals," whether or not they had much formal education, for their principal mission was to bring correct theory to the working class. Yet that role was an uncomfortable one for many radicals, including some with college degrees. The problem of teaching the worker without patronizing him caused chronic difficulties, among which was how to define the role and status of intellectuals in the movements.

Contrary to the impression conveyed by most accounts, the problem of defining the role of intellectuals was not peculiar to the SP and was not in that party restricted to the period after 1909, in which it tried to disassociate itself in the public mind from the IWW. In fact, this problem was and is inherent in "vanguardism," a theory that all radical movements in all countries and periods believe in: on the one hand, that a radical organization has the mission of teaching the working class and leading it to the good society and, on the other hand, that the working class has the mission of freeing itself. The potential irreconcilability of these two tenets may be discerned if the Chinese Red Guards' repeated admonition to learn from the peasants, to become "little students of the masses," is set alongside Mao Tse-tung's statement that "apart from their other characteristics, China's 600 million people have two remarkable peculiarities: they are, first of all, poor, and secondly blank. That may seem like a bad thing. But it is really a good thing. Poor people want change, want to do things, want revolution. A clean sheet of paper has no blotches, and so the newest and most beautiful words can be written on it, the newest and most beautiful pictures can be painted on it."[1]

Other Communist Parties, including the American, have sprinkled their pronouncements with injunctions to learn from the workers, but it is the blank-page theory that expresses their attitude most truly. This was stated explicitly by Lenin in 1902 in the famous passage in *What Is To Be Done?*: socialist consciousness among the workers "could only be brought to them from without. The history of all countries shows that the working class, exclusively by its own efforts, is able to develop only trade-union consciousness."[2] Lenin's book does not seem to have been known to the pre–World War I American radicals discussed here, but Karl Kautsky's writings were, and Lenin quotes Kautsky to the same effect.[3] The anomaly of self-described organizations of the working class that profess world views incomprehensible to the working class caused chronic and, as contended in Chapter I, insoluble problems in all three—the SLP, the SP, and the IWW. The famous controversy in the SP in the years before the recall of William D. Haywood from the National Executive Committee in 1912–1913 was merely the most publicized incident; its connection with the party's right-left factionalism has made it easy to assume that it was a tactical fight rather than a symptom of a fundamental problem.

That controversy has been used to buttress the thesis that the party was split between right-wing, middle-class intellectuals in the leadership, who had contempt for the workers, and left-wingers who were mostly true proletarians. As Ira Kipnis puts it, "It seemed to be the wage-working members of the 'proletariat' who gave the party leaders most difficulty because of their uncleanliness, backwardness, and stupidity. Party leaders warned each other that a socialist movement consisting of and led by unskilled workers, the 'product of the gutter and the slums,' could not gain victory because it could never enlist the support of enough voters. And even if such a rabble-led party were to slide into power, it would not have the intelligence to administer the co-operative commonwealth." [4]

Among the documents that Kipnis uses to support his characterization is an article by Carl D. Thompson, a leading "opportunist," which warrants close examination. [5] Thompson wrote in reply to an essay by Thomas Sladden, a prominent left-winger, in which Sladden had defined the proletariat in such a way as to exclude the skilled workers because they had interests to conserve. "Thus," wrote Thompson,

we have presented to us a working class with the entire organized trades union movement of America excluded. And we are to depend for our social revolution and Socialism upon the unorganized, unskilled workingmen. . . . Furthermore, we are told, this proletariat [sic] is a very low type of being intellectually. "He is uncultured and uncouth in appearance. He has no manners and little education." He has a religion, however—"the religion of hate."

In all of this Comrade Sladden is quite in agreement with Theodore Roosevelt, Mr. Parry, Sam Gompers and other enemies of Socialism that know nothing about it. They all say that Socialism is the product of ignorance, dirt and hate. They all say that no man with any brains would be a Socialist; that no person of intelligence or of any humane or kindly feelings towards humanity would ever join such a movement. And with its appearance all culture would of course disappear.

Then Thompson invokes the authority of the *Communist Manifesto*:

"The 'dangerous class,' the social scum, that passively rotting class thrown off by the lowest layers of old society, may, here and there, be swept into the movement by a proletarian revolution. *Its conditions of life, however, prepare it far more for the part of the bribed tool of reactionary intrigue.*" Marx at least realized that the social revolution would never be brought about by this class. . . . This idea that the slums cannot be organized for a constructive revolution runs throughout the literature of the Socialist movement. . . . It is absurd to limit the force of the social revolution wholly to one class. Much more so to limit it to any section of the working class. But it is worst of all to limit it to the lowest and least resourceful and least revolutionary section of the working class.

Thompson contends that the proletariat should be defined simply as "that class in society that does not own the means of its employment." But within it, the easiest elements to recruit are the organized: "Every force of their economic environment and every incident of their experience is drawing them with tremendous power toward the Socialist position." After them come the small farmers, and third come "the intellectual proletariat," who are college-educated but do not own the means of their employment. It is from that stratum that have come Marx, Lassalle, Liebknecht, Ferri, Vandervelde, Jaurès, and other luminaries of the movement, including some Americans. Then comes the passage that Kipnis paraphrases: "If we are to present Socialism as a product of the gutter and the slums, as made up only of those elements, and to be led by them, then I think we may well despair of its victory. Not only because it never would succeed in enlisting enough voters to capture the powers of government, but also because if it did it would be utterly incapable of organizing a social revolution, much less of administering modern social and industrial life and would very likely put civilization back a hundred years."

The article as a whole makes two things clear. First, Thompson is referring to the *lumpenproletariat*, although he does not use the word; and second, he is polemicizing not against the "slum element" but against certain socialists who glorified them. The "correctness" of Thompson's "constructivist" theories or of his predictions concerning the radicalization of the working class is not at issue here; at issue is a distinction that he and others on both the right and left made between those who worked (or tried to work) and the demoralized and criminal elements in the slum population. By erasing that distinction and substituting a distinction between skilled and unskilled workers, Kipnis persuades the reader who is unfamiliar with his sources that the strictures applied by both right and left to the *lumpenproletariat* were applied by only the right to all the unskilled workers.

Nor was this issue restricted to the SP. The SLP and IWW, which had no right and left wings to speak of, paid attention in their own ways to this question, for it was and is basic to the problems of the relation of "thinking to being," of theory to practice, or a vanguard organization to "the masses." One of its expressions ever since, in radical organizations and socialist countries, has been the ambiguous relation between ascribed and achieved "proletarian" status. For if the proletariat does not come to radicalism naturally, out of its own experience, what are the relative virtues of the horny-handed son of toil with proletarian "instincts" and of the intellectual who repudiates his class and becomes a Marxist?

That ambiguity found its perfect embodiment in Daniel De Leon, a middle-class intellectual and former college lecturer who, once converted to socialism, spent the remainder of his life in self-imposed poverty and unswerving devotion to the SLP.[6] In a 1905 editorial he denounced the intellectuals' "pernicious influence" in the world socialist movement. The intellectual, he said, was a "microbe," whose general feature "is superficiality, coupled, of course, with the usual accompaniment of vanity and conceit." He cannot think; he has only scraps of learning; he "sets himself up as a perambulating lump of wisdom."[7] The self-hate and projection discernible between these lines are found in many other such writings and speeches in all three of the organizations under study here, for the remarkable thing is that many of them, on both sides, were produced by intellectuals of middle-class origin. The problem would not have been very important had such people not constituted a disproportionate component of all three organizations and an even larger proportion of their most effective writers, speakers, and functionaries.

The simplest solution would have been to bar them on account of their ascribed class status. At the IWW's founding convention, a lawyer asked to be seated as an individual delegate, and some delegates acquiesced because the criteria should be beliefs and actions. De Leon and others countered that this was to be a workingmen's organization and lawyers were parasites.[8] But since De Leon was now technically a worker in the printing industry and other delegates had also achieved proletarian status by similar routes, the problem was only made worse, for now these petty-bourgeois elements were bringing the "pernicious influence" into the heart of the movement and the "microbe's" infection could not be prevented by simple definition and isolation. The difficulty engendered some shrillness. One working-class delegate at that convention deplored the ignorance of the workers whom the IWW must educate, for, as he put it, "Knowledge is power. Knowledge gives a man self-confidence. Knowledge shows the man where he stands. Knowledge puts him on his feet. It takes him out of the dust and makes him able to stand up against the so-called intellectuals. These lawyers and all this bunch of fellows that have been to college and got their sheepskins appear to have an advantage over the workman. Now, I am a workman. I have tried to get knowledge, and in all that I have read and in all that I have studied I make it my object to do this. Otherwise I amount to nothing."[9] Shortly afterward, Algie M. Simons, a college graduate, implicitly disagreed with that last sentence: "I have more faith in the rank and file of the working class of America, blind as they may be, mistakes though they have made, than I have in all the intellectuals and all the lecturers and all the soap box orators—and I have been one of them for years and expect to be—I have more faith in the rank and file and the spirit of revolt that springs out of the workshop than I have, I say, in all the theorists and would-be teachers of the working class of America. (Applause.) And I think that sometimes we who pride ourselves on our ability to teach, should go back to the masses to learn. (Applause.)"[10]

It was not long, however, before the IWW as a functioning organization found it necessary to make the kind of statements that Kipnis attributes solely to the SP's right wing, for evidently a fair number of disreputable people entered Wobbly ranks.[11] Wobbly writings soon became sprinkled with references to "booze-fighters" and "slummists" who the authors hoped would leave the IWW, voluntarily or otherwise. "It cannot be said," wrote one editorialist, "that a booze-fighter was ever welcome in our ranks." It is the logging boss who prefers "the spiritless wretch whose only thought is to 'hold down' the job long enough to get the price of a big drunk as soon as he gets back to town," whereas the IWW wants "the man of self-control whose spirit rebels against the beastly conditions around him."[12] And a month later:

It is up to every local union of the Industrial Workers of the World to see that the real "slum" element, the degenerates, the drunks, and those men who are so far gone that they have lost all manhood, are kept away from the halls and meeting places of the I.W.W. The element which make up the *drunks, and those who are too lazy to keep clean are simply a drawback to the human race* and a detriment to any union or association. The *sooner their wretched bodies are off* the earth the *better* chance will the fighters have. . . . It may be true that some old barrel stiff or booze fighter is "not to blame" for his filthy condition, but neither are we to blame for it. This is a union which is nothing, if not to *fight* the *employing* class. We have no place in our ranks for the degenerates.

The latter are not, he added, to be equated with the unemployed, for no one is permanently unemployed "except the infirm, the crippled and the degenerate." [13] The IWW's praise of the fighting proletarian implied and was often explicitly accompanied by statements that he did not need soft-handed intellectuals to do his thinking for him.

The SP too encountered the "intellectual" versus "proletarian" problem. Some of the intraparty polemics were evoked by reactions to Wobbly street speakers; many Wobblies also belonged to the SP, and it was not always clear to the public which organization a street speaker represented. In other cases the debates reflected the left-right split in general. [14]

In the *Call* of November 8, 1909, John Spargo wrote a long, thoughtful article, "What the Socialist Party Needs," disclosing that within the past three months nearly four hundred members of the party had written to him asking, "What is the matter with the Socialist party?" The writers represented all factions, both sexes, workers, professionals, and farmers. He listed a number of causes of the party's languishing, and among them was its faulty methods of propaganda: "Go into any of our cities and watch the progress of the Socialist propaganda. What do we find? Why[,] a speaker comes along, sent out by the national office most likely, and addresses—as he will tell you—the working class of the city. But we know that he does not reach the responsible, intelligent, self-respecting workers. Generally speaking, he reaches only the idle loafers to be found at street corners—that element of the working class which is least reliable, because least intelligent and least interested in social questions." The most likely recruits are at work, or at least not hanging around street corners. Yet the speakers there have "to pander to the ignorance of their auditors for the sake of applause." [15] Several writers complained that this pandering took the form of ridiculous flattery of the proletarian, disparagement of knowledge and culture, and a pseudodemocratic contempt for expertise. The most eloquent argument along these lines was made by William J. Ghent in the New York *Worker* in 1907:

When men in a delegate body take it upon themselves to extol ignorance and to decry knowledge; to speak contemptuously of one set of men as "intellectuals" and eulogistically of another set of men as proletarians, it is time to take stock of our principles and our personnel. . . . Socialism stands for the common diffusion to all men of all the results of the world's progress in knowledge. . . . Every Socialist movement welcomes to its ranks men of intelligence and capacity, and as a rule none are quicker to welcome these men than the sober-minded workers to whom learning has been denied.

The Socialist movement, we say, is a working-class movement. But what part of the working class does it represent to-day? It is our common boast that it represents that part of the working class which is most intelligent. Is intelligence then an evil or a good? . . .

No sober-minded Socialist idealizes the working class as he sees it to-day. We may say, without stopping for necessary qualifications, that its moral instincts are just, and that as these instincts are translated into ideas, it progresses towards its emancipation. But who are the men who translate these instincts into ideas? Who formulate its creeds, who carry its cause into public arenas, who define its mission, who point out its goal, who warn it what gifts and lures to reject, and what demands to insist upon, who tell it that its salvation is to come only by carrying on its combat without compromise?

I take it that those who do these things are the "Intellectuals." The uninstructed proletariat, unillumined and undirected by ideas, is the sport and plaything of its political and economic masters. . . .

There is no room in the Socialist movement for the demagog, literary or political. There is no room for the plea that ignorance is better than intelligence, that incompetency is better than efficiency, that the man who works with his hands is by reason of the nature of his employment better than the man who writes or teaches or organizes or plans, or who does any other useful service to society. . . . Every one who comes into the Socialist movement comes in, or should come in, on the same terms and he remains there on the same footing as every other comrade. . . . There is no room for class distinctions in the Socialist movement, just as there will be none in the Socialist Republic.[16]

Kipnis refers to this letter by saying that "when working-class members of the party protested against what seemed to them the conversion of the party into an organization for radical middle-class reform, the Center promptly replied that the 'uninstructed proletariat . . . is the

sport and plaything of its economic masters.' The 'chumps' and 'demagogs' in the party who insisted that the working class could furnish its
own leaders were blamed for failure of the party to increase its vote."[17]
The "chumps" epithet, which Kipnis makes much of, when placed back
into its context turns out to have an altogether different meaning: in the
middle of his article Ghent describes various

types of men from whom one can expect always to hear this exaltation of ignorance over intelligence. The first of these, to use a happy colloquialism, is the
plain "chump." He is a person without intelligence, and without the capacity for
acquiring it. He hardly knows what he means by any expression which he uses.
He will tell you, with an utter obliviousness of the implication contained in the
term, that he is a "scientific" Socialist; yet because he finds himself able to get
along without intellect he naturally doubts its value, and he speaks slightingly
of the "intellectuals." This type at least is comparatively harmless.

Ghent then lists other types: the literary demagogs and the political
demagogs (the worst of the lot); then follows the quoted passage in
which he argues that there is no room in the movement for any demagogs. Ghent's "chump" is therefore the pseudoeducated spouter of jargon, not the uneducated proletarian who wants the worker comrades to
furnish their own leadership.[18] And the protests against ideas like
Ghent's came largely, as pointed out before, from middle-class intellectuals. (It should also be recalled that until World War I, "intelligence"
was commonly used to mean knowledge and understanding, not a
fixed, innate mental capacity. Ghent is obviously using it in the old way;
he mentions the capacity for "acquiring" intelligence.)

Some readers misinterpreted what Ghent had said exactly as Kipnis
does. One member of the New York State Committee wrote that "as the
mouthpiece of the 'intellectuals' he [Ghent] virtually says that the working class is not to be trusted to work out its own salvation."[19] Among the
many other replies, some extended the cult of proletarianism into the
future socialist society. Not only economic classes would be abolished;
so would specialized work of any sort.

Once more Ghent explained at length, this time in the *Call* of December 4, 1909. Socialism would not abolish specialized occupations, he
prophesied; it would give people greater freedom than they now have to
shift from one occupation to another. But many occupations require

more than a lifetime to master. And of course individuals vary in talents.

The notion of a society in which a Darwin would be compelled to manipulate a linotype machine for five hours a day; or a Marx to handle a street-sweeper's broom for, say, four hours a day; or a Luther Burbank, or a Pasteur, or a Metchnikoff, or a Huxley, to sell goods in a state or municipal department store, is a notion which excites among normal men either derision or disgust. Such a social system would involve the immediate decay of scientific research and investigation, and the dismantling of our laboratories and museums and observatories. . . .

Is it not, on the whole, likely that under Socialism we shall have an enormous increase of social and intellectual service? . . . Is it not likely that we shall still have muscular men who can load a steamship, or fell a tree; skilful men who can run a locomotive or put together the delicate parts of a machine; deft and nimble-fingered men who can ply the arts; that most of these men will be able to do these things better than they will be able to do other things, and that for the most part they will do them to the exclusion of other things?

To those critics who had attacked him on a more personal level he replied that he had acquired his reverence for learning and respect for intellectuals as a printer, and the overwhelming majority of his fellow printers felt the same way; the composing rooms were unofficial schools where all subjects were discussed. Furthermore, "among men of all sorts and occupations with whom I have worked, or tramped across the deserts, or ridden on 'blind baggages,' or in freight cars, I have always found a thirst for knowledge and a respect for intellectual men. I say with shame and humiliation that I had to come into the Socialist party to find among the proletariat a savage antipathy to learning and to educated men, and to find disgruntled 'professional proletarians' playing upon this feeling for their own advantage." (See Supplement.)

Although their adversaries agreed with Spargo, Ghent, and their cohorts that the SP was languishing well before World War I began,[20] they disagreed as to the reason. Charles Kerr (publisher of the *International Socialist Review* and its editor after he shifted it to the left in 1908) approvingly quoted a resolution passed by Local Denver of the SP in September 1909 that blamed the party's leadership—"this cockroach element, composed of preachers without pulpits, lawyers without clients, doctors without patients, storekeepers without customers[,] disgruntled political coyotes and other riff-raff"—and announced its decision to withdraw from the party.[21] Not to be outdone, the editor of the *Call* in the following month closed an editorial with a blast at the "snobbish 'intellectuals,' who fawn on wealth and superficial refinement and reserve all their aspersions for the working, the fighting, the heroic proletariat."[22]

Such documents by SP members were sparse, however, for most of the statements that Ghent, Spargo, and others complained of were evidently made orally by street speakers. A page-by-page scanning of periodicals on the far left turns up occasional poems of the Hail To Thee O Proletaire! genre, containing locutions that must have sounded peculiar to John Q. Worker. Most of the few prose essays on the topic are similar to one by George Allan England (a socialist novelist and prolific writer in radical journals) in which he recounts attempts to convert educated men and their inability to understand the "irrefutable truth," and concludes that "the average workingman has more sense, more logic and more heart than the average holder of a sheepskin degree, the average professor or the average editor. Man for man, the so-called 'lower' class is infinitely superior to the misnamed 'higher' class. . . . Vive le proletaire!"[23] Also typical of the writings in this vein is Haywood's oft-quoted remark that "Socialism is so plain, so clear, so simple that when a person becomes intellectual he doesn't understand Socialism."[24] Spargo and Ghent accused the rabble-rousers of appealing to that portion of the population most easily swayed by crowd sentiment and least capable of weighing evidence. This preference for emotional appeals may be why the printed polemics against Spargo and Ghent's position rarely attempt the sort of reasoned exploration of the subject that they attempted.

Some of those printed polemics are more like odes and visions than discourses. They display a tendency to shift into the oracular mode (and therefore predictions in the present tense). For example, here is J. S. Biscay, a prominent Wobbly organizer and writer; after a lengthy denial that intellectuals have any special claim on radicals' indulgence, he pens this ode to the proletarian:

He does everything and gets the least. It is this despised prol when he begins finally to think for himself and organize from the hole in the ground to the top of the skyscraper, before whom the very earth trembles. He is the GOD over all we see, the creator. He has gotten tired of always giving: he is now preparing to demand what he has created. He does not aspire to be called "intellectual," as his intellect covers the earth. The whole earth is his college and experience his teacher. . . . The puny globe is his plaything which he is to take for himself. . . . A light breaks over his countenance and he quickens his pace. He sees. At last he understands.[25]

Another example of this genre is "The Revolutionary Proletariat," by Louis Duchez, a young journalist and agitator who died the following year. He explains in great detail how wealth is being more and more concentrated, the army of the unemployed is growing, competition for jobs is becoming fiercer and wages are declining as a result, and more and more women and children are taking men's jobs. But the unorganized workers are becoming the base of a revolutionary movement:

The minds of the producers are being impressed with the hopelessness of relief under the capitalist system and the futility and childishness of expecting anything constructive and permanent from or through the state. . . . A great revelation takes place. . . . It is the idea to give or withhold their labor power at will. . . . Strikes and mass movements become more numerous and far-reaching. Parliamentary wranglings are obscured and buried entirely by the thundering conflicts of the two classes arrayed in a final conflict on the industrial field. . . . A proletarian leadership is spontaneously developed with minds trained under the modern machine process; minds that are direct, definite and far-seeing, and unhampered by the ideals and baseless romanticism of the old society. The direct struggle sharpens the revolutionary appetite of the workers and stimulates within them a tremendous feeling of proletarian power. Revolutionary spirit blazes and the organization grows by leaps and bounds.

Eventually the capitalists "cave in."[26]

In the few reasoned arguments contributed to the "anti-intellectuals" side in the dispute, class resentment played a role. The lawyer Henry Slobodin, for example, contended that the antagonism within the SP between proletarians and intellectuals was due to the arrogance of some of the intellectual leaders who frequented banquet halls and pink-tea parlors instead of doing local party work. Some of these, he said, were inveterate "jiners," joining all sorts of nonparty organizations to socialize with rich radicals. Slobodin mentioned no names but was clearly referring to people like millionaire socialist Gaylord Wilshire and prosperous attorney Morris Hillquit.[27] *Intellectual* thus sometimes meant someone who was lucky enough to be exempt from the "real" work that was supposedly the source of proletarian virtues.

The linking of leftist Wilshire with rightist (or "centrist") Hillquit is significant in a different way, for, contrary to the impression conveyed by Kipnis, there was no consistent alliance, within the SP, between the prointellectuals and right-wingers on the one side, and between the anti-intellectuals and left-wingers on the other.[28] Nor can members' positions be predicted from their occupations; when the SP's National Executive Committee voted on whether to approve "Section 6," which barred advocates of sabotage from membership, there was no discernible pattern in the occupations of those who voted pro and con.[29]

II

The proletarian cultists' paeans to the brawny sons of toil have a certain abstractness about them; they do not address or describe real people. Their tendency to slide into the oracular mode, appropriate to a mythic vision, reinforces the impression that when such writers looked at John Q. Worker they did not quite see him; they saw what he was destined to become. Their faith in him, proclaimed so stridently, seems rather to have been a faith in their theory of society and history, to which he would soon convert, so as to play his assigned role. An essential part of that theory was that the worker would come to accept it. Hence, to lose faith that the worker would come to accept it was to reject the Myth that embodied it.

The socialists who belonged to the AFL unions were, by no coincidence, among those least prone to idealize the proletarian and least certain that he would soon convert, not only because for them reality overrode preconceived theory but also because the more one subscribed to the Myth, the more likely one was to stay clear of the AFL on the ground that it was not a bona fide working-class organization. The SLP members, having isolated themselves from the mass organizations of the working class and become rigid (although not consistent) in their doctrinal purity, kept and still keep that faith; there is no ambiguity in their perception of John Q. Worker, for the future always holds the same promise.[30]

It was the IWW, in this respect halfway between the SP and the SLP, that suffered the greatest ideological travail, for it lacked the SP's ideological flexibility (*chaos* might be a better word), yet was on principle always in close contact with unconverted workers. So we find something that ought not to be surprising—that the most numerous and vitriolic expressions of contempt for the unawakened worker came from the tongues and pens of Wobblies and those members of the SP who sympathized with the IWW. Why did John Q. Worker fail to play the role that radical theory assigned him? If the theory was not at fault—and there were compelling personal reasons why it could not be—then either John Q. Worker or his capitalist misleaders must be. But the theory also said that the capitalists' propaganda would fail as economic changes themselves made the workers receptive to the truth; hence John Q. Worker must be to blame. In an earlier period the Puritans would have called such a person a "sinner against his own conscience."

The radicals had nothing against conscience—*traitor* was a favorite epithet—but in the place where the Puritan put *conscience* they put *instincts*. The function of proletarian instincts was to make their possessor receptive to the radical evangel, which articulated what the worker obscurely felt and made sense of experiences that he could not explain. His mind may have been a blank sheet of paper, but not his soul.[31] All the radicals regardless of wing or class origin agreed that John Q. Worker was asleep and had to be awakened by his destined vanguard; the line of division, with respect to reactions to his failure to wake at the trumpet call, was not between right and left or between working-class and middle-class origin, but between those who subscribed and those who did not subscribe to what may be called the Myth of the Proletarian.

It is, I believe, only in terms of myth that certain features of their writings on this question can be understood: the absence from the proletarian cultists' writings of reasoned argument; the intense emotion invested in them; the automatic slipping—usually near the ends of essays—into the oracular mode, to portray a vision without secure anchoring in a particular time or place; the indifference to workers' and capitalists' own reasons for thinking and doing as they did; and the assumption that victory was imminent. As Robert Tucker explains in his brilliant analysis of the myth's operation:

The proper and worthy mode of conduct is as overwhelmingly plain as the reality luminously present before his [the mythic thinker's] mind in the myth. The answer to the question as to what should be done is given in the vision of what is happening in the world. This . . . is a vision of the inner as outer. A drama of the inner life of man is externalized and experienced as taking place in the outer world. The conflict of good and evil forces of the self, its constructive and destructive powers, appears to be resolving itself externally. . . . The thinker himself is intensely involved in the drama that appears to be taking place in the world outside him. Were this not so, he would never have engaged in the myth-making act in the first place. Once he has done so, however, his involvement becomes an involvement in what is now apprehended as a world-conflict. . . . The whole world, or alternatively the world of society, has become the battlefield on which the war of the self is being waged, on which the good forces are fighting for their life against the evil ones. . . . The mythic thinker cannot or will not reason with you about it. All he can do is to point to the world and say: "Can't you *see* what is happening?" He knows that if you *do* see, you will, just as he does, act accordingly. Therefore, his supreme concern is just to make everybody see what is going on under their eyes, to communicate the vision in an image of the world-process.[32]

The operation of the Proletarian Myth also helps explain why those SP members who were not captivated by it were denounced as false socialists, indifferent to the sufferings of the working class. The mythic thinker's perceptions of external reality were, to him, self-evident; and anyone suggesting that he was externalizing an inner struggle was directing attention away from the evils of capitalism. As Tucker points out, means and ends are, to the mythic thinker, combined in one vision; hence a socialist who disagreed as to means must really have had other ends in view than the overthrow of capitalism.

The most common object of the Proletarian Mythicists' praise and scorn was, however, not other radicals but John Q. Worker. As to praise, it is instructive to notice the grammatical tenses in the following document (one of many suitable examples):

The unskilled laborer knows without any telling that he is exploited at the point of production. . . . He challenges the whole structure of modern society at its base. . . . By means of the industrial union, [he] builds up a society within society. . . . Time . . . the great dispeller of illusions, has wrought its effect upon the mind of the proletariat. No longer will it satisfy itself with the belief that parliamentary action will bring the relief which it so earnestly deserves. On the contrary it grows more and more distrustful of mere parliamentarism. It has learned the lesson that political power is merely the reflex of economic power, and that political advantage can only be had through economic superiority; that there is no road to power save through the "will to power" and all that that implies.[33]

It is not always clear here whether the present tense implies a statement of present fact or a vision of the future expressed in the oracular mode; whether the laborer's mind referred to is the author's own or that of the still sleeping worker. The ambiguity is not due to careless writing; it expresses perfectly the writer's certainty that his understanding will shortly be universalized.

Or consider the following fantasy about the Pennsylvania coal miners. It ostensibly portrays the SLP through the workers' eyes but by that very fact inadvertently reveals how the miners appeared in the eyes of the writer (probably De Leon):

As time went on, the steady degeneration of the miners caused the more intelligent among them to look deeply into the hellish conditions that surrounded them, and looking, they saw; seeing, they agitated; and this was the song of hope they raised to their fellow slaves of the pick and lamp.

Miners of America, awake, rouse up! We have moved along wrong lines in the past. Our union is a rope of sand. Our leaders are scoundrels save where they are ignoramuses. . . . Our real strength lies in that powerful weapon that we possess—the ballot. . . . Up with the Socialist Trades & Labor Alliance, the New Trades Union, which has no Labor and Capitalist brotherliness about it[,] and its strong right arm, the Socialist Labor Party. . . .

The coal diggers were dazed when they heard this message. It was too good to be true. . . . The man who suggested such ideas was all right, probably, but he was a dreamer, yes he was impracticable [sic]. . . . Then the conflict grew fiercer. Up and down the coal mining towns of Pennsylvania, Ohio and Illinois the apostle of the proletariat went and lashed their enemies with whips of fire. . . . Then some strange things happened. The tenth anniversary convention of the United Mine Workers was held in Pittsburg, January 1899, and the delegates from the other States were astonished to find that in the greatest coal producing center of the nation there was practically no organization of their pure and simple Unions. THE MINERS WERE LEANING ON THEIR PICKS— THINKING.

The "pure-and-simplers" thereupon concocted a conspiracy to keep control of the men by arranging a dues checkoff with the owners. The writer confesses puzzlement as to why the rank and file acquiesced and sank back—temporarily, of course—into apathy.[34] His honest perplexity is a measure of his absolute faith in the imminent awakening of the working class.

Again and again leaders of the SP, SLP, and IWW told the world and one another that the truth was so simple and self-evident that only one who was willfully blind could fail to see it, especially after a radical had pointed it out. Yet there are the miners, leaning on their picks and thinking over what had been said to them—and soon relapsing into slumber. Why do they reject the saving message? These are not the booze-fighters or degenerates; they are the correlates, in the real world, of the Proletarian whose instinctive heroism has earned the radicals' devotion. If Tucker is right in seeing an inner struggle projected onto the outside world in the form of the titanic confrontation between the mythic Proletarian and the equally mythic Capitalist, the embodiments of total good and total evil, the rage scorching the pages of IWW documents and appearing occasionally in SLP and SP documents, in response to John Q. Worker's failure to heed their message, conveys more meaning than their authors were aware of.

Documentary Excursus I

The following excerpts are from the *Industrial Worker*:

1) A man that will not fight the employers and their stool pigeons, is a moral eunuch, and the sooner the boss works him to death the better for humanity. ("Perseverance," May 6, 1909.)

2) The American workingman is a composite of superstition, stupidity and cowardice. . . . In rare moments of lucidity, the American realizes that the wealthy leisure class is living by his toil, like a parasite sucking his blood. Yet when it is in his power to organize into the INDUSTRIAL WORKERS OF THE WORLD, he cast[s] his lot unthinkingly with the fat, jolly, smiling EMPLOYMENT SHARK, or Sammy Gompers' A. F. of H–ll. . . . When it comes to being patriotic he is the limit. He will shoot down his FELLOW WORKER for the magnificent sum of $13.00 per month. To hear him talk about his country? one would be made to believe that he owned and controlled the STANDARD OIL CO., when in fact he could not raise the price to buy harness for a mouse. . . . The more he is persecuted the more submissive he becomes. What he needs is INDUSTRIAL UNION literature, and plenty of it, for his cranium is so thick that a 13-inch shell would not penetrate it. (Wm. R. Sautter, "The American Workman," February 12, 1910.)

3) Attend a concert at one of the parks where there is a musical concert. There

you will find a representative American crowd. Take notice of the music they applaud. You will find that it is the frivolous, the meaningless, the worthless, that appeals to the mob. . . . The music of power and inspiration passes so far over their heads as to be hardly recognized. It is "casting pearls before swine." Yes, swine; or shall we say apes? Let a player "do a stunt," give a trick performance, and the inane attention of the average monkey is attracted. . . . Mental effort is pain and suffering to the apes. Wait until the ITALIAN band renders an American national air. A few schoolma'ams and counter-jumpers with sloping foreheads and pretty cravats, having been well drilled by their respective owners, jump to their feet to honor (?) the country of their masters. The other apes, with ape-like faculty of imitation, rise in obedience, to the spirit of mob-mind. Many of them do not know why they are standing, and continue to stand even when the band has passed from patriotic (?) airs to ragtime. . . . As it is with music, so it is with the revolutionary movement. The mass, the mob of so-called "progressives," play and paddle around in little puddles of half-baked "intellect." . . . They complacently prattle of "Liberty," the "cow-operative commonwealth," "man's future emancipation," etc., and smugly go home, their potato minds working with the sluggish maggots of these meaningless phrases. (Editorial entitled "Just Cattle," July 23, 1910.)

4) You say our benevolent fathers, the capitalists, give us jobs, and we couldn't live without jobs. Did you ever stop to think that it is you who support the capitalist class . . . ? No, you never tried to think in your lives. . . . You are brutally murdered and you piously roll up the whites of your eyes in thankfulness to god for it. What infinite ignorance! What a huge but ghastly joke you are! . . . Do you deserve pity? No, a thousand times no! . . . BLAME YOURSELVES. You are such ripe, juicy plums, who could help plucking you? . . . O, you miserable cowards! . . . You, who are so white livered as to fear bloodshed in the future, why can't you see it in the present? . . . We tell you the truth, and we don't care whether you like it or not. Perhaps, if you get mad, it will jar loose some of the moss that covers your brains and get you to thinking. (M. B. Butler ["Camp Delegate from Local 93"], "Stand Up! You Humble Slaves," September 10, 1910.)

5) Why is it that the greatest men of the ages have been nailed to the cross, bound at the stake, hung by the neck, shot to death against cold stone walls of a fortress? . . . Because the misinformation peddled to the workers in the guise of "education" has reduced them to the level of cattle. Their dumb worship of the law, their humble adoration of the morality of their masters, their slavish subservience to the fetiches set up by the boss, politics, religion, patriotism, etc., has practically castrated them intellectually, taking from them the fighting spirit of their ancestors who roared and raged [ranged?] the forests looking for a chance to dispute the supremacy of an antagonist. The modern wage slave is a creature of the yoke, fit only for the collar of subservience. He produces all, and smirks sillily when the boss hands him a certain stipend in the form of wages. He is a cringer, a crawler, a thing to be despised—and he is despised by the boss and by

the small minority who have left in their veins the virus of FIGHT. If it were not necessary that the smirking slaves have rebellion pounded into their heads in order to make possible the rebellion of the minority, they could go to the devil and none would mourn them. (Editorial entitled "Degeneracy," October 15, 1910.)

6) Stand up, Mr. Workingman! . . . Patience has long since ceased to be a virtue and if you are not in open rebellion against the wrongs inflicted upon you and your class, then you are indeed a consummate fool, a cringing slave and a cowardly knave. . . . We need not tell you that your food is adulterated, your clothing shoddy, your "home" a mockery, your wife a consumptive drudge, your daughter destined for a life of shame, and your children but spawn for the mill owners['] profit. You know these things! . . . Do you not desire to act? If not, then you are no man! Your misery is not enough. It should be heaped mountain high and you should be doubly damned by your betrayed class and by your children whose future[s] are blighted by your apathy. Yet your privation is our privation, your misery forces itself upon us, and we are forced to continue our appeals to you in order to free ourselves. (Editorial entitled "Rise! Workers! Rise!" April 4, 1912.)

The following excerpts are from some of the relatively few articles in the *Call* expressing contempt for John Q. Worker (other than items by Debs):

7) [The author gives statistics, gathered by the Russell Sage Foundation, on the cost of living and workers' incomes, and continues:] Do you understand, Average Man? Your money went to Russell Sage, and he piled it up in millions. Fate has decreed that it be used to find out if you could live in a decent way on what you were allowed in exchange for helping pile those millions. And your money, red with the blood of you and your children, is crying back truth to the world for you. . . . Do you understand, too, that such incomes are the natural result of our capitalist system? Not the result of our Russell Sages, not the result of our Republican party nor our Democratic party, but the result of the system under which industries are operated. [Now that Russell Sage is dead, his] money goes marching on. And crying truth as it marches. Will you remember that cry next time you go to the polls? Or will you with dull mind, unseeing eye, and deaf ear, do as the capitalists like to have you do, vote for an average wage of less than $600 a year, and poverty, and all the degradation that poverty means. It's up to you, who make these low wages. How are you going to vote? (Grace Potter, "How Are You Going to Vote," April 16, 1909. Potter was a very prolific writer in socialist periodicals.)

8) [In the issue of August 4, 1912, there is a large cartoon by Gordon Nye that comprises two pictures. The one on the left shows a hilltop on which are a crucified man and a hanged man in silhouette, and men in modern clothes in the foreground walking away. One is saying, "They were crazy," and another is saying, "Fools!" The picture on the right shows a big man with a pig's head; he is

labeled "Boss" on his shirt front and "False Ideals" on his stomach. He is directing a flock of sheep, labeled "Voter," into a building labeled "Polls."]

The following is in the SP's New York *Worker* of October 13, 1906:
9) Why don't they see how they are oppressed and misused and ill treated? See
how all the work they do is done for masters who have no right to their toil.
Masters who give them so little in return for their service that they never really
taste life at all. Why don't they see that there is no use in their working in poisoned, filthy, hot places in summer, and bitter, freezing cold places in winter?
Why don't they see that no one need work the weary long hours they do. Why
don't they see that they are wilfully killing themselves by slaving like machines
day after day?—yes, and night after night. Slaving—slaving—. Why don't they
see that there is no need for them to do all the work while their masters live
filled with beauty? Why don't they see that all men and all women and all little
children might be living that life? Oh, we have shown them so many times. Why
don't they see? If they won't see, they deserve to be slaves!

   Why don't they hear the protest of their own hearts against living in aching
want that others may live in sated luxury? Why don't they hear the cry of their
imprisoned souls? Why don't they hear their children begging for bread and
knowledge and love? Why don't they hear Nature calling them out of their
work-prisons into the fields? Why don't they hear us calling them brother,
pleading with them to break their chains, and bid their masters defiance? Why
don't they hear? If they won't hear, they deserve to be slaves!

   They deserve to be slaves, if they won't see and hear? Oh, cry tears of pity.
Let it wring your hearts, let it seem the saddest thing you ever knew! But they
can't see and they can't hear—because they are blind and they are deaf. And the
very system whose oppression we want them to see, and whose curses we want
them to hear, has made them so! O slaves, our brothers and our sisters, there are
those of us who see and those of us who hear. We give ourselves to you. (Grace
Potter, "They Are Blind.")

The following is part of a leaflet issued by the SP in Boston in 1906, now in the
Boston Public Library, entitled *A Squeezed Lemon*; it was, presumably, distributed
among workers. It begins by likening the factory worker to a lemon squeezed to
make the capitalist's lemonade and then thrown away; the dry rinds then go
from factory to factory begging to be squeezed again:
10) No slaves ever poured out so much sweat at their masters' feet, as we have.
   No slaves ever voluntarily wrecked their constitutions for their masters' sake
as much as we.
   No slaves ever got so small a proportion of what they created.
   No slaves ever made their masters rich so fast, and created over 4,000 millionaires in 30 years.
   No slaves ever began in freedom and worked themselves into bondage, vot-

ing and shouting for an industrial system that was plundering them of their liberties.

No slaves ever before held out their wrists for handcuffs, and danced with such thoughtless glee to the whipping-post, or sprang with such willingness on the auction block.

No slaves were ever captured with such ease, or duped with such empty phrases, or managed with so little trouble to their masters.

No slaves ever made the treadmill turn so fast, or were so deceived into believing that the chance to tramp on the treadmill was a blessing and a privilege.

Yes, we are a nation of hustlers. No nation ever rushed to plutocracy and revolution so fast. No herd of stampeded or panic-stricken buffaloes ever galloped so fast toward a precipice as we are speeding towards an industrial crash.

The following are excerpts from speeches and articles by Eugene V. Debs, containing expressions of contempt for the unawakened worker:

11) Too long have the workers of the world waited for some Moses to lead them out of bondage. He has not come; he never will come. I would not lead you out if I could; for if you could be led out, you could be led back again. . . . When you begin to think, you will soon begin to act for yourselves. . . . There will be a great difference between a strike of revolutionary workers and a strike of ignorant trade unionists who but vaguely understand what they want or how to get it. . . . When you join the Industrial Workers you feel a thrill of a new aspiration; you are no longer a blind, dumb wage-slave. . . . You are a working man and you have a brain, and if you do not use it in your own interests you are guilty of high treason to your manhood. (Applause.) It is for the very reason that you do not use your brain in your interests that you are compelled to deform your body in the interests of your master. . . . It is so simple that a child can see it. Why can't you? You can if you will think for yourselves. . . . I would not have you blindly walk into the Industrial Workers. . . . I would have you stay where you are until you can see your way clear to join it of your own free will. . . . [The chattel slave was better off, although now and then he tried to run away from his master.] You do not try to run away from yours. . . . When you run, it is in the opposite direction, when the bell rings or the whistle blows. . . . (*Industrial Unionism: An Address Delivered at Grand Central Palace, New York, Sunday, December 10, 1905* [Chicago: Charles H. Kerr & Co., n.d.], 3, 5, 11, 17, 19–20, 23.)

12) Workingmen, wake up! The time has come to open your eyes and see things as they are. You have been hoodwinked and robbed and enslaved long enough. Be a man and line up with your class in the great struggle for freedom. To train with the enemy, ignorantly or otherwise, as you have been doing, is treason to your fellow-man. To be the ally on election day of the class that lives out of your labor and holds you in contempt, is not only cowardly and contemptible, but criminal, and means death to your manhood and infamy to the name you bear. ("Class-Conscious Courts," *Social Democratic Herald*, July 4, 1903.)

13) [These remarks follow a description of poverty in Chicago during the garment strike:] If the workingmen of Chicago were not inert as clods, white-livered excuses for men, they would rise like a whirlwind in defense of these shivering, starving children at their doors. . . . Why in the name of all that unionism stands for don't they act? . . . When will these union men awaken? Or are they dead, except for the use of the city hall at election time? ("Help! Help!! Help!!!" *International Socialist Review*, XI [1911], 394.)

14) The Workers . . . never had a party of their own until the Socialist party was organized. . . . But the awakening came. . . . Class rule became more and more oppressive and wage slavery more and more galling. The eyes of the workers began to open. They began to see the cause of the misery they had dumbly suffered so many years. It dawned upon them that society was divided into two classes. . . . They began to think. A new light dawned upon their dark skies. They rubbed the age-long sleep from their eyes. . . . The world's workers are aroused at last. . . . The Socialist party . . . expresses their collective determination to break their fetters and emancipate themselves and the race. Is it strange that the workers are loyal to such a party, that they proudly stand beneath its blazing banners and fearlessly proclaim its conquering principles? . . . We do not plead for votes; the workers give them freely the hour they understand. ("Debs' Speech of Acceptance," *International Socialist Review*, XIII [1912], 304–306.)

15) All I have to say is that if you are a workingman and familiar with his [Taft's] record—as there is no excuse for your not being—and still vote to make him President, you stand in need of a political guardian. . . . It's about this season of the year, or a little later that the capitalist politician comes before you workingmen to tell you how delighted he is to have the opportunity of looking into your manly faces and telling you what bright and intelligent fellows you are. This is the politician who calls you the horny-handed sons of toil, and would have you proud of your misshapen hands, when as a matter of fact you ought to be ashamed of them. You ought to blush to look at your hand in the face, and if you do, you will find written in unmistakable characters an impeachment of your intelligence, and indictment of your manhood. If you would use your brains in your own interest you would not have to deform your hands in the interests of your masters. ("Debs' Speech at the Hippodrome," *Call*, October 5, 1908.)[35]

The reader may have noticed the difference in tone between the pure mythic perceptions of John Q. Worker in the writings of Duchez, Debs, and some of the other authors quoted above, and the nonmythic perceptions of him in the writings of Grace Potter and the author of the *Squeezed Lemon* leaflet and a few others. There were many degrees of mythic thinking between the former group and the totally unromantic types like Victor Berger and Morris Hillquit. And just as the latter did not cast John Q. Worker in a heroic mold, so the journals they dominated rarely expressed contempt for him when he failed to live up to that image, or—to use Tucker's concept of the inner struggle projected onto the world—when the submissive victim threatened to prevail over the virile world-conqueror. This is not to suggest that the nonmythic writers' perceptions of John Q. Worker were accurate or that they made no a priori assumptions about him and predictions about his "awakening." Rather, the differences between them and the Duchez-Debs type seem to have been chiefly differences of temperament and only secondarily of ideology.

In an entirely different category were those socialists whose perception of John Q. Worker seems to have had its source in noblesse oblige. Grace Potter's article in the *Worker* of October 13, 1906 (Document No. 9 above), is a specimen of this genre. She seems sincerely torn between scorn for the wage slave who refuses to see and hear, and pity for his victimization by the system that had blinded and deafened him. The only way to reconcile these conflicting impulses is the solution she adopts at the end, after the purely honorific bestowal of kinship on the victim: "there are those of us who see and those of us who hear. We give ourselves to you." The problem with that solution is that the infirmities that prevented the slave from understanding would also prevent him from accepting her offer of leadership; even if he did accept it, he would follow blindly, incapable of understanding where she led.

Two more examples will suffice to demonstrate the vast difference between the Proletarian Cultists and those self-appointed saviors who, despite all claims to the contrary, could not feel themselves as belonging to the working class, even in its mythic guise. The first is a pair of poems, written ostensibly from the worker's point of view. One poem is addressed to the socialists:

And now my mission great, wide, breaking on
　　My soul, I come to you, ye scorned, despised,
　　Ye prisoned, martyred men. Ye've stood with me
　　In lock-out, strike, in starving home. Ye've giv'n
　　Your lives for me. Aye, yes, I come enthralled
　　By your great light, virile with strength hard won

On desp'rate battle field. And hence with you
O Comrades dear, hands clasped around the globe,
I wage class struggle bold, invincible,
Till strong, impregnable, we build our State. . .

The other poem is addressed to capitalist politicians:

What base affront to come to me to send
Ye back to power again! Think ye to still
My holy needs with plea of Dinner Pail
Heaped high, aspill? Bourgeois Republican
And Democrat, ye know me not. I scorn
Ye both and all your grov'ling ways: your lust
For power, inhuman greed, ideals base.

Out of my awful toil, my barren days,
My strike, my starving home, has come a life—
Ye wot not of, whose glory flames my soul. . .[36]

A final example of the "noblesse oblige" attitude is an article written
for *The Harp* (organ of the Irish Socialist Federation) by Anna A. Maley,
National Organizer of Women for the SP, which was published in the
September 1909 issue. She addresses it to "you Catholics" who have
been taught to believe many false things, and closes with: "Awake!
awake! take mill, mine and factory out of the hands of the profit masters! . . . You blacken the face of your God when you claim that love of
him must be expressed by hunger, death and terror! A superstition may
be based upon tyranny and oppression but no religion was ever
founded upon such a rock!" The very grossness of this reference to the
readers' religion testifies to Maley's utter sincerity and hence reveals a
perception of the worker that no empirical evidence could counteract.
More important is the patronizing attitude suffusing the article. John Q.
Worker is here certainly not the proud world-builder of the Proletarian
myth.

The Wobblies poured vitriol on the worker who failed to live up to
the myth, but they never patronized him. Inevitably, the contempt expressed for John Q. Worker evoked protests in the columns of the *Industrial Worker*, where it appeared most frequently and in its most vitriolic
form. For example, one writer observed that an agitator would not get
the worker to listen if he told him he was a fool.[37] For a while the paper

moderated its tone. But the insults resumed, and in 1914 more protests were heard, now in *Solidarity*, the IWW's principal paper in the East.[38] But the editor of the *Industrial Worker* had already given his reply: "Some apologetic, half-baked industrialists [*i.e.*, industrial unionists] have written to the Worker asking that our language be moderated. It is suggested that 'you cannot catch flies with vinegar.' To this the Worker replies that we are not trying to catch flies, we are trying to overthrow the wage system so that we may be free. In this work we have no time to stop and 'patch fig leaves to hide the naked truth.'"[39]

The socialist papers were evidently receiving similar complaints, for an editorialist and a prominent SP member protested a bit shrilly in the New York *Worker* that their party did not have contempt for the unconverted wage earner. However, they equated that contempt with a loss of faith that he would convert to socialism; for their part, they proclaimed their faith that he would eventually awaken to the truth. Evidently this was the sole ground of their respect.[40] Perhaps the main significance of such disclaimers lies in the need to make them.

III

The myth that portrayed society as the arena of struggle between two contenders, the Working Class and the Capitalist Class, defined them solely in terms of their relationship to each other; neither had important motives, ideas, feelings, or relationships irrelevant to the other. But their relationship was even closer than that; the evidence reveals that the more a radical thought in mythic terms, the more he perceived the unconverted worker through the eyes of the capitalist—the Capitalist of the myth, that is. In fact, if really evil capitalists had not existed, this segment of the radical movements would have had to invent them. The irony is that in one crucial respect those flesh-and-blood capitalists who were the worst exploiters were far more monstrous than the calculating, amoral, and conspiratorial oppressors fabricated by the myth, for the real ones seem to have believed in the moral rightness of their role, as they presided over the barbarities of industrialization; they did not, by and large, have the saving grace of hypocrisy. But the Capitalist of the myth lacked the human propensity to believe sincerely in the rightness of his way of life. He had no function and no motive but to exploit and to oppress; he saw the proletarian as that which existed to be exploited and oppressed. When the mythicists complained of John Q. Worker's failure to convert to radicalism, they portrayed him in terms identical to those they used when portraying him from the standpoint of the Capitalist.

One common expression of this merging of the radicals' with the mythic Capitalist's perceptions of the nonradical worker was the use of metaphors that likened him to a fruit or an animal. The documents above excerpted include a number of these: swine, apes, cattle, sheep, lemon rinds, pluckable plums, buffaloes. (Elsewhere we find faithful watchdogs, chickens, etc.) More common, however, were the strictly economic metaphors, such as those used by Debs in an address delivered in 1905: "In capitalist society the working man is not, in fact, a man at all; as a wage-earner he is simple merchandise; he is bought in the open market the same as hair, hides, salt, or any other form of merchandise." The boss, he continues, calls you a hand, and "when you see a placard posted 'Fifty hands wanted,' you stop on the instant; you know that that means YOU, and you take a bee-line for the bureau of employment to offer yourself in evidence of the fact that you are a 'hand.'" [41] The animal and economic metaphors were combined in a resolution passed by District Assembly No. 11 of the STLA in 1898; it said in part that employees are "mere pieces of property, which the masters purchase in the 'labor market,' exactly as they purchase mules, asses, corn, pork or other commodities" and that it would be preposterous "to designate these pieces of property as American citizens." [42]

The perception of the worker as "hand" originated in the rationalization of production and the division of labor to the point where individual employees' personalities became irrelevant. But since this process was accompanied, in the society outside the workplace, by the proliferation of roles that each worker—as well as everyone else—filled, it cannot be assumed that the worker regarded himself or that his employer regarded him as *nothing but* a "hand." The radicals, however, automatically translated an economic datum into a basic element in a common ideology; on the same logic, they ignored or disparaged John Q. Worker's other roles. That the radicals' equations of John Q. Worker with merchandise were not merely propaganda devices to arouse him by appealing to his pride, but expressed the orators' or writers' perceptions, is shown by the otherwise inexplicable references to the employers' lack of respect for their employees, by the common assumption that the capitalists were omniscient and omnipotent, and by the even more common equation of human status with radicalism.

The strange prizing of the class enemy's respect is found, for instance, in De Leon's telling AFL members, "The ignorance, stupidity and corruption of the 'pure and simple' labor leaders is such that the capitalist class despises you. The first prerequisite for success in a struggle is the respect of the enemy." [43] Why not *self*-respect? De Leon did not explain; but his audience evidently understood, for the statement evoked applause. The editor of the *Industrial Worker* argued that, even if a fight is lost, the man who stands up and fights has "the satisfaction of knowing that . . . [he has] the respect of all the employing class." [44] And a few months later the same paper used the following as a space-filler: "Fight for your master and he will despise you. Fight your master, and he will respect you." [45] Another one-liner three years later read: "Curs are kicked, bulldogs are respected. Be a rebellious slave. Join the fighting union." [46] Neither in these documents nor in any of the others in which similar thoughts are expressed is any reason offered why the enemy's respect should matter one way or the other. Nor is any such statement accompanied by evidence that the unconverted worker, who was ostensibly the target of these remarks, actually felt ashamed of his status as "merchandise" or of being subject to authority. The conclusion is inescapable that among the reasons why some workers became radicals was a feeling of shame on account of their proletarian status, a feeling that their subordination to the owners of capital unmanned them. [47] What is significant is not only the content of the ideal Capitalist's perception of John Q. Worker; it is also the adoption of the ideal Capitalist's viewpoint, whatever its content. For who is more degraded than one who sees himself solely through a stranger's eyes—who in a sense accepts that stranger as his creator?

Whatever it was in the minds of the radicals that caused them to value the capitalists' respect also caused them to exaggerate the capitalists' power and understanding of society. Despite universal manhood suffrage—universal white manhood suffrage in the South—the capitalists were perceived as completely controlling the government; they concocted the Spanish-American War to divert the workers' attention from their own interests; they invented the phony two-party system consciously to dissipate working-class unity. Their understanding of the structure of capitalist society was, in fact, Marxist—Marxist, that is, according to these writers' construction of Marxism, which omitted the analysis, by Marx and Engels, of ideology as the sincere mental correlate of class interest and status, including a system of ethics genuinely believed in. Rather, the capitalists' omniscience and omnipotence are, in these portrayals, equaled only by their malevolence (see Supplement).

We own the earth, proclaim the American millionaires speaking through a socialist contributor to the New York *Call* in 1912. Why have we got away with it? "It's because we have fooled the people, of course. We have fooled the people into going to war for us and fighting for us and shooting each other down for us and dying for us. That was easy," because we own the press and can tell the people what we want them to do. "Oh, the dear people! How dear they are! Although we get them very cheap." And we own the legislators and executive officers on all levels of government; that's easy too. "The dear people vote so nicely and for our candidates. Just hear them shout and holler for our officials." When they became restless in one party we added another, so that if they complain about one we can boost the other and then vice versa. "What else is the tariff for? But now the horrid Socialists are in the field. They tell the workers of our game and show them how we own both the Republican and Democratic parties." So we invented the Progressive party. "That sounds good, and the dear people won't catch on for some time. . . . Teddy is our man. He is the best stoolpigeon we ever had. . . . Now watch the fool voters flock to Teddy. . . . How we will skin the slaves after they have voted for our candidates." When they get restless and hungry again we'll just go back to the two old parties.

The only thing to fear is the horrid Socialist party. It is getting awfully big and strong. . . . The worst of it is that the Socialists ask the people to read and think for themselves. We can't cope with that, for our only safety lies in the ignorance of the workers. If the workers get wise and think enough to take over the government, then they will soon take over the whole earth and our kingdom will fall. For the workers have the votes and the power and we have not. We are in pretty bad shape if the slaves should wake up. . . . For, when the workers become intelligent, they will unite in the political field and the industrial field and drive us out of both and capture the government and the industries for themselves. That's what we fear.[48]

How easy it was for some radicals to write from the "capitalists'" standpoint! All they had to do was to reverse the first- and third-person pronouns. If they were reversed again, this article would be similar to many radical analyses of the ruling class's hegemony and the workers' mindlessness that were written without sarcasm. Not only did such writers believe the capitalists had a Marxist understanding of society equal to their own; they even looked at John Q. Worker through the eyes of the mythic Capitalist. For, as was proposed earlier, the myth had two faces, the other face being that of the Proletarian, who was the Capitalist's worthy adversary, as John Q. Worker was not. Both halves of the myth—or to be more precise, the myth as a single entity with one mind but two opposite value systems—perceived John Q. Worker as passive, contemptible victim; the eyes of the Capitalist and the eyes of the Proletarian were the same.

Between them, the two faces of the myth preempted the ideological and ethical field. "They who are not wholly with us are wholly against us," thundered Debs, unwittingly anticipating Lenin who wrote two years later, "Either bourgeois, or Socialist ideology. There is no middle course."[49] As the zoological metaphors suggest, however, more than ideology was involved; it was a question of the worker's very manhood. One is reminded of the remark by James Truslow Adams, that "Puritanism was essentially a movement of protest, and so was largely negative. In fact, to such a degree was it a matter of protest and negation, that the Puritan became absolutely fascinated in his contemplation of that first great protestor and protagonist of negation, the devil himself. . . . Drama, or melodrama, was supplied only by the devil, who, from that standpoint, may almost be said to have been the saving grace of the Puritan doctrine. Men become eloquent over what appeals to their interest."[50] There is no doubt that in American radical literature the Capitalist is a far more interesting personage than the worker, although Adams's reference to Puritan eloquence reminds us of the danger of pressing the analogy too far. Most of the propaganda about workers portrayed their horrible *conditions*—the long hours, industrial accidents, squalid homes, disease—*i.e.*, things that were *done to* them, but it rarely showed workers acting autonomously. The capitalists are invariably portrayed as active agents, doing things. Despite the effort to portray a titanic struggle between them as the great theme of history, this literature often reveals the struggle to be between the Capitalist and the Radical—the Proletarian of the myth—with the worker as the passive prize, now owned by the Capitalist but inevitably to be won by the Radical. Except in the expressions of contempt for the unawakened worker, it is the Capitalist who most engages the radical's emotions; his hate for the Capitalist is real, whereas he must try hard to feel and to portray love for the worker. It is the Capitalist who is conscious, active, cunning, a worthy foe; the worker is inert, a victim, even in those labored passages in which he is depicted as heroically struggling against his oppressor. (I should remind the reader that I am discussing the mythicists, not those radical writers and speakers who did not subscribe to the myth. And even the mythicists in other moods repeated endlessly that the working class must emancipate itself and would do so once it had been penetrated by the energizing radical propaganda.)

By now another subterranean theme in the mythicists' thinking has been hinted at often enough to warrant explicit discussion—the noticeably frequent use of sex-role metaphors. The worker who was to be awakened and won by the radical may suggest Sleeping Beauty entranced by the wicked adversary. The sources quoted earlier, and others, contain references to John Q. Worker as "unmanly," "a moral eunuch," and "intellectually castrated"; his virile ancestors as men who "roared and raged [ranged?] the forests looking for a chance to dispute the supremacy of an antagonist"; and the capitalist as a cruel father. The worker's voting for capitalist parties, according to Debs, meant death to his manhood, and his misshapen hands were an indictment of his manhood. The implication was spelled out most clearly, as usual, by Wobblies when polemicizing against soft-handed intellectuals, even though—or perhaps partly because—a very large number of Wobblies were self-taught working-class intellectuals who frequented libraries as often as saloons and brothels.[51] One Wobbly advised the editor of *Solidarity* (July 25, 1914) to "let long-haired men and short-haired women talk of 'Zapatism,' 'Armed Uprisings,' 'The Sex Question,' etc.," and to stick to the job question, the only one that "the clear thinking wage slave" is concerned with. More significant, because it was written by a very prominent Wobbly writer and agitator, J. S. Biscay, is this attack on a former Wobbly who taught at Columbia:

Some of the members have taken the wail of the effeminate [Frank] Bohn, knocking the I.W.W. in the June [International Socialist] Review, entirely too seriously. . . . While an overdeveloped boy with an undeveloped feminine mind poses before ladies, old and young, as a hero of mythical exploits in the region of Mexico, we do not declaim. . . . He has the right to bore the bourgeois into insanity with his dime novel stories of the romantic West, which even the unsophisticated effete females take with a yawn. . . . But, when this creature loaded down with its own importance seeks to reason on the affairs of men, it is then that he provokes us to mirth. The feeling is the same as if some female insisted on wearing trousers. . . . I write this with due respect to the women, having no intention of classing such a little mind with the intelligent women. I only point to the spectacle of sister Bohn (with due apologies to all sisters) trying to act the part of a man while he is a failure as a woman whom he seeks to ape. . . . This hysterical sisterette admits the great onsweep of industrial unionism without being endowed with sufficient intelligence to understand that practically all the industrial agitation has come through the I.W.W. . . . We have to laugh at the thought of what those battles would have been like if we all were as ladylike as sis Frank. . . . Your tiny college where you practiced insane yells, platitudes, calisthenics and football is entirely too small to hold the philosophy of mental development of the proletariat. We developed our muscles by juggling railroad ties, playing with steel rails, transporting the means of life and doing the work of the world. . . . Peddle your funny stories to the bourgeois children and weak minded females. . . . Don't take yourself seriously, little one, we do not.[52]

In sum, passivity, cowardliness, and victimization were equated with femininity—although seldom explicitly—and activity, courage, and aggressiveness with virility; here the radical mythicists were employing images current among their nonradical contemporaries. The relative fewness of women in radical organizations in that period probably had little to do with the pervasiveness of this theme; perhaps if they had constituted a larger proportion of the membership, it might not have had as much scope to express itself. It is true that the western IWW paper, the *Industrial Worker*, was filled with expressions of frontier *machismo*. The editor of the New York *Call* recognized this style of thinking and protested against one manifestation of it:

Comrade [William D.] Haywood seems to think the class struggle is concentrated and epitomized in those desperate clashes in the mining regions of the West. Well, they are not. It is in that very region that the old-time individualistic possibility of successful enterprise has its greatest opportunity. And those who fight the fight are men, strong men. But Comrade Haywood, strong man that he is, and his companions, strong men that they are, heroic miners daring death day after day in the mines, more than probably each produces less social wealth and capitalist profit than the gray faced tottering mill hand who dies of consumption at the age of 30. . . . The class struggle is not merely a standup fight in which big men are pitted against one another. It is an insidiously comprehensive social mechanism in which countless workers are crushed. Comrade Haywood should study it, even on the basis of those things the despised intellectuals and the social theorists have advanced.

It is not coincidental that the editorial then criticizes Haywood severely for insulting women in the same speech that evoked this protest.[53] But this attitude was not restricted to western radicals; it seems to be an ingrained attitude that transcends differences in region or doctrine—or even era, up to recent times, at any rate. The former Communist Party functionary, George Charney, remarks in his memoirs, in a passage referring to the 1930s, that "we had a habit of identifying virility with radicalism."[54]

This sexual theme would be a mere curiosity but for its relationship with the inner struggle projected in the Myth of the Capitalist and Proletarian. The shrillness of Biscay's screed and the less emotional castigations of passivity by other writers suggest yet one more reason to suspect that some of the radicals felt a proud albeit unacknowledged kinship with the strong Capitalist who had earned their hatred, and feared identification with the passive worker who had earned merely their contempt. An unusually clear evidence for this is in William E. Trautmann's report, as General Organizer, to the 1910 convention of the IWW. The capitalists, he says, "have corrupted and emasculated all institutions that were originally planned to uplift the downtrodden, materially and mentally. They have prostituted men who have risen out of the ranks of workers, and thus made the craft unions an auxiliary in the protection of their interests."[55] Emasculation and prostitution are here opposed not to the workers' self-help but to paternalistic uplift on the part of the workers' vanguard. Clearly Trautmann's self-image is closer to his image of the capitalist than to that of the worker. His feelings are engaged by the capitalist, although his theory puts him on the side of the worker. The section of his report immediately following this statement describes in great detail the capitalists' omniscience and diabolical cleverness, which are matched only by the IWW's theoretical clarity, organization, and manly defiance.

All the symbols were beautifully combined by Arturo Giovannitti, one of the few possessors of genuine poetic sensibility among the radical writers (but whose poetry, atypically, sometimes expressed profound pessimism):

One power alone could raise its arm against the Steel Trust in these days when God and Demos are nursing their wounds in the field hospitals. Not the government, for the government is the head salesman and the toll collector of the Steel Trust. Nor Public Opinion, for the trust has given it a permanent job as head eunuch in the harems of its favorite actresses and odalisques. Not the press, for America has no press, but only penny paper counterfeits of the people's currency. Not the American Federation of Labor, for the helots of the Steel Trust are not laborers and cannot pay dues. No, not even the Church, even if it wanted to, for all those helots, half a million of them, are damned and belong forever to Him That Denies. Only one power could do it, for only one power was as godless, fearless and ruthless as the Steel Trust, as disrespectful of traditions, as disregardful of laws, as unafraid of gunfire and hellfire, as unappeasably hungry for power, as unslakably athirst with the passion of life—a power as blazing on the hilltops of the jungle of beasts—the I.W.W.[56]

The Steel Trust and the Wobblies, it seems, agree, have the same perceptions and spirit, and differ only in the values they attach to the facts; the others are not only blind or afraid but also less than men.

Although the radicals often explained that society could be understood only by radicals in the light of Marxism—or, as they more frequently said, economic determinism—at other times they credited the capitalists with that understanding. It followed that the radicals' task of awakening the workers was also the task of getting them to perceive themselves as the capitalists supposedly perceived them—as things, hands, dumb animals. Only then would they feel ashamed of their proletarian status and rebel. There could be no other, off-the-job source of justified self-respect; the economic relation defined the person. The trouble with John Q. Worker was that he insisted on regarding himself as a man. When fully awake he would realize that he deserved the capitalist's (and radical's) contempt, but from that moment on would no longer deserve it. He would become the Proletarian.

The radicals who thought in these either-or terms rarely tried to reconcile them with the occasional raises in pay, reductions of hours, beginnings of labor legislation, and other concessions by the supposedly omnipotent employers to the supposedly passive employees. The difficulty could be handled in either of two ways. Late in the Progressive period a few socialists decided that the legislated reforms were due to the capitalists' realization that "State Socialism" would benefit the capitalists and minimize the socialists' influence.[57] Most radicals credited themselves for whatever concessions the workers had won. For if there were only two ideologies—radical and bourgeois—any militancy on the part of workers had to be incipient radicalism regardless of what the workers themselves thought their objectives were.

In November 1900 the *Weekly People* had the unpleasant task of accounting for the minuscule SLP vote, but De Leon found the answer ready-made in the party's dual perception of an omniscient bourgeoisie and an enormously influential SLP. This year, he wrote, the SLP had to fight for its life. "The Party had become known, its uncompromising policy was feared, its unflinching attitude was noted with awe. It was to be destroyed—if such was possible. It was too dangerous a factor to be allowed in the field by the powers that be—if the powers they wielded could compass its annihilation. Accordingly, all that the political strategy of capitalism could do was set in motion. The conflict has raged throughout the length of the land."[58] The bourgeoisie's ability to foresee the future must have been as great as the SLP's, which, as the party often proclaimed, came from the science of Marxism. Why else would all the powers of the capitalist class be mobilized to destroy such a tiny party? This was not solely SLP paranoia, for the same reasoning, more moderately expressed, can be found in perfectly sane members of the SP such as Max J. Hayes, who wrote the "World of Labor" column for the *International Socialist Review*. In the issue of March 1903, he explained that the high vote received by the SP in the recent election had thrown the capitalists into a panic. They and their allies had therefore organized to educate the workers about the fallacies of socialism. The operative assumption in Hayes's analysis is that the working class's militancy signified the threat not merely of unionism but also of socialism: "the capitalists are fully aroused to the peril that confronts their class. They understand that the people are awakening . . . to the ravages of the

trusts and combines, and for that reason they will leave no stone un-
turned to keep labor subjugated. The capitalists [will do all they can]
. . . to stave off the political revolution that they dread. The prediction
of Senator Hanna about a year ago, to the effect that the next great political struggle will be between the Republican party and Socialism, bids
fair to be realized." [59]

The most significant expressions of this assumption of enormous influence of radicals on John Q. Worker, however, are to be found in the
speeches and articles of Eugene V. Debs, which warrant extended
quotation and examination.

Documentary Excursus II

The following documents are all by Debs.

16) They have not been critical students of the past [who regard the rising SP
vote as transitory], nor are they more than superficial observers of the present
transition period in which industrial evolution is transmuting competitive small
capital into centralized co-operative capital and recruiting isolated workers into
industrial armies, the forerunner of a new economic system and of a higher
order of civilization than this earth has ever known. Such astute politicians as
Mark Hanna see it. Said he: "The great political struggle of the future will be
between the Republican party and the Socialists." [Then Debs quotes the Reverend Lyman Abbott and J. Pierpont Morgan to the same effect.] ("Socialism's
Steady Progress," *Social Democratic Herald*, March 7, 1903.)

17) Standing in your presence, I can see in your gleaming eyes and in your
glowing faces the vanguard; I can hear the tramp, I can feel the thrill of the social revolution. The working class are waking up. (A voice, "you bet.") They are
beginning to understand that their economic interests are identical, that they
must unite and act together. . . . The revolutionary movement of the working
class will date from the year 1905, from the organization of the INDUSTRIAL
WORKERS OF THE WORLD. (*Industrial Unionism: An Address Delivered at Grand
Central Palace, New York, Sunday, December 10, 1905* [Chicago: Charles H. Kerr &
Co., n.d.], 2.)

18) The working class can no longer submit to the lawless despotism of the capitalist courts in the United States. The only alternative left to them is revolt. The
courts of law, so called, under the capitalist system, exercise the most despotic
power to maintain capitalist misrule. . . . To submit to such outrages in a republic would be basest cowardice and the rankest treason. Hence this declaration of revolt. . . . [The people] now propose to submit no longer like dumb
driven cattle, but to give emphatic notice that the limits of their patience have
been reached, that their meek submission is at an end, and that from now on
they are in open revolt against the power that is trampling upon their rights and

destroying their liberties. The arbitrary imprisonment of Fred D. Warren, the editor of a working class paper [the *Appeal to Reason*], without the slightest warrant of law, is the climax of a long series of outrages perpetrated by the courts to muzzle the press and silence protest against corporation misrule. . . . The ruling class has always been the enemy of a free press, free speech, and a free people. . . . February 12, the anniversary of Lincoln's birthday, cannot be more patriotically celebrated than by the inauguration of a national demonstration of protest against the despotic encroachments of the capitalists' courts. ("Cry of Revolt Sounded by Debs," *Call*, January 4, 1911.)

19) The trade union is outgrown and its survival is an unmitigated evil to the working class. . . . The trade unions hold out against the unification of the workers notwithstanding the multiplying evidences that craft unionism is not only impotent but a crime against the workers. The reason for this is not hard to find. Craft unionism is backed by the ruling capitalists for the very purpose of preventing the workers from uniting in a class organization. . . . It is in the name of the rank and file that I write. . . . About all . . . [the leaders] are good for is to keep the workers divided. . . . Of course, I am with the nine thousand striking cigar makers at Tampa, . . . and I want them to win and will help them in any way in my power, regardless of the past, but I insist that they shall profit by its appalling lessons. ("The Crime of Craft Unionism," *International Socialist Review*, XI (1911), 465–68.)

20) [On the arrest of the McNamara brothers, charged with bombing the Los Angeles *Times* building and killing some *Times* employees:] With the general strike we can paralyze the plutocracy from coast to coast. Hundreds of thousands will join eagerly and serve loyally in the fight. We can stop the wheels, cut off the food supply and compel the plutocrats in sheer terror to sue for peace. We need only to have the manhood to be true, the nerve to do our duty. . . . Arouse, you working men and working women of America! Sound the tocsin of revolt that the hosts of labor may rally to their Comrades and thwart the satanic conspirators who are thirsty for their blood! A few men may be needed who are not afraid to die. . . . No greater calamity could befall us than to succumb to the paralyzing influence of cowardice and see our brothers perish before our eyes without an effort to save them. Let us be men and women, not worms of the dust! . . . Roll up a united Socialist vote in California that will shake the Pacific Coast like an earthquake, and back it up with a general strike that will paralyze the continent. . . . Let us once hear from Boston and let the Common again resound with the portentous cry of a hundred and fifty thousand revolting workers. "*If the McNamaras die, twenty million workingmen will know the reason why.*" Let the workers of New York turn out in such unvanquishable masses as will strike terror to the Steel Trust barons of Wall Street! ("Debs Sounds Battle Call to the Workers," *Call*, September 11, 1911.)

21) With an inspiration born of necessity, the toilers of America are uniting under the crimson banner of Socialism for the final struggle of human emancipa-

tion. From factory and mine, from field and farm, the gladsome cry of freedom echoes on and ever on. Faster and ever faster the battalions of labor's hosts are wheeling into action; with the irresistible onward sweep of the ocean's tide the workers of the world march upon the political citadels of capitalism, the defiant cry of unconditional surrender upon their lips, the unquenchable light of liberty in their eyes. No longer divided by the false political prophets of capitalism, united as they have never been before, the slaves of factory, mill and farm are bent on victory on every political battlefield. For the first time in the political history of this nation the workers of every occupation are realizing the oneness of their interests and their cause and they are recognizing as never before the common cause of their common impoverishment and oppression. . . . [The issue is not Wilson, Taft, Roosevelt, or their parties, but capitalism.] Close up the ranks, oh, ye toilers of earth! Stand true to thine own class, for the battle of the ages is at hand. Hearken to the trumpet voice of liberty, for it summons you to the accomplishment of your own emancipation! ("The Issue," *Call*, August 18, 1912.)

Even after allowance is made for the odd way that the oratorical style of the Age of Bryan strikes the modern ear and for the understandable assumption that the McNamaras had been framed, these documents remain astonishing products of a mind out of touch with reality. Let us examine a few of their most remarkable characteristics.

First, Debs had no way of knowing that Fred Warren would receive a presidential pardon before the date on which the national demonstration called for in Document No. 18 was to take place, and he would certainly not have called for it if he had imagined that few workers would show up. Nor could he know that the McNamaras would plead guilty. Therefore he must have expected masses of workers to obey his calls for nationwide demonstrations, in the one instance, and for a general strike, in the other. Members of an organization or movement normally tend to overestimate its impact on the outside world, but Debs and some other radicals carried this bias to an extreme. This was not a mere rhetorical device, for he would not knowingly have risked appearing the fool. He believed that the working masses considered him their leader and teacher. How else can we read his statements that "I insist that they shall profit" from the lessons of the past, that it was "in the name of the rank and file" of the craft unions that he denounced their own organizations, and that his appeal for Warren was made "in behalf of" the enslaved workers?

Second, Document No. 19 is only one of many in which Debs showed that he considered the rank and file of the craft unions passive pawns of their leaders. At other times he agreed with others on the far left that members of craft unions consciously elected the leaders who suited them. The difference between the two positions is not as great as it may seem; it could be expressed as the difference between seeing a worker as sleeping quietly and seeing him as sleepwalking. But this is a minor element in Debs's perception of the working class. The major element appears in documents such as No. 17 above, in which he unthinkingly equates his audiences with the entire American working class. The very combination of the two clauses in the first sentence shows this: the first refers explicitly to his audience in whose glowing faces he sees the vanguard, but in the second he hears the tramp of the awakening workers who do not happen to be present. Too little attention has been paid to the facts that Debs was a bona fide worker for only a few years in his youth [60] and that during his mature years his efforts in behalf of his radical organizations were restricted almost solely to writing articles and speaking to large, self-selected crowds composed in large part of admirers who could hardly have felt offended by expressions of contempt for the sleepers and cowards. In fact, such expressions paid tribute to the wakefulness and courage of most of those who were present to applaud. Traveling about the country on speaking tours, his appearance heralded in advance, he probably had little opportunity to meet many who did not agree with him. [61] How could he know that the huge, cheering crowds represented a small percentage of the working class? Later historians have no such excuse. The many references in the literature to the enormous significance of the 6 percent of the vote that Debs received in 1912 may be read as unwitting admissions of the sad state of radicalism throughout United States history. Even if some votes cast for Debs were "counted out," what of the other more than 90 percent, of which most were doubtless cast by workers and poor farmers? And how many of the 6 percent were cast by nonworkers, or by people who would not have voted for Debs if they had thought he might win? Can we be sure they were outnumbered by those who would have voted for him if they thought he might win but declined to throw away their votes? [62]

Third, Debs's acceptance in Document No. 16 of the authoritativeness of Hanna, Abbott, and Morgan, which was common among radicals at that time, should be juxtaposed to his innumerable proclamations that the revolution was at hand—a topic that will be discussed in Chapter VII. It is, of course, easy for a reader almost eighty years later to smile at his naïveté, but the fact remains that the empirical evidence could have been—and was by other contemporaries—interpreted differently. But Debs thought the breakdown of the System was so obvious that a child (or Mark Hanna) could see it.[63]

Debs's contemporaries and later historians have not erred in paying tribute to his generosity and warm humanity, which induced him on one occasion to give his coat to a stranger. The problem is not to explain away the expressions of contempt for the unawakened worker and the illusions of vast influence as exceptional, but to explain their place in the mind of a man who was justly loved by so many. Perhaps we should distinguish between his attitudes toward those people he met and those he saw only in his mind's eye. The former were real and evoked his genuine love and compassion—and his tendency to overgeneralize. The latter were material for mythologizing in terms of his vision of the Victim and Hero.[64] Debs's lifelong faith in the power of the ballot to bring peaceful revolution in a political democracy with wide suffrage may help explain his occasional anger at workers who did not fulfill his expectations. After the 1920 election he complained, "The people can have anything they want. The trouble is they do not want anything. At least they vote that way on election day."[65] H. Wayne Morgan interprets this as evidence that Debs had become pessimistic and bitter;[66] yet the documents excerpted earlier show he had been making similar statements for decades. The more one believes that the people can get anything they want, the more one will see their "enslavement" as their own fault. Debs could not conceive that the "anything they wanted" could be anything other than what *he* wanted for them—socialism. He seems to have been unable to consider any belief, feeling, or hope that he had to be just his own; it was always the awakened workers thinking, feeling, and hoping through him. Or, to put the suggestion differently, he mistook a projection for an echo. He indeed felt pity and compassion for workers, *i.e.*, the feeling that he would have evoked in others if he had been as deprived as they. What he did not feel was empathy, the understanding of their situation in their own terms, their wanting many things and acting purposefully to get them.

To return to the exaggeration of the radicals' influence on John Q. Worker: Debs of course was not the only one who made this error. *Solidarity* announced on September 14, 1912, that "on Sept. 14 the nationwide Ettor-Giovannitti general strike will receive the endorsement of the workers of Greater New York." The Lawrence strikers and their Wobbly leaders who were framed on a murder charge won strong support throughout the country, but no one with his feet on the ground could have anticipated a general strike or imagined that "the workers," with no limiting adjective, would walk out in response to the IWW's call. The important inference, from this article and many other comparable documents, is not only the exaggeration of the radicals' influence but also the misperception of John Q. Worker. Just as the contempt reflected the rage and intolerable uncertainty engendered by his refusal to play the role that the theory assigned him, the fanciful statements about his rebelliousness represented the wishful thinking that he had assumed that role and vindicated the theory.

The capacity to imagine not what one would feel and think in the other fellow's circumstances but what the other fellow feels and thinks in his own circumstances—in a word, empathy—is perhaps the one trait that the competent social and intellectual historian shares with the effective politician. It is a trait that cannot coexist in the mind with a myth about the Proletarian as either Hero or Victim or both. It is incompatible with the pity evoked by a belief that the people are asleep and passive, for that attitude and belief rest on the assumption that rationality and purposefulness are possessed only by adherents of one's own world view. Empathy permits the recognition that another person may have a world view different from one's own, or even antithetical to it, and yet be rational and purposeful. The mythicists felt compassion or pity not for real people but for the Heroes and Victims, and what evoked it was ultimately the workers' failure to become not what they might become but what the myth required them to be.

Furthermore, it is clear that the superhumanity of the Proletarian was as inextricably combined with the subhumanity of the squeezed lemon, etc., as it was with the superhumanity of the Capitalist of the myth. Yet the whole fate of the radical movements—and, therefore, in the radicals' eyes, the whole fate of society—hung on John Q. Worker's decision. Nothing the capitalists could do short of killing the radicals could defeat their movement; indeed, the theory insisted that repression of the radicals would ultimately fail of its purpose. But John Q. Worker could defeat them simply by turning away. The radicals perceived the capitalists as ruling them, but in reality it was the sleeping, blind, deaf wage-slave who held their fate in his hands and at the same time was the least predictable actor in the drama (in the short run, that is, before his inevitable radicalization). It is no wonder that they looked to the future not only for the vindication of their theories, but also for the relief from the contradictions and inner doubts of the present, and that prophecy occupied a large place in their writings.

VI   The Radicals' Perceptions of Nonwhite and Women Workers

One of the long trends in United States history has been the successive widening of public rights to include groups other than the property-owning white men who at first monopolized them. The negative expression of this widening of the definition of sharers in the public power has been the decay of the legitimate authority of one category of the population over others. As an indirect result of the shake-up of certain values associated with the development of large-scale industry, by the end of the nineteenth century, the authority of whites over blacks and of men over women had become problematical. Another result of that shake-up, this one direct, was the temporary florescence of the radical movements, which challenged the authority of employers over employees. Yet the two developments were partly independent of each other, for the radicals' theories would have been equally suitable—or unsuitable—if the American population had consisted entirely of white men. The ideological and moral heritage that the radicals elaborated in constructing their movements equated radicalism with the "liberation" of white male workers. Just as the radical theories at the turn of the century covered a group that had won inclusion in the public power two generations earlier, it was not until two generations later that American radical theories came to cover also groups that had won inclusion—albeit incompletely—earlier. In both generations radical theory trailed the achievement of the groups that had won or were winning inclusion by their own efforts.

This statement is not a moral judgment; it reflects the fact that a group's demand for inclusion is reformist, not radical—a demand to participate in the public power, not overthrow it. A radical says, in effect, "I want a share of power, but I believe I cannot get it within the present scheme of things." The overwhelming majority of black and women activists, like the overwhelming majority of white male working-class activists, believed they could get their share of power within the existing scheme of things. The reason blacks and women were proportionally underrepresented in the radical organizations may be that the initial demand for inclusion, in a country that has a very broad suffrage and defines public power in terms of the suffrage, is the demand for enfranchisement. In such a country, some members of a large group may become radicalized not because they cannot vote but in part because they can.

In the radicals' eyes, however, the women or blacks who were demanding the suffrage and other rights in the shake-up period were "asleep," as John Q. Worker was. They were asleep not because they devoted much of their energy to demanding the right to vote but more basically because they defined themselves primarily as women and as blacks, whereas the "worker" was the sole category of oppressed people that the radical theory recognized. Hence the radicals' perceptions of nonwhite and women workers can reveal certain implications of the fact that their theory obliged them to define all people according to class, even while those people—and to a certain extent the radicals themselves—spontaneously perceived them according to race and sex. Race and sex pertained to the private sphere, the sphere of family, neighborhood, and social relations. The conflicts between feelings and theory over these two questions are thus highly revealing of the radicals' attitudes toward the distinction between the private and public spheres.

I

Of all the splits and expulsions that the radical organizations underwent in the course of the shake-up period, not one was due to a dispute over the race or woman question. Most members doubtless were indifferent to these issues. But the disputes within the SP suggest that some members' feelings about them went deeper than their feelings about socialism. The failure of these issues to disrupt the party shows that the positions taken on them were peripheral rather than core positions *for the party*. Even those SP members who felt very strongly on them rarely suggested that their positions be made a condition for membership, part of the very definition of a socialist. Several believed that contrary positions conflicted with the party's ideals, but that was as far as they went. Conversely, if the SP had made a particular stand on the race or woman question an official part of the creed, a large bloc would have withdrawn, for the contrary stand was a core tenet to them *as individuals*. Because some tenets were core tenets for the SP but peripheral tenets for some of its members, and others were peripheral for the party but core for some members, a different set of terms will be used in the following discussion so as to avoid confusion. *Defining* issues were those on which the movements wanted to distinguish themselves from the environing society; these were issues on which *the movements* called the *society* deviant. *Nondefining* issues were those on which the movements did not distinguish themselves any more than they had to. Defining issues were bonds of fellowship for the members; those bonds were weakened when nondefining issues were controverted within the organization and caused members to ally themselves with nonmembers. But whether the Negro question or the woman question was core or peripheral to an individual radical, it was a nondefining issue for the movements. That is, none of the radical organizations differed from all nonradicals on either of these questions.

To understand the real significance of the race and woman questions in these movements during the shake-up period, several customary assumptions should be discarded. First, the vacillations, ambiguities, and evasions by members of the SP were not just opportunistic sacrifices of principle to expediency, for no official principles on these questions had yet been worked out (with the partial exception of the SP's stand on woman suffrage in 1912, to be discussed below). Second, if radical theory is not a Platonic Form, approached step by step as Historical Progress marches ever onward and upward, then it is whatever a radical movement declares it to be at any given historical moment. The teleological approach implies that the vast majority of those socialists who wrote on these questions had an inadequate understanding of their own theory. But if so, where was that theory to be found? Who were its custodians—the minority of the writers with whom current radicals agree? Third, the history of Communist Parties has accustomed us to assume that radical organizations by nature encompass all aspects of their members' lives. But the movements in the shake-up period were not administratively totalistic; they never expelled members for deviating from a prescribed pattern of social relations or a prescribed doctrine relating to those aspects of their members' lives.

If we reverse each of these three common assumptions, we can perceive the chief significance of the race and woman questions here. First, they help us interpret what was defined as radically anticapitalist at that time by showing what was excluded from the definition. Second, they demonstrate the time-boundedness of radical theories in that generation and, by implication, in all generations. Third, they reveal the discontinuity between the radical movements of that time and some present-day ones, between movements that did not and movements that do dominate the nonpolitical and noneconomic—*i.e.*, the cultural and social—aspects of their members' lives. It was the SP, with respect to theory the most heterogeneous and latitudinarian of the three organizations, that pointed toward what would be the modern totalistic pattern, for by engaging in open disputes on noneconomic and nonpolitical issues it forced examination of their relationships with the more strictly class issues. It may thereby have also facilitated, among those who later joined the Communist Party, an acceptance of the doctrinal authoritarianism and extreme System-thinking that took the burden of having to think through each issue from individual members' shoulders. Fourth, and most important, the race and woman questions exemplify the fundamental problem of System-thinking: how to integrate all important aspects of the society into the System paradigm, despite contrary evidence and even some radicals' own feelings. It is this fourth theme on which this chapter will focus.

In the ensuing discussion, the political and economic spheres and the issues associated with them will be referred to as the *public sphere*, and the woman question, the family, culture, religion, and social relations will be called the *private sphere*.[1] The public sphere was central to the radicals' thinking. Yet the System paradigm generated a drive toward comprehensiveness, as is shown by some radicals' theorizing about the capitalists' use of group prejudice, religion, and sex distinction to divide and mislead the working class. But it was largely their inability to convince John Q. Worker that the private sphere should be perceived in relation to the public sphere that prevented them from converting him to their ideology.

The theoretical dilemma posed by private-sphere issues was this: if the System and the ruling class did not invade, corrupt, and determine private-sphere relations, thoughts, and feelings, the radicals could not contend that the capitalists' power was as pervasive and dangerous as they insisted it was; nor would they have been able to make such sweeping assertions about economic determinism as they did (these will be discussed in Chapter VII). But if the System did dominate the private sphere, it must have dominated that of the radicals' as well, for there was little to distinguish most radicals from nonradicals there. Either the capitalists and their ideology ruled the radicals' own private sphere or they ruled no one's. Most radicals, of course, never gave these questions any more thought than they gave to any other theoretical questions; nor did the theorizing minority spell them out in this manner. Yet the debates among that minority on these questions should be interpreted within this framework, if we are to make sense of them, for otherwise we should expect the radicals to have unanimously agreed to ignore them completely, as irrelevant to their mission.

The SLP and IWW came close to doing so. Before 1897—that is, in the period when the SLP was the principal socialist organization—its narrow base of membership and its need to concentrate on hammering out a basic theory made private-sphere questions irrelevant. By 1908 or so, it was so small that the doctrinal rigidity that had once been a cause of its weakness had become the last and only bond holding its minuscule membership together. The SLP could ignore the private-sphere questions because of the homogeneity of its membership and its isolation from everyone else. As to the IWW, it was self-consciously iconoclastic on private-sphere issues—ridiculing the timid family man, calling clergymen "sky pilots," and provocatively defending the red-light districts of the mill towns in the Northwest. The core of the IWW membership in the West were single men without family ties anyhow—that is, without an institutionalized private sphere—and they believed that as time went on the working class as a whole would become like them. In short, the ability of SLP members and Wobblies as individuals to brush aside the theoretical implications of the private sphere exempted their organizations from the theoretical dilemma that troubled some members of the SP. SP members had all the personal ties that many Wobblies lacked, the contact with the unions that the SLP lacked, and the seeming prospects for political power and organizational growth that demanded solutions to theoretical problems that the other two organizations could evade. For these reasons the ensuing discussion will deal mostly with the SP.

Since the System paradigm in principle incorporated all important social phenomena into the capitalist System and required the radicals' theories about them to be subsumed under a single theory, the question was, were the race and woman questions "important" in this sense? As was noted before, they clearly were not important to the majority. But among the minority to whom they were of utmost importance, some, including several whose names have become well known, devoted their major energies not to the party but to organizations working for reforms on nondefining issues and were relatively inactive as socialists. Florence Kelley, for example, was a socialist, but her heart was in the movement to abolish child labor, in which she found more common cause with nonsocialists than with her comrades. Similarly Margaret Sanger, the crusader for birth control, and W. E. B. Du Bois and Mary White Ovington, founders of the NAACP, and others.

Here lay the danger. Nondefining issues had to be played down as far as possible, and the more fiercely the members differed on them, the more urgent it was to shove them into the background or to agree on evasive compromises. The vague generalities agreed on settled nothing and offended few; they could become the bases of policies or substitutes for policies, as tactical needs might dictate. Take feminism, for example. The more the issue was spotlighted in the SP, the more divisive it would be, not because of the depth of feeling it evoked but because every position taken on it by socialists was taken by some nonradicals. This does not mean that the socialists' views on feminism were "bourgeois" any more than it means that nonsocialists' views were "socialist." [2] At that time there *was* no "socialist" position on the woman question beyond some vague generalities. Most socialists favored woman suffrage, approved of motherhood, marriage, and the family, and thought women should be free to earn money if they wished to. But no one suggested expelling those who believed otherwise. As to the IWW and the SLP, they had even less to say and never experienced controversy over feminism. Their most authoritative pronouncements consisted of ritual repetitions that there was no woman question (or Negro or Asian-immigration question), but only the class question; translated into the terms used here, this meant that all private-sphere questions were really minor aspects of the public-sphere questions.

For practical reasons, no radical organization could engage in all-out campaigns for all its goals. So far as the defining issues were concerned, this did not matter, for there was nowhere else for a member, if he was deeply interested in one of them, to go. But when the organization failed to exert itself on a nondefining issue, a member passionately concerned about it might drop out or retain only nominal membership, finding his really kindred spirits in a nonradical organization devoted to that particular cause.[3]

At the outset of our discussion, there is a fourth common assumption that should be discarded, along with the three noted earlier—that rhetorical racism or "sexism" is devoid of meaning if it is endemic throughout the society. Consider the phrase "nigger in the woodpile," which writers in all three organizations used, although not as often as writers in the popular press. It may be argued that they were engaging in merely verbal racism similar to the merely verbal anti-Semitism common among the Populists. But to say that the latter was less extreme than non-Populist anti-Semitism is merely to say that anti-Semitism was endemic among Americans in the 1890s and that the boundary between Populism and non-Populism lay elsewhere. There is a point beyond which a metaphor becomes so automatic that it ceases to refer to any image in its users' minds. But the picture of the Jewish conspirator-capitalist clearly did not belong in that category, and so long as it corresponded to an image—as Populist cartoons prove it did—it had and conveyed real meaning. The same observation applies to the expression "nigger in the woodpile" in radical periodicals, especially since users of that metaphor sometimes went to the trouble of inventing cute variations and more especially since the phrase was never used in articles on the Negro question. (See Supplement.)

The same comments apply to the stereotypical portrayals of other groups. For example, in the April 1, 1909, issue of the *Industrial Worker* a cartoon showed a brogue-speaking Irish cop arresting a Wobbly street speaker; an article called three small businessmen "sheenies";[4] and a headline announced "Whites Cheaper Than Chinks." The article under that heading described in respectful terms a Chinese seamen's strike and did not use the epithet in the text, and in the same issues in which such things appeared, the paper repeatedly denounced racial and ethnic prejudice. It was unquestionably sincere; the IWW earned its reputation as the most consistent champion of equality (among men) of the three organizations. But it earned it by forcing egalitarian theory to overrule members' stereotyped attitudes. Its partial failure, however, resulted in a gap between members' attitudes and official theory. The reason why theory usually prevailed will be explored later. Whatever it was, the SP did not share it. Max J. Hayes, for one, had no compunctions against calling Chinese cannery workers in British Columbia "the pig-tails"; commenting on the defeat of their effort to prevent new machines from taking their jobs, he noted, "Hundreds of the Chinks are now coming across the border to see Melican man."[5] Nor did Thomas A. Hickey, SLP national organizer, hesitate to sneer at certain dissidents as "the Debsy Jews" and imitate the accent of one of them whom he called "this typical Debsy Jew."[6] Nor did De Leon comment on a poem he published in his *People* in 1900, which included every current libel on the Chinese.[7]

Women were rarely given contemptuous labels; instead, we occasionally find references to "the gentler sex" or "the fairer sex." The metaphors used in discussions of all three questions correspond to the images of all three groups—blacks, Asians and other immigrants, and women—common among white male Americans and to their statuses in American society. The rhetoric thus tells us something important about the content and strength of its users' egalitarian beliefs.

Use or nonuse of such metaphors does not consistently distinguish the egalitarians from the nonegalitarians, however. Blacks and their strongest defenders among the white SP members never used them. But neither did Victor Berger, an unabashed racist. Those images appear most often in the newspapers published by the organization that was most militantly opposed to racism, the IWW. Impressionistic evidence suggests that Wobbly papers' use of them reflected their "tougher" journalistic style and that the SP papers usually eschewed them because of their more genteel style. (The SLP's *People*, with a style somewhere in between, used them occasionally.) This impression gets some support from the fact that Negro-dialect jokes and poems, which at that time were considered socially proper, appear in the highly respectable *Call* and *International Socialist Review*. (See Supplement.) The point is not that radicals at the turn of the century were deplorably insensitive to racism compared to us enlightened moderns; it is that the spectrum of acceptable rhetoric and of the sometimes unconscious feelings it revealed has shifted since then. The boundaries—at both ends—of acceptable rhetoric within the radical movements were close to the boundaries of acceptable rhetoric in American society.

Individual SP members formulated two opposing positions on race, consistent with both the party's basic principles and their own predilections, and in so doing confronted the party with a dilemma. It could not adopt one and repudiate the other, because to do so would have defined as heretical a view that many otherwise orthodox members fervently adhered to. These issues could not be likened to, say, the tariff question, on which two socialists who were strongly interested in it could have genially agreed to disagree even if the party had promulgated a tariff theory. What, then, was so different about the Negro and Asian-immigration questions?

Part of the answer is that, for that minority of articulate socialists who felt strongly about them, they held profound implications concerning the future. Most of the socialist writers, and all the Wobblies and SLP members who expressed views on these questions, were environmental determinists. They assumed that if blacks and Asians were behind the white race, conditions were to blame and they would in time catch up. Of the very few who speculated in public on whether this meant intermarriage in the distant future, most thought it would not but that the races would be much like ethnic groups—distinguishable but friendly. The innatists, on the contrary, held that social equality must lead to intermarriage, and although some of them thought Asians were equal in talents to whites, they dreaded any policy that would bring Asians, not to mention blacks, into continuous proximity to white families. They had no difficulty incorporating their theory of social evolution into the basic socialist paradigm. Only the white race, they argued, had reached that stage of socioeconomic evolution at which the capitalist-versus-proletarian class struggle took place. As Berger's *Social Democratic Herald* put it, "When Marx said: 'Proletarians of all countries unite!' he meant the proletariat of civilized countries, not of Shang-Hay and Timbuctoo."[8] Although the eastern Europeans were a bit behind, they would catch up quickly as they lived and worked in an advanced capitalist country. According to some innatists, the Asians never would; but according to others, they would soon begin the long climb up to that stage, both in their homelands and in the western United States. To a true racist, this belief evoked greater dread than his perception of the permanent inferiority of the blacks, for it made miscegenation both more likely and harder to prevent. As R. Laurence Moore points out, "No necessary connection existed between the Asian and Negro question[s] or, for that matter, between the Asian question and the whole issue of prejudice. A socialist could with some semblance of consistency (and many did) urge the party to adopt a policy of actively seeking Negro members and still favor immigration barriers."[9] But there was one issue on which the two nonwhite groups merged in the racists' minds: the postrevolutionary future—bluntly put, the question of miscegenation. In sum, the racists were neither contradicting the ideals of their movement nor manifesting inconsistency when they perceived the class struggle as a sort of private affair among whites—or, to many, white *men*. What saved them was innatism and evolutionism. Innatism made everything they said about the class struggle apply to whites only; it attached a tacit proviso to all the statements that environmental determinists considered universalistic. Evolutionism restricted all statements concerning classes in an advanced capitalist society to those groups that had evolved up to that stage.

Women, Asians, and blacks are remarkably absent from the beautiful visions of the postrevolutionary future that we find here and there in the documents. All the delightful depictions show or imply white men doing things—working four hours a day, enjoying culture, and so on. The reason may be discerned if we note how a few writers dealt with the question of the future of the white immigrant groups. Would they retain their separate identities, or would they blend into the composite American population? Consistently with their heavy emphasis on class and indifference to culture (in the anthropologists' sense), most writers brushed it off, willing to accept either outcome. If those groups retained their separate identities, the unity of the working class would not be endangered, for all ethnic animosities would disappear with the exploiting class that fostered them. Radicals' positions on this issue were quite similar to that of the "immigrant gifts" school of nonradical thought. National culture was interesting and had a certain value but was not critically important. The radicals' automatic acceptance of the usual assumptions about national character—Irish quick wit, Jewish intellectualism, German diligence, and so on—was therefore not always the tip of an ominous iceberg, even when factional hostility transformed them into Irish tippling, Jewish aggressiveness, and German fondness for beer.[10] The radicals meant exactly what they said over and over: those workers had far more in common with each other than with the capitalists of their own national groups. There were only two nations, the capitalist and working classes, the world over.[11] And the postrevolutionary future would put this slogan of solidarity into practice, whether or not it would homogenize the white workers.

It was quite otherwise with the radicals' images of Asians and blacks. Many of the radicals could not complacently wait to see what the Co-operative Commonwealth would bring; here the rhetorical and cartoon images *were* the tips of icebergs. Abstract theory did not require the amalgamation of the races any more than it did the homogenization of the ethnic groups. In fact, the positions that modern readers find most obnoxious were defended on solidly socialist grounds, owing to the need to bring all theorizing under the System paradigm.

II

With respect to blacks, this point is perfectly illustrated by a letter to the *New Review* from the state secretary of the SP in Mississippi, Ida M. Raymond, in 1913. The southern Negroes, she explained, are the same as they were during Reconstruction,

with the exception that some few have received an education, and at the present time are engaged, with the assistance given quietly by our most active Socialists, in trying to reach the masses and training them up to the standard where they may be organized into locals, with the intention of showing them wherein the Socialist party is the only party that will give them the proper assistance to obtain their political rights. . . . They are always scheming whereby they may get the advantage of the white man, and should they be given the rights granted them by the Constitution and not be restricted by the state laws, and not be educated to the principles of Socialism, they being in a vast majority in Mississippi, would begin a time the like of which has never been known outside of the Ku

Klux Klan days of Negro supremacy. . . . The proposition to place the Negroes so they may "meet on equal terms with the whites" here in the South . . . will only do harm, until the education, both of the whites and the blacks, will reach the point where both classes will recognize the position each must occupy in the economic and social distribution of the classes.[12]

One of several readers who responded to Raymond could not understand how anyone with her views could be a socialist so long as socialism meant "Equality, Democracy, and Human Brotherhood." And Mary White Ovington wrote, "as a Socialist to Socialists," that "class solidarity should be preached as a world movement and not as a doctrine 'for white consumption only.'" In her rejoinder, Raymond agreed that there would be no classes under socialism; there would "be divisions, as there are no two races or individuals endowed with the same natural talents." Capitalists and workers must be educated to the point where the working class will tell the capitalists to get off its back and go to work; men must be educated to relinquish their superiority over women; so too white men in the South must be educated to acknowledge the brotherhood of men including the Negro. Socialism means equality of opportunity and justice; it does not mean social equality.[13]

Three key aspects of this exchange should be noted. First, Raymond was no obscure rank-and-filer, but a leader in one of the SP's state organizations; second, she integrated her racism with the accepted socialist ideals and principles of her time; and third, even the comrade who could not understand how someone with Raymond's views could be a socialist did not intimate that she should be expelled. The reason could not have been that expulsion of the racists would have decimated the party, although this would have happened. Anyone who truly believed that the Co-operative Commonwealth must by definition be racially integrated would simply have concluded that the party would be well rid of people whose presence would prevent the ideal from being realized. Radical organizations have always considered their occasional mass expulsions or splits over principle as strengthening them, as divesting them of impediments. Clearly, the SP as a whole did not consider its racist members impediments or the race question important enough to justify a split.

All these points are especially notable in view of the radicals' belief that the revolution was imminent. Obviously, those who believed that blacks could, by following in the white race's footsteps, evolve up to equality must have assumed this process would take place under a workers' regime and therefore under the white workers' tutelage. Neither the environmental determinists nor the innatists expected blacks to play a decisive part in the revolution, although some urged a problack policy on the ground that, if the radicals did not enlighten the blacks, the capitalists would use them against the radicals.[14]

De Leon simply dismissed them as a factor in the impending conflict. The southern states' constitutional conventions, which imposed voting qualifications that disfranchised most black men, were ominous, in his eyes, because they augured the disfranchisement of white workers. "The disfranchisement of the negro," he wrote, "does not hurt the revolutionary party in the least. The negro vote in the Socialist Labor Party is unimportant, and the negro is so tightly stuck to the Republican party, and so completely befooled by the fakirs of his own race in the pulpit and press that he is not likely to play an important part in the revolution."[15] This reasoning makes sense only on the assumption that the revolution was around the corner, which De Leon did not have to mention here since he stated it so often elsewhere. It is, however, implied in his assertion in the same article that "the property qualification cannot be made sweeping enough to be effective. The capitalist class is doomed." He must have known that the white workers in those states were as "tightly stuck" to the Democratic party by that time as the blacks were to the Republican. He could not believe the blacks would "awaken" in the foreseeable future, but he certainly assumed the whites would, in sufficient numbers to make the revolution within a few years. Since elsewhere he repeatedly expressed egalitarian views, these differing perceptions imply that he believed the white worker had had greater opportunity to learn the truth. In another article, however, De Leon wrote that the English workers' apathy and ignorance were due to their partial disfranchisement, since a person tends to be interested in something he possesses.[16] Nowhere did De Leon apply the same logic to the blacks in the South and oppose the southern conventions on the ground of the effect that disfranchisement might have on black men.

The vision of the future interacted with theoretical speculation about the present in still another way. Neither environmental determinists nor innatists thought their movement had anything special to offer blacks before the revolution—the environmental determinists because the abolition of exploitation was the only cure for present inequalities of achievement, and the innatists because even that would not help. The former foresaw a society in which all would be workers, with rather unimportant individual differences based on talent. The latter foresaw a society in which private-sphere distinctions would remain as sharp as ever. The innatists, of course, expected the workers' regime to treat the blacks far more equitably than the capitalists' did.[17]

Documentary Excursus

As the following documents (most of them excerpts) illustrate, the various positions taken on the Negro question by SP members in the 1890–1917 period bear little resemblance to any taken by current radicals (or nonradicals); nor do the more egalitarian and less egalitarian positions correspond neatly to the authors' positions on other questions such as a modern reader would expect if he read the current clustering of theories back into that period. For example, southern socialists who by present-day standards were racists divided into "right" and "left" on defining issues just as their egalitarian comrades did. John Spargo, for instance, a leading right-winger, was staunchly antiracist, and the left-wing *Appeal to Reason* took a segregationist position.[18] Whether these positions were exceptional will be known only after a survey of party members' attitudes on race, matched with their positions on defining issues, has been made.

1) The Brownsville affair, we admit, was disgraceful and indefensible, but it cannot be said that it was due to race discrimination. . . . The officials of the Western Federation of Miners were not negroes, but white men, and yet they were kidnapped by conspiracy of the Republican Governors and by sanction of President Roosevelt at the behest of the Mine Owners' Association. It is not a question of race, but a question of class. . . . When the negroes, the great mass of whom are wage workers, develop sufficient intelligence to understand their true economic and political interests, they will join and support the Socialist party. . . . There is no negro question outside of the class question. Abolish capitalism . . . , give negroes economic freedom so that they may have the right to work and to receive and enjoy all they produce and the race question . . . will be known no more. . . . The Socialist party wants every negro vote it can get, provided it represents the intelligence, dignity and honesty of the man who casts it. ("Not Racial But Class Distinction, Last Analysis of Negro Problem—Debs," *Call*, August 27, 1908, a letter from Eugene V. Debs to the Rev. J. Milton Waldron, president of a black organization.)
2) White men and boys, some less than sixteen years old, work, associate and eat with negroes, eat after negroes, drink after negroes, sleep by negroes, live and dress like negroes, on a real "social equality" with the lowest class of

negroes. And this is enforced by ever-present guards with guns, dogs and whips, backed by all the power of city, county, state and national government, and upheld by all the governments of earth. . . . This will very probably continue as long as it gives pleasure and profit to the owners and rulers of the country—probably until capitalism passes away and gives place to [the] co-operative commonwealth. ("North Carolina Jails Worse Than 'Galleys,'" *Call*, October 13, 1908, article by a socialist who had been in one for fifteen days.)

3) A few weeks ago The Call came out editorially for negro social equality with the whites. . . . Does the Socialist party propose to say that its members shall or shall not associate with negroes or anybody else . . . ? Isn't it better to answer questions from negroes on this subject by saying that every man chooses his own associates, and let it go at that? Social equality means that whites would invite negroes to their homes, and that of course would result in marriage between whites and blacks. Does The Call advocate the addition of black blood to the American "melting pot"? . . . The Socialist party is new to the negro and he is now trying to use it to break down this sentiment against black and white marriages. Any man who knows the negro knows that it is the all-absorbing, overpowering desire of every negro to possess a white woman. . . . Because Socialism is founded on the brotherhood of man, must it solve the negro problem in America by breeding a nation of mongrels? . . . The missionaries have long since learned that when the influence of the white man is removed from the negro he immediately falls back to his original state regardless of learning and culture. There have been several cases of negro missionaries who, finding themselves in the midst of their savage ancestors, have thrown away their high collars and long trousers, grabbed a club and gone harem hunting. Whenever the capitalist papers succeed in branding Socialism as the negro party it is absolutely dead so far as America is concerned. (Southern Socialist, "Race Equality," *Call*, January 24, 1911.)[19]

4) [Equality of rights does not entail the obligation to invite blacks into whites' homes, or intermarriage; it merely entails all the opportunities that whites now have.] . . . The important question to consider, for the negro as well as for the Socialist, is what Socialism will do for the colored man. . . . He is bound to discover, sooner or later, that the Socialist movement is radically different from every other movement of the past or present. It is the only movement that cannot succeed without freeing everybody from exploitation. . . . It is bound to open the doors of the trade unions to the negro workers, who are to be placed on a footing of perfect equality. To the unions this is, indeed, a necessity of their very existence, for to exclude negroes from equal participation in the struggles of labor for immediate improvement is equivalent to the artificial breeding of strikebreakers. But a successful Socialist movement will do for the negro infinitely more than this. At the very best, negro equality under capitalism can be only equality with his fellow workers in wage slavery. But a Socialist state of society is the only society in which the negro will be given, for the first time in

recorded history, the opportunity to develop all that is best in him, physically and mentally. And if that best should, after all, prove to be inferior to the white man's best—and no one can now predict whether it will be better or worse or of the same quality—the negro will therefore be looked upon not as a fit and proper subject for ruthless exploitation, but as a weaker brother, to be helped on the upward path of progress and enlightenment by his white brothers as well as those of his own race who have manifested an unusual or special degree of ability. . . . It is the duty of the Socialist movement everywhere to champion the rights of the negro, which are the same as those of the white man, in every possible way, and to demonstrate to the millions of negro workers that their only friend in this country is the Socialist party. This course, which is the only one we can take, will undoubtedly retard our growth in the states of the South. But steadfast adherence to principle has been demonstrated again and again to be the only course that leads to Socialist success. And in the long run our success in the South is as certain, as preordained, as our success in the rest of the country and in the world. ("The Negro and Socialism," editorial reply to Document No. 3, *Call*, January 24, 1911.)

5) Socialism offers economic equality to everybody, the full product of one's labor and a voice in the government of his job. That is what we preach to the whites. Should we preach something else to the blacks? Should we go out and tell the negroes that if they come into the Socialist party we will fix it so they can enter the parlors of the whites, ride in the cars with the whites, send their children to the same school as the whites, in short, guarantee a general mix-up with the whites? If that is what we must do—well, excuse us Southerners. . . . If the negroes were such intelligent people . . . why should they pine for the culture of the whites, why not establish a culture of their own? . . . Just so far [as] the negro question is an economic question, Socialism will settle it; just so far as the negro is economically oppressed, will Socialism free him. . . . We don't propose to have any one who knows practically nothing of the conditions here to bring discredit upon our movement by sending negroes and sentimentalists here to inflame the colored population with a desire for social equality in the name of Socialism. (Nat L. Hardy [a Texas socialist], letter responding to Document No. 3, *Call*, February 14, 1911.)

6) Socialism without the idea of democratic equality is unthinkable, except as a reactionary nightmare. . . . The present social inferiority of negroes in several states of the South, as expressed in Jim Crow cars and separate, inferior and inadequate educational facilities, is due entirely to the existing economic and political inferiority. It is a heritage of the days of slavery. Does Comrade Hardy really imagine that a people economically and politically free would tamely submit to such insults . . . ? He might just as easily imagine the women of today, and even more so of the future Socialist society, tamely submitting to all the restrictions and disabilities of the patriarchal family. (Editor's reply to Document No. 5, *Call*, February 14, 1911.)

7) [Prejudice is not due basically to the Negro's economic and political disabilities, nor will socialism eliminate it. If socialists obtained control of governments in the South they would allow more home rule to localities.] In the South, where a practical race war between the white and colored laborer exists, the white voters of a municipality would be quite capable of passing a law that would force the negro to be educated in a different school from that in which the white children were educated. Race prejudice has more than once shown its power to overcome class consciousness. In the above case Socialists and race prejudice would walk arm in arm together. . . . [Race prejudice] . . . is the principle that Nature uses . . . to prevent the mixing of white and black blood, a thing which Nature and I regard as manifestly evil. The same thing applies to the yellow races—the mixing of yellow and white blood. (Louis H. Wetmore [frequent writer on the arts in the *Call*], "Race Prejudice," *Call*, February 21, 1911, responding to Document No. 6.)

8) [A] proper attitude towards the negro problem is one of the most important problems before the Socialist movement in America. . . . But unfortunately there does not appear [to be] any great interest in the matter among the active membership. [To arouse interest, he offers an article (part one of a two-part summary of a long series that had been published, under the name I. M. Robbins, in the *International Socialist Review* in 1908–1910). It includes the following:] It is easy to conceive of a solved negro problem in a capitalist society, or at least the absence of all racial friction in such a society; it is also possible to conceive, though perhaps somewhat less easily, of a negro problem, or some race discrimination[,] surviving after the introduction of a co-operative commonwealth, as, for instance, the relegation of all negro citizens to the worst paying occupations. This is all hypothetical, of course, but it is purposely stated here to underscore the fact that the connection between race prejudice and Socialism is not self-evident. (I. M. Rubinow, "Socialism and the Negro," *Call*, May 12, 1912.)

9) [Blacks have never asked for social equality or intermarriage.] This phase of the negro question is pure fraud and serves to mask the real issue, which is not social equality, but economic freedom. There never was any social inferiority that was not the shrivelled fruit of economic inequality. The negro, given economic freedom, will not ask the white man any social favors; and the burning question of "social equality" will disappear like mist before the sunrise. I have said and say again that, properly speaking, there is no negro question outside of the labor question—the working class struggle. Our position as socialists and as a party is perfectly plain. We have simply to say: "The class struggle is colorless." The capitalists, white, black, and other shades, are on one side and the workers, white, black and all other colors, on the other side. . . . We have simply to open the eyes of as many negroes as we can and bring them into the socialist movement to do battle for emancipation from wage slavery, and when the working class have triumphed . . . the race problem will forever disappear. . . . [The next convention should repeal the resolutions on the Negro question

passed in 1901.] The negro does not need them and they serve to increase rather than diminish the necessity for explanation. We have nothing special to offer the negro, and we cannot make separate appeals to all the races. (Eugene V. Debs, "The Negro in the Class Struggle," *International Socialist Review*, IV [1903], 257–60.)

10) There can be no doubt that the negroes and mulattoes constitute a lower race—that the Caucasian and indeed even the Mongolian have the start of them in civilization by many thousand years—so that negroes will find it difficult ever to overtake them. The many cases of rape which occur wherever negroes are settled in large numbers prove, moreover, that the free contact with the whites has led to the further degeneration of the negroes, as of all other inferior races. . . . The barbarous behavior of the American whites toward the negroes, and the contempt evinced for their human rights, is due to the fact that in this country men are judged chiefly according to the amount of capital which they possess. . . . The man pronounced superfluous by capitalism changes all too easily from an element of civilization to an enemy of civilization. Society refuses to him the legitimate means of existence and of pleasure, so he seeks for himself those of an illegitimate nature, and becomes an assistant of the universal passions and vices of speculation, or else a dangerous criminal. And in the case of the negro all the savage instincts of his forefathers in Africa come to the surface. (Victor L. Berger, "The Misfortune of the Negroes," *Social Democratic Herald*, May 31, 1902.)

11) The old idea that the people were by nature bad was a fearful slander on the race. The struggle of humanity to break through all sordid and corrupting restraints proves that it was not and is not true. People are what their surroundings compel them to be. (Editorial note in Victor Berger's *Social Democratic Herald*, June 14, 1902.)

12) There was a time when organized labor in the main was hostile to the Negro, and it must be admitted with all candor that certain unions [still bar him]. . . . But in spite of all such influence, the labor movement in general, in America and throughout the world, stands unequivocally committed to receive and treat the Negro upon terms of absolute equality with his white brother, and where this is not the case the genius of unionism is violated and investigation will disclose the fact that corporate power and its henchmen are at the back of it. The Socialists, who represent the political wing of the labor movement, are absolutely free from color prejudice, and the labor union, the economic wing, is rapidly becoming so, and in the next few years not a trace of it will remain even in the so-called black belt of the Southern States. (Eugene V. Debs, "The Negro Question," *Social Democratic Herald*, July 25, 1903.)

13) Whereas, The economic conditions under the present capitalist system of industry cause the race hatred which leads to many of the lynchings, and also foster the brutal instincts which lead to lynching in general and to the crimes for which the lynching is perpetrated, therefore be it Resolved, That it is the sense

of the national quorum that the Socialist Party of the United States abhors and condemns the practice of lynching both of negroes and whites, and that it abhors and accuses the capitalist system which begets freaks instead of types, and then when the natural moral sense of society is outraged by one of them, a portion of society becomes resistlessly enraged, and the mob and the lynching follow. The Socialist party points out the fact that nothing less than the abolition of the capitalist system and the substitution of the Socialist system can provide conditions under which the hungry maniacs, kleptomaniacs, sexual maniacs, and all other offensive and now lynchable human degenerates will cease to be begotten or produced. ("The National Quorum Meeting in Omaha," *Social Democratic Herald*, November 21, 1903; the meeting passed several resolutions, this one in response to an inquiry by the International Socialist Bureau as to the SP's attitude toward lynching.)

14) [There is nothing in the SP's position] that would promise to the negro the right to force his society on those that objected to him, BUT ON THE CONTRARY THE INDEPENDENCE THAT SOCIALISM PROMISES WILL MAKE IT ABSOLUTELY THE PREROGATIVE OF EVERY HUMAN BEING TO ASSOCIATE WITH THOSE ONLY WHO ARE AGREEABLE TO HIM. Can this be said at this time? You know that capitalism never examines the color of the skin when it buys labor power and I have seen white men walking the streets of the city of Dallas side by side with negroes when the heat of summer was such that if the negro could ever be offensive to a white man he must have been then. Moreover I have seen WHITE and BLACK working thus under A NEGRO FOREMAN. . . . I can show you whites and blacks of the working class FORCED INTO BEING NEXT DOOR NEIGHBORS. Why? Because capitalism has forced exactly the same conditions of work and wages upon them and they could not help themselves, although I know personally that the black people objected to it as strongly as the white people, for they said the poor white trash was forever nagging them. . . . [If the blacks have any desire to mingle with whites it is only because the whites live better; if the blacks had the same means to clothe themselves, eat well, get an education, and pursue leisure activities as the whites, they would prefer to live by themselves,] as they understand each other better and that subtle attraction of race that makes Jewish quarters and Irish quarters and German quarters and Swedish quarters, etc., in all our large cities would draw them together. (John Kerrigan, SP National Committeeman from Texas, "How International Socialism Views the Negro Question," *Social Democratic Herald*, November 21, 1903.)

In the light of the documents of which the foregoing are a sample, it is not surprising that the SP's actions with respect to the blacks were generally initiated by black members. The often-quoted resolutions on the Negro question passed at the founding convention originated with black delegates.[20] The plan to organize Harlem blacks, which Hubert H. Harrison succeeded in getting the New York party to approve, was finally aborted by the sheer indifference of his white comrades.[21] There were, by no coincidence, too few blacks in the party to force it to adopt a positive program, and some of them opposed any special recognition of blacks and their problems by the party.[22] If foreign comrades had not inquired, the resolution on lynching (Document No. 13 above) would not have been written. The brief flurry over the Louisiana state party's decision to organize jim crow branches fits the pattern too.[23] In a word, whatever the SP did or said on the Negro question was *reactive*.

When documents referred to the SP as though it were a group of whites,[24] they were reflecting not merely the statistical facts, but an image of the party that was taken for granted. Among the whole assortment of self-delusions it fell victim to, the notion that the SP was the "vanguard of the Negro people" was not one of them, as it has been in the thinking of the Communist Party. Nor did it have an authoritative center that could have handed down a decree, as the CP leadership did in 1949, to "root out white chauvinism." The SP before World War I was, by contrast, larger, more influential in the labor movement, nontotalistic, able to elect many officials in municipal and state governments, and autonomous. That these facts also mean it was more racist is precisely the point: the American CP has been free to spin whatever theories it or its foreign mentors wished (a few of which by chance became popular later), without the slightest effect on its role in American life. Neither the SP nor the CP has ever had the power to alter white Americans' attitudes on race; the SP's greater success in recruitment was due in part to the larger area of its prior agreement with nonradical whites, not to any greater success in playing a "vanguard" role.

Since it faithfully reflected the spectrum of nonradical opinion on nondefining issues, the SP also gave full freedom of expression to members who argued against racism. A New Jersey comrade, who wrote to the *Call* in response to "Southern Socialist's" essay (Document No. 3 above), was one of the very few, however, who argued that white socialists should be taught that racism hurt themselves; "Let us . . . educate our white members," he concluded, "to work with him [the black recruit] and thus overcome the habit of race prejudice." Another correspondent, thoroughly atypical, wrote that there was no place in the SP for people with "Southern Socialist's" prejudices.[25] Almost all the antiracist documents merely urged the white members to enlighten black workers.

Debs's views are of interest not only because of his eminence but also because they mirror the party's ambivalence on the issue. As Document No. 9 above shows, he brushed it aside by reducing the Negro question to the class question.[26] Therefore, he contended, the party should repeal the "Negro resolution" passed at its founding convention. Yet two months later, replying to an extremely racist comrade, Debs accused him of not understanding the philosophy of socialism, and to prove his point he quoted that very resolution.[27] Since in that period any recognition of group differences was potentially dangerous to a member of a minority, especially a black, Debs's apparent wish to define the Negro question out of existence doubtless made some sense. (Perhaps the wish to maintain what today is called a "low profile" accounts for some black comrades' insistence that the party not give special recognition to the Negro question.) But in view of the incredible fantasizing and circular reasoning he indulged in in Document No. 12, it is doubtful that he had thought through the problem in this way. His attitude, say Spero and Harris, "actuated as it no doubt was by lofty idealism, was an escape from the reality of the relations between the white and Negro workers rather than an assault upon race antipathy."[28] Debs's tolerance of comrades who disagreed with him here (he never suggested expulsion of racists), however, contrasts with his belief that a union should expel a member who voted for a capitalist party.[29]

One socialist who evidently struggled with his own feelings was I. M. Robbins, also known as Rubinow, who wrote a long, thoughtful series in the *International Socialist Review* examining all aspects of the Negro question and pleading for an "aggressive" party policy, although acknowledging that personally he felt revolted by the thought of intermarriage.[30] The last article in the series contained a unique revelation of what lay at the base of the difficulty. Referring to the racists' repeated invocation of the specter of social equality, he pointed out that "the 'social' life, concomitant upon Socialist organizations, (*i.e.*, entertainments and festivals) have [*sic*] often been urged as an unsurmountable difficulty against admitting negroes to Socialist locals. . . . It is no secret, that in cities with a mixed population the festivities and entertainments of the Socialists are conducted on national (and for all I know may be conducted even on religious) lines." [31] This admission throws light on black comrades' repeated complaints that black potential recruits were reluctant to attend party meetings. Thomas Potter, a black socialist from New Jersey, wrote that "we must try and make him [the Negro] feel at home in the party. On account of his past and present position he is timid in joining anything but a race organization." And when the effort to organize the "Colored Socialist Club of Harlem" was under way, and black organizer Hubert H. Harrison published an invitation to white socialists in the vicinity to come to the meetings, he included the remark that they would provide "an excellent opportunity . . . to learn something of the psychology and history of the negro." In another article in the same issue of the *Call* that contained that announcement, Harrison gave detailed advice on how to act when talking to Negroes; he urged the white comrades to treat them simply as human beings. [32]

The issue of whether the party should have separate clubs was debated for a time. W. E. B. Du Bois argued strongly against the plan for the all-black branch in New York. "It must not be forgotten," he wrote, "that while colored people from long and bitter experience submit to segregation and separate institutions rather easily, that they do this, not because they wish to avoid their fellow men, but because they wish to avoid insult and oppression. There should not be, and [there] is as yet no such barrier in the Socialist locals and, therefore, the argument that negroes want separate locals is absurd." [33] Yet many documents indicate that there was indeed an invisible barrier against comfortable association between black and white comrades even in New York, from which none of the extremely racist articles and letters emanated. Potter posed the problem perfectly when he explained that timidity but at the same time opposed separate branches. Obviously the only way to reconcile both his points would have been a sustained effort undertaken voluntarily by the white members to change their own feelings. As has been pointed out, this was out of the question. But in the atmosphere of that period, if they had done so and succeeded, their recruitment of whites would have plummeted.

This fact cannot be overemphasized: no whites joined the SP because of their attitudes on race, one way or the other. Anyone desiring to fight racism would have sought a different vehicle—after 1909 it would have been the NAACP.

The most egalitarian position that could win majority support within the party was spelled out in a *Call* editorial in 1908, in response to the statement in the Boston Negro paper, *The Guardian*, that many blacks wished to leave the Republican party for the SP but were not sure how they would be received. "In reply," the *Call* explained,

it should first be said that, DIRECTLY, the Socialist Party is doing NOTHING to secure the negro vote. . . . The Socialist party does not vote its supporters in blocks. . . . Socialism, instead of destroying initiative, develops individualism and encourages men to think and vote and otherwise act for themselves. It is essentially a propaganda movement; its mission is to make SOCIALISTS, the vote being a consequence. . . . As to what Socialism has to offer the negro, it offers him exactly what it offers any other member of society. . . . Socialism is frank with the negro. It tells him that in the Socialist movement human nature is not different from what it is elsewhere. Some Socialists have a personal prejudice against the negro. Perhaps their number is not relatively great and possibly their prejudice is less pronounced, for every Socialist is to some degree a philosopher, and prejudice is not a part of philosophy. But these men are not the SOCIALIST MOVEMENT. Nor does Socialism make the negro any specious pledges. It does not promise him equality. . . . Socialism will give the negro equality of opportunity. . . . We are all creatures of environment. . . . Under Socialism he will be what he may make [of] himself. What Socialism has to offer the negro, or the members of any other race, is . . . "A white man's chance to each and all."[34]

The IWW underwent no such troubling controversies. From time to time Wobbly papers published scathing denunciations of racism. "Prejudice," proclaimed the *Industrial Worker*, "is the reason of fools." On another occasion it castigated the Brotherhood of Locomotive Engineers in Georgia for striking against the employment of blacks. And in its convention of 1906 the IWW unanimously passed a resolution "emphatically protesting against the brutal outrages and murders committed on our class, the negro wage earners of the south."[35]

Unlike the SP and SLP, the IWW in its day-to-day organizing tried to serve blacks' economic needs. The rhetorical racism noted earlier suggests that this record may have been made at the cost of some members' feelings. And traveling organizers in the South were quite capable of sending report after report to headquarters without mentioning black workers. Yet the distinction between the IWW and the two socialist parties is undeniable. One reason for the difference was suggested earlier—the Wobblies' consciously cultivated iconoclasm. Many Wobblies delighted in outraging genteel society, and a willingness to defy racial conventions could easily fit into the pattern.

More important is the fact that the IWW was a union, whereas the SLP and SP were political parties. Each of these parties regarded itself as the political arm of the labor movement; its immediate practical aim was to win votes and governmental offices. Before World War I the vast majority of blacks lived in the South and were disfranchised, legally or extralegally. In the North, enfranchised blacks were too few to help much, especially since a policy to attract their votes would have scared off many whites' votes. But the IWW's aim was always to organize unskilled workers regardless of whether they could vote. In short, the two parties had little incentive to examine their own attitudes on race, much less fight them, but the Wobblies' organization's very reason for being gave them that incentive.

III

It was in the far West that that incentive was tested, because the newness and prevalence of extractive industries in that region made it the Wobblies' most promising field for recruitment, and it was also where most Asian workers lived. A political party had nothing to gain by defending them and little to lose by ignoring them, for not only were they disfranchised but the organized labor movement had a tradition of hostility to the Chinese for allegedly threatening white workers' living standards. In fact, as Alexander Saxton has shown, anti-Chinese sentiment had for some time been a bond of solidarity in the white labor movement. Later, the anti-Japanese campaign had the same effect. Progressivism could be quite compatible with anti-Asian sentiment, as was shown in 1900 when the conservative widow of Leland Stanford ordered the firing of Populist-Progressive professor Edward A. Ross from Stanford University for making an anti-Japanese speech. Some non-Progressives defended the Asians because they were more satisfactory employees; others on grounds of religious principle; still others out of loyalty to old-fashioned American values of progress and assimilationism. Yet they lost ground as time went on and the anti-Japanese movement grew irresistible, in large part because of the "bogey of miscegenation."[36]

The AFL's opposition to Japanese immigration gave the revolutionary union an added incentive to take the opposite position. Scholarly defenders of the IWW have played down evidence that it was a dual union, out to destroy the AFL, and contended that it wished merely to organize the workers whom the AFL ignored. Among the many evidences to the contrary was a remark made by a Wobbly leader at the 1907 convention, immediately before the passage of a set of strong resolutions defending Asian workers. William E. Trautmann declared, "The most important thing to do is to undermine the power of the capitalist institutions, such as the United Mine Workers of America, . . . the Machinists' International Union, . . . the old Brotherhood of Railway Employees and . . . the Longshore and Maritime Workers. We must . . . build up our organization from the disgruntled and discouraged members of those organizations, and . . . minor organizations . . . will fall in line just as soon as they see the others are lining up." This hostility to the AFL may have influenced the IWW's position on the Asian-immigration question. Shortly after Trautmann's speech, the convention passed a resolution condemning persecution of Asians in the West as contrary to the common interests of all workers. It went on to blame the master class for thus dividing the workers so as to keep them in slavery. The last clause condemned "the A.F. of L. as well as other so-called labor organizations who have in this respect aided the masters."[37] In 1906 the Wobblies' consistent opposition to racism earned the thanks of a Seattle Japanese paper, which predicted that the IWW would become the most powerful labor organization in the world.[38]

The Wobblies' western weekly, the *Industrial Worker*, was sprinkled with little items from time to time praising the militancy of the Japanese, often contrasting it to the timidity of white workers. In fact, the contrast seems sometimes to have been the point of the articles. "If the porters' union [in Spokane]," it remarked, "were but half as class conscious as the average Japanese worker, there would be better wages and better conditions for the porter[s] than the wretched ones they now are forced to submit to." A few months later, in an editorial lauding the militancy and solidarity of the Japanese in Hawaii and California and denouncing the prejudice of white workers, it added, "The personal cleanliness of the Japanese workers is one of the highest and surest marks of their inborn intelligence and their natural refinement of disposition. Compare the bunk house of a gang of 'stiffs' on the average railroad with that of the next Japanese extra gang. The difference can easily be detected a half mile off—especially if the wind is in the right direction." [39]

The same concentration of the Japanese in the West that induced the IWW to welcome them had the opposite effect on many members of the SP (by the time the anti-Japanese agitation peaked, the SLP was too small to matter). Whatever chance the party might have had to ignore this public controversy disappeared when the Second International, meeting in Stuttgart in 1907, proclaimed the principle of free migration of workers. [40] Both the 1908 and 1910 conventions of the American SP experienced long and bitter debates in which a few of the top leaders, including John Spargo and especially Morris Hillquit, tried to find common ground on which the warring delegates could stand. The debate took place in the socialist press as well.

No one believed the party must accept the International's dictum— or even Karl Marx's opinions. Those who invoked their authority did so to strengthen the positions they believed right; their adversaries had the same motive when they declared their independence of foreign or earlier authority. [41]

If the participants in the convention and press debates are sorted according to the reasons why they favored or opposed the exclusion of Asian immigrants, we find that the theoretical bases for the positions at the opposite extremes were the same as those in the controversies on the Negro question. Here too we discover concern for the future American society, innatism versus environmental determinism, and the threat or absence of threat to the home and family. All three themes are neatly combined in two of Ernest Untermann's convention speeches. Presaging a later generation's totalistic party, he argued (inaccurately) that every socialist writer agreed that the SP was concerned not only with the economic question

but with all phases of social life. But when the race question comes into discussion this reasonable declaration is quickly forgotten and the whole debate turns upon the economic factor, without taking the slightest notice of the racial aspect of the question. . . . Those comrades who merely consider the economic point

of view forget that every argument that can be brought against oriental exclusion from that point of view can also be brought against the immigration of
every other race. Only when we take the race issue into consideration along
with the economic factors do we get any satisfactory solution of this question. . . . I am determined that my race will not go the way of the Aztec and the
Indian. I believe in the brotherhood of man, regardless of races, but I do not
believe in extending that brotherhood to the point of eliminating myself voluntarily from the struggle for existence and turning over this country to my brothers of other races. I am determined that my race shall be supreme in this country
and in the world.[42]

When it comes to the question of whether we shall be permitted to live in our
own house or whether we shall voluntarily abdicate and let somebody else come
into our house, I should think every sensible man would stand for his own
house and for the right to live in it, rather than voluntarily emasculate himself
and let somebody else in.

Untermann intended the second speech to support his statement that
Oriental immigrants should be excluded from the United States, because a struggle was taking place not "between different classes, but . . .
between the same class of different races."[43] It was the image of the
home and family—each man's kingdom, as suggested by the word *abdicate*—that came to his mind when he tried to express the urgency of
the threat, and it is significant that he expressed it by associating the
race question with autonomy, power, the sanctity of the home, and
masculinity.

Mrs. E. D. Cory, a delegate from Washington, complained that the
easterners did not understand the situation in the West. "While you
with your idealistic theories of what the Chinaman or the Jap may be
accept him as one of the brotherhood of mankind I will concede nothing
of the kind." Those people work in filthy canneries, smoking opium
while processing the fish you then eat, she said, whereas you in Chicago see only the Chinese student or businessman. "A lady told me
in this hall . . . that she would just as soon one of her daughters
would marry a Jap or a Chinaman that she had seen here in the college
as any white man on earth. Do you realize, my comrades, what this
means? . . . Can you realize what it would mean if the blood of the orient were injected into the Caucasian blood of our country? It is a race of
people that we are discussing."[44]

Untermann was logical in refusing to base exclusionism on economic grounds—the main economic ground being the oft-repeated argument that the Asian immigrants, by working for very low wages, threatened American workers' living standards (which on other occasions were said to have hit rock-bottom in many industries). On this one topic economic determinism had to go and environmental determinism had to give way to innatism, for the exclusionists did not want to bar the European immigrants. Some of the exclusionists frankly accepted this logic but denied that their acceptance of innate racial differences implied prejudice. Their adversaries insisted it did, for in that generation Americans commonly applied the term "race" to white ethnic groups as well (although as we have seen Untermann did not), and everything the exclusionists said about the Asians had been said about the European immigrants. Winfield Gaylord of Milwaukee inadvertently confirmed their contention when he said, "One of the things necessary for political organization is . . . homogeneity. . . . We must be as much alike as possible, and the more different classes and the more different nationalities and the more different kinds and habits of life and language and food and clothing and living and everything else that you introduce, the harder it is to" raise the standard of living. I used to preach the distant utopian dream when I was in the pulpit, he went on, but now I preach from the socialist platform, for bread and homes and clothes now. In the recent municipal elections, "I went down in the Italian ward and spent the whole of election day there watching to see that those crooked Irishmen did not lead the Italians around by the nose. Victor Berger took an automobile and went from one Polish precinct to another to see to it that those same Irish politicians did not lead the Poles around by the nose. . . . These men are difficult to organize and get to the polls because they are scattered and have no home. They have lost their stake in the country and they are getting desperate. But, comrades, men that are desperate and driven by hunger are not the men that have the capacity to build a new civilization." [45]

That the desired homogeneity could not be achieved by intermarriage was made clear by Guy E. Miller of Colorado in his plea that the delegates consider the "biological" as well as economic and sociological grounds for exclusionism. "There has," he said, "never been a mixture and amalgamation of races that did not end disastrously for those amalgamated. (Applause.) And I want to say to you that it is capitalism that fosters and creates conditions of that kind," namely, the forced mingling of people of different races, who would prefer to spend their lives "among the people of a common descent." The SP could not, he added, promote its ideal of brotherhood "by sinking mankind to a common level." [46] Miller and some others expected socialism to bring about homogeneity by ending the forced association of unlike peoples, not by fostering intermarriage.

The "Negro problem" could not, of course, be solved by means of immigration laws, but the "Asian problem" could, and on good socialist grounds. All foreign proletarians who were so dissatisfied with their lot at home would do better to stay there and fight their own nations' capitalists. They could do so more effectively, for at home they knew the language and customs and could not be used by the capitalists against other ethnic groups with different standards of living. As Victor Berger said at the 1910 convention, "Now I believe in the motto of Marx that the proletarians of all countries should unite, absolutely. But he did not say nor would he say if he lived to-day, that they should unite in Milwaukee or Chicago or New York. We unite in spirit; we fight in the same cause; but do not come together in the same place unless it is absolutely necessary." [47]

Despite Untermann's warning that recourse to economic arguments cut the ground from under the exclusionist position, delegates at both conventions used them repeatedly, sometimes without apparent racism. The gist of the argument was that capitalists induced Asians to immigrate because they would work for wages that no American would accept. Such contentions evoked two types of response—general appeals to brotherhood and, more rarely, the assertion that capitalism tended inexorably to drive wages to the minimum required for subsistence all over the world. In a typical speech along these lines, a California delegate said that if American wages were higher than those in other countries, the jobs would emigrate, so that "either the laborer will be brought to the job or the job will be taken to the laborer." Interestingly, he linked the egalitarian position on immigration with the theory of increasing impoverishment. The abstract appeals to brotherhood evoked from one delegate the advice to postpone the brotherhood of man to the future; in the meantime the capitalists were importing labor and exporting indus-

tries, and "the class struggle is the main factor." To which another countered that "class runs deeper than either blood or race," apparently substituting wishful thinking for the evidence of his own ears at that very
convention, to say nothing of the views of nonsocialists outside it.[48]

As to the economic arguments, an older delegate recalled the Know-
Nothings' prediction that immigration would impoverish the workers;
the prediction had been proven wrong because unionization had enabled American workers to raise their living standards despite massive
immigration. Another delegate retorted that the standard of living had
dropped since his own arrival; the cause, however, was not immigration
but new machinery.[49] Meyer London of New York, representing "the
Jewish Section," excoriated all forms of innatism that had been expressed; they had, he complained, obscured the only relevant question,
the class question. "There is," he maintained,

one fundamental point in this case, and one of the things that pained me in the
discussion today was the attitude taken by two women Socialists in this matter. I
expected the women to favor something in the direction of sentiment, in the
direction of international brotherhood, in the direction of the greater side of Socialism, and yet they are the most practical on this proposition, the most conservative, the most orthodox, and they seem to have surrendered to race prejudice and race division. . . . When you say we will exclude people because they
are Japanese and . . . Chinese and . . . Hindoos, you violate the decalogue, one
of the elementary principles of international Socialism, and you will have declared the bankruptcy of Socialism.[50]

Most of those who refuted the exclusionists' economic arguments contended either that the immigration of very poor workers did not really
harm the American working class or that if it did the effect would be
temporary.[51]

As these excerpts from the debates in the SP's 1908 and 1910 conventions indicate, the arguments on both the exclusionist and antiexclusionist sides were so various—only a few are included above[52]—that
summary is difficult. Any theories that can be teased out of the speeches
were clearly expressions of delegates' personal feelings, hopes, fears,
and experiences. Nor was there a consistent division between the left
and right wings. Leftists tended toward the antiexclusionist side and
rightists toward the exclusionist side, but there were too many "exceptions" to warrant an identification of either "wing" with either side, ex-

cept in the case of the Wobblies and their sympathizers, all of whom strongly opposed exclusion. Right-winger Victor Berger and left-winger Ernest Untermann favored exclusion, and right-winger Meyer London and left-winger Thomas F. Kennedy opposed it.[53] A slight geographical pattern may be discerned: the delegates from the Rocky Mountain states were most consistently for exclusion. Those from the Pacific Coast were split, the Wobbly sympathizers consistently against, and the anti-Wobbly SP members (right and left) generally in favor. More important were the ethnic patterns: representatives of new-immigrant groups, such as the Jews and Finns, opposed exclusion, whereas a somewhat disproportionate number of those with English names, probably native-born Americans, lined up with the foreign-born Untermann and Berger on the other side.

The antiexclusionists often accused their adversaries of opportunism, but the exclusionists' remarks suggest that most of them would have taken their position regardless of consequences.[54] Some who argued on the basis of expediency obviously did so in order to win other delegates' support for the positions they themselves believed in sincerely. Some of them were obviously clothing their feelings in theory; but the same is true of some of their opponents. Scientific authorities at that time were divided; egalitarianism was a matter of faith, not scientific judgment about empirical data.

This point must be stressed because it is natural for modern readers to assume that radicals' early-twentieth-century egalitarianism had the same rationale as it does now. But consider the statement by Leo Laukki of Minnesota, a left-winger and opponent of all discrimination: "The Asiatics when thrown into the industrial mills of America cannot forever remain Asiatics; they will get the habits of the American industrial worker; they will undergo the same sufferings in the same hell and so into their hearts will grow the same hatred and the same desires as in the hearts of the Western workers. Economic life itself arrays them against capitalism."[55] The current reader is tempted to assume that, because he (probably) shares Laukki's antiracism, his reasons are the same as Laukki's. Perhaps for some readers they are; but intervening advances in the social sciences show his position to have been unempirical and economic-determinist in its view of the relation between culture and economics. The comrades against whom he was arguing, however, proved better prophets when they foresaw a long life for race feeling. That view was propounded in the majority report of the committee on immigration at the 1912 convention. Untermann, speaking for the majority, contended that "race feeling is not so much a result of social as of biological evolution. It does not change essentially with changes of economic systems. It is deeper than any class feeling and will outlast the capitalist system. It persists even after race prejudice has been outgrown. It exists, not because the capitalists nurse it for economic reasons, but the capitalists rather have an opportunity to nurse it for economic reasons because it exists as a product of biology." [56] If "ethnic" were substituted for "race," and "cultural" for "biological," that statement would come close to what social scientists now consider the truth. Both Laukki the antiracist and Untermann the racist were clothing their feelings in the garb of theory and predicting what they hoped would happen. An accurate perception of this long past controversy entails the reader's perceiving both the disputants as meeting the challenges of their own time with the intellectual resources available in their own time. Those resources did not equip them for prophecy, and hence if the prediction of either of them comes true, it will be not because he had the right theory but because of events and conditions he could not see or foresee.

IV

By now it should be clear that the Co-operative Commonwealth or Socialism was the name radicals gave to their visions of what American society should be, contrasted with what they saw around them that they felt to be unnatural and unjust. To some, the mingling of unlike peoples was unnatural; it followed that the Co-operative Commonwealth would separate them. To others, the estrangement of those groups was unnatural; the Co-operative Commonwealth would cause them to mingle naturally. To some radicals, women's working in factories was unnatural; the Co-operative Commonwealth would return them to their natural sphere, the home. To others, women's confinement to that sphere was unnatural and unjust; the revolution would abolish sex-defined spheres.

The woman question, as another of the nondefining issues, gave rise to a variety of incompatible theories but never disrupted any of the three organizations. On this question too, only the SP experienced controversies, for the IWW and SLP simply brushed it aside owing to their single-minded focus on class.

The Wobblies' western paper, the *Industrial Worker*, however, repeatedly played up one theme—not the subject of controversy—that throws light on its writers' attitudes toward women, the home, and the family. That theme was the "blanket stiff's" lack of a family and his consequent patronage of prostitutes in the towns of the far West.[57] Early in its publishing life, the *Industrial Worker*, written mainly for workers in the Northwest, defended the lumberjack and transient worker, who were often accused of being immoral for consorting with prostitutes. They were, the editorialist explained, deprived of a normal social life.

Marriage and a family life is the natural state of man. The South Sea Islander leads a fuller and more natural life than the men who work in the pens of the railroad contractors and logging companies. . . . The negro slaves on the average plantation had their cabins and their homes, such as they were, and they changed wives no oftener than the modern divorce maniacs. On the whole the negro slave had the best of it. Then, too, we are advised to marry and settle down. This is a joke. Perhaps the laborer, who has difficulty making a living for himself, has too much manhood to be willing to half starve a wife and children. . . . The "social evil" is caused by the luxury of the rich and the poverty of the poor. Settle the bread-and-butter question and men will live like men. Why not? The only thing then, worth living for, is to fight the employing class and improve our condition materially; the rest will settle itself.[58]

This editorial contains all the themes that were to be repeated over and over in subsequent issues of the paper—the contempt for the docile family man in contrast to the single man who was willing to fight; the ambivalence about family life, wished for yet considered a drug that dulled the radical consciousness; the defiance of genteel society's values; the justification of prostitution; the belief that the potentially most radical workers were those who had nothing to lose; and, one might add, the ingrained conventionality revealed in the phrase "divorce maniacs."

Two of these themes were spelled out a year later, by a weekly contributor who explained that in a strike in the East, the family man was tied down, but

the more rebellious of the unmarried men go west. . . . These young and unmarried men have within them the spirit of unionism. . . . These are the real proletarians. Of them it can truly be said, "you have nothing to lose but your chains." . . . They are irreligious. . . . The one, last tie that binds other workers to society is lacking; there are no family ties. . . . This is the class that the masters fear. . . . A yawning gulf separates them from the slum proletariat of the great cities. . . . It is to this class . . . that the I.W.W. must turn for material to organize. . . . It expresses the idea which they have long felt and it gives new life to the hope nursed within their breasts.[59]

Shortly before, however, the *Industrial Worker* had argued that each point won by the worker against the boss prepared him to fight to win the next, that "the man who is absolutely 'on the bum,'down and out completely for the time being, with no clothes, no money, not even a clean skin," was the slowest to try to rise, whereas the man with something to lose rebelled "at the idea of allowing it to slip away from us from the lack of a little effort."[60] That both attitudes found expression so often in the pages of the *Industrial Worker* shows a real ambivalence, and one of its most frequent foci was the relation of the "floaters" to prostitutes.

The singleness that sometimes was credited for the transient worker's militancy was just as often included among the grievances against capitalism. An editorial addressed to "you workin' plugs" asked, "Do you LIKE to be crummy and filthy and hungry and cold and hot and miserable and down-and-out and weary from overwork and starving. . . . and homeless and wifeless and childless and brutalized from living like a beast of burden?" But another editorial in the very next column praised the hobo and the prostitute as defiers of conventional morality in contrast to "the CONTENTED wage slave."[61] That praise of the prostitute was no unique departure from custom; for example, a few months later the paper's first page had a cartoon showing a blanket-stiff with his bedroll on his back, walking by an open window and saying, "Gee, my feet are sore!" In the window is a young woman with almost bare breasts; she says, "Come inside, kid!" The caption reads, "He can't afford to have a home. She never had a chance. That's why they are both selling themselves to the highest bidder."[62] It should come as no surprise, then, that the *Industrial Worker* had nothing but scorn for the then-current propaganda in favor of large families to counter the threat of "race suicide," that it favored legal dissemination of birth-control information,[63] and that it thought the anti-white-slavery crusaders were misguided. "Modern industrial conditions," it explained, require many migratory workers in the farming, railroad, lumber, fishery, maritime, and other industries. They have the same sexual desires as do workers with homes and families. If those needs are not met, "degeneracy, disease and insanity" result. "The prostitute is a physical necessity to the 'blanket stiff' and the 'blanket stiff' a financial necessity to a large portion of the prostitutes." After all, working women also have natural desires, among which is the desire to eat, wear clothing, and have shelter, but many are paid too little to afford these. "Therefore there is a beaten path from the low wage establishment to the brothel." Whereas the migratory worker cannot marry, more and more city workers are refusing to, and low wages are causing increasing numbers of wife-desertions. "The desire for a good time is born of the monotony of the daily toil and is the same source from which flows the greater part of drunkenness. There is not a case of prostitution on record that cannot be traced directly or indirectly to economic conditions."[64]

This editorial touches on another theme that must be kept in mind if we are to understand why this problem was so important to the *Industrial Worker*. It is the assumption, to be discussed in Chapter VII, that the conditions in the far West at that time were intrinsic products of the capitalist system and destined to spread eastward. The footloose young man with nothing to lose but his independent spirit, yet yearning for permanent and lawful family ties, was thus not necessarily in contradiction to the settled husband and father who was scorned and envied at the same time. The revolution would abolish the contradiction by enabling all men to settle down, in a society in which families to support would not pose a danger to their self-respect.

Such articles, of which there were many in the *Industrial Worker*, evoked no protests from a readership that on other matters proved quite contentious. If *Solidarity*, the IWW's eastern weekly, had published them, protests would probably have poured in. It cannot be accidental that the sort of articles that seem to have been acceptable to the westerners who read the *Industrial Worker* appeared very rarely in *Solidarity*, whose readers, actual and hoped-for, were generally family men with more or less permanent homes.[65]

Perhaps that is why it was a reader of *Solidarity* who protested against a theme that appeared occasionally in the *Industrial Worker*— that the revolution would return women to the home where they belonged (some articles even called upon male workers to refuse to work with women, because they deprived men of their jobs). "Woman Toiler" addressed her article to her male fellow workers: "You say you want us girls to keep out of the factory and mill so you can get more pay, then you can marry some of us and give us a decent home. Now, that is just what we are trying to escape; being obliged to marry you for a home. And aren't you a little inconsistent? You tell us to get into the I.W.W. If we got out of the shop, the mill and the factory how are we to get into the I.W.W.? an organization for wage workers only." To go back to the home, she added, would be to exchange one form of servitude for another, whereas the best thing that had ever happened to women was the need to leave the narrow confines of the home and enter industrial life.[66] "Woman Toiler" spoke to the winds, for within two years a front-page call to "Arise, Textile Workers!" to defeat the frame-up of the leaders of the Lawrence strike, declared that "the workers will never be satisfied until all the wrongs they suffered under are righted, until the mother returns from factory life to a home restored for her and the children."[67] Both papers agreed, however, that there was no "woman question" any more than there was a Negro or Asian-immigration question; there was only the class question.[68]

On this principle the SLP agreed. De Leon put it this way: "There is no woman question, neither man question; there is no race question, nor color question, nor religious question. What there is is the Humanity Question,—the SOCIAL QUESTION. To take up sex, color, creed or race is to fritter away energy at the twigs of the tree whose trunk should be attended to. All these so-called 'questions' are but the fruit or flower that betray with their poison-taste or smell the nature of the poison-tree from which they spring. That tree is Capitalism, the poisoner of the human race."[69]

Yet if there was no woman question, for De Leon and his fellow members of the SLP, there was an image of woman. One way of reconstructing it is to note the change that came over the *People* from 1890 on. At first the paper was conventional, full of nonpolitical and nonradical human-interest features. For instance, issues in the spring of 1891 revealed "Secrets of Voudoo," described April Fool's pranks of past years, and showed how to make a laryngoscope out of a candle and a tablespoon—and contained a regular woman's page.[70] In the April 5, 1891, issue a woman's-page column provided helpful hints on "How to Make Some Pretty Things for the House." Another, "On Wife and Mother Rests Man's Respect for Women," reported a clergyman's lecture, without comment from the editor. The regular "Etiquette" column, in the issue of May 10, gave instructions on addressing unmarried women, and they show an acceptance of social ranks. Each issue in that period ran articles of this sort, while the labor pages published articles on working women and their oppression and struggles. Evidently it was middle-class women who came to mind naturally when the editor and staff thought of Woman, whereas they thought of working-class women when thinking consciously in terms of party theory.

In time the *People* became more austere. De Leon's wit was restricted to political articles, the jokes used as space-fillers disappeared, and so did the woman's page, the science page, and human-interest material in general. The inadvertent revelations of deep-seated conventionality no longer appeared, and references to women from the middle 1890s on must be considered conscious expressions of beliefs that the writers deduced from the party's basic theory. Since according to the theory there was no woman question, articles on women and the family were published very seldom thereafter. One of these reminded the opponents of woman suffrage of their own argument that suffrage would cause women to leave their natural sphere; this, the article stated, "is a valid argument against that very capitalism which they love. If the weaning of women away from their sphere is bad, as it surely is, these anti-suffragists should exert themselves against capitalism. . . . It is only under capitalism that the mother has to yield to the female wage slave, by abandoning her family to look for starvation wages. It is only under capitalism that woman is forced to leave her home for the factory. It is only under capitalism that she-towns and he-towns spring up, blasting woman's sphere." [71]

The New York *Call*, which started publication on May 30, 1908, also had a "Woman's Department." In the issue of August 27, 1908, that title was accompanied by a drawing of a matronly woman with muscular arms and with hair gathered up functionally; she was wearing an apron, sitting with a bowl in her lap, and peeling a potato. (Three weeks earlier the paper had announced the formation of the Socialist Women's Society of the State of New York to educate women in socialist principles and prepare them to join the SP.[72]) The same sort of human-interest material that the *People* published in the early 1890s was in the *Call* as well, much of it remaining in later years. For example, the first issue had apolitical columns devoted to "Our Boys and Girls" and "Hints for Health." Two days later the sports column appeared; it became a permanent feature of the paper. The next issue pictured fashions in hats and a pattern for a little girl's frock. We also find advice to the lovelorn by Betty Beeswax, a column on babies, instructions on "Home Care of the Piano," and so on. The *Call* (like the *Social Democratic Herald* in Milwaukee) obviously wanted to fill the need for a general newspaper as well as for a party paper and propaganda organ. It featured general news articles and departments indistinguishable from those in nonradical papers. The sort of material just mentioned may thus suggest what the staff believed would attract the readership it wanted.

It would not, however, be correct to say that the image of the matronly housewife was the *party*'s image of woman, for the SP was as divided on the woman question as on the other nondefining issues. It could not dispose of it by mere diktat, as the SLP did, for, lacking a leader of De Leon's authority, it permitted the free expression of widely differing opinions throughout the period covered here.[73] But wholehearted feminists were not likely to devote their main energies to the party even if they believed that only socialism would eliminate the woman question. The bohemian comrades too remained peripheral to the party's life as it remained peripheral to theirs. The spectrum of beliefs most frequently expressed on the issue was thus somewhat narrower—the "left" and extreme "right" ends were missing—than in the environing society. SP feminists used most of the same arguments used by nonradical moderate feminists and especially suffragists.[74] The main one was that women had never been given the chance to develop their intellectual faculties, but that recent achievements in the professions proved their innate equality with men. On the question of innate emotional and temperamental differences between the sexes, however, both sides accepted and rejected innatism as the need of the occasion dictated.

Despite the passage, at the 1912 convention, of a resolution committing the party to woman suffrage, no one (so far as is known) was ever expelled for violating it. Hence it should be regarded as a nondefining issue throughout this period. Crushing indifference remained, and so did occasional expressions of what is now called sexism.

A survey of these persisting attitudes could start early in the party's life, with a speech delivered in 1904 by the prominent Milwaukee socialist Franklin Wentworth:

> As we regard the ready sympathy of woman; as we read countless tales of self-denial and sacrifice of mother love; as we detect in the rare gift of intuition with which she is so generously endowed, a wondrous spiritual faculty whose possibilities are beyond our ken, we are lost in wonder that they have not long since changed the brutal aspect of the world and ushered in a reign of peace and love. . . . It is because around every woman's life there has been raised an invisible wall of mental tyranny, that has turned her noblest attributes to selfish ends; and obscured our vision. Behind this barrier woman has been locked in what is called her "sphere"—a region vast in pettiness and futility, until the slow mental grinding of the centuries has dwarfed her, enfeebled her body and shrouded her soul in webs of superstition.

Her dependence, he went on, induces her to adopt her husband's opinions of women, and she transmits them to her sons. Woman is innately the intellectual equal of man, yet modern woman does not want the vote; she just wants to be kept by a man. Economic necessity, however, is making her independent, and this in time will make her intellectually independent.[75] The first sentence quoted above can be found almost word for word in countless speeches and articles by both feminists and antifeminists, suffragists and antisuffragists, in the same period. The intuitive, self-sacrificing image could justify exclusion of women from public affairs as well as a demand for their enfranchisement. Nothing in Wentworth's speech could identify him as a socialist.

The same is true of the eighth installment of Joseph E. Cohen's series "Socialism for Students," in the *International Socialist Review*. Cohen explained, "The impulse below intellect is intuition, which is developed further in many animals than in man. . . . And because woman is nearer to the lower forms than man, intuition is more deeply seated in the female of the race, enabling her to peremptorily pass judgments that the male arrives at only after laborious thought. Intuition is often spoken of as a feminine attribute." Comrade Lida Parce retorted, two issues later, that Cohen's views were not part of the socialist philosophy. Her analysis of the nature of intuition and its relation to intellect was, however, identical to that in scores of nonsocialist propaganda tracts, and the entire controversy was identical to scores of others in nonsocialist publications.[76]

Before the woman suffrage movement began to make headlines and force political commentators of all hues to take a stand on it, both men and women leaders in the SP expressed views typified in an editorial by Victor Berger in his *Social Democratic Herald*. He predicted that socialism would take women out of the factories and stores and return them to the home. Earlier socialists had prophesied that every adult would do an equal share of work in the public service, including manual labor. They were "ignoring the idea of *'function,'* the idea that everybody is to do the particular work for which he or she is best adapted by nature, sex, and training." But, he added, "Modern Socialists have never claimed that *all* women will be in the service of the collectivity. In fact I do not believe that the majority of them ever will be, except in the sense then that they will be mothers and wives." They will have the same opportunities as men; yet most women will want to marry, and, "I suppose, that as now so then the married woman, daughter and mother will want to be supported by husband, father and son." Kitchen drudgery will go, for each block will have a public kitchen where varied foods will be prepared and sent to individual homes, "if so desired." Some women will serve the Commonwealth part-time as doctors or teachers or in other ways. Exceptional women then as now will choose to remain single and will find suitable work. "And furthermore, whenever a married woman, or daughter[,] will get tired of her dependence, all she will have to do is ask to become a public functionary." Socialism will also enable couples to marry young; this will encourage chastity and abolish prostitution and "commercial marriages."[77] Berger's essay shows how the woman question would appear to a thoughtful socialist who did not deliberately think through the woman question per se but merely made the requisite deductions from general socialist ideology. Socialists favored technological progress and expected it to continue; therefore manual tasks such as housekeeping would be mechanized. Socialism would inaugurate equality of opportunity for all; hence individuals of all races and both sexes, with special talents frustrated by capitalism, would develop them. Socialists blamed prostitution and "commercial marriages" on capitalism;[78] socialism would free women from that sort of oppression.

This was the ideological atmosphere when the party's 1908 convention appointed a committee to look into the relation of women to the socialist movement. Mila Tupper Maynard's report in behalf of the committee shows that its appointment was as reactive as were the party's actions concerning the race question. The party, she said, must announce a position on suffrage because of the many requests for an official statement, as well as because it had to have a policy on propaganda among women within the party. The majority report recommended the appointment of a well-funded special committee to oversee organizational work among women, a paid woman organizer, and other such administrative provisions. Laura B. Payne of Texas submitted a minority report opposed to the party's devoting time and money to women. The development of capitalism, she said, was having the same effect on women as on men; disfranchisement did not put women in a different relation to the socialist movement, since in some states many men were virtually disfranchised by property and residence requirements; and the only cure was socialism and the only issue the class struggle. The ensuing debate dealt more with tactical issues than with theory,[79] as did the longer debate at the 1910 convention. The principal issue at both meetings was whether the party should work with the nonsocialist suffragists for suffrage. But underlying the tactical problem were attitudes that found expression from time to time in sneers, jokes, and laughs at women's expense, to the point where Algie M. Simons asked his comrades to be serious. Their attitude, he protested, was precisely what was at the root of women's position. Among the male delegates, Simons was clearly in the minority in considering the woman question a serious issue worthy of grown men's attention.[80]

"Hebe," a frequent contributor to the *Call*, admitted that

if the test time came to cast a vote at the polls for woman's suffrage many Socialist men would vote against the measure. We Socialist women have experienced time and again at meetings and discussions that one or several Socialists will take the floor to argue against the political emancipation of women. Some try to check our ardor by the rather antiquated and unsatisfactory assurance that woman's suffrage will come without any effort on our part after we have Socialism, and others base their a[d]verse criticism upon the assumption that woman's enfranchisement would only tend to strengthen the political power of the ruling class. The fact is that many who are Socialists in name still grope in darkness as to the true spirit of Socialism.[81]

But the true spirit was what was at issue, since many comrades defined it differently from the way "Hebe" did. (See Supplement).

In view of these attitudes, Hillquit's claim that the SP's exertions in behalf of the woman suffrage amendment in the New York State constitution were decisive in its passing in 1917 should be interpreted with great care.[82] If the party did make the difference its effort was probably due to tactical considerations, for it is unlikely that attitudes had changed much since 1912, when a socialist member of the state Assembly wrote, "Equal suffrage advocates of middle class or plutocratic affiliation do not fail to accuse Socialists of apathy and indifference to their cause. They do not appreciate that economic justice is infinitely more important than the mere political enfranchisement of their sex."[83] The editor of the *Call* agreed with those critics:

Academically we Socialists have accepted the idea that the just or equal franchise was the right thing. Placidly, fatuously we have gone ahead and done practically nothing to make it an actuality. Our women were permitted to work as collectors of funds. . . . At the same time we have remained so marble-browedly—the old classic term for bone-headedly—supine that we do not realize what is actually happening in the world about us. Woman suffrage is a menace. Not to the capitalists, for they are going to use it if they can. It is so to us. For we who have so long pretended that we stood for it have done nothing to advance it, and all the magnificent opportunities that a fight for it might have given us have been up to the present passed by. Our own working women who favor the suffrage and who should through their fight for the suffrage form a splendid addition to our ranks, are being led elsewhere because we have been doing nothing—well, except "thinking, thinking, talking, talking—and forgetting what we thought we thought."

It is time, he concluded, that the party work for "what is actually one of its basic ideas."[84] Perhaps this reiteration (or should it be called this "protesting too much"?), by those who believed it was one of the party's basic ideas, made it so in after years.[85] That eventuality was probably due more to the rising tide of independent feminism, to everyone's realization that equal suffrage was the wave of the future (of which socialists considered themselves the proper custodians),[86] and, in part, to some conservatives' habit of discrediting feminism by equating it with socialism and discrediting socialism by equating it with feminism. They did so not because there was a natural affinity between the two causes but because both were, at that time, outside the boundary of acceptable doctrine—although feminism was closer to the boundary and soon crossed it.

The pro- and antifeminist division, like those on the Negro and Asian-immigration questions, did not correspond to the right-left division on basic issues such as trade-union policy and violence. For example, when the 1912 convention officially declared that advocates of sabotage could not belong to the party, William E. Rodriguez of Illinois and Anna Maley of Washington both voted yes. Only a short time before, the two had clashed over whether the party should commit itself to woman suffrage. Rodriguez said he favored woman suffrage but thought it should not be a condition for membership because it was not a fundamental question. "There are," he said, "men in the Socialist Party that I know who do not favor woman suffrage, and I honestly believe they are good Socialists." Comrades have the right to disagree on other issues, he added; why not on this one?[87] He was, in short, arguing that the woman question was not a defining issue for the SP.

The reason many feminists in the party resorted to most of the same arguments as nonsocialist feminists used is that they were responding to socialist antifeminists' thinking that was identical to nonsocialist antifeminists' thinking. Here as on other issues it was the enemy's categories that determined the rebel's. But one essayist, Theresa Malkiel, added something new: men must be taught to see that they have the duty to fight for workingwomen's political freedom as much as workingwomen should be taught to make common cause with men of their class. On this point Malkiel approached the theory on which many of her comrades based their argument that there was no woman question at all, but only the class question. She did not draw that inference, for evidently her own feelings impelled her to insist on the importance of the woman question. "Even the most progressive of our men," she complained bitterly, "are still considering woman as the being who, chained by a thousand fetters of dependency to man-made conditions, broken in spirit and in health by her long degradation and continual maternity, became a weak, thoughtless being that was neither man nor beast. They do not take into consideration that the woman of today has marched forward on the road of evolution." There were fifty thousand dues-paying members of the party, she added, and only two thousand of them were women. Only about one of every thirty men in the party brought in a female member of his family or of a friend's family. The other twenty-nine were not socialists at home. Surprisingly, however, she ended with the remark, "I know my sex and will admit freely that woman still looks to man as the guiding spirit of her life path and it is therefore for him to direct her steps into the party membership where she belongs—side by side with him." [88] Perhaps this was merely her clever way of placing the responsibility wholly on the men.

If twenty-nine of every thirty socialist men were not socialists at home it was probably because they did not consider socialism relevant to what went on in the home, as Malkiel did; that is, they believed they *were* socialists at home because to be socialists did not entail recruiting their wives or changing their attitudes toward women and the family. In other words, Malkiel was including the private sphere within the boundary of socialist concerns, whereas most of her comrades believed socialism had to do only with the public sphere.

It is here that the woman question can be seen to differ profoundly from the Negro and Asian-immigration questions, although on the level of theory all three centered around the issues of innatism versus environmental determinism, the vision of the postrevolutionary society, and the relation of the public to the private sphere, especially the family. With respect to the race questions, both innatists and some environmental determinists foresaw a segregated Co-operative Commonwealth. Even the most egalitarian rarely proposed "social equality" for the races, usually arguing merely that political and economic equality would not deprive anyone of the right to choose his friends and houseguests. In arguing thus, however, they were digging a chasm between the race and woman questions, for the family and woman were the core of the private sphere and hence constituted the core of the issue of social equality. It was the home and woman that were to be protected from invasion—protected either by a segregated social structure or by each family's autonomy. [89]

That consistent socialists could be antifeminists becomes more understandable when we note certain underlying themes in the ideology of the antisuffragist movement during the decade or so before World War I.[90] One theme was hinted at earlier: the bohemians with their flouting of sexual convention could never have found a secure home in the SP or SLP. The reason—aside from tactical disadvantages—is implied by the importance that many socialists placed on social control and predictability (to be discussed in Chapter VII); the use of *anarchist* as an epithet hurled at big capitalists (discussed in Chapter IV); and the need, felt by many of them, to comprehend (in both senses of the word) all the world in a single, systematic theory, which is to say, to be in intellectual control. As some scholars have observed, this characteristic accounts better for the chronic tensions between radical parties and their creative artists than does any fear the former may have that the latter will promulgate false theories. It also helps account for the chronic suspicion that radical doctrinaires often have of psychology, of a belief in a private, elusive basis for behavior, not externally controllable. The intuition and spiritual faculty that Wentworth found so wondrous were also inexplicable and unpredictable, and, as Cohen made clear, "below" intellect, placing woman closer to the animals than man was. This does not mean that socialist writers of Wentworth and Cohen's generation exalted nature over technological society. Nature was the abode of the savage,[91] of forces as yet uncontrolled; and the envisioned future had drained the wetlands, irrigated the deserts, and tamed all nature in obedience to the planning intellect.

When some socialists took it for granted, because they could not even conceive of the alternative, that in that future the private sphere would remain sharply demarcated from the public sphere, they were showing themselves to have more in common with the antisuffragists than either group could have imagined. To both, the prospect of women's entering the public sphere threatened not only to allow the public sphere to enter the private sphere, but also to make it even harder to control. Thus, in addition to the first theme—that of control—the antisuffragist movement shared with some socialists the concern to prevent the blurring of the distinction between the home and the world outside.

They shared still a third concern—skepticism about the ability of enfranchised women to reform society. As has recently been pointed out, when suffragists asserted that voting women would improve the tone of politics and help enact reforms, antisuffragists countered by pointing to conditions in the equal-suffrage states; "figures on divorce and prostitution proved that California and Nevada had become less moral after giving women the vote." [92] Others challenged the suffragist contention that voting women could help enact labor-protective laws, by asking why workingmen had not been able to use their votes in that way. [93] Socialists who elsewhere maintained that only limited improvements could be gained by workers' votes so long as the capitalist System lasted could not consistently advocate woman suffrage on the basis of any sweeping changes it might effect. In fact, they rarely used that argument, and when they did it was without much conviction. They thereby permitted their nonfeminist comrades to rely on the unprovable and undisprovable doctrine of innatism. But generally, they did not bother to argue at all. [94]

V

When conservative Mrs. Leland Stanford opposed Progressive Edward A. Ross's anti-Japanese racism; when right-wing socialist John Spargo championed women's equality against some of his left-wing comrades; when "bourgeois" feminists' views in the turn-of-the-century generation resembled those of the present day more than some socialists' of their own day; when the controversies over the Negro question found socialists sorting themselves out into categories different from those that defined the right and left wings of their party—they were repeating a phenomenon as old as the Republic. Again and again conservatives on economic-class questions had manifested egalitarian attitudes on racial and sometimes sexual questions, and economic-class radicals and reformers had manifested inegalitarian attitudes on racial and sexual questions. [95] This pattern does not require us to reverse the currently fashionable identification of economic with racial and sexual egalitarianism and of economic with racial and sexual inegalitarianism, for the historic pattern would not support the opposite generalization either. It may not be coincidental, however, that the one radical organization that has had the closest ties to the organized labor movement and, in some localities, to John Q. Worker in general—the SP in the shake-up period—manifested the greatest inegalitarianism on those issues.

A modern radical reading the sources sampled in this chapter is likely to exclaim, "See how contradictory those people were! They organized to fight the injustices caused by capitalism but failed to engage in special struggles against two of the greatest of them!" This contradiction would exist in that radical's own activity if he omitted sexism and racism from the issues he tackled, for he perceives them as injustices and caused by capitalism. But if a past radical did not perceive what is now called sexism or racism as an injustice, or did not attribute the treatment of women or nonwhites to capitalism, he did not contradict his radical ideals by not approaching the question in the same way as the modern radical does. This is why it is so important to discover the past people's perceptions and values if we are to avoid the natural inclination to impute what would be a contradiction in current radicals' thinking to people for whom it may not have been that at all.

If, as one historian contends, the fact that a thought was in one person's mind means that "its time had come,"[96] then in the shake-up period the time had come for many thoughts we now reject. The inarticulate John Q. Worker held many beliefs that few accept today, as did radicals, reformers, and others. We may best understand the continuing selection process if we attend to all the menu items available in the shake-up period, not just to those that happened to get accepted and become generally approved in our own day. A comprehensive analysis of the process of choice in that period, for instance, would have to include the liquor question, which as Norman H. Clark has shown, was involved in all the great domestic issues of the day and was supremely significant in the evolution of present-day values and beliefs.[97] Its "time" had definitely come—and then it passed. But neither with respect to prohibition nor with respect to beliefs in higher esteem today could contemporaries be expected to predict the future, and even if they could, future acceptability and goodness are not synonymous.

If we discard the method of seeing history in terms of the evolution of values and beliefs most approved of today and stop seeing radical movements as their avatars becoming more and more consistent as time goes on, the nondefining issues take on great importance. On the issue of race equality, the NAACP was by present-day criteria more "advanced" than the SP, SLP, even IWW; on the issue of sex equality the

National American Woman Suffrage Association and other suffragist and feminist organizations were by present-day criteria more "advanced" than the SP, SLP, or IWW. On other nondefining issues such as the shorter workday, the abolition of child labor, workmen's compensation, and mine- and factory-inspection, reform organizations and individual reformers were not more "advanced," but they were more energetic in working for change. To one of the greatest reforms of the time, prohibition, the radical movements were indifferent. In sum, if we discard the equation of radical movements with opposition to social injustice in general, we are free to see those movements as a few among many, which differed somewhat in how they defined injustice, what they attributed it to, and what injustices they chose to fight.

Another form of historical teleology that the nondefining issues can help elucidate is the "false consciousness" thesis. Some radical historians hold that racism among white workers manifested capitalist ideology, the purpose of which was to divide the working class. They link the workers' receptivity to the racial myths to their ideological "backwardness" in general. The assumption implicit in the term "backwardness" is that they would eventually see through those myths, with the help of the radicals whose anticapitalist ideology enables them to unmask all the means by which the ruling class exercises its ideological hegemony. The trouble with this theory is that it cannot explain some radicals' "racism" and "sexism," not to mention their basing them on their own socialist or syndicalist ideals and theories.

Jack London, for example, has always been a problem to modern radicals, for he was both an extreme racist and a left-wing socialist. A classic expression of the fallacies discussed above is an article by Art Shields in *Political Affairs*, the Communist Party's theoretical magazine, in 1976. After lauding London's deep understanding of the class struggle, deeper than that of most socialist leaders of his time, and his ability to see through the disguises of power, Shields says, "Unfortunately this bold people's artist did not escape some negative influences from his environment, which gravely marred his work at times." Shields blames the virus of racism prevalent in London's childhood. "In Jack's case the disease was often suppressed by a powerful antidote—the revolutionary movement. White supremacy didn't enter his socialist writings and speeches. He spoke of the brotherhood of workers of all races instead. But the virus would break out again, and this involved him in acute contradictions."[98]

Three comments will suffice, although many more could be made. First, to Shields "the movement" is different from its members. No one has ever surveyed the whole SP in London's day to find out if the majority opposed racism as currently defined; such a finding would be the only warrant for counterposing "the movement" to any individual member's racism. So far as the articulate members are concerned, most fall far short of the standards that Shields would apply. Hence "the movement" to him is a Platonic Form; its representation in the real world is irrelevant. Second, the virus and disease metaphors show that, to Shields, London's racism was a foreign body. Whereas London is portrayed as a passive victim with respect to beliefs Shields disapproves of, he is portrayed as active and in control with respect to those Shields approves of. Bad things are due to the environment and not intrinsic parts of London's belief-system; good things represent transcendence of the environment and are intrinsic parts of London's belief-system. (It would be as logical to postulate the reverse—that the socialism was the "exception" or "defect" to be explained; as is well known, London himself said, "I am first of all a white man and only then a socialist.") This is a constant among American radical writers, and it would be interesting to see an investigation of how it relates to another constant—their strong environmental-determinist bias when they argue for the malleability of human nature. Third, if an economic reactionary had written London's racist statements, Shields would link them with his reactionary ideology; this shows that for Shields, race is not a defining issue any more than it was for the old SP, unless he is merely making an exception for London.

To return to the pre–World War I radicals: they were psychologically and ideologically predisposed to challenge anything that the capitalists approved of or that enhanced the latter's power. They assiduously exposed all the "capitalist myths," yet were themselves susceptible to what latter-day radicals regard as some of them. The theory offered nowadays argues that everyone in American society is influenced by the racially poisoned atmosphere, including radicals. But since they seemed to be immune to other ideological poisons, it does not explain why some are harder to resist than others. This is a most curious omission, in view of the supposed integration of all important features of the society into the System and the correspondingly comprehensive and all-inclusive nature of the radical theory. In particular, it does not explain why the myths that are hardest of all to resist have to do with the private sphere, "social equality," sex.

Notice an interesting fact: the racists in the SP, like racists outside it who also favored economic and political equality, strenuously denied that it entailed social mingling. Some nonracists in the party, for prudential reasons or out of conviction, argued similarly. Yet no one, inside or outside the SP, ever reversed those positions and favored social mingling but opposed economic and political equality. In fact it is hard to conceive of such a combination of beliefs. The reader is invited to imagine it; he will, I think, discover that social mingling automatically entails all forms of equality except for disqualification based on immaturity or mental defect. That is, it is the last form of equality a person will accept.

For most people a century ago, there was another exception. Women were the one category of persons whom men could conceive of as friends and relatives without automatically accepting them as political and economic equals. The reasons are complex[99] and need not be explored here, but this asymmetry between racial and sexual inegalitarianism demonstrates three crucial facts. First, there is no such thing as egalitarianism per se, encompassing all humanity, such that a person who favors it for one group is inconsistent if he does not favor it for another—except in highly abstract theorizing that has no apparent contact with the real world. The claims to equality of racial groups and of women had different bases, just as arguments for their inequality did. Second, that asymmetry makes understandable some past radicals' egalitarianism on one but not the other issue. Third, it shows how the claim to equality for one of those categories could, with ideological consistency, be based on the inequality of the other. Either way—that is, whichever of the two categories was assigned a separate sphere—the perceived danger, in the eyes of many people, of invasion of the family and corruption of its racial purity would be prevented.[100] This concern, even in the recent past, went far deeper than opposition to economic or political inequality. In this respect most radicals in the shake-up period resembled most of their contemporaries, and this is why the race and woman questions were nondefining issues to the radical movements of that day.

It is also why SP members rarely urged their comrades to struggle against their own reluctance to accept blacks or women as equals, but generally argued that the party's task was to convince blacks and women that it was in their interest to join the party. The former notion posed the aforementioned threat; the latter did not. Anyone who accepted the defining tenets—the attribution to the capitalist System of everything defined as an injustice and the need to inaugurate a radically new social order—was a bona fide socialist, whatever else he might believe or do. By the same logic, party members could not agree with the judgment of blacks or women who refused to join on account of the party's stand or lack of a stand on the race or woman question. First, people who refused for those reasons to join would be making an independent and substantive issue of what the party considered secondary, and second, they were ignoring the only criteria of bona fide socialist commitment and thus showing that they did not understand the true theory. As Debs said, any worker who understood socialism would be a socialist and join the party. The assumptions underlying this conviction, which all other radicals shared—Wobblies and SLP members merely substituting their own terminology—will be explored in the next chapter.

VII   The Radicals' Perceptions of Themselves

Despite their disagreements, all three radical organizations were sure their predictions were grounded in a science of society and history that assigned them the role of leading the working class into the future. These three themes—prophecy, scientism, and vanguardism—comprise the key ingredients of the self-image of the radicals in the shake-up period.

I

Although most Americans at that time did not suffer from "future shock," enough articulate people did to produce a large corpus of documents showing that the need to dispel disorientation by predicting the future was not confined to the Left.[1] American society's relative fluidity and lack of overall structure made some see it as especially vulnerable to disintegrating forces. The political system itself, in that situation, was perceived as a potential source of weakness, for it sanctioned activities that could ultimately destroy it. Not socialism but anarchy was, to some, the next step beyond republicanism (see Supplement), for they believed that the American political system permitted as much freedom as a society could tolerate without disintegrating and that its very reliance on the will of the people opened the door to disaster should the people be misled by radicals. Some conservatives predicted an enormous increase in the socialists' strength and warned that capitalism must reform itself if it was to retain the approval of the people; a few saw no hope and resigned themselves to the coming cataclysm.

It might be expected that the main difference between the nonradicals and the radicals was simply that the latter hoped for what the nonradicals feared. But a few socialist leaders were oppressed by cataclysmic visions too; they agreed with Marx and Engels, who in the *Communist Manifesto* had predicted that the class struggle would end "either in a revolutionary reconstitution of society at large, or in the common ruin of the contending classes."

This small minority of the socialist leaders can be represented here by Victor L. Berger and Ernest Untermann, of the SP's right and left wings respectively.[2] In Berger's view the socialists were racing against time. American society was fast splitting into two nations: "One nation will be very large in number, but semi-civilized, half-fed, half-educated and degenerated from overwork and misery; the other nation will be very small in number, but over-civilized, over-fed, over-cultured and degenerated from too much leisure and too much luxury." The outcome "will be a volcanic eruption. The hungry millions will turn against the over-fed few. A fearful retribution will be enacted on the capitalist class as a class—and the innocent will suffer with the guilty." Socialists should not look forward to this cataclysm: "WE SHOULD NOT GET A BETTER SYSTEM, FOR THE DEGENERATE BARBARIAN WOULD NOT BE ABLE TO GIVE IT TO US." If socialism comes, it will come by evolution, having been built brick by brick. To expect socialism within a few years would encourage actions that would more likely result in civil war or a man on horseback. "The people may have to have bloody skirmishes with plutocracy before Socialism is reached, but there is a deal of education necessary before they will be able to come out of such contests right side up. There is good reason for believing that a Social-Democrat will occupy the presidential chair in 1912, but that would not mean Socialism. It would only mean that the people were ready to use the government to hasten the advent of Socialism."[3]

But there was not much time. Never before, he wrote in 1902, had rulers and ruled had equal political rights; how long would the American capitalists allow the workers to keep the suffrage? In some states they were beginning to take it away.[4] And a year later, Berger advised the workers to use the ballot in their own behalf while they still had it, for the time might not be far off when the capitalist class would take it from them. And then they might be forced "to fight with dynamite, dagger and rifle," for their political rights as well as industrial rights.[5] The workers should arm themselves, he stated, for as their standard of living fell they would be forced to resort more and more to their only weapon, the strike; but the growing, permanent reserve army of the unemployed would doom most strikes even during prosperous times. If every citizen were armed, the capitalists and their government would not dare to provoke their wrath. History shows, he said, that an armed people is a free people.[6]

Throughout Berger's writings on these themes runs an apprehension that history was closing in on the American working class. He repeatedly painted pictures of workingmen driven to unprecedented depths of misery and vagabondage, their wives and daughters forced into prostitution, while their oppressors reveled in gluttonous degeneracy. Yet he was also a leading spokesman for step-by-step socialism, insisting that a few benefits such as an old-age pension and the eight-hour day could be secured before the revolution,[7] and that "in the world's history there are no sudden leaps."[8] His admonitions to his comrades to educate the people imply an extended time perspective. How long that perspective was, however, can be inferred from his statement in 1905 that "of course, we do not expect the millen[n]ium in three years or even in seven years."[9]

Untermann too felt history closing in. "How," he asked in 1904, "will the development of society proceed within the next decade? Will the Socialists have time to penetrate with the light of reason into every nook and corner of capitalist society? Or will history rush down upon us with unforeseen events which will bury the flower of the revolutionary proletariat in an avalanche of blood, before we are fairly prepared to meet the storm?" Even if the SP won control of several states and then the presidency, the capitalists would still control the army and most of the states and would be better prepared than the socialists for the ensuing civil war. Every socialist group should therefore arm itself and learn to shoot, for "if the Socialist majority is unarmed and badly organized, we shall see ourselves balked at the very threshold of victory."[10]

Daniel De Leon also thought the capitalists were plotting to disfranchise the workers. They had begun by pretending it was only the blacks whom they wanted to bar from the polls, but the southern constitutional conventions were merely the first step.[11] At the end of 1899 he announced that the capitalists were planning a coup d'état, because political democracy threatened their power. "There is to-day, in America, a race being run between the Socialist Labor Party and Capitalism: the former to seize the existing democratically organized public powers, the latter to overthrow them. Which will first reach the spot where the roads fork: the spot whence one road leads to the utilization of the present democratic forms for the enlargement of freedom by rearing the SOCIALIST REPUBLIC; the spot whence the other road leads towards the checking of freedom by rearing up MILITARISM?" Time will tell, but the chances are at best even that the revolution will be peaceful. The capitalists might fire the first shot. At this point De Leon resumes his usually optimistic tone, for he knows that his party will remain loyal to the true doctrine and will "drill our people for the possible emergence of EXTRA PARLIAMENTARY ACTION. . . . THERE SHALL BE NO COMMUNE DISASTER IN AMERICA. The day Capitalism shall sound the signal for civil war in America it will be promptly confronted with the solid ranks of the proletariat, moving as one body, held by the only bonds that can hold men together under such circumstances—a clean-cut purpose, born of clean-cut training." Two and a half years before he wrote this document he asserted that a correspondent's prediction that the masses would be forced to fight for collectivism or starve would be "substantially verified" before the end of the nineteenth century.[12]

Like Berger, De Leon accepted the theory of increasing impoverishment of the working class and believed that his party's progress would be gradual, "in the sense that it will capture successively offices now held by the capitalist class."[13] The difference between his confidence and Berger's forebodings may have been due to De Leon's fantastic overestimation of the strength of his party and the radicalization of the workers, which is understandable in view of the SLP's total isolation from the working class by this time, in contrast to the close relations between Berger's Social Democratic party and the Milwaukee labor movement.

This conjecture gets some support from a comparison between Berger's reaction to the 1905 Russian Revolution and that of Debs, who was almost as isolated from the American labor movement by that time as De Leon. Berger predicted the revolt would fail because the economic basis for socialism was lacking; all that the striking workers of St. Petersburg wanted was more bread, and their uprising had taken the Social Democrats by surprise. On the same page as Berger's article, Debs proclaimed, "The Russian Revolt No Surprise!" In the article under that headline he explained that the workers' conditions had been known for some time and that "the time may be near when the workers of all lands . . . will inaugurate a universal strike, at the ballot box as well as in the factory, mill and mine and not cease striking until the struggle is victorious and labor is free throughout the world." [14]

Perhaps the difference between De Leon's and Debs's thinking, on the one side, and Berger's and Untermann's, on the other, can be expressed as the difference between the conviction that the working class *was* becoming radical and the conviction that it *had better* become radical very soon. Both judgments were deductive. They were based on a theory that the capitalist System was collapsing, not on empirical observation, and it is this perception of capitalism that accounts for the extremely short range of the predictions found in the writings and speeches of all types of radical leaders.

Late in the period under study some of them lengthened that time span. In 1917, for example, Austin Lewis of the IWW foresaw better conditions for the workers after the war, owing to the cutoff of the capitalists' supply of cheap immigrant labor and to employers' discovery that long working hours impaired efficiency. [15] From 1912 on, Charles Kerr, publisher and editor of the *International Socialist Review*, conceded that many reforms that radicals had assumed would be impossible under capitalism could now be expected from the Democratic administration. Roscoe Fillmore, frequent writer in the *ISR*, in 1916 reflected upon the collapse of the Second International and concluded that "we don't know anything about the coming revolution," that the golden age of capitalism might even be in the future, and that the revolution could be a century or several centuries away. Mary E. Marcy, a leading socialist writer, admitted in 1915 that making the revolution would be harder than she and many others had thought. Others had begun warning against the revolution-around-the-corner style of thinking a few years earlier. [16]

But they were rejecting an integral part of their movements' thinking. Tommy Morgan, old Chicago socialist whose frequent autobiographical speeches at conventions made him the butt of ridicule, [17] delivered an impassioned warning against this attitude, which he mistakenly attributed only to young hotheads. At the SP's founding convention in 1901, he told his comrades:

I have heard the impatient prophecy that the revolution would come next year. . . . I was told that 27 years ago by men just as good as any that ever sat in a Socialist Convention. Their morality, their good sense and everything could not be questioned, but their desires outran their reason. Some of these men committed suicide. The editor of our Socialist paper committed suicide. John McAuliff, one of the best agitators we have had[,] blew his brains out. Leo Milebeck, one of our best representatives, cut his throat. William Kemke, our German agitator, took the morphine route; Hirth, a cigar maker and editor of the first Socialist paper we had, poisoned himself in Detroit. After those men had nominated candidates and cast their votes and the candidates were elected to the legislature or city council and their votes were counted out, they gave up the struggle in despair, and went into the physical force movement and went to making bombs. . . . Their eagerness, their enthusiasm carried them beyond the bounds of reason, and they shattered our Socialist movement into fragments.

It would be a long time, he maintained, before the socialist state would come.[18] Morris Hillquit warned his comrades too, but his concern was for the effect that false expectations would have on the nonradical workers. At the same convention he declared (erroneously) that socialists were the only people who suffered from the "delusion" that the United States was practically ripe for socialism. "If we ever attempt to go before the working class and promise them the co-operative commonwealth in two or four or five years, and if they wait six or ten years and see no chance of its realization, then we will be much worse off, for they will lose faith in your propaganda." Let us admit that we do not know whether our ultimate aim "will be reached today, tomorrow or in ten years or half a century—if you show them, in other words, that all we know is the general tendency and all we can do is to work along these lines and that all we can call upon them to do is to co-operate with us along those lines, then real progress is begun."[19]

If "half a century" seemed a long time to Hillquit, who was totally immune to mythic visions, the suicides that Morgan recalled become understandable, for there must have been many radicals who believed they were living in the midst of the revolution. Predictions of the imminent overthrow of capitalism are, in fact, among the most common themes in the radical literature of that period. Debs was forever dating the beginning of the end from some important event, such as the founding of the IWW in 1905, the election of Berger to Congress in 1910, or the Ludlow massacre of 1914.[20]

Although most such prophets based their predictions on the theory of increasing impoverishment (see Supplement), others based theirs on the expectation that increased affluence or the granting of some immediate demands would whet the workers' desire for the entire product of their labor (see Supplement). This is but one of many proofs that the conclusions preceded the evidence for them. Another is the reaction by radical periodicals to election results: a rise in the radical vote proved the irreversible radicalization of the working class, whereas a decrease was a temporary setback (see Supplement). Every event could be fitted into a theory that clearly was not based on empirical data but, rather, used them for illustration; the assurance that the revolution impended had other sources. Those sources doubtless varied from individual to individual, but a temperamentally cautious member of a radical organization must have been affected by the optimism of his co-workers, to the point where only an independent and strong-willed person could retain a long-range view.[21]

Documentary Excursus I

The following excerpts illustrate the faith in the imminence of the revolution. (In addition, see Supplement.)

1) Now that the capitalist system is so palpably breaking down, and in consequence the political parties breaking up, the disintegrating elements with vague reform ideas and radical bourgeois tendencies will head in increasing numbers toward the Socialist party, especially since the greatly enlarged vote of this year has been announced and the party is looming up as a possible dispenser of the spoils of office. (Eugene V. Debs, "Danger Ahead," *International Socialist Review*, XI [1911], 414.)

2) Capitalism is rushing blindly to its impending doom. . . . Poverty, high prices, unemployment, child slavery, widespread misery and haggard want in a land bursting with abundance; prostitution and insanity, suicide and crime, these in solemn numbers tell the tragic story of capitalism's saturnalia of blood and tears and shame as its end draws near. ("Debs' Speech of Acceptance," *International Socialist Review*, XIII [1912], 307.)

3) This [the 1900 election] will be one of the last convulsions of capitalism before the social revolution sweeps it out of existence. . . . The next four years will witness the development of socialism to continental power and proportions. (Eugene V. Debs, quoted in H. Wayne Morgan, *Eugene V. Debs: Socialist for President*

[Syracuse: Syracuse University Press, 1962], 56.)

4) The coming alignment [resulting from the 1904 election] will be between the Republican party representing the capitalistic interests, and the Social Democratic party representing the working classes. . . . From now on, every move on the political chess board, whether so designed or not, will be in the interest of Socialism, and promote the growth of the Socialist movement, and it is entirely possible that in four years more the Social-Democratic party may sweep the United States. (Eugene V. Debs, untitled statement in *Social Democratic Herald*, November 12, 1904; the original is in italics.)

5) Revolution is in the air! Pity the poor wretch who does not feel it throb in his heart, burn in his bosom, glow in his eyes and leap in his veins! His is a dead soul in living fetters. (Eugene V. Debs, "Half-Century Parallels," *The Worker*, December 21, 1907.)

6) Only the victory of the Democratic party in this election can prevent the masses of the people from turning to Socialism for 1912. . . . Socialism is coming. The vanguard of the army of workingmen sees the breaking of the dawn. Every year, every moment, every day that passes, added thousands see that light and cheer its coming, and step bravely forward, shoulder to shoulder, on the upward and onward sweep. (Editorial entitled "Mr. Watterson Is Half Right," *Call*, November 2, 1908.)

7) [The workers] have lost confidence in the existing parties they know of, and they are seeking desperately for the party of their class. . . . In the crash that . . . is now just ahead of us, our steadfast Socialist organization will alone stand intact above the ruins; there will then be a stampede to our party—but only upon revolutionary lines can it achieve this; upon lines of reform it can never be victorious. (Daniel De Leon, "Reform or Revolution" [1896], in Daniel De Leon, *Socialist Landmarks* [New York: New York Labor News Co., 1952], 59.)

8) Had . . . [the IWW] been in existence the revolution would have been accomplished in 1903. The workingmen's pulse beat high. The class instinct was there; the revolutionary spirit was there; but the army of labor, like the Czar's army, which also consists of workingmen, was captained by the lieutenants of the capitalist class. (Applause.) . . . The times are ripe. (Daniel De Leon, in IWW, *Proceedings*, 1905, pp. 147–48.)

9) [The capitalists know we are] the first and gathering nucleus of the army that shall overthrow the plutocracy [and they will turn all their weapons upon us. It will be] a hard, bitter, desperate fight that may last out your lives. (Algie M. Simons, in IWW, *Proceedings*, 1905, p. 169.)

10) [How long will it be before New York's workers revolt?] I don't know. But it is not many years away. The momentum for the revolution in the great cities, especially for New York, will develop in the two basic industries—that of mining and the metals and machinery. The workers in the Pittsburg district, and Pennsylvania in general, will lead the way. . . . Out of this collective struggle in production, there springs a collective aim, a direction, a definite plan, a tremendous

confidence in each other, and a feeling of working class power which is uncon-
querable. But New York City in itself is not as hopeless as the superficial observer would think. . . . Everywhere I saw, perhaps I should say felt, the spirit
of revolt. A battle cry is listened for. A spark is needed—expected. . . . We have
reached a point in capitalist development where capitalist oppression only stimulates revolt. . . . The millions in New York City and everywhere else, for that
matter, are not going to stand for capitalism much longer. (Louis Duchez, "New
York City and the Revolution," *International Socialist Review*, XI [1910], 174–76.)
11) We confidently anticipate that within thirty years the people of the United
States will have committed themselves definitely to industrial REORGANIZA-
TION on lines of Socialism. ("What We Anticipate," *Social Democratic Herald*, December 21, 1901.)

Any doubts that the revolution would come soon would have been
especially hard to retain in view of all the radicals' perception of American society as a System. Most important reforms were incompatible
with the System and could not be accomplished before the revolution.
For example, Berger's *Social Democratic Herald* asserted in 1904 that tuber-
culosis, largely a working-class disease, would not begin to disappear
until the workers had been emancipated.[22] A front-page article in the
Call of March 25, 1909, entitled "White Plague with Us until the Present
Social System Is Abolished," quoted a doctor who had "said that he did
not think consumption will be wiped out in forty years, as it had been
prophesied. While the present social and economic conditions exist the
human race will be subject to this horrible disease." The other direct
quotations that follow also show that the doctor had blamed tuber-
culosis on bad *conditions*, not on a System. The headline writer missed
the distinction because he automatically equated the two.

Among the other conditions intrinsic to capitalism were the employment of girls eight years old in factories; the power of millionaires permanently to block an income-tax amendment; the capitalist class's
power permanently to prevent enforcement of labor laws; the existence
of a gigantic reserve army of the unemployed always on the edge of starvation; a twelve- or sixteen-hour workday; a seven-day working week;
the death of 939 persons out of a thousand without property to be-
queath; a 55 percent mortality rate among workers' children below five
years of age; the impossibility of a rise in real wages; the creation of
"'he' towns and 'she' towns" according to the need of industry for par-

ticular sorts of workers, forcing hundreds of thousands of adults to "pass their lives in enforced celibacy"; the impossibility of workers' obtaining good wages without aiming at "full earnings"; court decisions invariably in the employers' favor; and the progressive replacement of adult male workers by women and children.[23] Each of these conditions was well known to reformers; they, however, did not assume them to be intrinsic to a System.

Another corollary of System-thinking was the class nature of politics. Until late in the Progressive period, all the radicals would have approved of De Leon's statement (if not of his metaphors) that "legislation favorable to labor is a fruit that can be strained through the loins of a capitalist Congress as little as a Kentucky stallion can be strained through the loins of a Texas coyote. . . . The scientific deduction that capitalist government is there for the benefit of the capitalist class; that it is a government of, for and by the exploiter; flows from shiploads of facts." The prophetic essays and speeches contain countless statements that the Republican party represented the big capitalists, the Democratic party the small capitalists or middle class, and the SP, SLP, or IWW the working class. The organizational and ideological shifts of the major parties in the shake-up period were interpreted as the disintegration of the capitalist party system itself. Either the Democratic party would disappear owing to the erosion of its middle-class base, or capitalists big and small were about to merge the two major parties in one bourgeois party that would share the field briefly with the SP or SLP.[24]

A third basis for the predictions was the invention of machinery that made industrial skills obsolete. Women and children were replacing adult male workers whose strength was no longer needed; strikes were becoming futile because employers for the first time could hire unskilled scabs to replace any workers and because the concentration of capital massed employers' power against the workers; products made by machines would be too expensive for workers to buy, while their incomes declined and the reserve army of the unemployed grew. The most common sort of article on this theme consisted of a report of a new invention and a calculation of how many skilled workers it would displace. Max J. Hayes's monthly department in the *International Socialist Review*, "The World of Labor," carried such news in almost every issue. Rarely did these writers add that the new machines might create new jobs; De

Leon did, but he calculated that the net loss of jobs would amount to 25 percent.[25]

The sum of all these beliefs and the point of all these predictions was the almost universal conviction (there were a few dissenters) that capitalism had reached the limit of its mechanization and expansion, and its ruling class the limit of its power. As Algie M. Simons explained in 1905, at the start of one of the great surges of reform in American history:

Capitalism seems to have reached its limit, to have perfected society as far as its social mission will permit. . . . All over the world comes the same story of a stoppage in all reformatory liberalizing movements. . . . As long as any ruling class feels perfectly secure in its position as a ruler it can still afford to grant concessions in order to prevent the rise of any effective opposition, but as soon as its actual domination is threatened, and then its existence as a class, it looks upon every position which it occupies as of probable value in its coming conflict for life,—consequently it is not disposed to yield even the apparently most unimportant post. . . . In America, as in Europe, the last three years have been marked by a more stubborn resistance on the part of the plutocratic rulers of society. . . . We are now about to enter upon the beginning of the end.

Untermann put it more concisely: "capitalism is nearing the time when it cannot expand much further without bursting."[26]

Documentary Excursus II

The following excerpts illustrate the tendency to assume that an existing condition or situation is permanent or intrinsic to capitalism. (In addition, see Supplement.)

12) Machines are now displacing. . . . almost every kind of worker there is. This process will not stop. On the contrary it will go on ever more rapidly. The unemployed army will grow greater and greater. Women and children wage-earners will more and more take the place of men. . . . The wages of the American worker have gone down one-third in fifteen years because he can no longer get away from his master. . . . *Nothing but socialism can prevent the condition of the American workers from becoming just as bad as that of the working people of Europe, or even worse.* (William D. Haywood and Frank Bohn, *Industrial Unionism* [6th ed.; Chicago: Charles H. Kerr & Company, 1911], 5–6, 23–24.)

13) [Berger's call for workers to arm is unwise, for modern weapons, including guns that shoot seven miles, would make the workers' rifles useless. Furthermore,] Americans have been so enamored of the achievements of the Wright brothers that too little attention has been paid to the development of the balloon by Zeppelin. Yet . . . it has evolved into the most perfect and formidable fight-

ing machine ever dreamt of. . . . It is more than probable that the development of these machines will eventuate in an armed truce from military conquest by the international capitalist class, the consecration of the flying machines to the old task of holding in check the working class, and the making safe and profitable all sorts of attacks upon social and political rights. (James Connolly, "Ballots, Bullets, or—," *International Socialist Review*, X [1909], 356.)

14) FELLOW WORKERS: In the lurid light of recent events do you not at last perceive that you have no rights, either as laborers or as citizens, that the capitalist class, possessed of all the means of life and armed with all the public powers, is bound to respect? . . . Do you not yet see that with the natural development of capitalism into powerful trusts, the strike and the boycott have become antiquated weapons, of no more effect against monopoly than the old flintlock against the Gatling gun?[27] ("Manifesto to the Toiling Masses of America," *People*, August 5, 1894.)

15) This new means of transit [the horseless carriage] will drive thousands of men upon the streets to swell that already large army of unemployed. What of our pure and simple unions of platers, harness makers, coach drivers, and the like? As purely economic organizations they must crumble to pieces as soon as the "horseless carriage" makes its triumphant debut. (H[arry] Carless, "Machinery and Invention," *People*, January 31, 1897.)

SP members generally agreed with the above reasoning. One, however, drew an atypical conclusion from the economic trends:

16) [President Roosevelt and some churchmen have called for the abolition of child labor, but it will be abolished only when it becomes unprofitable. The most advanced industries employ few children.] The tendency is in the other direction, to engage the highest priced men in the labor market, men with more than ordinary ability, intellect and technical knowledge—in short, experts. . . . It is not the poorest paid, but, under proper circumstances, often the highest paid labor that brings in the best results, that can bring in the greatest return for the output in wages, that permits of the greatest exploitation. . . . "Public opinion" is soon to be moulded by our "public press" against the abominable institution of child labor. The abolition of child labor will be another blow at small investments, it will be another sign that capitalism, the ascendancy of large enterprise, is in control. (Joseph E. Cohen, "Child Labor," *Call*, December 15, 1908.)

Few of these writers described the Co-operative Commonwealth as they envisioned it, but we can infer some of its features by merely reversing the assertions as to what they believed could not be accomplished before the revolution. Most of the explicit predictions had to do with what appear now to be rather small changes. The reason is that the prophets' extremely short perspective caused them to draw surprisingly sweeping conclusions from a single defeat of an effort to win a reform. Consider De Leon's reaction to the New York State legislature's refusal in 1894 to enact woman suffrage. "It was and continues to be a Utopian dream on the part of woman," he wrote, "to expect emancipation from the class whose economic interests demand her subjection. . . . Freedom for woman can be the award only of Socialism."[28] This editorial is one of many indications of the enormous importance De Leon always imputed to political rights, for he not only equated the suffrage with freedom but considered the disfranchisement of woman essential to the capitalists' tenure of power. But the more interesting implication is that he drew a basic lesson about the System from that one legislative defeat. In De Leon's world there was no room for the give-and-take of politics, for accidents or logrolling or personal conviction. Whatever existed was an aspect of the System and therefore permanent until the revolution, and one event was as significant as a dozen.

System-thinking would seem to require the radicals to predict their own defeat when they worked for particular reforms here and now. Naturally, they did not do so. But at the very least the theory of capitalist ripeness produced ambiguous attitudes toward immediate demands. They might tell one another that the chief benefit of a strike or the struggle for a reform was educational; they could hardly tell that to the unawakened worker who joined the effort not to get an education but to win the particular demand. But the winning of a reform or a strike was equally troublesome for radical theorists, especially if the object of the struggle had been one that they had considered unattainable before the revolution.

In the period under study the conditions that brought in the recruits were relatively new, and many nonradicals agreed with the radicals that certain reforms that have since been effected were unobtainable under capitalism. The *Call* spoke for many when, in an editorial on November 15, 1909, it offered a long list, including the end of the wanton slaughter in factories and mines, enactment of labor laws, government inspection of workplaces, limitation of the workday especially for women and children, employers' liability, unions' control of their own treasuries, legalization of the boycott, and abolition of the labor injunction. These immediate demands, it declared, "are so revolutionary . . . that they only have to be properly formulated and persistently agitated in order to bring about such a tremendous forward movement as has never before been witnessed on this continent," and their enactment would require such an extension of government power as to require "what is tantamount to a political revolution." The implication was that it would amount to an economic revolution too, for the government was the instrument of the capitalist class.

If the revolution could be brought about that easily, the capitalist class must indeed have been tottering. Yet all varieties of radical from right to left generally saw their adversary as wielding immense power in all sectors of the society. As they saw the situation, John Q. Worker may have been asleep, but the capitalists were fully awake to the danger and plotted continuously to keep their power beyond their appointed time. One means was to offer judicious "concessions" in response to rising discontent. Although the capitalists thought such concessions would strengthen their rule, the radicals knew they undermined it (although from time to time they expressed fear that the stratagem would lull the workers back to sleep). Thus, the conviction that social evolution proceeded inexorably upward and onward, despite whatever the capitalists did, often encouraged excited predictions of what a large socialist vote would accomplish. Max Hayes speculated in 1908 that a million SP votes in the coming election would force a long list of concessions that governments would enact "in fear and dread that two million might follow" in 1912. That million "would sound the tocsin that the working class had repudiated the Pharaoh of capitalism and was preparing to march into the promised land of the co-operative commonwealth." As it happened, Debs received comparatively large votes in 1908 and 1912, the reforms came, and the SP began to decline, for it was the "concessions" that most of its voters had wanted. Hayes and his comrades automatically imputed to John Q. Worker their own assumption that each "step" had no real value except with reference to the next, and the next. As Sidney Hook explains, "If, in the face of the strong opposition of capitalist interests, the state adopted social legislation . . . this did not invalidate the doctrine that the state is inevitably the executive committee of the ruling economic class. It only showed th the state was acting out of fear and making concessions. That the power to compel the state to make concessions indicated a substantial measure of control over the state was denied or ignored. Everything that transpired in the world was either a necessary step forward to socialism or merely a temporary setback."[29]

The obvious way out of the contradiction was to regard the benefits and rights conferred by the "concessions" as illusory or of little value, and radical movements have argued thus in all periods from the earliest to the present. It is implicit in the term "wage-slave," which tells the worker that his freedom is merely freedom to change masters. It appears in the discourses on the essential identity of the two major political parties. The civil liberties and opportunities that John Q. Worker possessed were lullabies to his radical instincts, having no value in themselves. Radical periodicals were full of news items intended to prove the illusoriness of these rights and benefits. Perhaps the articles were motivated by propaganda needs that justified some hyperbole. But they could hardly have had the desired effect in view of John Q. Worker's persistent delusion that his family more often than not retained its integrity, that freedom to change masters often brought a raise in pay, that schooling for his children was a good in itself that he might reasonably look forward to, and that the suffrage, freedom from military service, and freedom to worship represented a real improvement over what he had had in the Old Country. (Not all immigrant workers are covered by these generalizations; they vary in applicability from ethnic group to ethnic group.) But these propaganda items more likely expressed their authors' sincere conviction that they were portraying the essential, deeper truth: that all such rights and opportunities were merely superstructural, conceded by the masters to keep the slaves contented. This is, however, less true of those on the SP right than of the SLP and IWW; and De Leon is a partial exception, in that he repeatedly lauded the democratic heritage of the United States.

The contradiction between the enormous power of the capitalists and the ease with which they might be overthrown was noted long ago by John Graham Brooks, whose comment on the Wobblies applies to the members of the SLP and most members of the SP as well: "On the one hand we are assured that capitalism has reached senility. Though never more prolific of depravity, never more active in parasitic lecheries, its real power is so near its end, that a few years of adroit and vigorous assault and it will tumble of its own weight." On the other hand, "others speak as if the strength of capitalism was never so great. The proof offered is that three generations of social and other legislation meant to curb its power have obviously failed."[30] In fact, the same people said both things at different times. Both parts of the contradiction were indispensable—the optimistic outlook, for the psychological ground of continued activity and commitment; and the perception of the capitalists' power, to account for the indifference of John Q. Worker to radicalism. But there was another reason for the belief that the revolution would be a rather quick yet totally transforming event—the "expectation that the socialist economic arrangement would of itself create and sustain the millennium," as Martin Diamond puts it. "Socialism," he adds, "promised the most extraordinary of results by the simplest of means." "In short," adds Will Herberg, "American socialism, like socialism everywhere, has held freedom, justice, and all the other social virtues to be sufficiently guaranteed by the abolition of capitalist private property and the inauguration of the new Co-operative Commonwealth. . . . Once the revolution has wiped out economic injustice . . . [all other social] ills will of course disappear, for with the removal of the cause the effects must go."[31]

II

Many of the empirical facts on which these prophets based their predictions were not in dispute; nonradical periodicals discussed them copiously and often ventured predictions of future consequences as erroneous as the radicals'. But even most of those who regarded poverty, the industrialists' raw power, and other phenomena as threatening the continuation of the social order generally assumed that reforms could solve the problems; they did not perceive the problems as inherent in a System. What distinguishes the radical prophets was the theoretical framework into which they incorporated the empirical data and predictions.

Only a minority of the writers and lecturers explicitly dealt with that framework, but those who did sometimes called it a "science." Even those Wobblies and pro-IWW SP members who cared little for theory generally assumed that their various tenets and tactics hung together as parts of a theoretical system. They all perceived themselves as the bearers of this special knowledge about society, its past, present, and future. It enabled them to speak with amazing self-assurance on a large assortment of subjects—from child-rearing under socialism, to the inevitable psychological effects that labor struggles would have on workers, to the future of racial and ethnic feelings—a certainty all the more remarkable in view of the confusing variety of doctrines among and within their organizations.[32] Difference of opinion is of course no disproof of scientific competence. What disqualified the people under discussion was the purely deductive route they usually took to their conclusions.

Some of them would have been disqualified in any case by virtue of their calling socialism or Marxism "a science" (see Supplement)—not a theory *within* a body of knowledge called a science of society. If socialism was a science, any assertion about society that was antisocialist was *ipso facto* unscientific and a priori untrue. It is as though Newtonian theory were regarded not as a body of theory within the science of physics but physics itself, not a set of propositions to be evaluated by criteria independent of it, but rather the ultimate criterion by which all other propositions in physics must be evaluated. Before examining this feature of the three movements' writings, we should first reconstruct the assumptions that underlay it.

In *The Devil's Dictionary* Ambrose Bierce defines prophecy as "the art and practice of selling one's credibility for future delivery." We may note an application of that epigram in the radicals' asking John Q. Worker for faith, since integral parts of their message were predictions and hence undemonstrable. They needed the authority of science, God being unavailable for most of them, to back up their right to make the predictions. Science, which explains the apparent by the unapparent, necessarily goes behind commonsense observations (as, for example, in the aforementioned delusory rights); only the possession of a science could enable the radicals to insist on the correctness of their predictions and analyses, and their special access to the Truth.

At the base of their theoretical structure lay what they variously called economic determinism, the materialist conception of history, sometimes Marxism (some Wobblies would have substituted Bakunin for Marx[33]). A writer in the *American Socialist*, for example, refers to "the idea of economic determinism (materialist conception of history)" and calls it the application of evolutionary theory to society. William D. Haywood and Frank Bohn, in their pamphlet *Industrial Unionism*, boast that socialism is "a complete system of thought with regard to human society and social progress" and entitle one of the ensuing expositions of it "Economic Determinism."[34] Another writer, in 1907, imagines himself writing to a friend in 1920 and describing "the last days of the System." The socialists, he "recalls," had been working quietly for a long time. "With their knowledge of social evolution, their economic determinism, their materialistic conception of history, they alone held the key to the future. Under the direction of their leaders, men of thought, science, and scholarship, who saw and foresaw the trend of natural laws," they quietly prepared while "the class-conscious workers presented a united but peaceful, dormant, and unaggressive front to Capital." In the same year Charles Kerr deplores some SP members' ignorance "of Marx's law of economic determinism," which, according to Algie M. Simons several years earlier, "is simply a recognition and statement of the fact that economic relations determine all other social relations."[35]

Many documents said the same things in other language. Daniel De Leon proclaimed, "Relentless is the logic of events. Never did JOHN STUART MILL make a worse slip than when he claimed that exact scientific principles are inapplicable to sociology. . . . As logical as biologic formations, so are sociologic formations. The action of masses of men obey[s] laws as relentless as those that build up the granite rock and that scatter the sands."[36] The far left did not have a monopoly on inevitablism: Hillquit wrote a few years later that "the workers of America, once set upon the path of labor politics, will draw the last consequence from that step—they will not stop at the Democratic party. The sheer force of logic will soon force them into the only true labor party . . . the Socialist party." And the editor of the *Call* pronounced the success of the SP in the South to be "preordained."[37] But on this subject it is De Leon who must have the last word: "The laws that rule sociology run upon lines parallel with and are the exact counterparts of those that natural science has established in biology. . . . The Socialist Labor Party cannot, in our country, fulfill its mission—here less than anywhere else—unless it takes a stand, the scientific soundness of whose position renders growth certain, failure impossible, and unless its disciplinary firmness earns for it the unqualified confidence of the now eagerly onlooking masses both in its integrity of purpose and its capacity to enforce order."[38]

Order is indeed the point.[39] Where many American intellectuals and reformers saw rampant disorder throughout their society, the radicals saw an oppressive order—the System—beneath it. In fact, it is a plausible conjecture that those who could not tolerate psychological and theoretical incoherence were the ones who became radical. This does not mean their outrage at poverty and exploitation was not genuine. But reformers, Progressives, and social workers had similar feelings and motives; only the radicals felt theirs needed the rigor and justification of a "science" that explained all and that ruled out chance and choice not only in current affairs but also in the future. The word "inevitable" appears again and again in their writings, including those by people like Berger, Untermann, and De Leon for whom an alternative did exist—cataclysm, the epitome of disorder.

To be able to see the invisible System beneath the apparent disorder was to possess a special gnosis, a pair of spectacles that made all things clear.[40] When Debs and others proclaimed that the truth was so plain that a child could see it, they were not contradicting their claim to superior knowledge. They were expressing the absolute certainty and clear perception possessed by anyone who looked at society from the standpoint of Truth. (It was, as was shown earlier, possessed also by those capitalists who knew the truth because they ran the System.) They could not have been that certain if they had conceded indeterminacy to social "evolution." Past, present, and future comprised a single entity, with the future almost as determined as the past. Hence the occasional excursions into genetics and anthropology by radical intellectuals with no other qualifications in those fields but their gnosis.

An especially interesting such excursion was made by the prominent SP leader, Kate Richards O'Hare:

Since civilization is but the slow process of evolution it is but natural that we should have failed to pick the Indian up out of barbarism and land him at one leap into civilization. It took some thousands of years for the Anglo-Saxon to reach our present civilized state and it is the height of presumption and folly for us to expect the Indian to reach it in a few decades. . . . The Indian is neither the "Noble Red Man of the forest," the angelic hero sentimentalists are wont to rave over, [n]or the blood thirsty thief and murderer he has been painted. He is just a man in the childhood of the race as our ancestors were, just a little parcel of the fargone past, ruthlessly tossed into the hustling present and as a natural result he does not fit into the ways of the white man, hence is being trampled out of existence. . . . The Indian is fast disappearing . . . [owing to] the law of the survival of the fittest.[41]

It will be noted that the reason the Indian does not fit into the ways of "the white man" is not that he has a different culture but that he is a living fossil from the white man's own past. Anglo-Saxon civilization equals the present—a remarkable equation even if Anglo-Saxon civilization had been worldwide in 1906 when O'Hare wrote this passage. It follows that other cultures are not adaptations to their environments—although O'Hare as a professed Marxist materialist endorsed that theory—but are "the past." By linking the normative idea of economic progress with time, she can see Indians as children or as fossils somehow existing out of their proper time dimension.[42] Although it is not clear from the essay whether she believes that adults effect the economic progress or that economic progress makes cultural "children" grow up, only the second alternative is consistent with her economic determinism. Yet her implicit theory goes beyond economic determinism; her equation of a particular stage of civilization with a particular moment implies that somewhere in the Book of the Universe the page numbered 1906 bears a description of the technology that fits just that year, even though only a tiny portion of the human race possessed it.

Debs did not engage in such analyses but restricted himself to such statements as: those who regarded socialist sentiment as transitory "have not been critical students of the past, nor are they more than superficial observers of the present transition period . . . [to] a higher order of civilization than this earth has ever known." An editorialist in the *Industrial Worker* was more scientific (if not more modest); he appropriated a current catchphrase for the IWW's hard-boiled philosophy to write, "The argument of the hungry stomach is the same the world over. The survival of the fittest is the kindly cruel rule of Nature. . . . Industrial Union of the workers is alone fitted to survive."[43]

Several writers in the *International Socialist Review* attempted to synthesize Darwinian theory with their own versions of Marxism, to account for the influence of both heredity and environment on social institutions, or to incorporate current discoveries in biology in their social theories. One such author rejected Lamarckian evolutionary theory on the ground that it would have made socialism impossible by transforming into hereditary characteristics all the bad traits fostered by centuries of oppression. Weissmannism implied that most people could be raised to the socialist level within a generation; therefore it was the correct theory.[44] A more sophisticated attempt to ground socialist theory on scientific authority was made by Algie M. Simons, one of the chief intellectuals in the SP. He found it in the recent work on mutations, by Professor Hugo de Vries of the University of Amsterdam.

Simons sees an analogy between biological mutations and social revolutions. The pseudoscientists who maintain that there are no leaps in nature, he explains, have already been refuted in geology and other sciences, but the new discoveries in biology are much more significant. The struggle for survival in nature parallels the history of class struggle, with long periods of slow growth and slight variations (called reforms) culminated by sudden change (revolution). As if uneasy over his invasion of scholarly territory, Simons follows this article with an editorial in which he condemns capitalism for stifling science by making it esoteric; popularization, he argues, is essential to true science. He is glad that the artificial separation of science into narrow specialties is breaking down and the unity of all things is becoming more and more obvious. The same laws govern all phenomena, and one universal law is "that only the necessary happens"; in biology every organ or trait furthers survival. "Consequently all organs are determined by the necessity of getting a living, which after all is but the biological statement of the economic interpretation of history." The second great law is that everything changes. Hence, "the sociology of the future must draw its laws to a large extent from the field of physical and biological science."[45]

Biology and economics were not merely analogous; they were ultimately one science, different expressions of one basic law—the supremacy of environment. A *Call* editorialist drew this conclusion from the report of the Immigration Commission in 1909, which showed physical differences between immigrants and their children owing to the homogenizing effects of the American environment. "Whatever may be the role of heredity in biology, or the strictly physical life in the social life," he added, "it is purely passive, assuming the form of established institutions, usage, and traditions, and giving way before the active force of economic development." [46] Here was an obvious allusion to John Q. Worker's traditions as passive drags on evolution and to the revolutionary movement as the active force destined to supersede them.

What enabled all these writers and lecturers to speak with such assurance was their certainty that they were not engaging in theorizing at all but simply reading the bare facts that all could see. Indeed, from time to time they scolded one another for not sticking to the empirical evidence. Robert Rives La Monte, the most determinist of all, criticized another Marxist's book on the ground that its method was "the reverse of scientific, as he first states his theory and conclusions and then starts to scour the universe for facts to support them, instead of first collecting the facts and letting them impose the theory upon his mind." [47] In 1900 it was still possible to consider this the scientific method. The significance of La Monte's criticism lies in his assumption that the positivist method was the one he himself and all good Marxists followed, that his own writings were nothing but expositions of fact. As a modern writer points out, one characteristic of rationalistic theories is that they accord precedence to "deductive argumentation . . . over evidence and testing." [48] The paradox of highly rationalistic theorists' insisting that their theories were merely reflections of raw data reveals a way of thinking so devoid of self-awareness as to purport not to be concerned with theory at all.

Associated with that assumption was economic reductionism. It was inconceivable that cultural or psychological phenomena intervened between naked economic fact and radical doctrine. In this respect, La Monte was typical of the radicals of all varieties discussed here. The largest single category of articles in their publications consisted of descriptions of oppressive conditions in factories or mines or cities, followed by the prediction that the workers would soon wake up to socialism and abolish them. The middle term of the chain of reasoning is invariably missing: proof that the workers could not draw other conclusions—for instance, that they could abolish the conditions without abolishing capitalism—or that the same facts could not fit into other belief-systems. Since the radicals' belief-systems were self-evident, mere reflections of raw facts, unmediated by culture or attitude, those workers who drew other conclusions perceived the facts inaccurately.

The radicals had to emphasize unmediated fact for another reason. That the working class, though in process of waking up, was not voting socialist by heavy majorities or flocking into the IWW was demonstrated in every election and by the IWW's own membership figures. Clearly, it had not yet sloughed off the capitalist ideology or capitalist-induced fear. But if the oppressors could exert such influence now, through their economic power and false teachings, how could one be sure they could not continue doing so indefinitely? One common answer, that the System itself was breaking down, did not suffice, for it did not entail the proletariat's enlightenment. There had to be something that would inevitably rend the veil of capitalist ideology, and that was sheer fact—whether that fact was increasing immiserization or multiplying victories producing rising expectations; both theories filled the need for scientific certainty that the workers would see the truth of the radicals' propaganda. But in minimizing the influence of the ruling class's ideas in the long run, the radicals also had to minimize the influence of the working class's ideas, since the latter merely reflected the former, so long as the workers remained enthralled to the capitalist System. Hence a universal feature of the radicals' thinking was the denial that an autonomous working-class culture, neither capitalist nor radical in content, could exist. Sheer fact working directly on the will made the workers strike or join unions; it determined the essential meaning of those actions regardless of what the workers themselves thought. The function of the radical, in this context, was to see the facts plain, unobscured by culture, theory, or ideology, and to explain to the workers the meaning of their own acts. For, as a Wobbly editorialist remarked, "On what does the power of the employing class rest, if not on the traditional respect for the laws, customs and methods of society which are founded by the ruling class to enslave the minds and paralyze the courage of the workers?"[49]

The denigration of culture as either superstructural or an unnecessary veil hiding economic fact can be read between the lines of all the excursions into historical anthropology published from time to time in the *International Socialist Review*—in Mary E. Marcy's historical series for children, in essays on primitive societies, in human-interest travelogues about exotic lands. One of the latter, for example, entitled "Socialism in the Arctics," explained that the Eskimos of Greenland had long ago, without contact with Christianity, worked out its best principles. The Eskimo was "a natural man leading a natural life on natural principles.

No law tells him he must not lie, yet he never lies; no law tells him he must not kill, steal, or cause suffering among his tribe, and yet he never kills, steals, or causes trouble." The editor appended a comment that of course we socialists know that that is not socialism; it is primitive communism.[50] But he did not quarrel with the author's implication that the Eskimos were cultureless and that the "natural" man is the one who behaves as all will after the Co-operative Commonwealth has been established and the ideological accretions of class society have been peeled away.

When the modern worker was the subject of discussion, this assumption found expression in the tenet that he had nothing to lose but his chains. A certain circularity may be discerned in these essays. If, as happened rarely, someone suggested that in many localities the worker had valuable cultural institutions and interests, that he was more than an Economic Man,[51] the reply was that those things were either unimportant or delusory. Since "interest" was defined in exclusively economic terms, cultural "interests" were defined out of existence (see Supplement). As Louis Duchez put it, the worker "lives and moves and has his being in the shop, not in the legislative halls." Duchez evidently could not imagine a third possibility.[52] For present purposes the most significant feature of this style of thinking was the way it helped shape the radicals' self-image in relation to John Q. Worker. The worker in relation to whom they defined themselves was, however, a set of traits deduced from the basic postulates of the theory. Chapter V showed several aspects of this perception; it remains to fill out the picture.

The Co-operative Commonwealth could not be inevitable (or, for some, the only alternative to a general smashup) or the theory a science, or evolution a single-lane highway, if John Q. Worker was free to remain nonradical or to create a society unanticipated by the radicals. Subject to the laws of social evolution, he *had* to become radicalized by strike struggles, his joining unions *had* to be a step toward the revolution. No matter what he thought he was striking for, his strike was essentially a bid for power. This essentialism is a pervasive trait of the radicals' thinking, for they could not entertain the thought that they were and would remain an ideologically deviant sect, rather than the generals of an inevitably victorious army.

By *essentialism* I mean the practice, common among the radical theorists, of interpreting a particular institution and the behavior of its members or participants in terms of their "essence" as set forth in the theory, rather than in terms of its actual operation and the motives of the members and participants. The "mission" of the working class was to abolish capitalism and create the Co-operative Commonwealth, every strike was a revolution in embryo, and workers' actual motives could be deduced from their interests as defined by the theory. Wobblies would add that the essence of an industrial union was revolutionary, and the AFL was not a true working-class organization. Haywood, for instance, angered some SP members by declaring that since a trade (*i.e.*, craft) union was not founded on class-struggle principles, "no Socialist can be a trade unionist."[53]

The direct perception of fact facilitated by scientific understanding permitted its possessors to get behind appearances not just to explain them but even to contradict them, as, for instance, when De Leon in 1896 explained "the existing popular apathy"[54] (in the face of twenty years of militant strike activity and reforming third parties). The "apathy" of course meant the working class's nonradicalism. Other writers took it for granted that most immigrant workers were disappointed at what they had found in the United States,[55] even though these same workers inexplicably kept urging their friends and relatives to follow and sent passage money in enormous amounts. And during and after the great textile strike in Lawrence, Massachusetts, in 1912, the *Industrial Worker* filled its columns with exposés of the AFL, the employers' "benevolence," the "legal" socialists, and the Catholic Church; it mentioned the strikers mainly in speculations about how they must learn the lessons that the struggle had to teach. It did not examine the strike from the standpoint of the workers' own objectives. When the newly recruited members of the IWW dropped out after the struggle, a few Wobbly writers deplored the organizers' failure to remain in Lawrence long enough to put the local on a permanent basis. They rarely suggested that what to the IWW was failure was, to the strikers, a victory, or that while the IWW was using the strike to teach revolution to the workers, the workers were using the IWW's leadership and organizational abilities to achieve their own goals. As in so many other episodes, the radicals viewed the particular struggle only in terms of the "next step." If they had viewed it in John Q. Worker's terms they might have seen that he felt no need to "learn lessons" from the struggle if it won for him the gains for which he had waged it.

Instead, the writers generally focused on what members of all three organizations called "the mission" of the working class, for the behavior of real workers had to be measured at all times and in every circumstance by the degree to which they recognized their mission. All three organizations used virtually the same language; as a Wobbly editorialist put it, "It is the historic mission of the working class to overthrow capitalism and to establish collective ownership and management of industry." A member of Berger's section of the SP, running for alderman in Milwaukee, called upon the workers to "Awake! Awake! to a consciousness of the strength of your class on the political field, learn how to use the ballot in your own interest, that you may fulfill the mission of your class." De Leon told the founders of the IWW that "the mission of Unionism is to organize and drill the Working Class for final victory." Debs was "opposed, not to the . . . [AFL] or its members, . . . but to those who are restraining its evolution and preventing it from fulfilling its true mission." Charles Kerr combined three of the radicals' favorite metaphors—"awakening," "army," and "mission"—in a typical expression of radical teleology: "Revolutionary sentiment in the mass of American workers is as yet dormant, waiting for the occasion to awaken it. . . . The historic mission of the Socialist party is to develop and organize the awakening spirit of revolution among the American wageworkers—to weld them into a compact, resistless army." Capitalism too had its mission, explained De Leon in 1905: to build up the country's productive forces. During that process, "pure-and-simple" unions had "wandered" from *their* mission, which was "to drill" the working class in discipline. One prominent Wobbly's version of this thesis was that "a labor union is essentially an army of occupation." [56]

On those rare occasions when the theorists mentioned John Q. Worker's own motives for joining unions or striking, they usually discovered them by deduction from essentialist definitions of unions, capitalism, and the workers' interests, rather than by generalizing from empirical data. Morris Hillquit reasoned that the socialists' appeal touched the workers' "material interest, and we are, therefore, more likely to succeed with them." It is Hillquit's *therefore* that reveals the combination of economic reductionism with the deductive basis for socialist optimism. William E. Trautmann of the IWW was bolder: "The purpose of a labor organization on the industrial field," he declared, was, in addition to obtaining better conditions, to develop the workers' intellectual and physical faculties so that they would want to abolish wage slavery and have the power and intelligence to do so.[57] The further left an author was, the more apt he was to use the present tense and omit qualifiers such as Hillquit's *likely*. Wobbly theorist Austin Lewis explained that *because* the unskilled worker had no vote, he had "no illusions about the value of political action," and that *because* he had nothing in common with the skilled workers, he was "not subject to the ethical and patriotic concepts which have drugged the minds of the organized skilled workers." Facts would force him to revolt; and facts would teach him the method of revolt. Indeed, Lewis asserted in another article, "The real Marxian idea of the government as being the mere mirror" of economic power "has completely entered into his consciousness."[58]

The wishful thinking discernible in that statement can be seen as well in an untitled editorial in the *Industrial Worker* of May 13, 1916, concerning seven strikes; it explained, "Every strike is an embryo revolution, showing that the workers realize their struggle with the boss will have to be fought out on a basis of their power against the power of the boss." The hypothesis with which the writer began his analysis determined the very definition of the facts he observed. If he had not believed a priori that a strike was an embryo revolution, he never would have seen these seven strikes as such, for there is nothing in the account of any of them to show they were anything but strikes.

The concept of mission implies that the purpose of an organization is not determined by its members. This is, of course, clear in the radicals' assertions that the mission of the unions was this or that, regardless of what the members thought—in other words, that the rank and file could not formulate the unions' mission but must merely discover it. But the same is true concerning the radical organizations' missions. If a group of radicals had the right to confer and decide in the light of their own wishes what their task was to be, the unity of socialist science would be imperiled. Therefore, even the fully awakened could only discover the mission of the organizations they themselves founded.

A few dissenters asked for recognition of culture along with economic interest, of feeling along with reason, and of the dangers of wishful thinking along with the rewards of commitment (see Supplement). But their warnings were lost in the chorus of scientific disquisitions and confident predictions, for these were far more consistent with the radical activist's mind-set, as illustrated in the following documents.

Documentary Excursus III

The first two excerpts illustrate economic determinism.

17) If the philosophy of economic determinism is true (and if it is not the whole philosophy of socialism must be recast) then it is in the United States that socialism should reap its first great victories. ([Algie M. Simons], "A New Milestone for American Socialism," *International Socialist Review*, II [1901], 233.)

18) The most basic of Socialist theories is economic determinism. By this we mean that the mass actions of people, the religious or political ideas which they agree in accepting, the customs and laws which they make for themselves—all these are the direct result of the changing *methods of production*, through which people supply themselves with food, clothing and shelter. . . . We Socialists owe to Marx and Engels a knowledge that the most important acts of human beings . . . are as necessary and inevitable as the movements of winds and waters, plants and animals. Rightly applied, this law of determinism will give us a clearer insight into passing events, a more steadfast optimism in the face of apparent misfortune, and a broader sympathy for all workers, no matter how misguided they seem. (Charles Kerr, "The War through Socialist Lenses," *International Socialist Review*, XV [1915], 433.)

The following two excerpts illustrate the manner in which workers' motives and desires were deduced from their "interests."

19) Living in constant struggle with the capitalist class and capitalist institutions which must array themselves in the struggle on the part of the capitalist class, he [the worker] learns to hate these institutions and the whole ideology of the capitalist class. Being thrown on his own resources he begins to think for himself, to form his own ideology. But every ideology must have its base in the material conditions under which it is formed. The new ideology is based on and is the reflection of the new economic forces, the socialized means, modes and methods of production and distribution, and the growing collective control over them. His ideology is collectivism. . . . At the same time the working class is steadily advancing in economic power and independence in the sense that it takes possession of more and more responsible positions in the economic life of the nation, diverts to itself, by means of the corporation and otherwise, all the growth of the concentration and centralization of capital, and particularly with the development of the corporate form of economic activity, the capitalist class abdicates its functions, the proper functions of a ruling class, those of economic management, into the hands of the working class. *The working class thus not only*

becomes revolutionary in its ideas, desires and aspirations, but it has the organizational power to carry the revolution into effect, and is fully equipped to take hold of all social and economic activities and functions the day after the revolution, and carry them on successfully. (L. B. Boudin, "Will the Workers Bring Socialism," *International Socialist Review*, VII [1906], 170–71.)

20) When the worker, either through experience or a study of Socialism, comes to know this truth [the economic basis of all social formations], he acts accordingly. He retains absolutely no respect for the property "rights" of the profit-takers. He will use any weapon which will win his fight. He knows that the present laws of property are made by and for the capitalists. Therefore he does not hesitate to break them. (William P. Haywood and Frank Bohn, *Industrial Unionism* [6th ed.; Chicago: Charles H. Kerr & Company, 1911], 57, 60.)

The next excerpt illustrates teleology and the mission theme.

21) When the workingman awakes to class-consciousness, he receives a new soul. With him mankind also awakes to a new conception of life. In the measure in which the working class becomes conscious of its historic mission, in that measure does all mankind become conscious of the mission of the human race as the determining and conscious factor in the evolution of the world. Only when class rule and exploitation of man by man is abolished, can mankind rise to the task of conquering the forces of nature. (Untitled editorial, *Social Democratic Herald*, April 2, 1904.)

The remaining excerpts all relate to the scientism theme.

22) Verily the walls of the capitalistic Jericho have fallen before the trumpet blasts of the socialist philosophy without striking a blow and it only remains for us to enter in and possess the promised land in the name of all the producers of wealth. . . . All along the line the outposts of capitalism are capitulating to the logic of events and admitting that that logic has won the argument for socialism. ([Algie M. Simons], editorial, *International Socialist Review*, I [1901], 745–48.)

23) The finish of the capitalist system is imminent. . . . With the same accuracy and assurance that a Copernicus or a Kepler could predict the appearance of new heavenly bodies years before their actual appearance, so unerringly does the Socialist Labor Party predict the downfall of Capitalism and the advent of the Socialist Republic. . . . (SLP's National Executive Committee, "Cuba, the Philippines, China, and the Working Class," *People*, October 20, 1900.)

[In reply to a letter, *The People* clarified the remarks above:] Nothing would justify the conclusion that Socialism is inevitable in the sense that it is bound to come whether the people are educated for it or not. . . . The human agency is necessary at this stage of social evolution. That the human agency will be sufficiently enlightened, thanks to Socialist Propaganda and S.L.P. work, is considered certain. If, however, this proves false, then a social catastrophe will follow, similar to the catastrophe that would overtake the pregnant woman for whose accouchement no preparation was made, and whose "ailment" was not understood. ([Daniel De Leon], "Letter Box," *People*, November 3, 1900.)

24) If economic conditions shape the thought of men so forcibly as to compel them to a definite line of political action, then it must be shown that the whole human soul life is indeed nothing but a response to material stimuli, and not only to economic stimuli, but to all stimuli coming from the social, terrestrial, and cosmic environment. . . . Class-struggles in human society, thus brought about by material stimuli on human brains, are but a human portion of the struggle for existence, which runs through the whole of the universe. . . . [If the teachings of Marx, Engels, Darwin, and Dietzgen are combined, we get] materialist monism as a conception of the universe, with the class-conscious proletariat as the historical champion of this historical monist science. . . . To the extent that the evolution toward socialism continues, this monist science will gradually become the accepted guide of a greater and greater portion of mankind, until the inauguration of the co-operative commonwealth of the world will make materialist monism the light of this world and replace theological religious and metaphysical ethics. . . . [Many well-meaning socialists do not claim to be Marxists but are socialists out of sentiment or idealism, but they are] harmless, because there is no danger of their ever being taken seriously by the class-conscious proletariat. . . . [All parts of Marxism are connected, such that it is impossible to accept one and reject another.] For if the materialist conception of history does not suffice to explain all phenomena of social evolution, then some of them must be explained by a method which is not materialist, and which can therefore only be an idealist method. But this is an irreconcilable contradiction. (Ernest Untermann, "Marxism or Eclecticism," *International Socialist Review*, VI [1906], 589–97.)

25) [The following was later reprinted as a leaflet, presumably to be distributed to workers:] This diagram roughly illustrates the political history of this country since the revolution:

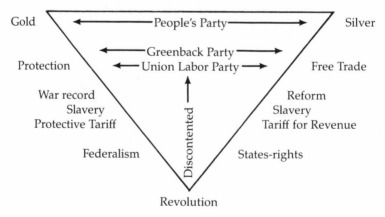

[There follows a political history of the United States and of the "principal issues set up to divide the voters," as graphically arranged to the right and left of the triangle. The parties inside it were "crude expressions of the rising discontent of" various groups. Then came the statement that the SLP wanted the reader to understand the situation.] This diagram may help you:

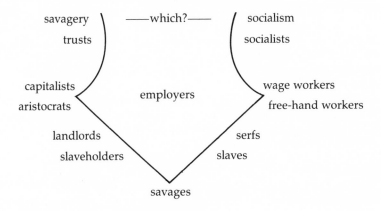

Read from the bottom up. [There follows a history of the human race.] ("A Word to Wage Workers," *Socialist Alliance* [organ of the Socialist Trades and Labor Alliance], I [October, 1896]. Copy drawn by the author.)

26) A mission of the Trades unions is to drill the membership of the Working Class in the habit of self-imposed discipline. The mission of capitalism . . . is so to organize the mechanism of production that wealth can be so abundantly produced as to free mankind from want and the fear of want, from the brute's necessity of a life of arduous toil. . . . American conditions, however, . . . have revealed a subsidiary mission of capitalism, to wit, the mission of KEEPING ORDER, while the revolutionary class, the Working Class, is gathering the needed qualities for itself to assume control. . . . The Working Class, a propertyless class, . . . lacks an element that is a drilling force in itself—property. The defect must be substituted [supplied?] from another source. Thorough education in its own class interests is valuable, is indispensable, but it is not all-sufficient. The habit of self-enforced discipline is an essential accompaniment of class-consciousness. . . . That "pure and simpledom" neglects the drilling in class-consciousness, aye, prevents it, has been amply shown. . . . As that division of the Labor or Socialist Movement in which none belongs but the wage slave, the facilities enjoyed by the Trades Union as an Academy for drilling its membership in the two essentials for the emancipation of their class—discipline and class-consciousness—are matchless. . . . The Working Class still is a tumultuous mob. NO REVOLUTIONARY CLASS IS EVER RIPE FOR SUCCESS

BEFORE IT HAS ITSELF WELL IN HAND. Until the Working Class of America shall have taken itself in hand, the Capitalist Class has a mission to perform, to KEEP ORDER. . . . It is one of the missions of the Trades Union to drill its class into the discipline that civilization demands. (Daniel De Leon, "A Mission of the Trades Unions" [1905], in Daniel De Leon, *Industrial Unionism: Selected Editorials* [New York: New York Labor News Co., 1944], 16–20.)
27) I am wearied unto death listening to Socialist speeches, and reading Socialist literature about materialism, and philosophy, and ethics, and sex, and embryology, and monogamy, and physiology, and monism, and Platonism, and determinism from men to whom the more immediately important question of unionism is a sealed book. . . . I am inclined to believe that when the working class really takes hold of the Socialist movement as a weapon in their industrial warfare, and ceases to regard it as a mere propaganda of idealism, they will make short work of the philosophers. (Item in the "Harp Strings" column by Spailpin [pseud.], *Harp* [organ of the Irish Socialist Federation], II [May, 1909], included here for its atypicality.)

III

When the radicals presented prophecies and scientific analyses to the working class they were also presenting *themselves* as people assigned a special mission by History. This is obviously one reason why they grasped at every sign that the working class was "waking up."

Anyone who reads page after page of the three organizations' newspapers may be tempted to suppose that their typesetters kept a few standard headlines set up and waiting for use when this or that place or group was to be referred to. In the *Call* we find "China Waking from Age-Long Sleep," "Kansas Awakens," "Ohio Town Waked Up," "Turkish Workers Awaken," and "Southern Timber Slaves Awakening." The *Industrial Worker* announced "Giant Labor Awakening," "Women Are Awakening," "Miners Waking Up," and "New Zealand Waking Up." The *People* preferred the light breaking, but it too observed Philadelphians "Waking Up," and called upon the "Maryland Proletariat, [to] Awake!" Berger's *Social Democratic Herald* joyfully greeted certain resolutions passed by the Wisconsin State Federation of Labor as evidence that "Labor Is Awakening!" but later discovered "Old Rip Van Winkle Beaten! As a Sleeper, the Workingman Beats All Records"; however, on another occasion it again announced "Labor's Awakening!" *Solidarity* used this metaphor throughout its lifetime but it appeared most often as the paper's subscription list shrank; thus one finds "East Waking up,"

"Awakening of Marine Transport Workers," "Awakening of Steel Workers," "The Awakening of the Workers of the San Joaquin Valley," and, a bit anxiously as the authorities prevented IWW meetings from taking place, "Workers, It's Time To Wake Up!" (see Supplement). It hardly needs to be added that the alarm clock was usually the radicals. This theme, the third major element in their self-image, is "vanguardism."

There are two reasons why we cannot consider this metaphor simply an automatically-used device with little content. First, many articles and speeches that used the wake-up metaphor sustained it at length, with variations. For example, Joseph E. Cohen wrote, "The sleeper has awakened. But his first movements are awkward; he stumbles and falls. Yet he renews his exertions; he strives on step by step; his eyes become accustomed to the light. It cannot be long before he will stand erect and snap his chains!" The subject here was a strike in Philadelphia. Debs, writing to a black leader, explained that "to awaken the negro, the same as the white man, who works for a living, to open his eyes and to educate him along true lines is now the great problem to which the Socialist party is giving itself with all the means at its command." As to the white workers, Debs said in 1904 that they were "just beginning to awaken from the torpor of the centuries (applause). The most hopeful sign of the time is that from the dull, dim eye of the proletaire there shoots forth the first gleam of intelligence, the first signal that he is waking up." [59]

Obviously not all the implications of the "awakening" and "asleep" metaphors were conscious, yet unless we assume their presence in the minds of the users their ubiquity is inexplicable. In theory, the difference between perceiving someone as mistaken and perceiving him as asleep is merely the difference between a literal and a metaphorical statement of the same thought. But so far as the perceiver's attitude is concerned, there is a world of difference. In the first case dialogue is possible; in the second, not. The views of a sleeper need not be taken seriously (unless they are dreams of liberation), nor, it should be stressed, are those of the awakener subject to critical scrutiny. As Peter Berger points out in a discussion of a currently popular phrase, this attitude involves "what one may call the hierarchical view of consciousness. . . . There is . . . an affinity between 'consciousness raising' and the Marxist concept of 'false consciousness.' There too the intellectual identified with the 'vanguard' lays claim to a cognitively privileged status. . . . If the hierarchical view of consciousness simply referred to levels of information on specific topics, there would be no need to quarrel with it. . . . [But] those who employ the concept in their rhetoric usually see themselves as genuine democrats, close to the throbbing life of the 'masses,' and emphatically 'antielitist.'"[60] The second reason for our taking the awakening metaphor seriously is that the English language is rich enough to have supplied these writers and orators with whatever metaphors best expressed their thoughts and feelings, and, although some came to use this locution unthinkingly, they were following the lead of others for whom it was one of several related metaphors that, combined, expressed a basic element in their self-image.

Of these, a second very important category originated in military usage. Class society was war, the proletariat an army, its officer corps the SLP, SP, or IWW, and a strike a battlefield. A third category of ubiquitous metaphors was borrowed from the field of education: labor unions were "the kindergarten of the proletarian movement"; the radicals were the teachers who must fit their instruction to the level of the pupils, offering the simplest—bread-and-butter—lessons first, and only later proceeding to more scientific explanations. The military and educational metaphors were combined in the favorite word *drill*—i.e., it was the task of the class-conscious vanguard to drill the workers in discipline and correct theory. This metaphor is especially interesting in that it is sometimes impossible to tell whether the image is of the drill sergeant or the teacher; quite likely both.[61]

When we peer behind the metaphors to discover why some seemed so natural as to become ingroup jargon, the double meaning of *drill* turns out to be significant. In the users' self-image the roles of drill sergeant and teacher were fused—to be a vanguard a movement had to be both organizer and purveyor of truth, leader both in the present battles and of the post-"war" peace. The double image created problems, however. An army could not consist only of officers. Yet the necessity of leadership clashed with the tendencies toward egalitarianism implicit in these writers' animus against capitalism for its supposed elitism.

It has become customary to regard the Wobblies as consistently anti-leadership. They deliberately filled the jails during the free-speech fights in the far West and, when the authorities asked who their leaders were, replied, "We are all leaders!" and demanded to be arrested. The facts are correct but the antileadership inference is not. Dozens of articles in IWW papers show that the Wobblies regarded themselves as the leaders of the unorganized working class. But the leadership principle operated as fully within the IWW as it did within the SLP and SP. As Melvyn Dubofsky notes, it "even took over George[s] Sorel's syndicalist concept of the militant minority." [62] The word *even* is misleading, for the concept of the militant minority did not conflict with other Wobbly principles; it was implicit in the organization's very reason for being.

This does not mean all Wobblies accepted it easily; in fact, some controversy arose over how to distinguish between leadership and elitism. On the organizational level the problem took the form of the question of centralization versus local autonomy. On the ideological level—the one that concerns us here—it went to the very heart of the Wobblies' images of themselves and of John Q. Worker. [63] The IWW, of course, had a problem that the two socialist parties did not, for it aimed to be a union as well as a radical vanguard. Therefore a large majority of its recruits had to be unawakened workers who would join for the same reasons that would induce them to join any other union—the hope of obtaining more pay, shorter hours, and better working conditions. The IWW had to include a rank and file at a far "lower" level of ideological awareness than the SLP's or SP's membership; consequently it had to develop a theory of vanguards within vanguards. "It is well and good," said the *Industrial Worker*, "to tell the average wage slave that you are building up an organization which in time will take over the means of transportation and distribution and administer them for the workers. But if you want the worker to join your organization just tell him that you are organizing for the purpose of getting more beefsteak. That's what will strike him. You bet it will. Heap savvy beefsteak revolution." [64]

It did not, however, follow that in time the entire working class, or even a majority of it, would rise to the level of the current vanguard, for, said the *Industrial Worker*, "the majority is always a hopeless proposition . . . [and] has in all history persecuted the revolutionary minority." [65] On a later occasion the same paper used a metaphor that revealed more than it could have realized, when in an editorial entitled "Leadership" it explained, "A flock of sheep led by a lion are as bad as a flock of lions led by a sheep. What is aimed at is a body in which all are active fighters, fighting collectively, but each feeling that the battle depends upon their [sic] own personal efforts. . . . To deny leadership is to fall back on the utopian theory that all men are equal in ability and enterprise. The I.W.W. seeks equality in nothing but opportunity." [66] "Democracy," it declared a few months later, "is only a beautiful theory. It has never been a fact. . . . With a militant minority to direct the efforts of those who are in line with the organization, but who do not yet fully comprehend its purposes[,] the admission of new members is a source of strength. . . . Within the militant minority, and ahead of their fellows in thought and activity, are still a smaller body. They are the minority within the minority. . . . The I.W.W. is designed to bear the same relation to the rest of the workers outside it, as its militant authority does to the new recruits." [67]

De Leon split with the IWW in 1908 over issues other than the principle of the militant minority, for on this he never wavered. At the IWW's second convention, in 1906, he argued that the IWW could not expect to organize all the workers and in fact would not have to, to make the revolution; if it recruited just the militant and dedicated minority that had always made the revolutions, "the indifferent mass" would follow. [68] One expression of the SLP's militant-minority theory is in an article written in 1897 by Henry L. Slobodin, who later went over to the SP. He argued that the size of the vanguard party was not a crucial determinant of the forces of a revolution if economic conditions and intellectual development were suitable. Indeed, if plebiscites had been held before the English, American, and French revolutions, the overwhelming majority of the people would have voted against overthrowing the government. It was the task of the clear-sighted minority to diagnose the illness of the body politic and apply the remedy. "The passive majority looked on, where it was not forcibly led" to take sides. It was therefore a principle in "political science that, no matter what the form of government may be, active minorities rule passive majorities. . . . Socialism will be sustained by the Reason of Impartial Philosophy, by the Ideal of the Poet, by the Logic of History, and by PHYSICAL FORCE. . . . The Socialists are the makers of history for the time being." He concluded that only 30 percent of the American people need be for the revolution for the socialists to take power. [69]

When Slobodin switched to the SP he did not have to abandon his militant-minority thesis, for that hospitable organization included both minoritarians and majoritarians. One of the former, Isidor Ladoff, divided the human race into philistines, kickers, and cranks. The philistines, the vast majority, lived by tradition, authority, and precedent, and became furious when "forcibly aroused from their mental lethargy" by the kickers and cranks. Kickers, though instinctively rebellious, were only half awake, but did not object to being aroused. The cranks were the innovators, the "advance guard" and "controlling force" of history; "they supply consciousness and clear vision . . . and . . . drag the philistine humanity forward." Hillquit agreed that the workers "need[ed] guidance, cohesion and support" by the vanguard but felt sure that the socialists' message would "appeal to the workers" (no limiting adjective); "OUR MOVEMENT CANNOT SUCCEED UNLESS WE HAVE THE MASSES OF THE AMERICAN PEOPLE WITH US." In fact, it could not win in the face of the "opposition or even passive indifference on the part of the bulk of the laboring classes." The *Call* agreed with Hillquit; "we never can have Socialism," it editorialized in 1908, "until a majority of men are Socialists—until they have gained an intelligent conception of the Socialist philosophy and can interpret its vital significance."[70]

The reader will have noticed that the three organizations' positions on the militant-minority thesis correspond to their attitudes toward John Q. Worker as described in Chapter V. They agreed on vanguardism, but those who held the dimmest view of John Q. Worker found most reason to regard him as unnecessary to the revolution. Others on the left solved the problem, which this view obviously presented to any sincere champion of oppressed workers, by going to the opposite extreme of painting John Q. Worker in mythic colors that covered up the absence of a theory. Except for the mythicists, it was the SP right wing that saw him as most easily aroused and hence could see him also as indispensable. But that belief was as aprioristic as that of most elitists, for it rested on the highly rationalistic assumption that the economic "facts" alone would make most workers receptive to the radicals' message.

Will Herberg sums up this issue accurately when he points out that

All—socialists and syndicalists, gradualists and revolutionaries—have agreed on seeing the movement as at once a militant crusade to usher in the new society and a prefiguration of the future society within the present social order: as at once, so to speak, both the Saving Remnant and the beginnings of the Kingdom of Heaven. . . . In answer to the question "Who makes the revolution?" a large number of American socialists—including the I.W.W., left-wing elements in the Socialist Party, and most of the early communists—insisted that the dynamic factor was a revolutionary elite, the "conscious minority" in the frank syndicalist phrase. . . . The predominant feeling, however, has always been that the revolutionary act would somehow be the work of the masses, of the "vast majority of the producers." By and large, it may be said that the more radical the sentiment, the more it has inclined toward some form of elite doctrine; only gradualism, in fact, has been able to give much concrete meaning to the "mass" theory through its conception of the revolution as the accumulation of piecemeal reforms achieved through the democratic process.[71]

Herberg's use of the words *feeling* and *sentiment*, whether or not he deliberately chose them in preference to *theory*, suggests the uneasiness that even some on the far left felt on account of their own vanguardism. From time to time we even find one radical accusing another of having appointed himself the savior of the masses; perhaps this indicates that the problem was conscious even if awareness of it was evoked mainly by polemical needs.[72] One of the most revealing polemics went as follows:

A thousand and one "saviours" are found in all directions at present, trying to get the working class to place its destiny in their hands—in the hands of politicians, reformers, sectarians and other inconsequentials and incompetents, from the middle and professional class. All of these "saviours" strike the same attitude toward the wage slave: the slave is ignorant; he lacks initiative; is too narrow and bigoted in his ideas; needs a broadminded and capable leader; I and my creed fill the bill. Don't depend upon yourself; you don't know enough to manage your own affairs; put me on the job as your saviour, or rather recognize me as such since I have already assumed the role, and we'll have the cow operating the commonwealth or something else just as lovely in the near future. The siren song of the "labor saviour" is doubtless very alluring to many slaves. It must be so, else the grazing for such cattle would not be as good as it is, in the pastures of the labor movement. . . . Yet the slaves should have learned from their own experience, if not from history, to steer clear of such a dangerous illusion.

The true leader, concluded the writer, comes from the working class, embodies its tendencies, and "never dreams of being a 'saviour.'" If the reader perceives this screed as an accurate portrait of Wobbly vanguardism, he is right, except that it is an unwitting self-portrait; it is from an editorial in *Solidarity*.[73]

The problem could not be solved by polemics, for it inhered in all varieties of radical theories, including the part that was earlier called *essentialism*. So long as the radicals perceived themselves and their organizations as embodiments of the workers' future course, they had also to perceive the workers' present organizations as contrary to their members' own interests. The nonradical unions were not, to some of these writers, true working-class organizations, even though all their members were workers. Algie M. Simons reasoned the same way with respect to political parties: what defined a working-class party was not that its members were workers but that its principles accorded with the working class's interests, expressing the mission of that class, which of course only the radical minority understood. The initiative for the formation of such a party did not have to come from workers.[74] An editorial in the *Industrial Worker* concurred, with respect to unions:

The American Federation of Labor is not the labor movement. . . . It has a membership that is but a small percentage of the working class. . . . It in no way voices the sentiment of the aggressive minority who would overthrow capitalism, nor do its ideas appeal to the vast majority now outside of any organization. . . . The masters perpetrated it, nursed it, and foisted it upon the labor world. . . . In contrast to the A.F. of L. the I.W.W. . . . strikes direct for the goal of industrial freedom. It is the voice of the militant worker and is destined to be not only the labor movement of America and the world, but also the means of carrying on production when the wage system with all its rotten supports, including the A.F. of L., has been swept into oblivion.[75]

The first two sentences are true. The others, however, make it clear that the writer would not consider the AFL a bona fide labor organization even if it comprised the majority of the working class, for he ascertained the genuineness of a labor organization not by the degree to which its policies met the approval of its membership but by the degree to which it was revolutionary even if they were not. In effect he was criticizing the AFL for being democratic.

Those who possessed the theory "represented" the workers even if only the former knew it. Lucy Parsons evoked no objections when she told the other founders of the IWW that each individual present represented all the toilers of the earth. Debs denounced the craft unions as an "unmitigated evil to the working class." Only late in this article did he mention the rank and file at all, and then to say that it was the victim of its misleaders, and he added that "it is in the name of the rank and file that I write." Debs was writing not of the disfranchised and unorganized, unskilled workers whose wishes might be difficult to ascertain, but of members of AFL unions whose votes kept the misleaders in office and only a minority of whom ever voted for Debs.[76]

That Parsons and Debs could perceive themselves as representing the entire working class or speaking in its name bespeaks not closeness to but isolation from it. Those socialists who were personally involved in the labor movement were the most aware of the variety of actual workers' beliefs and hopes.[77] The SP's opposition to the war is, of course, the best proof of relative isolation from organized labor, and it was the least isolated of the three organizations. It was free in April 1917 to stand on the principle of proletarian internationalism because it was, in Martin Diamond's words, "unburdened by the need to protect mass institutions or by participation in government as were many of the European parties."[78]

It is hard to see how people not in intimate contact with workers and their thoughts and problems could have perceived themselves as the teachers of the workers and destined to be accepted as such. Yet the evidence that they did so perceive themselves is abundant. A socialist journalist commenting upon a convention of the National Negro Business League explained: "We Socialists feel that the most important truth for negroes to grasp is the fact that their problem is the problem of all the exploited and disinherited, . . . and therefore we can accept as a leader of the negro race only one who has this understanding of the problem of his race." A delegate to the 1906 convention of the IWW opposed the motion to delete the political clause from the constitution, on the ground that "if you adopt this amendment it will give them [the workers] a license to be divided." Debs wrote in 1902 that, during the period in which the AFL was evolving into a true—i.e., socialist—labor movement, he favored the SP's policy of "allowing it to manage its own internal affairs." The SLP's labor affiliate, the STLA, was less patient: "the American working class," intoned one leader, "cannot be left to the mercy of the leaders it has had. . . . The whole of this labor movement must become saturated with Socialism, must be placed under Socialist control." In the meantime, those workers who were radicalized by socialists within the old unions frequently fell back under the influence of conservative leaders, he explained. "We saw, therefore, that it was necessary[,] in order to keep the recruits we were gaining, to remove them from an atmosphere hostile to us, and to place them in a Socialist atmosphere"—the STLA. And a prominent member of the SP, after pouring vitriol on the "sheep," "cattle," and "twelve million big American six-footers" who "toil on in a trance," asked, "Who shall speak the electric word to rouse these millions to a hot, blazing consciousness of their wrongs . . . ? Those and those only who are already roused from the cursed trance that numbs and stuns the mind of the working class—the Socialists! Five hundred thousand . . . evangels to that 'dark continent,' the working class intellect of this country."[79]

"We make no violent professions of friendship for you," added another SP leader in 1907, "for the reason that we are of you, a part of your class, workingmen like yourselves, and WE SPEAK TO YOU AS WORKINGMEN TO WORKINGMEN. We do not regard you as a lot of helpless creatures who must depend upon what we promise to do for you. We speak to you as full grown men, not as a flock of silly sheep who need a shepherd. We speak to you as people who have the power to help themselves, and who need no shepherd or saviors." Whether or not the author of this piece wrote it to cancel the effect of Grace Potter's patronizing article in the same journal exactly a year earlier (see Chapter V, Documentary Excursus I, item No. 9), he evidently did not consider it ironic that a proletarian party's spokesman had to make this disclaimer in order to get his fellow workers to learn the lesson he had to teach them. He was not the only socialist troubled by that problem, however; a few months before, the *Worker* pleaded with socialists to show more respect for their pupils, for "if some workingmen are slow to learn what we would teach them, let us not forget that all the institutions in society have had their influence in shaping their beliefs to accord with capitalist society." We should have "infinite faith" in their wisdom and capacity to change the world, the editorial concluded.[80]

Yet despite the best of intentions, some writers' metaphors betrayed them. Franklin Wentworth, for example, likened the working class to a rabbit about to be devoured by either a big dog or a little dog—*i.e.*, the Republican party or the Democratic party. Neither the dogs nor the rabbit assumed it had the right to live. But the growth of the socialist vote signaled "the coming of the rabbit to consciousness."[81] Wentworth did not explain how even a conscious rabbit would stand a chance in that predicament. The significance of the metaphor in the present context is that it indicates that the radical was the protector as well as the teacher of the working class. But in so doing it reinforced the image of John Q. Worker's essential passivity.

IV

The radicals' self-perception was one part of a three-part picture, including a particular perception of John Q. Worker and of their nonradical rivals for hegemony over him. The triptych is neatly summed up by Linda K. Kerber in a comment on the Protestant missionaries to the Indians in the nineteenth century: they were "apparently unaware that the Indians' lives included any meaningful relationships except with the missionaries themselves on the one hand and with whiskey dealers on the other."[82] By sheer coincidence Kerber's point, made with reference to Indians, is illustrated by Kate Richards O'Hare's article quoted herein (see page 223). It is appropriate at this point to draw one more conclusion from that remarkable essay: it is one of many evidences that the radical theorists were not as far from the conventional view of their generation as they thought. Their ideological deviation, extreme on certain issues and nonexistent on others—and, on still others, located on all points in between—was deviation within a framework set by the conventional ideologies. For example, O'Hare was arguing against racists and for understanding of the Indians' plight. Neither she nor those whose attitudes she opposed could know how close the two sides were and what large ground they shared. The only observers who can know that are those who do not share the assumptions that both took so much for granted that they did not recognize that they shared anything whatever. Modern historians who see the radicals as links in a chain stretching through time to the present, assuming they have more in common with their radical ancestors and descendants than with their own contemporaries (and who see current radicals in the same light) miss the most important fact—their time-boundedness (and that of current radicals too). For it was not a long-lived System called capitalism, "essentially" the same through all its stages, that lay at the foundation of the radicals' world view. What lay there was the same for them as for everyone else of their own generation—the general ideological and cultural milieu of their time and place. It shaped the radicals' perception of what they called capitalism, the features they ascribed to it, and their image of the radical.

Neither they nor their class enemies foresaw the reforms that were to come in later years within the capitalist economic framework. The capitalists and their spokesmen turned out to have been shortsighted; they could have conceded more to their employees than they realized. But the radicals believed these transitory policies were scientifically discovered, structural elements of the System. In sum, for all the claims to scientific grounding, their analyses perched on nothing more substantial than their class enemies' narrow perception of their own class interest. Or, to put the point differently, the radicals mistook the capitalists' intransigence for the voice of historic necessity.

Kate Richards O'Hare thought of herself as an iconoclast on the Indian question, and in a sense she was, but we know that her idols and those she smashed belonged within the same temple. As to other issues on which the radicals differed to a greater degree from their contemporaries, there too it was the conventional world views that set the terms of their dissent. They were, in an ironic sense, more closely tied to the conventional American world view than was John Q. Worker (usually a recent immigrant), who often did not even know what the conventional world view of Americans was, and who rarely joined the Americans' ideological debates.

VIII   The Radicals and
American Democracy

According to Arthur Bestor, the typical communitarian of the early nineteenth century "conceived of his experimental community not as a mere blueprint of the future but as an actual, complete, functioning unit of the new social order."[1] The future society would not be the experimental community writ large; it would comprise many small, largely self-sufficient communities. By the 1880s, however, improvements in transportation and communication and the development of a national economy had made the prospect of a countryside dotted with almost self-sufficient and self-governing communities obsolete, and in so doing had created the problem of the relation of scale to democracy. The radical organizations studied here were, in some respects, communities like those Bestor wrote about: membership in them was voluntary, they were small enough for each member to "count," and they possessed a strong bond in the form of a commitment to a radical creed. But unlike the antebellum experiments, these organizations were intended as models for the society as a whole rather than for duplicated segments within it. The radicals had no way of knowing that what they would have abolished, if they had achieved power, were the very conditions in American society that made it possible for their organizations to exist as democratically run, voluntary groups bound in fellowship by a distinct ideology. For the conditions that made these things possible were the smallness that gave every member a significant role, the feeling of "we-ness" that resulted from the deviance of their ideologies, and the opportunity for dissenters to withdraw without being exiled from their country.

By aiming to eradicate, for purposes of public policy, the distinctions that made the United States a pluralistic society, and to make everyone define himself primarily as a worker, they were inadvertently designing a polity in which public policy could not be decided from below. The word *inadvertently* must be emphasized; no one at that time could have foreseen what a truly mass, totalitarian society would be like. Furthermore, the radical organizations of the 1890–1917 period, unlike the antebellum communitarians, did not assume authority over their adherents' family and social relationships, that is, over the private sphere. Hence the democratically arrived at will of the group possessed far less scope in the radical organizations than in the experimental communities, which tolerated no wall between the private and public spheres, no privacy, no multiplicity of memberships for each person. What saved those communities from being tyrannous was also the aforementioned possibility of secession, a possibility that does not exist in a society that is the organization or community writ large.

The relation among these three themes—democracy within the radical organizations, their attitudes toward democracy within American society, and the connection between democracy and the private sphere—must remain largely a matter of speculation. The radicals paid no attention to it as a distinct problem and little attention to its component issues.

I

The radicals, as we have seen, perceived themselves as possessors of the true doctrine—most called it a science—to which they must awaken the workers. Many thought this science enabled them to predict the course of social evolution. Someone who knows nothing about these organizations could reasonably conclude that they constituted a unitary movement guided by a single body of doctrine. This was also implied by their common perception of a unitary capitalist System and their certainty that the workers—or, in the case of the IWW, the unskilled workers— had a single common interest in destroying it. All the radicals were certain that true theory and effective practice could not in the long run conflict. As De Leon said, "Large masses cannot feel and move as one if they are in error. Error is manifold; it scatters. Truth alone is single; it alone unites."[2] Yet, with doctrinal unity implied in the radicals' very perceptions of their society, themselves, and their mission, and at the same time seemingly unattainable, it is pertinent to ask, what were their attitudes toward doctrinal diversity itself? Where did they draw the line between unimportant issues on which disagreement was tolerable or even useful, and important ones on which unanimity was essential?

A year after the IWW was born it was still unclear to some leading members what industrial unionism meant. At the 1906 convention, a delegate rose to say, "What I want to know is what is an industrial union?" Next year another delegate asked for an explanation of "what has created so much confusion in this convention, namely, Karl Marx's Economics." Another objected, saying he cared nothing for Marx; we are here, he declared, to push the organization and get results. A third took offense at the sneers at Marx. A fourth had no objection to Marx; let those who wished to study him do so, but there are "as many different brands of Marx as there are of Heinz's pickles, 57 brands." The job of the IWW, he added, was to organize the working class. "There is no need of our floating in the air. . . . It is well that the working class has a knowledge of Marx," but "we do not want, when we are here for the purpose of doing practical work towards building up our organization . . . to be treated with discourses on Marx."[3] Yet the questions continued; virtually every issue of *Solidarity*, year after year, contained at least one article discussing basic theory. By the middle of 1913 the issues were filled with examinations of the very meaning and mission of the organization. The problem became critical when not only the SP but also many thoughtful Wobblies decided that advocacy of sabotage must be repudiated. The IWW's tolerance of advocates of sabotage and even violence had attracted to it some people whose membership and influence increased the confusion about what the organization's basic theory was. Wobbly writers repeatedly explained that the IWW was not anarchist; but there were members who were anarchists. Some argued that it was not syndicalist, although other members said it was. Some called it socialist; others implicitly denied this by predicting it would usher in a society in which each factory would be owned by its own workers rather than by the nation. As Vernon Jensen writes, "The mark of the I.W.W.

was that it had no 'line.' . . . There was a wide variety of notions all passing as the I.W.W. position or program, when the fact of the matter is that the I.W.W. had no central program except destruction of the hated capitalist system."[4]

Neither did it have an official attitude toward doctrinal diversity. It contained members of the SLP in its first three years, as well as others who also yearned for unanimity. But it also contained, for its entire lifetime, anarchists and near-anarchists who abhorred the very idea of a central headquarters or authority. Furthermore, its articulate members always included many who were stridently anti-intellectual, and therefore it attracted more of such people. Some of them had no patience with theory of any sort but merely kept repeating that they were in the IWW to wage the class war.[5] Others were doctrinaires, each believing passionately that his own theory should guide the IWW but none of whom would accept a majority vote as determining which theory would in fact guide it. The IWW recognized no ideologue authoritative enough to set forth an orthodox theory of the organization that included a theory concerning theory itself.

The SLP's attitude toward doctrinal diversity changed over the years. When it had the secular-socialist field to itself, its criticisms of wrong-thinking people were calm and self-confident. In the pages of *The People* during the early 1890s one finds few expressions of contempt for the sleeping workers, no polemics against other varieties of socialists, frequent calm denunciations of Gompers and other labor leaders, and many attacks on Democrats, Populists, and reformers in general. By the end of 1895 the paper's tone had become shrill and dogmatic, for the long series of factional fights and expulsions had begun. By April 1896 the party and the paper were equating theoretical error with disloyalty.[6] In the issue of June 20, 1897, De Leon accused the current dissidents (the immediate issue was whether the party should control its Yiddish-language press) of secretly wishing to be free to print articles contrary to party doctrine and policy. Repeating the telltale phrases "conspiracy" and "deliberate acts," he stressed that the party must be able to establish order or it would be destroyed.[7] Two years later the principal dissidents were the "Kangaroos," who disagreed with the party line mainly over trade-union policy and had also been alienated by De Leon's dogmatism. These eventually joined with other socialists to found the SP. To

De Leon and his supporters, the Kangaroos were not socialists with different views; they were "a conspiracy of long standing against the
Party," with secret motives, who "undertook the job" of destroying the
party by destroying its national paper *The People*. And since De Leon
equated the SLP with the socialist movement, these plotters were therefore antisocialist.[8]

But De Leon did not explain the doctrinal dissension solely in personal terms. It was, rather, "The Class Struggle within the Party." "We
recognize," he said, "the fact that material interests determine men's
views. When we apply this scientific principle, every capitalist numb-
scull [sic] politician charges us with being 'personal.' The charge of 'personality' should never deter us." The material interests in the present
case were the dissidents' desire for alliance with "pure-and-simple"
unions. "Every pure and simpler with a job or expecting a job on a label
committee or strike committee; every pure and simpler who fears for his
sick and death benefit; all such are incommoded by the [Socialist Trades
and Labor] Alliance; like veritable caricatures of the middle class they
clutch their 'illusion of property;' scared to death about losing it, they
are willing to let the fakir ride them and to stand by him." Then, listing
the foreign-born leaders of the conspiracy, he showed "it was no accident that" each of them was more interested in his homeland than in
the United States and that some planned to return.[9] De Leon was not
the last polemicist to discover that an environmentalist psychology
could promote an *ad hominem* attack to a defense of the people's interests. His certainty that the dissidents had bad motives arose primarily,
however, from his certainty that his views were so obviously correct that
no intelligent man could sincerely dissent from them.[10] And because
they presented themselves to the public as socialists, the SLP's worst enemies were other radicals.

It followed that agreement on all important questions was a sine qua
non for a true socialist party. De Leon said as much:

If . . . the S.L.P. is what it claims and has proven itself to be, then it cannot,
neither may it, brook a divided allegiance. The conclusion is irrefutable: that organization, whose principles and tactics are in any essential particular at vari-
ance with the Party, is wrong. The same person cannot belong to both. . . . The
surest way to insure dissension . . . is for men to blur the lines that divide them.

The ERROR, on which either, or both, may build, would thus never be discovered; nor the TRUTH, that either may hold, become apparent to the other. The path to Harmony lies across the sharpest demarcation of differences. The sharper the dividing line, the clearer will both *error* and *truth* transpire. Thus what seems to be the course of DIVISION is in fact the course of UNION, what seems to be the course of DISRUPTION is in fact the course of HARMONY. . . . Socialism is the veritable harbinger of harmony.[11]

As to the SP, David Shannon correctly calls it "a collection of quite diverse and often warring groups, held together only by what proved later to be a poor adhesive, common hostility to industrial capitalism."[12] Just as the IWW's extremely militant tactics attracted the sort of recruits whose presence raised questions about whether its fundamental theory could accommodate terrorism, so the SP's tactical moderation attracted the sort of recruits whose presence raised the question whether the party's theory could accommodate demands that would barely be considered even reformist.[13] That the socialism advocated by the SP did not come to mean the ideals of the family farmers or of the skilled craftsmen or of the middle-class professionals or of the Christian clergymen or of any other large component of the party was due merely to its heterogeneity. The party was, in this sense, the nation writ small, a propaganda field for members with strong convictions. William English Walling, for instance, urged his comrades to replace Marx with Veblen as basic theorist. Jack London preached the law of the survival of the physically strongest, which would not be repealed by the revolution. May Wood Simons, speaking for the Woman's Committee on Education in 1912, announced that "domestic training is necessary today for all girls." The Resolutions Committee at the 1908 convention blamed the evils of alcoholism on capitalism and said that excessive drinking weakened the workers in their struggle. Charlotte Perkins Gilman advocated what the 1930s would call a Civilian Conservation Corps, for blacks "who do not progress," in a setting that would remove "the strain of personal initiative and responsiblity."[14] All these suggestions and scores of others bore implications for the party's guiding theory. As to the relationship between socialism and the nature of the universe, an exasperated book reviewer described his party's membership thus, in recommending a new work by materialist Ernest Untermann:

In a party where every third person is a spiritualist or swedenborgian or theosophist or seventh day adventist or divine healer or astrologer or a believer in the great gospel or "message" that "Man is God" or "I am it" or "I am that I am," the appearance of [Untermann's] "Science and Revolution" is a boon to make one wish that a few of the defunct gods were still alive that we might give them thanks. It would, no doubt, be wholly impracticable to make a careful study of such a work as this a condition of party membership, but it is to be hoped the time is not far distant when some such test will be applied to party orators, soap box and others, before they undertake the enlightenment of an ignorant public.[15]

The SP's attitude toward doctrinal diversity was shaped by the party's origin. Some of its founders had rebelled against the doctrinairism of the SLP—they called De Leon "the Pope." In its early months *The Call* (which spoke for them), like the early *People*, contained no polemics against other radicals, but preached socialism only in very general terms that all socialists could agree with. When the Reverend Charles Stelzle gibed that there were fifty-seven varieties of socialism, the editor retorted that there were fifty-seven varieties of religion too. Besides, he added, it was not true; there were socialist parties with different names in different countries, sometimes more than one in a country, "with considerable friction between them." Yet they met at International Congresses, and on important occasions they acted in unison. "All are clearly recognizable as divisions of the same army, advancing against a common enemy, advancing along slightly different lines, but under a common plan of campaign." The SP does not, he went on, waste "its strength on internecine warfare" and thus fall prey to sectarianism. It debates freely yet retains "an effective unity of action."[16] It should be emphasized that the differences in theory between the SP and the SLP were rather small, probably not large enough to warrant two parties; or, if they had been, not such as to preclude their working in friendly rivalry as the editorialist said the European parties were doing. What principally divided the American SP and SLP were their respective attitudes toward doctrinal disagreement. Each party's attitude matched its perception of the nature of American society. Although both perceived a unitary System presided over by one class with one overall ideology, within that unitary reality most of the SP's theorists perceived distinctions and complications that were real and important. Members of the

SP generally thought that the true interpretation could best be discovered by free debate.

Of course, this latitudinarianism resulted in the party's containing some members who opposed latitudinarianism. What Stelzle ridiculed some socialists denounced. *The Call* criticized those comrades who insisted that nothing short of the full program of socialism had any value. "Let us not," it concluded, "in our eagerness to hold fast to the cardinal principles of Socialism, make the mistake of . . . saying: 'He who is not for us is against us.'" (It should be recalled that Debs said just that.) "Let us not make the mistake of saying that everything which is not Socialism in its completeness is bad or worthless. Let us not make of our movement a sect, segregated from the affairs of life and living only in the pious contemplation of a beautiful future. . . . Let us have our ultimate goal so clearly in mind, and understand so well the road by which it is to be reached, that we need not dread taking 'a step at a time,' but can take each step with the assurance that it leads us toward that goal."[17]

When the majority of articulate members, three years later, moved toward drawing the boundary of tolerance so as to exclude William D. Haywood, *The Call* insisted that it was the Haywoodites who were trying to impose doctrinal orthodoxy, as when Big Bill announced that no socialist could be a trade unionist. Earlier, during the long controversy leading up to Haywood's recall from the National Executive Committee, Local Saugus (Massachusetts) called for a referendum to recall Victor Berger, Job Harriman, Morris Hillquit, and John Spargo. *The Call* ridiculed the comrades who, apparently thinking that socialism was a mathematical formula to be accepted or rejected, went heresy-hunting:

Comrade Haywood, who is a member of the National Executive Committee, seems[—]like the rest of us—afflicted with the zeal to have everything uniform, regular, orthodox and right. . . . And, on the other side, there are Comrades for whom Haywood is not good enough. Evidently we have arrived at the point where the following are essential: No speaker should speak until he has been examined, not as to his fitness, but as to his orthodoxy. His orthodoxy shall consist of his being revolutionary and conservative. . . . All members shall be obliged to believe in contradictory things, and if they do not they shall be driven from the party, and if they do they shall be expelled for heresy. . . . Instead of trying to bring people into the party we must bend all our efforts to driving people out or keeping them out. . . . We cannot disguise from ourselves that we are reaping the fruits of our endless and silly dissensions. At the present time, when the [election] campaign should be in full swing, when we should all be facing the enemy and pushing forward our line of advances, it is a fact that the campaign languishes, that it is almost impossible to get any work done. . . . As many good contributors to The Call have pointed out, our recruits more speedily learn our petty, worthless, internal politics than they learn about Socialist politics as a whole.[18]

But where was the line between silly dissension and valuable dialogue? The editorialist was trying hard to defend freedom of discussion and the value of open debate, rather than one side in the particular debate. Events proved this to be an impossible position to maintain, for, his sarcasm notwithstanding, he had unwittingly noted the consequences of a real dilemma.

During the months in which the referendum on Haywood's recall was in progress, Dr. M. Baranov (whose articles in the Yiddish socialist paper The Forward were sometimes published in translation in The Call) denied that free speech was at issue. We do not, he argued, propose to let Emma Goldman or Samuel Gompers propagandize from inside our party; hence the charge that we are cutting off Haywood's freedom of speech is nonsense. "A Socialist party is like an army in war time. On the field of battle all have to be united, not only on the purpose of the war—to destroy the enemy—but also on the plan as to how to accomplish the purpose. Every general who goes around among the soldiers and ridicules the accepted plans of war is a traitor. He demoralizes the army, he befogs the officers and soldiers. He weakens their belief in themselves, their courage, and thereby helps the enemy. He deserves to be shot—for the welfare of the entire army and the war." The SP does not shoot traitors, but it should exclude them from leadership. "Free discussion? With the greatest of pleasure. As much as you want, only not over the existence of our party. And to allow free discussion over the necessity of political action is the same as to allow a discussion on the question: Has our party a right to exist?" A political party that does not engage in political action is like a union that does not believe in strikes. Yet that is what Haywood proposes for our party.[19]

De Leon could not have said it better. All the radicals used military metaphors, but De Leon most often, as would be expected of one who insisted on military conformity in the face of a united enemy. Yet there is a difference between Baranov's and De Leon's positions on theoretical diversity; the SP members who voted against Haywood in the referendum did not thereby transform the SP into another SLP. Haywood was indeed becoming an opponent of political action, and Baranov was right—a political party could not oppose political action. It could, and did, continue to include advocates of a wide variety of theories on other issues after the Haywoodites had departed. On doctrinal issues the SP continued to be impaled on the "right" as the SLP was on the "left" horn of a series of theoretical dilemmas.

A similar contrast between the SP and the IWW was brought to light by the controversy over Haywood, who for a time was a leading member of both. Whereas the SP dealt with the problem of developing a consensual theory by means of debate, the IWW dealt with it by means of power struggles. (This refers to dominant tendencies only; the SP too experienced power struggles, and the IWW too debated theory.) There was therefore more continuity in the SP than in the IWW. For where theoretical disagreements are handled by debate and voting, minority theories retain potential legitimacy; where they are handled by power shifts, neither the majority nor the minority theories possess potential legitimacy to their opponents. In the light of this difference between the two organizations, Haywood's refusal to argue his case during the recall episode takes on significance: he was acting within the SP the way Wobblies acted within the IWW, recognizing no legitimacy but only power. This is shown by another passage in the *Call* editorial on Haywood quoted above: "Haywood is, of course, not active in Socialist politics, in working class politics, though he is active in Socialist party politics, that is, in the internal matters of the organization, and in spite of a certain personal libertarianism as regards his own conduct and own ideas, he has not shown any degree of liberalism and understanding where the opinions and actions of others are concerned. . . . Comrade Haywood would probably be the last person in the world to claim that he considered Socialist political theories of any importance to him." At the end of the long referendum *The Call* again expressed regret that Haywood had chosen not to defend himself. "Either he regarded an explanation as uncalled for, or the demand for it an impertinence, or he had no time or he did not care." And this despite the desire voiced by many fair-minded comrades to get the information to guide their votes. There is, the editor continued, no disgrace in opposing political action; there is, however, disgrace in lacking the respect that each member owes the party.[20] Thus the SP's vote, in delegitimating advocacy of violence, also condemned a type of intraparty behavior inconsistent with the party's way of handling differences of opinion.

The foregoing contrasts between each of the three organizations and the other two reveal that, on the question of the importance of theory, the IWW leaders stood on one side of a dividing line and the two socialist parties' leaders on the other. This distinction throws additional light on why first the SLP and then the SP became hostile to the IWW. Even though they disagreed over how intraparty theoretical disputes should be handled, the two parties agreed that theory itself was important. In fact, their opposite attitudes toward disagreement manifest this respect for theory equally. As was implied in the discussion of the debate between anti- and prointellectuals in Chapter V, the metaphor of "awakening" meant slightly different things to different radicals. The "anti-intellectual" minority in the SP leadership and most articulate Wobblies tended to assume that John Q. Worker was incipiently radical and that radical *organization* and *agitation* would soon show him the essentially revolutionary nature of what he dimly felt. Some, as we saw earlier in this chapter, considered debate over theory a luxury that could interfere with a radical's real job. The "prointellectuals" in the SLP and SP put more emphasis on *propaganda*, implicitly assuming that although John Q. Worker had revolutionary "instincts," they must be supplemented by a set of beliefs brought to him by bearers of true theory. This distinction is a matter of emphasis only, but it helps to explain why the IWW experienced power struggles where the SP experienced mainly doctrinal debates; why Wobbly leader Haywood did not deign to argue for his doctrine within the SP during the recall referendum; why most of De Leon's life as a socialist was spent in explaining Marxist theory to workers; and why most Wobbly leaders thought *their* time was better spent in organizing and agitation.

There is no reason to believe that the doctrinal wrangling was a major cause of the failure of all three organizations to recruit the millions of workers they sought. True, members complained in letters to the organizations' press that new recruits sometimes left in disgust when they found the older members more concerned about theoretical minutiae

than about propagating doctrine. Yet we cannot know whether these recruits were not outnumbered by others who relished such debates (this
does not apply, of course, to that majority of temporary recruits to the
IWW who were never radical). The contempt for the unawakened
worker and the theoretical disputes may even have held an attraction
for some whose old belief-systems had ceased to give meaning to their
lives and who had become receptive to socialism. These disputes and
essays could, for all we know, have symbolized to some recruits the
privilege of crossing the line between the unenlightened, on one hand,
and the possessors of the truth, the vanguard of the working class, the
heralds of the future, on the other.[21]

Yet few people could have joined any of these organizations solely
because of doctrinal agreement. Not only were the doctrines of the SP
and IWW unclear, but the organizations' reason for being was activism.
Many Americans doubtless accepted the basic tenets but felt no urge to
act on them and remained unaffiliated sympathizers. And inside the organizations, most theorizing was carried on with reference to practical
problems of agitation, propaganda, and tactics. In fact, most of it consisted of rationalizations for preformed approaches to practical problems.[22] The diversity of views on theory thus reflects, by and large, the
diversity of views on practical issues and, of course, differences in
temperament.

There was one exception to this subordination of theorizing to attitudes oriented toward tactical preferences—theorizing about the in-
eradicable distinctions of race and sex. The System-thinking that characterized the radicals and that produced their hope for a future society
containing a rather uniform population with perhaps minor cultural
variations, ran head-on into the ingrained approval, by many of them,
of race- and sex-defined social roles. Contrary to their opponents'
charges, the secular radicals' class theory was not a way of dividing the
people; it was a way of defining away distinctions. Their writings
abound in approving references to the American melting pot, in efforts
to show that ethnic differences were minor or temporary,[23] and in demonstrations of uniformities in different nations' histories. Yet, for most,
the universalist attitude stopped short when it touched women, and for
many, it did so when it touched nonwhites. The homogeneous future
society they looked forward to would be complicated by the persistence

of these two distinctions. They could not be erased by a definition having to do with a person's relation to the means of production. More important, many radicals could not *feel* that a woman worker or black worker was a worker first and a woman or black second, any more than most nonradicals could. This was not a contradiction in theory; it was a conflict between two feelings, one—the universalist—ratified by theory, and the other irrelevant to theory. The race and woman questions both affected the private sphere—the family and social relations, the realm in which feeling properly dominated—in a way that class theory did not. Hence all the earnest attempts that were made to bring economic and political reason to bear on these problems failed, so long as the private and public spheres remained distinct. That they remained so for most SP members manifests a limitation on the area within which their radical ideology and organization exerted authority over their lives. And to a modern reader who has learned of the horrors of totalism, that limitation has interesting implications, for within the area left free by the limitation of public-sphere authority both good and evil can flourish.

II

Before we examine the relations between the public and private spheres, however, we should ask the obvious question evoked by the radicals' inability to agree or unite: if *they* could not agree on what tenets their "science" entailed—and they certainly could not suppose that truth could be ascertained by the counting of millions of sleeping heads—how did they believe truth was to be ascertained? Was there a relation between their mode of attempting to achieve consensus within their organizations and their attitudes toward American democracy?

As to the second question, the ways in which the radicals dealt with differences of opinion within their own organizations might not reveal how they intended to deal with them within American society once they had won power, or how they felt about American democracy in their own day, if it were not for four facts. First, the Wobblies regarded their movement as prefiguring the postrevolutionary society, and the socialists seem to have expected their party to be the leading institution for a time after the revolution, although they rarely theorized on this topic. In either case the organization was a sort of model for the future society at large. Second, environmental and economic determinism attributed fundamental differences of opinion on important questions to opposing class interests; and the view of the class struggle as a form of warfare denied legitimacy to any opinions that could be identified as "bourgeois." Third, since John Q. Worker did not know his own interest whereas their own beliefs constituted a "science," the radicals bore the same relation to the working class as a whole as the most "advanced" members of the radical organizations bore to the less "advanced"—the former must teach and the latter learn. And fourth, their certainty that there was only one Truth and one human interest made most of them feel that variety of opinion was a bad thing; unanimity on important topics was their goal. Thus, the radicals' attitudes toward democracy, as a theory and as it existed in American society, corresponded to their attitudes toward disagreement among themselves.

All the radicals proclaimed their movements the heralds of true democracy, but they gave the word different meanings. Two principal attitudes may be discerned, each having several variants. First, SP members of the right and center—who acknowledged the difficulty of discovering which policy in a given situation was correct, those whose contacts with John Q. Worker or whose participation in politics had shown them that neat theories could not easily be made to fit the facts—tended to be majoritarian on the level of practical policy, although not always in principle. No radical could ever believe that *vox populi vox dei* (or His secular equivalent), but all knew that the workers would learn the truth from experience, with the help of the socialists. De Leon went even further in his support for majoritarian democracy. In his case it was isolation from the workers and his dismissal of the complexities of the American economy and polity that fostered his faith in the imminent conversion of most workers and the ease of instituting socialism, and thereby allowed him to be a majoritarian democrat (although at the same time an extreme vanguardist, as was shown in Chapter VII). The least doctrinaire and the most doctrinaire of the socialists, sharing this faith in democracy, hence accepted the place in American society that their nonradical compatriots willingly accorded them, as peaceful propagandists for a deviant ideology. Second, Wobblies and their SP supporters, whose ambivalence about the convertibility of John Q. Worker was discussed earlier, considered their vanguard role as authorizing, indeed requiring, them to employ coercion of the backward workers

when they had the power to do so. Democracy, to them, was a bourgeois trick. No leadership was legitimate except that exercised by the
enlightened vanguard. The sleeping or cowardly or misguided worker
had no "right" to be wrong. The Wobblies who believed this also believed that the capitalists had no rights that a worker was bound to respect. By a process of elimination, then, it would appear that only radicals had "rights," chiefly the right to adopt whatever means seemed
appropriate to their ends.[24]

The Wobblies did not justify terrorism; they insisted that only a
united, enlightened working class could end the endemic violence of
capitalism and peacefully take power. "The Industrial Union is the future government. The employers all belong to the enemy and so does
the law they make. . . . The class struggle is a physical struggle and depends on physical force." But only a fool would take the law into his
own hands as an individual. Organization is the alternative to terrorism. The IWW is not anarchist; it teaches "order, discipline and organization. There is not in the realm of Nature an organism or a species
which is without all three. 'Anarchy' is an impossibility." "Physical force
is the only thing that counts. The universe is ruled by it. It is up to the
workers to organize and apply physical force for their own benefit. An
organization that does not depend on physical force has never succeeded. . . . The control of the physical or natural forces is what distinguishes the man from the jelly-fish. Are you afraid?" Workers must
learn "that the end justifies the means, and that all things are fair for the
workers against the employers, who are robbers." That political power
is ultimately economic is shown by the fact that when maximum-hours
laws are enforced the employers reduce wages accordingly. Therefore,
"the only laws that are worth while are the ones made in the union hall
and enforced upon the job."[25]

Such views were anathema to De Leon and his supporters; they prevailed in the IWW only after the departure of the SLP members. At the
IWW's 1907 convention, De Leon pleaded for the retention of the political clause in the organization's constitution. "The sun of the twentieth
century civilization," he contended,

frowns down upon the man who would propose physical force only and reject
absolutely the theory of an attempt at a peaceful solution. . . . Civilization

means that men shall deal with one another as each expects to be dealt with. Civilization means that we shall utilize all the conquests of the human race that have enabled us to do what we are doing here today, talking, although we may disagree, peacefully, without jumping at one another's throats. [To the delegate who has asked whether we shall use the capitalist ballot box, I reply that t]here is no such thing as the capitalist ballot box . . . or such a thing as capitalist free speech. These are all conquests that the human race have wrung from the clutches of the ruling class, and for the same reason that I walk proudly and freely on the highway, and for the same reason that we advocate and exercise free speech, for that same reason we stand by the ballot box, not that it is the ballot of the capitalist, but it is the ballot of the civilized man.[26]

De Leon had been preaching thus for years before the IWW was born. In 1895, for example, he set forth the rationale for "the New Trade Unionism"—the STLA—explaining that it had been "born of American conditions, where the proletariat is armed with the ballot"; it "refuses to fight exclusively on the economic field where the proletariat is weakest, and transfers the main struggle to the political arena, where the proletariat is omnipotent."[27] Of all the radical ideologues, De Leon stands out as the defender of the genuineness of American democracy and, by no coincidence, had the keenest historical sense. At the 1900 convention of the SLP, he replied to another delegate's denunciation of the Founding Fathers, by arguing that the coming revolution was

intimately connected with the revolution that the so-called revolutionary fathers accomplished. . . . The revolutionary fathers were oncoming capitalists, they were bourgeois, but . . . they imagined that if you would allow a person free access to the opportunities of labor, his freedom would be guaranteed. . . . Statements of John Adams, Madison, Franklin, not to mention the more demagogic Jefferson, go far enough to indicate that these men, when they established the American Republic, did not mean to establish a republic of oppression. . . . Deprived of the presence of a large proletarian element, they could not conceive such a thing as wage workers by extraction, so to speak, and they opened the gates of the nation to the exploited and oppressed of others to come here and be free with them.[28]

The SP, as usual, showed the greatest diversity of opinion on the cluster of issues having to do with democracy and force. The debunking view of the Founding Fathers, against which De Leon argued, was as popular within the SP as among the Progressives. Algie M. Simons' works in this vein are well known. John Spargo, of the SP's right wing, praised J. Allen Smith's *Spirit of American Government* for showing how evil the Founding Fathers were. Smith, wrote Spargo, described the writing of the Constitution "from the viewpoint of the Marxian theory of economic determinism"; he showed how "the progressives" were excluded from the Constitutional Convention, in a "deliberate effort" to protect the rich against the poor; almost all delegates to "that reactionary body" considered democracy an "unmitigated evil"; and so on.[29]

On the one hand, De Leon seems to have believed that, despite the capitalists' domination of the nation throughout its history, a supraclass evolution of "civilization" had been occurring as well and that the workers had participated in creating it.[30] Spargo, Simons, and other socialists, on the other hand, tended to perceive American history solely as the work of the capitalists. Both approaches to history corresponded to perceptions of current democracy. Victor Berger, for example, doubted the ability of the most oppressed workers to vote intelligently.[31] Yet he repeatedly urged that the socialists educate the workers; for if they did not, the sequel would be blind rebellion and the destruction of civilization.

Others of the SP's right and center shared Berger's horror of the Wobblies' contempt for law and order. When Wobbly leaders Haywood and Bohn publicly stated that a worker who came to understand the economic foundation of modern ethics and jurisprudence lost all respect for property rights and did not hesitate to break the law, Hillquit responded angrily. Such doctrine, he wrote, was anarchism, the opposite of socialism, "and not even a remote cousin to the theory of economic determinism." True, the law was mainly class law, he acknowledged, but socialists want to change it by means of lawful procedures.

The laws of political democracies in the last analysis always represent the will of the majority of the people. They may be conceived in ignorance or procured by fraud or purchase, but in that case they exist only because the majority of the people and voters are so indifferent, ignorant or corrupt as to sanction them or at least acquiesce in them. The remedy of the minority aggrieved by the law is to convert their fellow citizens to their own views—to turn their minority into a majority, and thus get possession of the legislative machinery for the interests and policies represented by them. Whenever we will obtain control of the legislative machinery of the government, we will exact obedience to our laws, working class laws, upon precisely the same grounds upon which we now yield obedience to the capitalist laws. . . . We fight in the open as an organized, trained and intelligent army, with clean weapons and for a great cause, and not as a gang of petty criminals.

Hillquit apparently saw no incongruity between his military simile and his argument. But Haywood did; in reply he asked whether Hillquit did not realize that the war between capitalism and socialism was already going on. Did he not know that the 145 victims of the Triangle Fire were casualties in that war, among thousands of other victims of the capitalists' "rapine, murder, debauchery, bribery and all of the crimes on the calendar in the present battle against the working class? . . . Is it necessary to call Comrade Hillquit's attention to the spirit of revolt animating the workers in every city of the world at the present moment? Is it necessary to build the barricades on the asphalt pavement before the door of the building where his law offices are located before he will be brought to a realization of the fact that the fight is now on?"[32] Haywood's logic, at least, was correct: during a revolution votes are meaningless and only force counts, and the problem of democracy does not arise except as a problem for the future.

On what other logic than that the revolution was in progress could left-wing socialist Henry L. Slobodin have answered Hillquit by distinguishing between "ordinary crimes . . . committed for individual ends" and those "committed for social ends"? The latter were committed, he wrote, for the good of the people. Whether they were politic or wise in a given situation was a separate question. "Every act that furthers the interest of the working class is sane and wise, law or no law." As to Hillquit's statement that the laws of political democracies were ultimately the will of the people, Slobodin expounded a theory that went to the heart of the question of democracy: "no man has a will, i.e., exercises a free choice, in anything unless he is fully conscious of the nature of the thing. And so long as the workingmen are not class-conscious, i.e., not conscious of the real nature of the class struggle and their position therein, they cannot have a will in any social sense."[33] How are we to reconcile Slobodin's justification of "social" crimes with this statement? There seems no other way but to infer that, since a crime committed by a non-class-conscious worker was likely to be for "individ-

ual ends," only class-conscious workers—by which he meant socialists—had the moral right and duty to commit "social crimes." It goes
without saying that they would not commit them against the non-class-
conscious worker. Yet they certainly would commit them against his
wishes.

In the present context Slobodin's last statement above is critically important, for the conviction that the overwhelming majority of voters did
not understand what they were doing, had no will of their own, were
not exercising free choice, follows from the vanguardism and scientific
pretensions that all the radicals shared. Berger, as far to the right as
Slobodin was to the left, expressed the contradiction between this "scientism" and democracy perfectly: "Scientific discussions of theories as
such cannot at best be decided by a majority vote of any [SP] convention. Scientific facts have never yet been decided by majority vote—
and economic facts and philosophical problems no more than mathematical or historical facts and problems. All such matters ought to be
discussed for months or even years in the party press,—in fact they
ought to be discussed continuously."[34] If even Berger, ordinarily lucid
and logical, could produce such an incoherent statement, the problem
must have been insoluble. If scientific facts were decided by scientists
and not by majority votes, his proposal would make sense only if the
participants in the party's conventions and discussions had been scientists, with as specialized knowledge of the "science" of society as mathe-
maticians had of mathematics. To be scientists they must have qualified
themselves by years of study and testing of hypotheses. But the party
press and conventions were open to all who accepted the few basic tenets of the party or chose to write letters to editors, and it was their consensus that Berger was willing to accept. Yet that consensus could be
arrived at only by means of majority votes, which he realized could have
no scientific status. If this problem was so confusing within the SP, what
could the socialists have thought about the meaning of majority votes in
the country at large? Berger tried to answer this question partly by faith
fortified by italics:

We are speeding toward it [Social Democracy] with the accelerating velocity of a
locomotive. . . . It is only a convincing confirmation of this view, that the "*social
question*" now stands everywhere in the *foreground of public discussion.* . . . We

want to *convince* the *majority* of the people. As long as we are in the minority we of course have *no right to force our opinions upon an unwilling majority*. . . . No true Social-Democrat ever dreams of a sudden change of society. . . . Yet we do not deny that *after* we have *convinced the majority* of people, we are going to use force *if the minority* should *resist*. But in every democracy the majority rules, and must rule.[35]

All the italics in the font could not convince the Wobblies that such a policy could succeed. As we have seen, they generally subscribed to the theory of the "militant minority," and we may recall it here because of its implications for the question of democracy. One editorialist explained that in any gathering or organization a few people always lead the rest, even in the SP, an organization "that hugs the delusion of majority rule." The IWW does not consider it necessary to recruit the majority of workers to overthrow capitalism. "We simply hope to get enough militant workers together to be able to form the foundation for the next social order. We are the militant minority of the working class."[36]

The reader will have noticed a tendency toward authoritarianism in most of the statements quoted. Wobblies and left-wing socialists often admitted it frankly and justified it. Right-wingers were sometimes troubled by it and tried to reconcile the implications of "the science of economic determinism" with their genuine belief in democracy. One solution was to predict that in the postrevolutionary society the coercive state would wither away. Right- and left-wingers cooperated in this enterprise and would all have agreed with *The Harp's* advice that socialist propagandists "lay more stress upon the structural form of the new social order, to emphasise it as democratic in practice in the workshop. This would kill all the fear some finer intellects have of Socialism as a huge state machine dominating the souls and bodies of all people."[37] Wobblies Haywood and Bohn proclaimed that under socialism "government will concern itself only with the management of industry, with the promotion of public education and with other public activities which are of benefit to the workers." Since "Socialism is industrial democracy" and "industrial democracy is Socialism," presumably the future government would be democratically run.[38] Even this limit on government's functions was not enough for the editor of the *Industrial Worker*, who equated "State Socialism" with state capitalism and accused the political socialists of working for this undemocratic goal. He predicted that when the workers got control of industry the state would "commit suicide."[39] Whereas most socialists predicted that industry would be administered nationwide, the IWW predicted that each workplace or industry would be run by its own workers. Several socialists called this merely a form of capitalism, for it would mean that each group of workers would exploit the other groups in the marketplace.[40]

Berger was unusual, however, in admitting that true socialism could be "consistent with the most fearful tyranny the world has ever seen" because the ruling powers would possess far more control over people's livelihood than the capitalists had. And capitalist Switzerland had an almost pure political democracy. Socialism and capitalism were economic, not political, phenomena, he explained, and each economic system could be combined with a variety of political systems. Berger's goal was "Social Democracy," which meant collective ownership of the productive forces by the whole people and also political rule by the whole people, and it could be inaugurated only by the willing majority of the people.[41]

In sum, advocates of both the two main attitudes toward democracy—the majoritarian and minoritarian—contradicted themselves or betrayed uncertainty. This is hardly surprising, for a contradiction lay at the heart of these notions of democracy. On the one hand the radicals accepted the popular definition of democracy as majority rule—either openly, or obliquely as when they portrayed the majority as willingly following its natural leaders. On the other hand they identified democracy with the true interest of the working class, which meant that a majority vote cast by people who did not understand their true interest was not really democratic.[42]

The procedural and substantive definitions necessarily conflicted during the period in which the radicals were still trying to convert the workers. In practice the double meaning of democracy engendered a series of dilemmas. For example, should a socialist elected to public office before the start of the revolution represent his constituents' views, or should he use his office to further radical objectives that his constituents disagreed with? In the former case he would betray his vanguard role; in the latter case his constituents would vote him out of office. Should a revolutionary union leadership that had won a strike bow to its members' desire for a contract, or should it refuse to thus legitimate the employer-employee relationship? In the former case it would be acting like any other union; in the latter case it would lose its nonradical members. Each such choice was a choice between procedural and substantive democracy. Only after the start of the revolution could the two meanings of democracy coincide, for only then, presumably, could the procedural democracy be relied on to yield substantive democracy.

This problem could exist only in a society that already had procedural democracy, a society in which socialism could not be brought about by a palace revolution or one staged by a small party that won mass support by promising "immediate demands" irrelevant to socialism (such as peace, land, and bread). In the United States or any nation with broad suffrage, such an attempt would be regarded as antidemocratic regardless of the substance of the radicals' ideology and program. In a society without procedural democracy, a revolution could be the only way for the working class to obtain "immediate demands"; in a society with procedural democracy, the agitation for and winning of the immediate demands could have the effect of reinforcing John Q. Worker's faith in democracy and in the social order in which democratic procedures could win those demands.

Some radicals tried to circumvent this difficulty by asserting that most workers only seemed to support the capitalist System and that they were really coerced into acting as though they did. Hence, a radical action that appeared to be coercive—such as sabotage or a union's expulsion of members who voted for capitalist parties—would help to free the majority to pursue what they recognized as their real interest. The radicals would organize the workers and show them they were strong enough, if united, to take power from the exploiting minority. Unfortunately for those who reasoned in this manner, white male workers did not, apparently, believe their votes were coerced except in several specific situations that reformers publicized and denounced as deviations from the norm. All such radical theories, in fact, must fail in a society with very broad suffrage and the right of minority dissent, a society in which the people believe the majority rules, for such belief is self-validating. That is, a polity that depends on the acquiescence of the majority in the results of frequent balloting after free debate is *ipso facto* one in which whatever policy prevails in the long run is at least acceptable to the majority, and hence what the majority believes to be true about the extent of acquiescence in a policy is *ipso facto* so.

But the radicals' assertion of the gap between procedural and substantive democracy was far more plausible in the shake-up period than it has been at any other time. Their claim was given substance by the raw power of the big capitalists and their corruption of legislatures, by the disfranchisement of a large number of white male workers who often moved from job to job or who were recent immigrants, and by the precariousness of unskilled workers' employment. Radicals believed that these conditions were permanent features of capitalism. Nonradicals replied that the immigrants would soon get the vote and that migratory workers lacked the stake in their communities that voters should have. As to the corruption of legislators by capitalists, nonradicals maintained that this flaw in democracy could be cured by a mobilized public opinion that would purify democracy by restoring the traditionally approved wall between the economic and political spheres. Here too belief in majoritarian democracy was self-confirming. Radicals replied that political power always served economic power, whether overtly or covertly. Hence the cure for the capitalists' illegitimate power over the government was not to repair the wall between the economic and political systems but to demolish it and put both in the hands of the working class.

III

The radicals' project of amalgamating the political and economic systems under working-class hegemony was not part of a larger project of amalgamating the public sphere (government and the economy) with the private sphere (social relations, family, religion, community). That is to say, the general outlook of most radicals was not totalistic. They were unfamiliar with the Leninist conception of the party as composed of "professional revolutionaries" whose personal amalgamation of political and economic concerns with private concerns prefigured the postrevolutionary regime's authority over all citizens' private lives. Even those radicals who manifested the most authoritarian tendencies, such as Haywood and Debs, at this time agreed with their cohorts that, once the capitalist class and its System had been done away with, the private sphere would revert to its proper autonomy, purified by the elimination of the capitalist System's illegitimate intrusion and influence. A woman would work or be a housewife, as she chose; everyone would be free to choose his associates; everyone would have the economic security and time to pursue cultural and recreational interests without dictation or the corrupting influence of capitalism. Forecasts of the postrevolutionary society occupy a minor place in the radicals' writings largely because they assumed that the revolution would be mainly a dismantling process. Economic and environmental determinism fostered their belief that their task was mainly negative: once the principal means of production had been placed in the workers' hands, ideology and feelings would be rectified automatically. The radicals' felt need for an all-encompassing theory could avoid clashing with their negative approach to the private sphere only because their beliefs and attitudes concerning most parts of the private sphere did not differ from those of their contemporaries. In other words, their all-encompassing theory, all fifty-seven varieties of it, did implicitly encompass the private sphere but did not demand basic change in it and hence could ignore it.

One might suppose that the radicals' hands-off attitude toward the private sphere would help them win recruits. John Q. Worker might have reasoned that his conversion to radicalism would not force him to alter his private-sphere values and relationships, but would merely require him to support the overthrow of the System that corrupted these values and relationships. So the radicals assumed, and so they repeatedly told him when they blamed the System for prostitution, sickness, excessive hours of work, crowded tenements, false religion, and the economic need that drove women and children into the factories. But they misperceived both the "System"—its domination of the private sphere—and John Q. Worker's attitude toward it.

Compare the radicals' ideas of what a political party should be with John Q. Worker's. The radicals assumed that each political party represented a class—the Republican the big capitalists, the Democratic and Progressive the little capitalists, and (to most radicals) the SP the workers. But John Q. Worker, once naturalized, seems to have adopted, consciously or unconsciously, the traditional American perception of the party system as virtually the only institution in an extremely segmented nation that transcended—as well as expressed—distinctions of class, community, ethnicity, and religion. Socialists misread their compatriots' attitudes toward politics when they played up the major parties' agreement on fundamentals and proposed a radical party that would introduce debate over fundamentals into political contests. Such debates had long since been assigned to other media of public discussion—the press and voluntary associations—and so long as the radicals agitated in their press and their own associations they were accepted as legitimate contributors to this continuing process. They were the only ones who considered radical movements a sign of the nation's sickness; many articulate Americans seem to have considered them a tonic helping to keep the society healthy. Like the nonradical press and nonradical associations, theirs too contributed menu items that became parts of the major-party platforms, which in turn became expressions of a nationwide unity overriding and therefore in a way legitimating the much wider differences among groups within the nation.

That most Americans, including workers, have viewed the political system in this way can be inferred from many indirect evidences. Readers who are old enough to remember World War II may recall a theme repeated over and over in war movies—the military unit portrayed as a microcosm (white) of this nation of immigrants, each man fighting for "freedom." What did freedom mean? To the Italian taxi driver from Brooklyn it meant the right to root for the Dodgers; to the WASP farm boy from Kansas the chance to save money and buy his own farm; to the Irish lad from Chicago the chance to take a civil service exam and become a policeman; to all of them the prospect of marrying the girl back home and raising a family. America was the country in which each man could strive for his own goals, and its freedom was the umbrella under which the individual goals could be pursued. Those movies were, to be sure, sentimental and propagandistic, but they struck a chord that resonated with the viewers' own hopes and values. They were expressing in effect a belief so taken for granted as not to need defense: that procedural democracy was Americans' most precious public possession because it restricted political decisions to public-policy questions, leaving the private sphere semiautonomous. The radicals' proposals, on the contrary, implicitly required the adoption of a large assortment of collective goals and values pertaining to the private sphere, to be enforced in the public sphere.

Debs, for instance, proclaimed, "The time is near at hand when a member of a union will be expelled just as promptly for casting a scab ballot, that is to say for supporting the party of the enemy of labor, as if he took the place of a member while out on strike."[43] He was here giving politics a substantive, value content, contrary to the conventional American norm and, moreover, happily prophesying the abolition of the right of political dissent among the future minority. Since in that period when a union might have the power to expel a member for voting "wrong," union membership would surely be a prerequisite for a job, Debs was in effect announcing that John Q. Worker would have to be politically orthodox if he wished to support his family. To the objection that a union had no more right to control its members' politics than to control their religion, Debs would reply that religion was a private affair but politics was not, because if a man used his vote to fasten slavery more securely on his fellow workers they had the right to interfere with his behavior to protect their own interests. Debs obviously did not notice that, on the same logic, belief in religion too could become a subject of public policy. The very procedural democracy, with its assumption of the self-limitation of the power of majorities, which permitted Debs to agitate, would be abolished.

Far more common, however, were predictions by members of all factions in all the radical organizations that the socialist government or administration would have no authority whatever over the private sphere. Typical of such statements, but significant because one of its coauthors manifested authoritarian tendencies in other contexts, was this remark by Haywood and Bohn: "Socialist government will concern itself entirely with the shop. Socialism can demand nothing of the individual outside the shop. It will not say to the worker how he shall use his product. Socialism has absolutely nothing to do with either religion or the family."[44]

Even more explicit disclaimers were made by delegates to the SP's convention in 1910. John M. Work, in his "Report on Organization," suggested that the party send out lecturers on health, hygiene, and other topics concerning individual welfare. Party locals should hire socialist physicians to look after members' health, their salaries to be reduced whenever members fell ill. Capitalism, he explained, induced people to harm themselves with "liquor, tobacco, patent medicines, confectionery, soda counter abominations, unwholesome diet, excessive sexual inter-course, lack of ventilation, unsanitary homes, ignorance of the require-ments of their bodies, etc. . . . Being below the intellectual plane, . . . [many people] have no impulse to spend leisure in any way except in dissipation. If we left them on the lower plane, the leisure brought to them by Socialism would speedily work their entire degeneracy. We cannot begin too soon to develop their higher natures."[45] Some dele-gates protested the "insult" to the workers; some feared ridicule; others found Work's report unobjectionable.[46] The ensuing discussion ranged over several of his proposals, showing that the benevolent authoritar-ianism implicit in his vanguardism did not shock all the delegates. Yet John Spargo seems to have expressed the majority view when he ob-jected to the party's concerning itself with such matters before the revo-lution. "We will," he added, "attend to these other questions in due time."[47] Many others, however, thought the SP should never concern itself with private-sphere issues.

By far the most common disclaimer of authority over the private sphere had to do with religion,[48] a question of extreme importance within the SP. A scanning of *The Call* from the period 1909–1912 will turn up at least one article or letter on it in virtually every issue. Because the Catholic hierarchy, some priests, and the Militia of Christ propagan-dized against socialism, socialists had to distinguish carefully between the Church as an institution and religion as belief; they felt free to attack the former because it was moving out of what the nonreligious socialists concerned its proper (private) sphere and into politics. Some socialists went so far as to argue that they were thus helping to purify John Q. Worker's genuine religion. The *Social Democratic Herald* and *Industrial Worker* made the same distinction and took the same line. The radicals' attitude toward the relation of religion to their ideologies was not due to their holding conventional beliefs concerning it, as was the case with their attitudes toward the race and woman questions. Most of the lead-ers seem to have been atheists or agnostics, but they assumed religion would die out after the revolution. Moreover, they knew it would be bad tactics to attack John Q. Worker's religious beliefs, and they re-garded his economic and political beliefs as more vulnerable to propa-ganda anyhow. Besides, the Christian Socialists in the SP were numer-ous and valuable. (See Supplement.)

The American radicals, in sum, did not foresee the totalistic implications of their attraction to ideological comprehensiveness. They were not out to *make* John Q. Worker live morally; they were out to *let* him do so. It was a later generation of radicals that, once in power in other countries, discovered that private-sphere values were dangerous to the public-sphere authority and that therefore transformed the radical movements' educational efforts into socialist regimes' coercive imposition of approved beliefs. All loyalties intermediate between the individual and the state, and the semiautonomy of the private sphere, turned out to be limitations on the loyalty of the worker to the state and had to be eradicated or made instrumental to the power of the state. Even earlier, however, the Leninist conception of the party, which introduced a large element of will and therefore the chance for error and which partly freed behavior from material determinants, made state dictation of private-sphere values and behavior necessary. The purification of belief and behavior could no longer be assumed to follow automatically from the inauguration of the "classless" society. Perhaps the most delicious irony in the history of the radicals in the shake-up period is that their "science" of economic determinism, which exculpated them from the future totalistic consequences of their own System-thinking, was linked in their minds with the belief that they could foretell the future. The fact that they were not good prophets also saved them from confronting the ultimate conundrum—whether a country could be both socialist and democratic.

IX   The Radical Mind, 1890–1917: Some Speculations

When all the inferences concerning beliefs, commitment, hope for the future, compassion for oppressed workers, and the demands of propaganda and agitation have been drawn from the radicals' rhetoric, there remains a strong sense that it manifests something more. That something is the personal meaning of radicalism and of the particular organizations for their members—or, at any rate, for those leaders and writers who produced the documents. The thesis of this chapter is that radicalism and the organizations were ends as well as means, that, except for radicals by birthright and some right-wing socialists, radical ideology rationalized certain individuals' ways of coping with their own "shake-up period" and that their organizations functioned as surrogate communities for people who did not feel themselves integral parts of ethnic, religious, or neighborhood communities.

Whatever generalizations can be made about the radical mind must take account of variety, exceptions, and qualifications. Even an attempt to simplify by sketching the main types should be accompanied by the proviso that these are only ideal models, which individuals resembled in varying degrees. No more is claimed for these conjectures than that I believe they make sense of a mass of documentary evidence that cannot be adequately explained otherwise. The relevant evidence consists of documents, phrases, and statements other than the radicals' denunciations of the hideous conditions that evoked their compassion and anger and their demands for change, for in these respects they did not differ from their reformist contemporaries.

One reason there has been little intellectual history of American radical and reform movements is the belief that such probing is tantamount to discrediting; a good deal of the intellectual history that has been written on such movements is therefore defensive and one-sided. For example, a few years ago a reviewer criticized the author of a book on slavery for being hostile to the abolitionists; his "proof" was that the author considered John Brown insane—as though the factual evidence about Brown's mental state had any connection with a historian's attitude toward slavery and abolitionism. Another historian has "defended" the sincerity of certain abolitionists' commitment to their cause, by asserting that they were not neurotic, as though neurosis equaled hypocrisy. Moreover, there is no contradiction between neurotic (or other unconscious) grounds for a belief and its having a realistic content. The realistic content of parts of the belief-systems of the radicals studied here is proven by the eventual acceptance of most of their demands; they were responding to real needs, but then so were the reformers. (This statement says nothing concerning the rightness of those demands or of their acceptance.) As to their System-thinking, the disproof of the theory and the explanation of its psychological sources are separate processes involving distinct kinds of data. The genuineness of these people's commitment to their ideologies is not at issue; none of the various types of radical can be said to have been noticeably more or less committed than others, whether their commitment was due to acceptance of their parents' ideologies, to a reversal of them, to a mostly rational rethinking of their inherited ideologies, or to any of a variety of unconscious or even neurotic motives or needs.

I

One trait that all the radicals studied in this book shared was the need to systematize inner and outer reality. This need requires us to distinguish between the leftward and rightward directions; the act of leaving a radical movement is not comparable to the act of joining it. Most defectors from these movements converted to liberalism or conservatism, neither of which offered a believer a neatly catalogued world in which there were no ambiguities, insoluble problems, or unquestionable predictions of the future. To such a person, the earlier "choice" of joining, say, the SP—or in a later generation the CP—was no choice; he was more apt to feel that the Cause had chosen *him*, awakening him to the Grand Pattern of the Universe, shedding light that flooded all the

dark corners, and showing how everything was connected with everything else. To leave the movement was, on the contrary, an act of choice,
as free and yet protracted and agonizing as that of the child who lets go
of his security blanket and risks the world.[1]

Since the radicals perceived their society as a System, it is legitimate
to speculate that their perception was influenced by their own need for
what Egon Bittner calls "a unified and internally consistent interpretation of the meaning of the world."[2] If one believes that all parts of the
capitalist System work together like the wheels of a clock, so that the
breakdown of one wheel paralyzes the whole mechanism,[3] one is likely
to aim at opposing it with an equally well integrated ideology. And the
more integrated it is, the greater will be the perceived consequences of a
challenge to or disproof of any basic element within the theory. This
does not mean that the radicals never changed their minds; it does explain why they endowed each alteration in their thinking with enormous historical significance. The new bright light it shed on all the other
tenets was matched only by the depth of the ignorance or iniquity of
those who refused to see it.

Although, as I argued in Chapter III, American society was not
anomic, many individuals were. Some became demoralized; others became what William Kornhauser calls "mass men."[4] Some of these became radicals, blaming their anomie on the System and organizing their
lives around the goal of revolutionizing it. For them, the radical movements were the way out of their own "shake-up period." Alienated from
their communities of birth, they built or joined surrogate communities
of like-minded people.[5]

Still others became radicalized because of an ideological bent, a desire for theoretical formulae to explain the unprecedented events happening around them that had aroused their anger and/or their compassion for the victims of industrialization. In a shake-up period, radicalism
can be a rationally plausible destination for such a person—whether
he is a trained intellectual, a natural questioner of the conventional
wisdom, or a member of an ethnic minority possessing universalistic
ideals—the type who seeks large patterns hidden among the disparate
data that are so disturbing. Some of these people did not so much mis-
perceive John Q. Worker as misinterpret what they perceived. They interpreted his nonradicalism in terms of their own ideological require-

ments. The real John Q. Worker could seem to fit their image of him, for like most people elsewhere and at other times he was less interested in larger political and economic questions than they were, except when he felt that circumstances prevented him from living according to his values. Their error lay in their construing his different orientation as submission or somnolence. It should be added that no one at that time could have made the sort of analysis of John Q. Worker's culture and of the process of social change that social scientists have been working out only within the past generation. These radicals were theorizing before the development of modern sociology and anthropology, and their results were hardly less scientific than those of their scholarly contemporaries. But their methods were. Their certainty that their theory was a "science" had the opposite effect of the scientific attitude of such contemporaries as the Pittsburgh Project investigators in that, instead of questioning their own explanations and seeking data to test them, they were certain their theory gave the answers and obviated the need for empirical study.

We may recall here the assortment of evils that the radicals, along with reformers and many conservatives, perceived in their society but that the radicals alone assumed were intrinsic to capitalism, evils that have since been lessened or abolished. Certainly no one at that time could have foreseen this. All the same, it must be noted that the radicals had no empirical evidence for what they added to the empirical data that many reformers perceived and deplored. This also means that no one could have been converted to radicalism solely on the ground of commitment to end those evils—low wages, poor housing, and so on— for there was no empirical or logical connection between such commitment and postulation of a System in either thought or society. Correspondingly, there was no necessary connection between a person's becoming aware of and sensitive to the evils around him and his converting to a total belief-system that linked up all the disparate data. Since what the radicals added was a product of their own minds, it is obviously related to the way they felt the *urgency* to work for the abolition of capitalism. Some reformers have shown the same pattern of thinking—for example, a wing of the prohibitionist movement, whose sense of urgency was so great that they saw the Liquor Interests wherever they looked, in government, the economy, and society. Hence, they said, abolish the Liquor Interests and all good things will follow because the source of all bad things will be no more. There was no more evidence for the radicals' seeing the Capitalist Class wherever they looked in government, the economy, and society than for those prohibitionists' finding their enemies there. The ubiquity of the Enemy can be accounted for only by the tendency of the person possessed by the vision of the One Great Evil to make it dominate every social and historical datum in his field of vision.

That possession accounts also for the vision of the future society held by this type of activist. Since he felt diversity of belief to be intolerable, he blamed it on the System; truth, on the contrary, must be unitary, order the ideal, and error the result of plots or at best bad influences. The Good Society of the future must be envisioned as unified in thought and behavior under working-class hegemony, when the working class would have unanimously adopted (or passively accepted) the radicals' ideology. Presumably radical ideology itself would have become unified by then, by the refutation or suppression of rival, spurious radicalisms. The totalism implicit in some varieties of pre–World War I radicalism (and made explicit in postwar Communist Parties) would have become the norm throughout the society, which would have become the radical movement universalized.

Some—certainly not all—of the radicals seem to have been attracted to System-thinking because of a need for cosmic order and a perception of the phenomenal world as disorderly, chaotic. Hence this type of radical's superorderly System not only contradicted appearances but presupposed apparent disorder; without his "science," which justified his vanguard status, no one could see how things that seemed meaningless and discrete were really related and what they really meant. Where most people who were integrated in a living culture and community could believe that science explained unapparent principles that were *expressed by* phenomena, this radical System-builder saw the unapparent principles *hidden by* phenomena. This was one reason why he found it so easy to believe in malevolent conspirators.

II

Whatever else the radical commitment was, it was also a bond that performed for the radicals of all types the same function that neighborhood, ethnic, religious, or occupational communities performed for others. Having defected from those communities and declared themselves members of the larger society or of the international proletariat, however, they found these categories too pluralistic, amorphous, and abstract to replace what they had rejected. They plunged back into community, but in the form of artificial communities that they wanted to be far more unified than those they had left.[6] This is not to say that the chief motive for joining a radical organization was the need for such a community. Other groups or causes could have satisfied that need; hence a person thus motivated needed an additional reason for joining a radical organization—its ideology, its deviant status, the influence of friends or relatives, or any combination of these.

Once inside, however, and active, committed, choosing his friends mainly among his fellow members, he would find himself in a milieu that strengthened his commitment and decreased his contacts with those data that could refute his beliefs. The movement press would encourage him to interpret even those disconfirming data in the light of refutations already formulated, and the further this process advanced the more he would be likely to see all data as confirming his ideology. Even intramovement controversies would work toward this end, since they were predicated on prior agreement on the basic tenets and they mobilized emotions in their defense.[7] After a while his main reading was newspapers and books that expounded the movement's theories. This literature acted as a filter of potential meanings offered by the outside world. Everything in it reinforced assent to the Theory and opposition to contrary theories, "proving" again and again the correctness of the Theory and encouraging the member to direct feelings of love, pride, contempt, hate, and so on, toward the correct objects. Every piece of news or personal problem or question of fact or value that the Theory interpreted or answered was new proof of its correctness and of the benightedness or lack of comprehension of everyone outside the movement. If only all those people could be either defeated or converted (depending on their class), he would say, then his personal objectives, frustrated by the System, could be realized; he must do all he could to spread the gospel, to wake up other people as he had been awakened. By now he was capable of saying, "I can't conceive of living without the movement; how could I have lived in darkness for so long!"

All his associates felt the same way, used the same esoteric terms, read the same papers and books—and so he knew he was right. The hostility of outsiders reinforced this certainty, for it proved that they lived in the same darkness from which he had been rescued. The movement's function of screening out disconfirming data both contributed to and resulted from System-thinking. The radicals unified things that John Q. Worker permitted to remain discrete; they saw all social phenomena in terms of the radical mission. Their subculture, a reinforcing semiclosed environment, enabled members to see as unimportant those things that did not bear on their radical vocation. In other words, by focusing all the members' energies the movement fostered the perception of System. There was *nothing* that could not provide proof anew, each day, of the correctness of the Theory. Nothing, that is, but the loss of the group. The unaffiliated ideological deviant is a very rare person.

Consider a partly analogous situation that Dorothy Burton Skårdal describes in her superb study of Scandinavian Lutheran immigrants. "Identification as a member of a given church body," she explains, ". . . made possible easy classification of others according to their inclusion in or exclusion from a select group." Religion became more important to their self-definition as their ethnic traits faded and became unable to maintain group definition. "Within church groups sanctioned by God and the Truth, each individual could find support in the struggle to maintain his identity and uphold his worth against the threatening environment. To condemn its values as inferior to his own became part of his self-preservation. Some explanation of the dogmatic bitterness of Scandinavian-American church warfare can be found in the inner uncertainty and need for aggressive defense which are characteristics of the marginal man." By the beginning of the twentieth century, the Scandinavians were no longer marginal, and the church disputes cooled.[8]

Although the people Skårdal describes were much less single-minded than the radicals, her account suggests two analogies. The parallel with the radicals' internecine wrangling is obvious. In addition, since both John Q. Worker and an unknown but very large proportion of the radicals were certainly marginal in Skårdal's sense, the radicals may have helped John Q. Worker sharpen his developing sense of identity as a new member of American society, for he and they were both orienting themselves to the American economy, polity, and society, and each was an available negative reference group for the other.[9] John W. Gardner's statement applies equally to both: "Man is in his very nature a seeker of meanings." At one level the search is intellectual, to organize knowledge into patterns; but at another it is personal, "a compelling need to arrive at conceptions of the universe *in terms of which he could regard his own life as meaningful*. He wants to know where *he* fits into the scheme of things. . . . In the individual life, meaning, purpose and commitment are inseparable."[10] John Q. Worker found these three things in precisely the milieux and institutions that the radicals would have directed his attention away from: family; ethnic community and organization; sometimes church or synagogue—that is, those institutions that mediate between the individual and the public sphere and the decay of which makes people "massified," anomic, and "available" for messianic movements.[11]

The two functions of the movement thus worked against each other, and together they insured that the radicals would have a false image of John Q. Worker. On the one hand the personal function that the movement performed for its members required its semi-isolation; it required the frequent meetings and the reading mainly of movement literature that reinforced belief in the movement's tenets and image of the outside world, including John Q. Worker. On the other hand the proselytizing mission required contacts with John Q. Worker so as to convert and recruit him. If the first function had dominated, as it virtually did in the SLP, the second function would have proved impossible. If the second had dominated, the first would have proved impossible—which is why it is so important to note the sharp distinction the Wobblies themselves made between their radical core and their nonradical, temporary recruits.[12] Only if John Q. Worker had fitted their image could the radicals have performed both functions. But their "John Q. Worker" was a product of their esoteric ideology; when the real John Q. Worker failed to convert, the same ideology explained why. Thus, no matter what the result of the proselytizing turned out to be, it reinforced the ideology and obviated the need for reality-testing—in the short run, at any rate. Or, to put the point a bit differently, by painting John Q. Worker in their own double image (see Chapter V), the radicals glossed over the distinction between the causes of their movement's appearance and the conditions for its enlargement. It originated in the need, by a small minority

of alienated people, to change the conditions that produced their alienation. They assumed that John Q. Worker was similarly alienated from
the System, even if he was too oppressed to know it yet. In reality, he
was not alienated, and hence they offered him a solution to a problem
he did not have; they had to make him feel alienated and *then* offer him
their movement as the cure for his condition. But, not having the disease, he did not need the medicine.

The foregoing generalizations apply in different ways and to different degrees to the three radical organizations.

The SLP may be considered the limiting case of the closed "community," waiting for John Q. Worker to come to it and making only limited
efforts to reach out to him. SLP members magnified every distinction
among radicals as diligently as they erased all essential distinctions
among the capitalists. Their polemics were directed mainly against
other radicals and some reformers, and their demand for doctrinal
orthodoxy ensured that they would never be troubled by the choice between purity and popularity. Their attitude on this question is nicely revealed in a statement by Herman Simpson (who later went over to the
SP) at the SLP's convention in 1900. Arguing against the party's advocating any immediate demands, even in its municipal programs, to appeal
to the workers' current beliefs and wishes, he came close to plagiarizing
from Tertullian: insofar as the party platform's basic principles "appear
self-evident," he said, "they are of no effect. It is only so far as they appear absurd and paradoxical, the very reverse of all the previous experience of the race and working class under the thrall of capitalist domin-
ion, both material and intellectual—in so far only as it is revolutionary
and therefore strikes a man as something absurd and paradoxical, does
it stand, only in so far can it have the desired effect. In other words, the
revolutionary character of the platform should appear at first sight."
Therefore, the party should make it clear that its principles differ profoundly from all others.[13]

The IWW's core were extreme individualists who rejected not just
the content of the conventional community relationships but the social
bonds themselves, so that even as the IWW satisfied their need to belong to a collective enterprise it did so only tenuously. Its meeting halls
were social clubs, providing libraries, good conversation, shelter from a
hostile world, the safety of numbers, and the comforts of comradeship.

But as an organization the IWW was amorphous. John Graham Brooks expressed the point well when he observed, after talking with many Wobblies, that "the element of anarchy peculiar to the I.W.W. is its inherent dislike of organic restraint. No one uses the word 'organization' oftener and practices it less. . . . An impetuous individualism cannot endure organic relationships." He observed also that the Wobblies' tactics angered the very workers they wanted to recruit.[14] Yet the wish for these organic ties is poignantly expressed in the statement by a Wobbly journalist that "no working man can possibly sacrifice anything for the cause of industrial solidarity, no matter how much he does for it. For it is only thus, as we sink our personal aims and ambitions in the larger mission of our class, that life becomes invested with meaning for ourselves, and the living or losing of it is made worth while."[15] Such statements should be juxtaposed with the frequent disclaimers of idealism ("We want the goods!") in *Solidarity* and the *Industrial Worker*.

The contradiction was expressed also in the fact that on the one hand the Wobblies made it very easy to join, by assessing low initiation fees and dues and by issuing interchangeable membership cards, and on the other hand they antagonized their recruits by refusing to sign contracts and by countenancing inflammatory rhetoric. That the organization was in part an end in itself is suggested in Robert L. Tyler's depiction of "Wobblies trying to make sense out of their frustrating lives through an ideology of class conflict and revenge. . . . The confusion in . . . [the IWW's] goals, the conflict between revolution and industrial unionism, limited the appeal of the organization among average working men. To the average worker, such an act as joining the I.W.W. must have seemed tantamount to becoming a professional revolutionary, not something one did to improve one's economic position." Only the transient, deracinated, unskilled and semiskilled, with nothing to lose and "no neighbors to chide them for being Wobblies," were attracted in large numbers.[16] As was shown in Chapter VI, Wobbly writers both boasted of their liberation from those "neighbors'" values and yearned for the family ties that sustained them.

It is appropriate to recall that ambivalence here so as to relate it to the present subject, the radical organization as surrogate community. It will be recalled that the evidence reveals a double contradiction: first, writers repeatedly complained of their not having wives and children, yet declared that family ties made workers fearful and subservient; and second, they theorized that only the man with something to lose would fight to save it from the aggressions of capitalism, yet they also said that the worker with nothing to lose was free to defy capitalist intimidation. A typical article addressed the workers thus: "In our privation and hunger you and I have had higher dreams than bread. We have had dreams of home, children, wife and fireside. . . . For us today there can be no home, no children, wife and fireside. Every animal has a mate, someone to love and be loved by, but two—the migratory worker and the mule. You and I, brother, are the sexless slaves of a civilization we have built of the blood and toil and tears of generations of our class. . . . Organization is the road to independence and respectability." Both the "mule" image and the "respectability" theme were common in such writings.[17]

To say that the Wobblies' provocative behavior and rhetoric alienated potential recruits is not to say that moderation and conventionality would have had the opposite effect. The SP proved this. Its local headquarters too were social centers, and the party held picnics, concerts, and theatrical benefits as well. After an election a New Yorker remarked, "Judging from the experience of one of the most flourishing of the New York city branches . . . one naturally draws these conclusions: The branches are successful socially and in increasing the party membership. The branches are not successful, however, politically."[18] The social life was not necessarily a permanent recruiting device, for it depended partly on exclusiveness. The comrades did not consciously try to keep out newcomers, of course, but they seem to have done so unwittingly. The *Call* received letters from time to time complaining that an important reason for the big turnover in membership was that new members were not greeted and introduced to others when they arrived for their first meetings. Some of these letter writers implied that they wanted to form surrogate ethnic-type ties with their comrades.[19]

What the IWW and SLP accomplished by tactics that had to narrow their appeal to John Q. Worker, the right-wingers in the SP seem to have achieved by their moderation. The *Call* and especially the *Social Democratic Herald* barely challenged John Q. Worker to think about large issues in terms other than those conventional among AFL members. True, they preached socialism on every page (except the sports page), as the only solution to the workers' problems. The *Herald* in addition expressed real hate for the Catholic Church. But these papers used no jargon; they did not even suggest the worker would have to devote time to the party if he decided to support it. Mostly they asked him to vote for candidates for office who, if elected, would give him what he already wanted and would certainly have no power to institute socialism. This sort of appeal could win thousands of passive supporters and votes, but the mildness of the demands could hardly win millions of recruits to a party dedicated to overthrowing the System. That is, the result of this line would likely be two kinds of "socialists"—an undependable mass of electoral supporters, and a party cadre who had been converted by means other than the sort of propaganda that the *Herald* and the *Call* provided. Of the former sort, some would join the party but probably would leave as soon as more commitment and activity were demanded of them, especially if they continued to participate in their ethnic and neighborhood community activities.

The crucial role of the demands made upon the member should be stressed. For the casual member who had satisfactory outside relationships and meaningful activities, the organization's demands would be felt as an imposition. For the deracinated seeker after meanings who was described above, the organization's demands made him fully committed to the cause. For such a person a movement that did *not* place heavy demands upon him could not satisfy his need for new meanings; the demands were the link between him and the movement as the giver of meanings.

This predicament of right-wing socialists elucidates the contradiction between the need for a supportive community and the need for the constant contact with potential recruits that was necessary if the movement was to grow. Most of those whom the radicals perceived as potential recruits were involved in those very ethnic, neighborhood, and/or religious relationships from which the radicals had extricated themselves. To make the converts, the radical had to go where the workers were, and that was generally inside those milieux that gave the workers support in *their* beliefs. To achieve his goal, then, he must relinquish the social context that sustained his commitment to the goal; and to sustain his commitment to the goal he must focus his life in a social context that prevented the goal from being pursued.

This contradiction was most evident in the SLP, which demanded such unanimity on doctrine that members had no choice but to wait for the converts to come to them; political and economic realities would, they felt sure, awaken the workers very soon. They are still waiting. Such a radical, feeling isolated in his society, has three compensations: *present* membership in a worldwide movement, the expectation of *future* vindication, and identification with *past* heroes. Yet all three leave him isolated: his present tie is with people who are distant in place, and his past and future ties are with his own compatriots who are distant in time. Nevertheless, the sense of isolation is overcome by these imaginative extensions, these absent members, of his radical "community."

The IWW had a different problem. As a union it had to send its cadre among nonradical workers, and it is therefore not surprising that that core consisted of a small number of individuals whose commitment could not be shaken even by constant mingling with nonradicals. Moreover, the IWW's main base was among migrant workers and those in small, new, and isolated localities, people who tended to be hostile toward the social order even if not committed radicals. Association with them posed less of a threat to the organizers' ideology than would association with settled workers with developed community structures and loyalties. Nevertheless the Wobblies did lose committed members often enough to complain of the constant threat of what they called "corruption."

The SP faced the gravest threat of all, for unlike the IWW it did not write off the skilled workers, and association with them meant involvement in the very relationships and organizations from which the socialists had in effect defected. The only alternative was for individual socialists to engage in one-to-one propagandizing, and they did so especially within their AFL unions, unaware that most people, even if they are receptive to new ideologies, are convertible only in groups that retain their preconversion bonds.[20]

III

One of the principal ways of maintaining the boundaries that separated the radicals from outsiders—while leaving doors open to them—was the use of polemics against adversaries both within and outside the organizations. Frank Bohn caught the essence of this function neatly when he wrote, "Socialists are innately 'kickers.' If they are not fighting capitalists they are pretty sure to be fighting one another. . . . We are so much like a great family that we sometimes forget that we are after all only a political party." [21]

A phrase in the quotation from Skårdal, above, suggests why this was so. The "dogmatic bitterness" of the Scandinavian-American church quarrels, she points out, was due in part to "the inner uncertainty" the quarrelers felt. On rare occasions radicals came close to admitting this about themselves. One delegate to the SLP's 1900 convention, for instance, favored a prohibition of party members' belonging to trade unions, for he did not want to see any comrade "in a position where he can even be contaminated by the pure and simplers." Another comrade said that there were many young people present and others coming into the party, and "we do not want the young element to be contaminated by the pure and simpler in any form." [22] The same self-doubt can be read in the statement by Wobbly agitator Joseph Ettor that those radicals who tried to "bore from within" the conventional unions almost invariably were corrupted: "the most unscrupulous labor fakirs now betraying the workers were once our 'industrialist,' 'Anarchist' and 'Socialist' comrades, who grew weary of the slow progress we were making on the outside, went over, and were not only lost but, like our former comrades who are now politicians, became the greatest supporters of the old and most serious enemies of the new." [23] As to the SP, a delegate to its 1910 convention remarked that, instead of working wholeheartedly for certain reforms that were before the Colorado state legislature, her Denver branch was reluctant to say anything, "so afraid are we of agreeing with our neighbors on anything." [24] It is fair to speculate, then, that one motive for vanguardism, in addition to the desire to induce John Q. Worker to join the radicals, was to keep their distance from him.

The obvious question evoked by such fears of corruption is: if the committed radicals found it hard to fend off the ideology of the outside world, how could they have expected John Q. Worker, who lived there all the time, to become converted from its ideology? Moreover, if consorting with nonradicals posed such a danger, then those radicals who had been converted to radical ideology, rather than having been born to radical parents, could not have consistently attributed their conversion to the "obvious" shortcomings of nonradical explanations for social phenomena. They did so anyway.

For people who must maintain the boundaries that help them define who they are and yet have trouble locating them, the worst enemies are necessarily those closest by. It was easy to differentiate oneself from Morgan and Roosevelt, somewhat harder from Gompers, but where was the boundary between one's own ideology and that of someone who claimed to be as radical as oneself and yet disagreed on important issues? This question is the context within which the astonishing epithets that the radicals flung at each other should be understood. It also helps explain why such epithets were used most abundantly by members of the SLP. The SLP's tenets were not so different from the SP's as to preclude friendly rivalry, and many SP members agreed with the SLP's trade-union policy rather than with their own party's.[25] Hence differences in temperament must be included among the reasons for the SLP members' hatred for both the SP and those movements that the latter was closest to. A few examples will suffice.

The STLA's periodical commented thus on the Populists: "The easy virtue of this political hotch-potch was disgustingly exhibited as it rushed into the embrace of that hoary-headed and most repulsive of all political reprobates, the Democratic party." In the next issue the target was AFL leaders who through their magazine "vomit forth their venom."[26] De Leon's response to the coalescence of the Debsites and the Kangaroos went as follows, in part: "The vocal collection of freaks, frauds and incompetents was a true reflection of the dumb body that it spoke for. That body consists not of the raw material that a new social system is to be woven out of, but of the garbage-barrel material, the offal and refuse of society; the slum element in every sense: struggling small retailers, who cannot rid themselves of the habit of cheating, acquired in their trade; labor fakirs, to whom swindle has become a habit like breathing; international adventurers without either sense, honor or knowledge; etc. etc."[27]

Doubtless some of those who left the SLP for the SP did so partly to escape the atmosphere of suspicion and recrimination revealed in such documents. SP members tended to be less prickly, less obsessed with order and purity, with doctrinal precision, and with putting every person and thing and idea into precisely the right conceptual pigeonhole, than members of the SLP. As to the Wobblies, most of their epithets that expressed intense hate were directed against the unconverted worker.[28]

Just as common as the epithets were expressions of a mind-set that attributed enormous power, cleverness, and malignity to adherents of other belief-systems, and often grossly exaggerated the movement's impact on outsiders. One example of this mind-set, sometimes commented upon, was a grim pugnacity and lack of a sense of humor. De Leon was complex enough to escape this character trait, as his *People* demonstrated each week. But not his comrades, at least those who put out the STLA's *Socialist Alliance*.[29] Charles Dobbs recorded a conversation he had had with an SLP member, who was

fiercely arraigning all Socialists outside the pale of his party for what appeared to him as the folly of their tactics. He had rehearsed the whole catalogue of the crimes of the "Kangaroos" and the "Debsites," and had expressed the usual opinion that there is but one Socialist party and De Leon is its prophet, when I interrupted and gently remarked: "My dear Schmutz, the trouble with you is that you lack a sense of humor." The interruption, however, did not have the desired soothing effect. Instead of taking the remark as I meant it—that a sense of humor would enable him to recognize the absurdity of his party's claim to all virtue and wisdom—he thought I was pleading for a gentler warfare against social injustice, and he cried out: "There is no humor in the crimes of capitalism. It is no laughing matter to us poor devils who are shut out from the enjoyment of the good things of life to which we are entitled." Yes, capitalism is a tragedy, but it is beyond the ordinary human capacity to go on forever with one's teeth clenched in the frenzy of combat.

Perhaps Comrade Schmutz did see that Dobbs was denying the SLP's monopoly; to a Comrade Schmutz such an assertion *was* tantamount to laughing at the crime of capitalism. Dobbs missed that point when he concluded that "sanity demands an occasional cessation in the work of feeding the flames of our indignation."[30] That was true of most socialists; for a Comrade Schmutz, however, sanity demanded the perpetually clenched teeth.

De Leon epitomized the atmosphere in his party in one brief line: "In a movement like this, there is not one enemy MADE; but enemies are UNMASKED."[31] He was genial and accommodating when comrades disagreed on secondary questions, but incapable of admitting error on issues he thought basic. Those who disagreed with him on such issues were, however, not touching anything so personal as egotism, for "if any one thing more than any other is the distinguishing mark of the Socialist, that thing is veneration for FACTS."[32] Opponents on basic issues must have been conscious conspirators against the party (therefore against socialism) and in behalf of capitalist oppression. The result of this chain of logic was the unshakable belief that the capitalists considered the SLP their only enemy—and an enormously formidable one— despite its small numbers. The capitalists, he explained, perceived that only the SLP told the truth about the essential unity of all other parties, wherefore they were trying to capture it. But all who had attempted to do so had been expelled. So the capitalists misrepresented the party, to deprive it of its influence. All of the controversies and expulsions involved "carefully disguised emissaries" of the capitalists. The SLP, he insisted, was still attracting the intelligent workers, and that was why the enemy needed the Social Democratic Party as a spurious alternative to the SLP and why Debs must be exposed as the "bombastic, ignorant fakir" he was.[33] All this venom was not only excusable but obligatory, for its only motive was the defense of the workers' vanguard.

So long as a radical considered his movement the sole means to social salvation and assumed that the capitalist class agreed with him on that one point, discoveries of conspiracies followed logically. After the expulsion of the Shermanites from the IWW, a leader explained that that faction had intended, when it took possession of the headquarters, to destroy all evidence of its plot to hand the IWW over to the employers. But, as Paul Brissenden pointed out, when two years later De Leon split with the IWW, it was the SP leaders who saw a "deep-laid conspiracy," and now De Leon was the ringleader.[34] De Leon must bear the palm for imaginative accusations, however, in accounting for Sherman's behavior: he contrasted Sherman with Jesus. The archfiend showed Jesus all the kingdoms of the world and said he would rule over them if he bowed down and worshiped the devil, and Jesus refused. "The arch fiends of this movement gathered round Sherman, and they said to him, 'All these myriads of working men will we give you if you bow down before us and put the revolutionists out of the I.W.W.," and Sherman succumbed. "The conspiracy was deep laid. . . . It was a conspiracy to squelch the revolution in this convention and to start over again an A.F. of L." [35] It need hardly be added that Sherman's ouster did not clear the air, for this type of person carried his plot-ridden atmosphere around with him. At the next convention of the IWW, De Leon, pleading with his fellow delegates not to abolish the office of president, because the organization needed an executive, intoned, "We are surrounded by men who are intriguing. We are surrounded by pure and simple politicians. We are surrounded by pure and simple craft unionists, and we are surrounded by the hostility of the capitalist class that promotes the one and the other." [36] Other Wobblies perceived their organization in the same way. The *Industrial Worker* sometimes quoted from innocuous articles in "bourgeois" newspapers that supposedly proved that, as one headline put it, "The Master Class Is Trembling with Fear" [37] owing to the IWW's call for a general strike in behalf of the McNamara brothers or for some other action. In not one case do the quotations support the imputation.

The grim ferocity, exaggerated sense of the impact of one's own organization on the enemy, and inability to impute sincerity to other varieties of radical, all of which were so noticeable among the SLP members and to a lesser degree among the Wobblies, were rarer among members of the SP. Partly this must have been due to the natural inclination of people to associate with others like themselves; the existence of the SLP remnant after 1901 may have fostered the healthier atmosphere in the SP merely by providing the Comrade Schmutzes a coterie of their own. [38] Yet here and there a Comrade Schmutz turns up in SP documents—for example, the New Yorker who wrote to the *Call* to object to the sports department and its references to baseball as "our" national game. There are many young people, he wrote, who, instead of working to change conditions and study their causes, follow baseball to take their minds off those conditions. "Is not this one of the reasons why our young are so slow in 'taking hold' of Socialism?" [39]

IV

If radical movements satisfied the desire of many of their members to belong to groups of people with the same values, beliefs, and purposes, they in turn deposited their very selves in their groups. We have seen how several of the people quoted above identified themselves with their movements to the extent of interpreting hostility toward themselves as hostility toward socialism. The implications in the epithets require us, therefore, to return to the theme of the movements as surrogate communities and expand it by adding, to the function that the movement performed for the member, what the member gave it in return—to use Hadley Cantril's term, "ego involvement." The more a person feels "what he regards as 'himself'" is involved in his standards of judgment or frames of reference, says Cantril, the more intensely he will believe in them and reject alternatives, and the more he will devote time, energy, and money to getting his society to accept them.[40] Unlike John Q. Worker, who if asked to describe himself would name several roles and attributes—worker, machine tender, Catholic, Pole, resident of such and such a neighborhood, member of such and such a family, secretary of the choral society, etc., depending in part on the questioner and context—the radical would give his radical identification. Or, if he said "worker," he would mean something quite different from what John Q. Worker meant by it, for it would represent a Cause in addition to and more important than his occupation.

It is this "ego involvement" that made disillusionment so great a trauma, inducing most to blind themselves to disconfirming data and a few to commit suicide when such data could not be ignored.[41] Such a tragic outcome can be explained only by the monopolization of the person's very self by the movement; for the person whose self was, so to speak, distributed among several institutions and roles had some part "left over" if one of them must be abandoned. When Thomas J. Morgan told his comrades of the suicides of those socialists who had staked their very selves on their certainty of the imminence of the revolution,[42] and implored his hearers not to make the same mistake, he was touching on this danger of extreme "ego involvement."

In most of the radicals, of course, the process never went so far. We can see a milder form of it in statements such as that quoted earlier, by a Wobbly journalist, that "life becomes invested with meaning for ourselves, and the living or losing of it is made worth while," only as workers sink their personal concerns in the greater cause of the emancipation of their class.[43] The writer was projecting his own feeling onto John Q. Worker, who certainly did not feel that way. So totally had the Cause enveloped that Wobbly that he could not imagine that the nonradical worker could feel his life had any meaning.

The more a radical felt this way toward his movement, the more important must its basis have been to him. That basis was its ideology. Thus the wrangling over doctrinal minutiae is related in still another way to the "community" function of the organizations. Where an ethnic community is defined by a culture, a radical "community" is defined only by an ideology, a recently constructed intellectual artifact (although it possesses certain subcultural traits). Ideology can never be taken for granted as a true culture can; a true culture, precisely because it is taken for granted, can tolerate a good deal of ideological diversity. If the radical community had been truly the mirror image of the ethnic community, one would expect to find evidence that it tolerated a good deal of ethnocultural diversity. Yet this is not the case, because the radical ideology itself denigrated ethnicity as divisive and many members of radical organizations had clearly rejected their inherited cultures. (The various language federations and branches were unavoidable expedients, and the two socialist parties never felt comfortable with them.)

Projection is evident as well in statements such as Debs's reference to the "progressive heresy," that capitalists could be reformed.[44] Why "heresy" rather than "fraud" or "delusion" or any other of the many labels he could have chosen from the radical lexicon? "Heresy" has a particular meaning: a deviation from *the* truth, *his* Truth. Debs's choice of term reveals how totally he perceived the world from the standpoint of the One Center, the One Truth, beyond which all was darkness and error. Similarly, when he wrote that nonsocialist politicians "babble about the tariff and other inconsequential matters to obscure the real issue [wage slavery],"[45] he was assuming that his criteria of consequentiality were self-evident. The charge of ulterior motives followed logically.

Another form of the same mind-set was shown by a frequent contributor to the *Industrial Worker*. Revolutionary members of the IWW, he wrote, "bear in mind that there can be no peace between those who produce everything and get nothing and those, who get all and produce nothing. . . . Their dominant thought is the class struggle."[46] This was a Wobbly self-portrait projected onto all members of Wobbly locals, and, in the writer's imagination, onto all workers in the near future. The key point is the assumed connection between the two sentences. For a radical Wobbly the first entails the second; however, class-conscious but nonradical workers who believed the first statement had a variety of

"dominant thought[s]." But the life of a member of a radical "community" could easily shove other concerns into the background, if we can
believe the description of party activity written by a member of a New
York local of the SP. The active member, he said, devoted two evenings a
month to

assembly district meetings, two evenings to the general committee, two evenings to the agitation committee, and four evenings to the city executive committee. Four evenings are at present taken up by the Moyer-Haywood conference. That makes fourteen evenings monthly. To this must still be added
evenings spent in unions, sick-benevolent societies, Volkszeitung, Daily Call
conference, platform and literature committee, etc., etc. Numerous active members, after having worked hard for eight to twelve hours in their respective
shops, take part in most of the above enumerated meetings. So we certainly can't complain of negligence on the part of those who are active party
members.[47]

This letter was meant to show why the party did not progress and could
not keep most of its recruits. The writer did not consider the possibility
that only an atypical minority would be willing to sacrifice virtually all
outside roles and interests for the sake of the cause—or, to put it more
accurately, that only an atypical minority would consider the abandonment of virtually all other roles and interests to be not a sacrifice but the
discovery at long last of something that gave meaning to their lives. That
such statements implied a disvaluation of John Q. Worker's roles, interests, values, and very self-identification is clear; it is hard to imagine
that John Q. Worker did not hear it.

X   Epilogue: John Q. Worker

I

Among all the subjects of historians' theorizing, workers hold a special place: the beliefs, values, and motives of no other category of persons have been written about so deductively. The "Sombartian" approach discussed in Chapter II has not been monopolized by radical historians, any more than the passive image of the worker, prevalent in the period under study, was the sole possession of radicals. As was shown in that chapter, John Q. Worker's beliefs and values, where perceived accurately at all, until recently have been considered holdovers from the premodern past, obstacles to progress, and the like. In the absence of much empirical research, his life and thought were generally depicted in three general frameworks. The first was the misnamed labor history, which dealt only with the unionized minority.[1] The second was the Progressive paradigm, which depicted John Q. Worker abstractly as a participant in a struggle between The People and The Interests. The third was the Marxist portrayal of the proletariat as one of several historical "forces" and assumed that culture was secondary to economics and politics in shaping John Q. Worker's life and thought. The data that "the new social history" has been accumulating for the past twenty years have been revealing all such theories to be aprioristic.

Consider the tradition of historiography most relevant to this book, that of the radical historians who have perceived John Q. Worker much as his radical contemporaries did. Their a priori assumptions and their research method correspond perfectly. If all the Sombartian "obstacles" to John Q. Worker's radicalization are reversed, they produce the Old Left paradigm for interpreting working-class history. The effects of the Sombartian factors on John Q. Worker's attitudes are deduced from certain assumptions about what he must have been like, and those aspects of his life, thought, and history that do not fit the paradigm are absent altogether. In the Old Left histories, where are the studies of religion, ethnicity, family structure, immigration, community relations, recreational activities? The data for such studies have turned out to be more plentiful than had been supposed, but they have been discovered and discussed mostly by historians who have considered them worthy of study in their own right. Old Left historians have generally focused on union history, class struggle, radicalization: those good things that the Sombartian factors were obstacles to. It will be noticed that most of the obstacles are located in the private sphere.

Hence the apriorism; for religion, ethnicity, family, and community were those institutions that mediated between the individual and the public sphere of government and the economy.[2] They mediated in both directions, affecting John Q. Worker's attitudes toward the public sphere as well as affording him the means to affect it. A historian who ignores such institutions and John Q. Worker's beliefs and attitudes concerning them, who brushes them aside as "obstacles" or historical fossils, creates a documentary gap that he can then close only by means of a priori assumptions. But although John Q. Worker cannot answer back to these historians, he could and did refuse to enter the ideological pigeonhole prepared for him by his radical contemporaries.

When he did, he refuted the radicals' perceptions of him and thus bequeathed, to any modern historians who lack the blind spot that blocks out the meaning of the private sphere, a standpoint from which to perceive the radicals through John Q. Worker's eyes. This would not merely reverse the Sombartian approach; we need not assume that John Q. Worker's perception of the radicals was "correct" and that the radicals' beliefs and values were "obstacles" to *their* enlightenment. Rather, whatever the cognitive status of John Q. Worker's belief-system or the accuracy of his perceptions of the radicals, they are crucial data for a study of the radicals because the latter's belief-systems included beliefs about John Q. Worker's mind. If, on the contrary, those beliefs are taken as the standard of his rationality and the framework for interpretation of his belief-system, then the "results" of the research can produce no surprises. A historian who does not question the essential correctness of the radicals' message is not likely to consider the possibility that John Q. Worker was an active maker of his own history, and not just when he was struggling or thinking radical thoughts.

Just as radical historiography tends to perceive John Q. Worker both as inert raw material for capitalists and radicals to work on, and as the heroic Proletarian with an instinct for struggle against his oppressors, so nonradical historiography used to contain a double image of him: as the bewildered immigrant huddled in his ethnic enclave craving security,[3] and as the proud folk figure who sacrificed his own comfort so that his grandsons could become scholars and write filiopietistic histories in the immigrant-gifts tradition. The immigrant-success image is, ironically, very similar to the heroic-proletarian image in that, by denying widespread demoralization, they both minimize what the immigrant majority of the industrial working class of that period were up against and the inner resources they had to have if they were to cope successfully. By denying the failures, both interpretations trivialize the successes. The radical historian portraying the heroic proletarian as the norm thinks he is condemning the System, but he is really paying it an impossibly high tribute, for any System that permits such universal heroism and little demoralization must be the best the world is ever likely to see. It is hard to believe that if American society has been a System it can have been as good as radical historians have portrayed it. Or as bad— not in the sense that it could not have been so oppressive as they, contradictorily, have depicted it, but in the sense of forcing all its working-class members into a single mold. Even if that single mold had been heroic, moreover, any tribute paid to their heroism must be as meaningless as the medals awarded to every member of a graduating class in a school that gives only *A*'s.

Unfortunately, the new social history has turned up few documents in which John Q. Worker stated explicitly how he perceived the radicals. But we now have a mass of evidence about those institutions and beliefs that his radical contemporaries and Old Left historians tended to dismiss, and the interpretation of which can help us understand one datum about which there is no question: that John Q. Worker by the millions ignored the radicals. The new social history, however, presents its own problem: whereas Old Left historians and most political and economic historians focused solely on the public sphere, the new social history has gone to the other extreme of focusing almost exclusively on the private sphere. The new political history attends to both spheres, but mainly to show the influence of private-sphere concerns on political action, not the reverse at the same time.[4] The next stage will likely integrate the findings of the new social and political histories by means of hypotheses that relate the public and private spheres.

This chapter will proceed on the assumption that no wholly satisfactory theory has yet been formulated at this early stage of the new social history. It will assume that John Q. Worker's private sphere was subject to constraints and influences emanating from the economic and political power of the capitalist class in general and his own employer in particular, but that important aspects of his private sphere may not have been shaped by such constraints and influences. It will assume, further, that the object for which a person acts, the end for the sake of which he accepts certain means that to a large extent are beyond his free choice, determines the meaning of those means. It will assume that the historian cannot know what John Q. Worker's economic and political relationships meant unless he studies not just John Q. Worker's private sphere but also its relationship, in John Q. Worker's (not the historian's) mind, to the public sphere, and without preconceptions as to either their independence or their integration. And finally, it will assume that a portrait of the American working class of the 1890–1917 period should include the differences as much as the shared elements among the various ethnic groups.

On the basis of the foregoing assumptions and a large sample of the literature of American social history published before mid-1977, this chapter will discuss three general areas of John Q. Worker's life and thought: first, his private sphere as the locus of his values and relationships that provided him with his sense of identity; second, the reasons why he likely saw the public sphere as instrumental to those values and relationships; and third, how, in the light of those values and relationships, he may have perceived those people who attempted to convert him to their values and beliefs.[5]

II

To open the discussion of John Q. Worker's private sphere, we must stress one fact that the documents show clearly: his off-the-job life can

be discussed with very little mention either of his radical contemporaries or of ideological influences originating from outside his own ethnic group. Working-class communities were not, of course, isolated
from the rest of American society. Their members had to learn punctuality and other habits appropriate to an industrial society, had to ad-
just to urban living and daily contact with people of other cultures, had
to obey American laws, had to cope with all manner of unavoidable circumstances. These adaptations have been offered as proof that John Q.
Worker accepted the ideological hegemony of the capitalist class, but all
they prove is the truism that his belief-system was compatible with the
continued existence of the economic system. Unless the social order was
a System they prove nothing else. If, on the contrary, it was a Society,
John Q. Worker's belief-system may turn out to have been neither "bourgeois" nor "antibourgeois"—*i.e.*, not essentially describable in System
terms—but an autochthonous phenomenon.

The above hypothesis can be tested if we use the findings of social
history to portray the immigrant, first as he decided to emigrate from
the Old Country, and then as he participated in the construction of a
new community in America.

His very decision to emigrate proclaims the falsity of the common
radical perception of John Q. Worker as "squeezed lemon," "sheep," or
"asleep": each of the millions of immigrants made the decision to leave
his native land and undertake a long journey to a strange country. To be
sure, more than half of them returned during certain periods, but they
had intended to from the start. (See Supplement.) The decision and the
journey could not have been made by the willing slaves depicted in
Chapter V above, or in that school of historiography that emphasizes
the immigrants' bewilderment and therefore assumes that the ethnic
community was constructed for purely defensive purposes. One recent
commentator points out that emigration not only caused suffering and
culture shock but also provided "an occasion for many emigrants to live
for the first time outside of and in a reality completely different from
that of their old village, freed as it were from the restrictions of century-
old systems. However negative some of the consequences of this sharp,
if not brutal, 'liberation' may be, greater attention should be given to the
positive effects which it can have, providing for some the only possibility of complete renewal of their own convictions and orientation."[6]

Many became demoralized and degraded. Thomas and Znaniecki portray broken homes, drunkenness, and crime among the Poles; Hillquit depicts Jewish bakers reduced virtually to working machines; other writers add similar details.[7] But most migrants had the inner resources, individually and collectively, to cope with the unexpected situations they found themselves in, showing a capacity for innovation they must have had before embarking on the voyage to America.[8]

Their responses included the construction of "hyphenate" communities—the Polish-American, Italian-American, etc., ethnic communities—that adapted Old Country institutions and mores to new conditions, or invented new ones. In so doing they created something new, a cultural and institutional framework within which individuals found emotional support and guides to thinking and behavior, carried on social activities, married, and satisfied their need for sources of prestige and approval. (It should not be necessary to add that the resulting ethnic cultures and communities included meanness, superstition, prejudice against outsiders, etc., as well as courage, neighborliness, and other traits that are usually approved of. It *is* necessary to add this, however, in view of the assumption common in radical historiography that when The People do Bad Things it is only because they have been misled by their class enemies or corrupted by the System.) Since even English-speaking immigrants constructed hyphenate communities despite the absence of nativist hostility and language problems, such construction could not have been motivated solely by the "need for security,"[9] purely reactive and defensive. If it had been, ethnic consciousness would not be as strong today as scholars have recently discovered it to be but as John Q. Worker has always known it to be.[10] Its causes lay deeper in his psyche; they are to be found in the universal need for membership in a group of human size.

That community was "a staging area"[11] for immigrants and their children learning how to function in the larger society. The main vehicles for this learning were cultural, religious, and recreational institutions. (See Supplement.) All the detailed studies of hyphenate communities note the proliferation of mutual-benefit societies that were needed in the absence of workmen's compensation and unemployment insurance. But they also describe the many other societies, newspapers, and activities that had no economic function. Whether, as in Italo-America and

German-America, the societies kept the first generation fragmented according to village or region of origin,[12] or, as in other ethnic groups, produced a new national consciousness absent in the Old Country, they served to bind together communities that were both large enough to satisfy a member's primordial needs and small enough to permit him to play a recognized role; large enough to induce a recalcitrant member to support a strike but small enough to give him a voice in community decisions.[13]

The hyphenate communities that served these needs best were those that had the greatest class differentiation. They produced an intellectual and artistic group to run the newspapers and theaters and write the books and plays; a professional class to minister to religious, medical, and legal needs; and tradesmen to sell familiar goods. This petty bourgeoisie could also be exploitative, as was most notoriously the case with the Italian *padroni* and Jewish "sweaters" on New York's East Side. But the nonworking-class strata also located rungs on the economic and achievement ladders that John Q. Worker could envision himself or his children climbing, if he had the wish to do so, or, if not, a source of prestige for his ethnic group, and the financial means and voting solidarity for the group to be semiautonomous. And lastly, these nonproletarian strata made it possible, in time, for the group to acquire political clout, which members could not acquire as individuals; they thereby furnished members with incentives to retain their ties with the ethnic community.

It is appropriate here to recall the "ego involvement" theme discussed in Chapter IX. It was suggested there that John Q. Worker, if asked to describe himself, would have listed several roles and attributes, in contrast to the radical whose ideological commitment subsumed all other elements in his life and personality. The ethnicity concept here is not meant to be John Q. Worker's equivalent of the radical's radicalism. Unlike the radical, who of course also performed many roles, John Q. Worker did not subordinate all but one of them to that one. He did not generally manifest the "ego involvement" of the person who had committed his entire being to a Cause. His community permitted him to "distribute" parts of his personality among different relationships and functions. Hence, to suggest that his membership in that community and his acceptance of its belief-system made him unreceptive to the radical alternative is not to suggest that his ethnicity or value-system alone caused the unreceptivity; the very multiplicity of roles and relationships had that effect. This differentiation of functions is what made his a true community whereas the radicals' organizations were merely surrogate communities. However hard the radical tried to duplicate the cultural activities of the "outside world," by forming baseball leagues, running theatricals, and so on, these activities hung on the single thread of ego involvement in the one Cause. They were never integral aspects of the radical commitment, for the same reasons that the individual radicals' positions on the religion and Negro and woman questions—the private-sphere questions—were never fully accommodated to the *raison d'être* of the radical movements.

The construction of the hyphenate culture depended heavily upon the women's roles, for, as has been pointed out, "The cultural aspects of ethnicity are transmitted within the family largely through the woman, even without her conscious awareness."[14] During the industrialization process, the decay of craft skills had caused the separation of the public from the private sphere, which in turn entailed a greater distinction between the roles of men and of women. As Gareth Stedman Jones has described the process in England, it gave the wife more control over the depoliticized domestic sphere at the same time as that sphere came to occupy a larger place in the worker's life. The increased separation of the sexes extended even to recreation; pubs and clubs were all-male preserves.[15] One result was that fathers had less to do with their children's upbringing than before. In most ethnic communities the woman clung to the old language longer, having less need for English than the man did. Thus, the same process of sphere differentiation that was taking place in both the host society and the immigrant enclaves produced contrary effects. For reasons that are only now coming to be understood, it fostered in the host society a demand for equal rights for women.[16] In most ethnic enclaves the enhanced influence of women over the domestic sphere, consequent upon the men's working away from it, probably fostered the retention of the Old Country culture. The immigrants who generally declined to support the woman suffrage movement until its last decade were defending a separation of spheres that sustained their ethnic identities and hence their personal identities.

The crucial role of women in the evolution of the hyphenate community is strikingly demonstrated by what happened to the Scandinavians. Their young women usually worked in the households of Americans, where they learned customs and standards that they taught to their own families, thereby accelerating their acculturation. At the other extreme, Italian women were permitted fewer contacts with Americans, and the culture they transmitted to their children retained far more traditional ingredients. It would be interesting to see a study of how the degree and mode of acculturation of various hyphenate communities correlates with the roles of their female members. Unfortunately, we know little about immigrant women,[17] and the few published studies tend to stress what women of different ethnic cultures had in common, to the neglect of the differences.[18] But historians are starting to recognize what sociologists and anthropologists have always known: that a cultural heritage is much more resilient than economic-environmentalist assumptions have allowed.[19]

Those assumptions have been essential to radical historians' exaggeration of the ideological influence of the employer over John Q. Worker's belief-system, for the employer was supposedly the principal element in his "environment." Two chief corollaries have flowed from this contention: first, that the persistence of ethnic differences has been due to bosses' fostering of them and has retarded the development of class consciousness; and second, that the differences in the rates of mobility among ethnic groups are attributable solely to different degrees of discrimination against and opportunities afforded to immigrant workers. The first corollary can be disposed of merely by asking why John Q. Worker was receptive to the divide-and-conquer efforts.[20] Any answer to that question consistent with the assumption of the bosses' determining role must portray John Q. Worker as a blank page for cleverer people to write their own values on. The second corollary has been refuted by comparative studies showing the central role that immigrant values have played in mobility rates. For a long time even the asking of such questions was suspect on the left; it was "blaming the victim" or suggesting that the capitalist class wielded less power than the System theory required. But those assumptions had been undermined by social historians long before, and recent work has discredited them entirely.[21]

John Bodnar's comparison of the Irish and Welsh; Josef Barton's comparison of Rumanians, Italians, and Slovaks; Margaret F. Byington's comparison of Slavs, native whites, blacks, and miscellaneous Europeans; and many studies of Jewish mobility—all give evidence that immigrant groups in very similar circumstances climbed the income-and-class ladder at different rates.[22] The desire to earn more money is, of course, not the same thing as the desire to join the middle class, and John Q. Worker's actual mobility does not tell us whether he wanted prestige, or to afford to educate his children, or to leave the working class, or whether he had some other objective.[23] His motive may have been quite different from that offered him by the popular success literature of the day. Generalizations about Americans' attitudes toward mobility are customarily illustrated by quotations from Russell Conwell's *Acres of Diamonds* and Andrew Carnegie's *Gospel of Wealth*. There is no reason to suppose that John Q. Worker read these essays or would have been influenced by them if he had. We are more likely to discover his motives by looking within his own culture.

Among the discoveries that have resulted from this effort to discover John Q. Worker's own motives are the following: The Slavs whom Bodnar studied valued education for its own sake and as a way to transmit traditional values to their children, and not because they had bought the success ethic. The steelworkers whom David Brody studied accepted long hours and low pay not because they were cowed but in order to save money to return to the Old Country; that is, their submissiveness was a calculated aspect of their future-orientedness. According to Iris S. Podea, when the economic condition of the New England *Québecois* improved, they turned their attention away from preoccupation with getting a livelihood and to their survival as an ethnic group; in other words the work was important only so far as it implemented private-sphere values. The Scandinavians portrayed in the fiction that Skårdal surveyed did accept the goal of mobility and wanted to abandon their European roots, at the same time as they were determined to maintain a distinct way of life. The Italian gardeners studied by Rudolph Vecoli commuted all the way from Boston to their jobs in the suburbs because they wanted to live among their countrymen; according to Virginia Y. McLaughlin, Italians in Buffalo made similar choices, at the cost of financial sacrifice. A Norwegian quoted by Jon Wefald wrote that he and his friends did not expect to get rich but that the liberty to work as they chose was more important than wealth. Here and there such studies show the immigrants to have expressed distaste for American values as well as praise for American opportunity. That is, the opportunity did not necessarily foster the values; it sometimes provided immigrants more freedom to live by their own values than they could in the Old Country.[24]

Still another discovery made possible by the study of ethnic communities in their own terms is the surprising extent to which developments within them were not reactions to external pressures. A particularly suggestive example is Victor R. Greene's analysis of the evolution of localistic peasants into Polish-Americans. That evolution was due mostly to conflicts within the Polish-American community and churches. Greene speculates that a similar internal dynamic may have been decisive in other ethnic communities as well. If it was, he says, the enabling circumstances were "the underlying influences of a democratic society, church-state separation and ethnic federalism, which worked unseen on the immigrant's daily life inside his community."[25]

This orientation of individuals to the ethnic group rather than to, or in addition to, the environing society suggests that seemingly similar incidents could have opposite meanings. Consider the scolding that Joseph Barondess—a flamboyant character, union leader, and sometime socialist—gave his fellow Jews on New York's East Side. Berating them for accepting low wages, he called them idiots, cows, oxen, jackasses.[26] At first sight he seems to have been expressing the same contempt that Wobblies and some socialists manifested toward the unawakened worker, in the documents excerpted in Chapter V above. In fact, they convey opposite meanings. Barondess' harangue can be understood only in the context of the extraordinarily high degree of mobility among the Jews; he himself was an accurate barometer of their beliefs. They loved him for scolding them because in his words they heard themselves scolding themselves. Here was one of their own, with the same goals, goading them to pursue them more diligently. The radical polemicists, on the contrary, scolded John Q. Worker for having his own goals and pursuing them, or for having no goals at all, as they often assumed.

In fact, the more the new social historians have studied working-class communities in the latter's own terms, the broader the range of choices they have discovered existed. And the more choices they now know to have existed, the more they recognize that the choices that were made were made autonomously, in terms of the ethnic communities' own values, beliefs, and goals.[27] Let us recall the leaflet quoted in Chapter V, in which the socialists of Massachusetts told John Q. Worker that he was a "squeezed lemon," a dupe, a buffalo, stupidly going from job to job begging to be exploited. The findings of social historians suggest how he may have reacted upon reading this. He did not respond as the Jewish workers did to Barondess' scolding. He knew, as well as the socialists did, that he was sacrificing much for the sake of his family, neighborhood, and social club. But he knew, as the socialist did not, why he was doing so. Even though the means to his ends put profits in his boss's pocket, he was not a slave, so long as they served his own goals.

What did the demoralization of the minority consist of but the abandonment of independent goals? Those drunkards and criminals, those wretched bakers who lived only to work, those machine-like women with skilled hands and blank minds, had all given up the battle to separate the job and the private sphere and had become what the radicals said the entire working class really was: "hands." The very separation of work from family and community, consequent upon the decay of old crafts and the mechanization of industry, made it possible for unskilled and semiskilled workers to view the job as instrumental to goals located in the private sphere, to endow inherently meaningless work with a new meaning extrinsic to it.[28] Or, to put the point differently, John Q. Worker did resist the brutalization threatened by industrialization; he did so with cultural as well as with economic weapons. But the radicals interpreted the former not as barriers against dehumanization but as evidence of it.

A third reaction was possible, in addition to, first, John Q. Worker's instrumental view of the job, by means of which distinction he maintained his self-definition as a whole man, and, second, the demoralization that resulted if his self became identified with meaningless work. The third reaction was the radical's. It was halfway between the first two in that the radical had internalized, as John Q. Worker had not, the employer's supposed perception of the employee as a mere "hand," but resented this degradation, as the demoralized did not. The employer's use of a man as a "hand" or thing was resented to the degree that the man inwardly accepted that status short of total acceptance. The resentment, and the commitment to abolish the relationship, stemmed from the personality's struggle to maintain its wholeness. John Q. Worker certainly knew that his role in the factory was that of a "hand." But if he held fast to the goals for the sake of which he had immigrated and decided to stay in the United States, and if those goals remained embedded in a living culture and community, the "hand" role had little psychological impact upon him. For the sake of these goals he could put up with the miserable conditions of his job.[29]

It will be answered that the radicals' demand was not that the boss treat John Q. Worker as a "whole man" but that the System be changed so as to abolish the boss-worker relationship. The sources, however, show that the radicals gave little thought to the postrevolutionary job situation beyond predicting fewer hours of work and better conditions. They did not address the problem discussed here—the fact that the worker on the job was occupying one role that excluded all his others— beyond occasional paraphrases of Marx's fantasy that individuals would pursue many vocations in quick alteration. Another argument often encountered is that the loss of self-respect and morale, consequent upon long unemployment, proves that unskilled workers did identify themselves with their jobs. On the contrary, all it proves is that their self-identification included their role as breadwinners, regardless of the particular work they did. If the job was instrumental to the private sphere, its loss, by destroying the worker's ability to contribute needed money to that sphere, not surprisingly damaged his self-esteem. This distinction between being a breadwinner and occupying a high-status job is supported by the fact that John Q. Worker had, in some cases, been a proud paterfamilias in the Old Country although living in penury at the bottom of a class hierarchy that kept reminding him of his "place."

On the basis of the hypothesis that John Q. Worker's behavior in the public sphere should be interpreted in light of goals located in the private sphere, let us reexamine the latter so as to elucidate this instrumental attitude.

Except in the case of the east European Jews on New York's East Side, John Q. Worker's job generally required him to leave the neighborhood each morning six days a week and enter an alien world. Some of his co-workers were his coethnics, but his foreman probably was not, and his employer almost certainly was not. He was class conscious, but his class consciousness was a part of his ethnicity. That is, he knew himself to be a member of the working class even if he had been a peasant the year before;[30] the concept of class was familiar to him. But the social structure that gave the concept meaning was part of a culture rooted in the Old Country and not a theoretical abstraction defined by relation to the means of production. The increased conspicuousness of class divisions in the post–Civil War period was offensive to many Americans, and the American tradition of classlessness condemned the very fact of class divisions as unjust. John Q. Worker, however, generally came out of a tradition that took them for granted. He resented low wages, bad treatment, and other oppressive circumstances that could be changed while the class structure remained intact. The same cultural foreignness that made the immigrant worker an alien to American society made his class consciousness alien; integral to the social order that he had left, it could not be transplanted to America. In addition, the recency of the immigrants' arrival should not be forgotten. Most had not been in America long enough to have become convinced that their goals could not be achieved—even assuming that the radicals were correct in insisting that they could not be.

This may be why, in the only period in which there was a substantial number of working-class radicals in the United States—the period in which the vast majority of industrial workers were foreign-born—most of those who *became* radicals *in* America were native-born: the latter could feel themselves to be part of the American class structure. A commitment to fight against something is, after all, a form of acceptance— acceptance of the personal significance of what one is fighting. (One might even suggest that it was the radicals, rather than John Q. Worker, who labored under the ideological—or psychological—hegemony of the bourgeoisie.) The very high proportion of radicals in the Finnish and East Side Jewish immigrant groups was due partly to the presence of some who brought their radicalism with them to the United States and partly to the response of others to Old World experiences. The radical minorities in other hyphenate communities comprised mostly people who in Europe had been socialists or syndicalists and whose theories about capitalist society applied to whatever country they might live in.[31] Any large-scale class consciousness (in the radicals' sense of the term) among the immigrant workers would have had to be as new as the

multiclass hyphenate communities, as new as John Q. Worker's commitment to life in the United States. And it would have had to be an aspect
of the structure of real hyphenate communities, not the acceptance
of membership in the abstract, international proletariat of radical
ideology.[32]

A culture that in time ceases to satisfy the need for membership in a
group of human size will change or disintegrate, as its members find
their meanings elsewhere. It is in this context that we should view the
large proportion of immigrant Jews who were socialists. The cultural
change among the Jews of the Pale began in the Old Country and, for
thousands, pointed toward socialism, the universalistic appeal of which
was consistent with traditional Jewish values and centuries of Jewish experience.[33] "The Jewish labor unions . . . ," writes Moses Rischin, "were
far more than labor unions. In many respects, the Jewish labor movement represented no less than the aspirations of a Jewish world in tur-
moil. The early years of this movement paralleled the years of struggle
for the emancipation of Russia's five million Jews." In that struggle, they
were forced "to modify or to discard religious habits" and traditions,
which "gave way to a voracious urge for the most cosmopolitan modes
of thought," though adapted to the Jewish heritage. "Out of the debris,
Jewish immigrants forged a religiously-informed socialism and cultural
modernism," aspiring toward enlightenment, progress, science, and
knowledge as the key to freedom and social justice. "With the emotional urgency of a long-persecuted people, they envisaged a promised
land where differences of race, religion and nationality would no longer
divide mankind, where worldly goods would be apportioned equitably
and all energies would be devoted to the cultivation of the arts of
peace."[34]

The East Side Jews were unique among the "new immigrants" in that
a large proportion of their working population worked for coethnics
who were almost as new to the United States as they were, so that many
could spend the rest of their lives within the community.[35] The evidence
for this centripetal tendency, although much weaker in other hyphenate
communities, supports two conjectures concerning intracommunity
class differentiation. First, Howard P. Chudacoff has tentatively suggested that in addition to cultural traits, the different sizes of the ethnic
groups may help to account for their different responses to industrial-

ization. "In a heterogeneous American city," he asks, "was there a critical number above which a group was better able to re-create or approximate traditional life patterns and below which a group existed more marginally and more influenced by the host society?"[36] He believes this helps to explain the contrasting responses of the Italians, Slovaks, and Rumanians discussed by Barton in *Peasants and Strangers*, but the thesis looks especially promising when applied to the Scandinavians at one end of the assimilation spectrum and the East Side Jews at the other. As Skårdal shows, even when the Scandinavians were as new to America as the East European Jews were a generation later, they were more thinly scattered about the country, more willing to assimilate, and more quickly and deeply influenced by their neighbors' culture. The hypothesis—Chudacoff does not claim it is more than that—evokes a related thought: a large community was more likely than a small one to contain people with leadership talent and ambition and to give them opportunities to lead before they had mastered the American language and customs. The same is true of people with theatrical, journalistic, or business ability and ambition that would otherwise be frustrated or have to wait a long time to be realized in the larger society.[37]

Second, the fact that a large proportion of East Side Jews worked for other East Side Jews can, along with the factors mentioned earlier, help to explain both the large number of Jewish radicals after the first generation and the fact that the Jews have been "the most mobile of American ethnic groups."[38] As to their radicalism, Nathan Glazer, writing about the appeal of the Communist Party later, observes that "where the workers' institutions were part of, rather than separate from, the ethnic culture, where even the employers were part of the same ethnic world," especially in the garment industry, "even the employers were Jewish and could be influenced by public opinion in the larger Jewish community. Social life, work life, and union life were carried on in the same language and the same community. Here the situation of the Communist Party in the homogeneous nation was reproduced. Here the ethnic identification of the workers did not reduce their capacity to organize and fight as workers."[39] But that is only one side of the picture. If ethnic difference was not present to obscure the reality of class difference, neither could it obscure the reality of mobility opportunity, especially in view of the tiny gap between the "wealth" of the small contractors and the poverty of their employees, and in view of the many tiny gradations from the former up to the real wealth of the larger manufacturers. The Jewish bourgeoisie was both easier to fight and easier to join—many individuals chose to do both—than was the American bourgeoisie.[40]

By reversing these terms we can, I believe, discover crucial differences between the situation of other immigrant working-class groups in the United States and that of the same groups in their home countries, differences having to do with the function of the hyphen in their compound names (Italian-American, Polish-American, and so on). If the Jewish bourgeoisie was, for Jewish workers, both easier to fight and easier to join, it is also true that the American bourgeoisie was, for all immigrant workers, both harder to fight and harder to join than "their own" bourgeoisies. But this was true for more than economic reasons, important though these were. The ethnic difference, I suggest, made it easier in the United States than it would have been in the Old Country for John Q. Worker to separate the work sphere and the private sphere in his value-system. As a worker he may have been a militant union man and even believed that common ownership of the means of production would bring the justest rewards in the economic sphere. But he has rarely concluded that his relation to the means of production, shared with millions of others of various ethnic origins, should be the ground of his self-definition and should shape his world view. On the contrary, his perception of his worker role has been shaped by his culture. His importation of folk customs and religious practices into the economic sphere,[41] far from integrating the two spheres, seems to have been a way of keeping them distinct: it proclaimed that his work and work-related activities were merely instrumental to the private-sphere relationships and activities that were of paramount significance to him. This separation may throw light on John Q. Worker's religious commitment even where it did not run very deep. It may have been in part his way of announcing that none of the other roles he played or milieux he acted in, besides kinship, could claim more than a limited share of his time and attention, that none of them was the locus of his ultimate values or gave meaning to all his other roles. In other words, one function of religion, in this context, may have been to mark out a limit on the claims of the public sphere—religion being the formalization of his ultimate values, and kinship the practical arena for expressing them.[42]

For all these reasons, we may think of the hyphen, in the hyphenate community's name, as separating as well as joining the ethnic terms on either side of it. The "American" to the right of the hyphen represented both the necessary modification in the Old Country's culture and (the relevant point here) the public sphere that comprised everything outside the boundaries of the countrywide ethnic community. A society without traditions of deference and with large populations of immigrants who in Europe had deferred to people quite different from American factory owners, a country that evaluated class and prestige in quantitative terms, could not duplicate the kind of relationship between classes that existed in Europe.[43] The very rawness of the means of getting power over others, theoretically open to anyone, and the rarity of philanthropic obtrusiveness, left cultural space for various hyphenate associations as well as for the native-born American's voluntary associations that were also proliferating in that period.

If the "American" half of the hyphenate cultures' names represented the outward-facing aspects of the group's life, the inward-facing half— the left-hand term—represented aspects unique to the group. Consensual values in such a society would not include a cultural bond with a legitimate superordinate who owned the factory, especially if he belonged to a different ethnic group. They would include a common trait of all groups and classes: American citizenship and patriotism. This means, moreover, that the highest public-sphere values would be located in the nation as a whole rather than in a hegemonic class. The capitalists, intelligentsia, and clergy would be as vulnerable to criticism for deviation from them as anyone else. A militant struggle against the boss could be perfectly consistent with acceptance of the economic structure as the sphere where the dollar ruled and of the political system in which all white male citizens had equal votes, because the capitalists were not regarded as givers and exemplars of social values. It could even be argued that the very nakedness of the cash nexus and the technically equal political power of all voters would impede the capitalists' attainment of ideological hegemony by depositing it instead in the electorate as a whole, in a Society in which each vote was equal to every other as each dollar was equal to every other and, in a society that was beginning to accept pluralism, each ethnic culture was in theory equal to every other. The very fragmentation of such a society, the absence of a truly national ethnicity, made possible the ethnic islands (connected by many causeways with all others), designated by the left-hand term in the hyphenate name, in a sea of economic and political atoms designated by the right-hand term. And to John Q. Worker it was crucially important to distinguish between his public-sphere roles and his roles in his ethnic island, for the latter kept him from being submerged in that anonymous gray sea.

III

From the perspective of his ethnic community—a cultural, not necessarily a geographical entity—John Q. Worker could have perceived three groups of people who were inviting him to thus submerge himself: Protestant proselytizers,[44] Americanizers,[45] and radicals.[46] He can hardly have seen as much difference among them as they saw among themselves. They all shared one attitude of far more significance to him than their disagreements: they all disvalued the ethnic identity that he valued, and urged him to make some other trait—religious, patriotic, or class—the core of his identity. Their chances for success cannot have been helped by their unanimous perception of his values and beliefs as subtractions from The Truth. All three, assuming their own belief-systems to be universally true, evaluated his by its distance from *their* ideals. Those who perceived John Q. Worker's belief-system and culture as proof of his mental enslavement—to the Antichrist or an inferior culture or the capitalist class—were expressing various forms of their epoch's customary view of social evolution, as out of the shadows and into the light. But he never asked them to save him or to be his revolutionary vanguard, and he did not regard himself as in danger of damnation (unless he listened to the missionaries), or as a member of an inferior culture, or as hoodwinked by the bourgeoisie.

The Protestant missionaries made the fewest inroads. The Americanizers and radicals succeeded only to the extent that what they offered could be seen not as a superior alternative but as an ingredient in the new hyphenate-cultural composite. For example, the radicals' principle of working-class internationalism could be interpreted in either of two ways: as an ideal of brotherhood or as a deduction from the theory of Economic Man.[47] The ideal of brotherhood could stand on its own and be consistent with the retention of ethnic self-identification, as the history of Jewish radicalism shows; but the theory that ethnicity, religion, kinship, neighborhood patterns, feelings, beliefs, and values are epiphenomena of class relations could never be.

How would, say, a Polish-American worker react to the Alliance of Polish Socialists, "the only political organization for which Polish-American society was not an entity, a self-sufficient object of activity"? The PSA saw him either as a Pole or as a Polish-speaking American, never as a "member of an ethnically uniform and socially coherent body which is neither Polish nor American." [48] If he had decided to stay in the United States he knew he was no longer a Pole, but he was certainly not an American in all but language. He was either a lone, deracinated individual or a part of that "entity" the existence of which the PSA denied. The radicals understandably failed to realize that individuals converted from the values of their primary groups were not necessarily the first fruits of a bountiful harvest but were more likely to be mavericks. Moreover, there is a fundamental difference between John Q. Worker's accepting the leadership of a radical organization in a strike and his accepting its ideology—the difference between a tactical decision that left his own goals and values unchanged and acceptance of a total philosophy. In this respect the radicals were the rivals of the churches insofar as John Q. Worker's religion was something more than perfunctory observance. Silvano Tomasi puts the point this way: "The few Italian labor unions lacked the total appeal of the ethnic church while Protestant missionaries and socialist and anarchist groups were so peripheral to the immigrant mass that they produced a handful of exceptional figures and nothing else." [49]

The three types of missionary shared a second attitude that cannot have enhanced their chances of making mass conversions: individualism, not the advocacy of the individuality that is consistent with membership in a cultural community but the individualism that extracts a person from it. In this respect their efforts coincided with the policy of the government. For instance, Thomas and Znaniecki contrast the American and Polish ways of handling marital difficulties. In Poland the community had an interest in maintaining the family unit; when trouble occurred between spouses the community stepped in to uphold the marriage institution. In the United States the public authorities, by treating husband and wife as distinct individuals, induced each to consider the dispute as a contest and to try to get the best of the other. "This impression," the authors comment,

is strengthened by what seems to be the official and foreign character of the interfering institutions, making any appeals to solidarity meaningless, because the social worker or the judge himself is not a member of the community and has no direct, vital interest in the marriage-group. Moreover, the action of American institutions differs in nature from that of a Polish community by being sporadic and putting the matter on a rational basis, whereas the old social milieu acted continuously and by emotional suggestions rather than by reasoning.

Thus, direct or indirect state interference unavoidably *undermines* the institutional significance and traditional social sacredness of marriage.[50]

What the American courts "taught" when they administered justice on an individual-by-individual basis, the American economy "taught" by means of its competitiveness and its increasing bureaucratization, rationalization, and pecuniary criteria for success.[51]

Each of the three missionary types taught individualism in its own way—the Protestant by urging John Q. Worker to join religious "communities" so large and ethnically diverse that he could hardly have felt at home in them; the Americanizer by inviting him to abandon the language and customs that, by enabling him to perceive a "we" and a "they," formed a barrier against the threat of homelessness; and the radical by asking him to define himself in terms of an international proletariat so unimaginably large as to make its "members" in effect social atoms. The radicals in fact were the most individualistic of all. According to a Finnish socialist, "mankind was erasing all national barriers and instead was learning mutual help. Eventually, he predicted, people would find no need to be Finns but would rather be individuals deserving justice."[52]

So far as the individualizing influence of the public sphere is concerned, John Q. Worker could resist it by means of the wall partially enclosing the private sphere. That is, he could willingly accept the public sphere's norms as ruling his behavior in those roles that he played outside his community, while being guided by his community's norms when acting inside. This was made possible by the customary indifference, of government and employer, to the way he lived within his community. It was the missionaries who tried to enter his private sphere and who therefore obliged him to respond. And it is his response to them that reveals most clearly the needs that his membership in his ethnic community served.

To accept the new truths proffered by the missionaries would—with some exceptions noted already—have meant his subtracting from the solidarity necessary to the hyphenate community, as well as incurring the hostility of those who were the sources of his self-esteem and companionship. So long as his need for meaning and belongingness was satisfied by the hyphenate culture and community, he doubtless regarded the missionary either as a threat[53] or with indifference. Individuals here and there converted; every dense, complex, fast-changing society produces people who reject their groups' conventional world views and become receptive to deviant ideologies (this says nothing about their truth or falsity), some of whom even welcome their maverick status. The world views they convert to have social and historical significance only when the conversions occur in substantial numbers. When a large proportion of a group becomes receptive to a deviant message it is because the group's old world view manifestly can no longer satisfy what Geertz calls "man's need to live in a world to which he can attribute some significance, whose essential import he feels he can grasp."[54]

The radicals were not quite asking John Q. Worker to abandon his ethnic culture. Rather, they were in general suggesting he place a lower value on it and make his proletarian role the core of his self-definition. The reason he refused is suggested by their inability to effect that change in their own feelings. This part of their message was, in fact, inconsistent and ambiguous. At one extreme were the handful of Irish socialists whose organ was the short-lived *Harp*. They insistently linked Irish nationalism, culture, and history with their radical beliefs. At the other extreme were a few socialists and Wobblies who stridently disparaged national feelings and cultural diversity and happily foresaw their disappearance. Most radicals who wrote on the subject fell between these extremes. The SP, which contained the greatest ethnic diversity among the three organizations, could never formulate a consistent line. Like the Negro and woman questions, the ethnic question would, most party members seem to have hoped, solve itself some day after the revolution. All three questions, it will be noted, touched the private sphere and hence those innermost compartments of the radicals' own minds and feelings that had been least altered by their ideology. The letters columns of the radical press are full of evidence of uneasiness and ambivalence on these questions, and understandably so, since the writers were trying to find rational solutions for problems arising from a conflict in their own minds between their rationalistic ideology and the vestiges of certain nonrational bonds. (See Supplement.)

Unlike the Protestant and Americanizing missionaries, the radicals offered a message that John Q. Worker need not accept or reject wholly but that allowed for selective acceptance. One part of their message asked him to shift his basis of self-identification; this he rejected outright. A second part asked him to join with them to overthrow the System; this he generally regarded as irrelevant to his goals. A third part was an offer of leadership in his struggles for better conditions; this part he accepted from time to time (as he did the offers of reformers too). Although he probably did not make such distinctions consciously, there is good reason to interpret his responses in this way. For, as Herbert Blumer explains, "human beings interpret or 'define' each other's actions instead of merely reacting to each other's actions. Their 'response' is not made directly to the actions of one another but instead is based on the meaning which they attach to such actions." [55]

John Q. Worker's ability to interpret and select among the proffered messages and to define the scope of his leaders' authority returns us once more to the question of his alleged passivity. It may be objected that even if he regarded his job as instrumental to private-sphere values and goals, he was nevertheless passive in that he was dominated by his clergyman, who defined those values and goals for him. His radical contemporaries believed this to be often the case, and some modern historians agree. Marc Karson, for example, cites the opinions of priests on nonreligious topics and assumes he has demonstrated what their flocks' views were. [56] Yet if we ask the sources what John Q. Worker himself thought, we find many signs of difference of opinion within ethnic communities that testify to his ability and willingness to defy his religious, political, and community "influentials." [57]

The shake-up period that American society was undergoing, and the personal and group upheavals experienced by the immigrant majority of the working class, placed an unusual burden of responsibility on John Q. Worker. Neither the outside missionaries nor the leadership strata within his community enjoyed the presumption of authority as he devised ways of coming to terms with his new situation. If he proved capable of judging all these self-defined leaders by his own criteria, he must have been capable also of distinguishing between the capitalists' power and their belief-system. Yet it is because he was, so to speak, on his own that the radical movements won proportionately more converts in the shake-up period than in any other period before or since. The radicals' vanguardism, scientism, and systematization of experience proved attractive to an exceptionally large minority of workers and middle-class people for whom the majority's solutions were, for various reasons, inadequate. Hence the reasons for the radicals' relative success in the shake-up period were the reasons for their absolute failure at other times. John Q. Worker's solution—the construction of his hyphenate community—lasted longer than the radicals' surrogate "communities" because the former was an autochthonous adaptation of a traditional culture, with roots in the past and capable of creative response to changing conditions down to our own day.

IV

We have had to wait for the new social history of the past two decades to document an insight implied in Lenin's *What Is To Be Done?*, written in 1902 and quoted in Chapter V above: that socialist consciousness among workers "could only be brought to them from without. The history of all countries shows that the working class, exclusively by its own effort, is able to develop only trade-union consciousness." If the implied imperative—that socialist belief *should* be accepted by the workers—is dropped, Lenin's dictum is true and sums up the problem of the radicals of the shake-up period. Socialism—or any radical ideology—is not a natural product of a living culture; which is why, when the imperative is put back into the dictum, it produces the Leninist theory of the party, the vanguard that must impose its ideology and the transformation of society "from without."

"From without" means from outside John Q. Worker's community, for so long as the private-sphere institutions were functioning John Q. Worker was impervious to radical propaganda. The radical evangel is attractive en masse only to the extent that such institutions have decayed, or to those individuals who (for whatever reasons) have cut their bonds with their communities. The radical allegiance then becomes an antidote to anomie. What makes it attractive to the deracinated person is not the liberation hoped for but the hope for liberation—its function in the present, not the future realization of its program. The ideology of such a person, for whom everything has lost meaning, must embrace everything in a total system of meanings. This includes the private sphere by definition, but it can do so only by abolishing the private sphere's function, to be a giver of meanings.

The American radicals of the 1890–1917 period lived in a society in which private-sphere institutions were changing and shifting, not decaying. Some of those who could not participate in their reconstruction came to fit Kornhauser's description of "mass men" to one degree or another—the Wobblies most of all, the ethnic socialists least of all. The problem was most acute among the latter, who had not quite cut those ties, yet whose belief-system demanded comprehensiveness. (Comprehensiveness on the mundane plane, that is. The need for a religious faith is not germane to this point.) If the radicals' belief-systems had really been comprehensive, explaining all aspects of society and bringing them all within one systematic theory, why could they not formulate that part of it that pertained to the private sphere? The answer must be sought on at least two levels. On the level of their perception of John Q. Worker, the radicals' theory prevented them from perceiving the true importance and functions of his culture and community. As a result they lacked the incentive to grapple with the difficulties in formulating a theory. But there is every reason to believe that even if they had tried to formulate one they would have got bogged down in the same confusions and ambiguities that fill the extant sources. On the level of theory, their inadequate solutions to the problem of relating the private and public spheres in one consistent framework suggest that any private sphere capable of sustaining John Q. Worker's values could not be part of the society that the radicals envisaged. Their theories' pretension to comprehensiveness could be sustained only by their treating an entire sector of society offhandedly, but their misperception of John Q. Worker obscured this flaw in their ideologies.

John Q. Worker did not, of course, reason the problem out in this way, in response to the radical missionaries. But then, the fact that he did not have to is precisely the point.

Notes

Abbreviations

C   New York *Call*, daily and Sunday (SP)
ISR   *International Socialist Review* (independent radical monthly that supported the SP until 1908 and thereafter supported the IWW and its supporters in the SP)
IW   *Industrial Worker* (principal IWW weekly in the West)
NR   *New Review* (independent radical periodical)
P   *People* and *Weekly People* (SLP)
SA   *Socialist Alliance* (weekly of the Socialist Trades and Labor Alliance)
SDH   *Social Democratic Herald* (SP; Victor Berger's weekly, published in Milwaukee)
Sol   *Solidarity* (principal IWW weekly in the East)

Short Titles

   Note: organization proceedings will be cited as follows: SP, *Proceedings*, 1908; IWW, *Proceedings*, 1905; and so on, the full titles are:
Proceedings of the First Convention of the Industrial workers of the World Founded at Chicago, June 27–July 8, 1905 [New York], 1905).
Proceedings of the Second Annual Convention of the Industrial Workers of the World Held at Chicago, Illinois, Sept. 17 to Oct. 3, 1906 (Chicago, 1906).
Proceedings of the Third Annual Convention of the Industrial Workers of the World Held at Chicago, Ill., 1907, "Official Report" (printed in newspaper form).
Stenographic Report of the Eighth Annual Convention of the Industrial Workers of the World, Chicago, Illinois, September 15th to September 29th, 1913 (Cleveland, [1913]).
"Proceedings of Socialist Unity Convention Held at Indianapolis, Indiana[,] Beginning July 29, 1901" (SP), typescript in Duke University Library, microfilm at Tamiment Library, New York.
National Convention of the Socialist Party held at Chicago, Illinois, May 1 to 6, 1904 (Chicago, [1904]).
National Convention of the Socialist Party held at Chicago[,] Illinois, May 10 to 17, 1908 (Chicago, [1908]).
National Congress of the Socialist Party held in Masonic Temple, Chicago, Ill., May 15 to 21, 1910 (Chicago, [1910]).
Proceedings National Convention of the Socialist Party (Chicago, 1912).
Proceedings of the Ninth Annual Convention of the Socialist Labor Party . . . July 4th to July 10th, 1896 (n.p., n.d.)

Proceedings of the Tenth National Convention of the Socialist Labor Party Held in New York City June 2 to June 8, 1900 (New York, 1901).

Chapter I

1. By open-ended I mean questions formulated in a falsifiable way, permitting the evidence to suggest answers contrary to the historian's own preferences. It is sometimes argued that this is impossible, since we all have unconscious biases and assumptions. I believe this is a non sequitur, disproven by the fact that occasionally historians do change their minds in the face of the evidence.

2. Yet radical historians often insist that such inquiry is by its very nature discrediting, even if the resulting monograph portrays the subject favorably. What such inquiry does do is desanctify its subject, for the only subjects that on principle are not subject to scrutiny are either sacred or axiomatic, which in scholarship amount to the same thing. Scholarly inquiry into a subject is incompatible with its being taken for granted, and this is what seems to be the meaning of the objections—from which it is reasonable to infer that the nature of past radicals' belief-systems can be a subject only for historians who do not regard those belief-systems as axiomatic or sacred.

3. Along with that assumption we sometimes find another: that to study past radicals' ideologies and behavior is to divert the reader's attention from the squalid reality that they had committed their lives to changing. The squalor, oppression, injustice, poverty, inequality, and premature death that occurred on a large scale in the period covered by this book are of course proper objects of historical study. Their existence is not denied by study of another proper object: the radicals' modes of perception.

4. Since most quotations are from newspapers and magazines with narrow columns that required frequent paragraphing, I have generally ignored paragraphing. The only other alterations I have made are corrections of unintentional typographical errors.

5. See Frederic Cople Jaher, *Doubters and Dissenters: Cataclysmic Thought in America, 1885–1918* (New York: Free Press, 1964), 44, and Adam B. Ulam, *The Unfinished Revolution: An Essay on the Sources of Influence of Marxism and Communism* (New York: Vintage, 1960), 6, 17, for very similar observations. I am indebted to Ulam's book for the germs of several ideas, including this one, in the present work.

6. See, *e.g.*, William English Walling's review of Morris Hillquit and John A. Ryan, *Socialism–Promise or Menace?*, in *American Journal of Sociology*, XX (1915), 536, in which there is a reference to "radical but non-Socialist reform."

7. The background on the SP, SLP, and IWW, summarized briefly in this section, is set forth in such works as Howard H. Quint, *The Forging of American Socialism: Origins of the Modern Movement* (2nd ed.; Indianapolis: Bobbs-Merrill, 1964), David A. Shannon, *The Socialist Party of America* (1955; Chicago: Quadrangle, 1964), and Melvyn Dubofsky, *We Shall Be All: A History of the IWW* (New York: Quadrangle, 1969). Quint covers the period up to 1901 and thus includes the period in which the SLP was important; the SLP's later history, in the few remaining years in which it had some historical significance, is recounted in scattered passages in the Dubofsky book and in various articles that will be cited later in this study. An excellent survey of its history is David Herreshoff, *The Origins of American Marxism: From the Transcendentalists to De Leon* (New York: Monad Press, 1973), Chap. V. Useful for facts is Charles M. White, "The Socialist Labor Party in America, 1890–1903" (Ph.D. dissertation, University of Southern California, 1959). Shannon summarizes the SP's history between 1901 and 1909 but emphasizes the period after 1909. The years between 1901 and 1909 are covered in Ira Kipnis, *The American Socialist Movement, 1897–1912* (New York: Monthly Review Press, 1972), but that book is so unreliable that I believe it should be dropped from the list of standard works in the field. A casual follow-up of the sources cited in some of its footnotes revealed so many citations that either had no relation with the text they ostensibly supported or refuted the statements in the text that a systematic check of Kipnis' footnotes might discredit the entire book. In addition, as several

historians have pointed out, Kipnis tortures even legitimate evidence to prove his pre-formed thesis. The Quint, Shannon, and Dubofsky books provide the necessary factual background for the discussions of the three organizations' histories in the present work. A controversial but always thought-provoking interpretation is Daniel Bell, *Marxian Socialism in the United States* (Princeton: Princeton University Press, 1967). So far as John Q. Worker is concerned, there is no single synthesis of the latest scholarship available yet. I have relied not only on studies of separate ethnic groups but also on several ground-breaking articles by Herbert G. Gutman, most of which are reprinted in his *Work, Culture and Society in Industrializing America* (New York: Knopf, 1976). On the relationships between radicals and unionized workers the most valuable work is John Laslett, *Labor and the Left: A Study of Socialist and Radical Influences in the American Labor Movement, 1881–1914* (New York: Basic Books, 1970). Briefer than the Dubofsky, but valuable as an introduction to the IWW, is Patrick Renshaw, *The Wobblies: The Story of Syndicalism in the United States* (Garden City, N.Y.: Doubleday, 1967). Helpful for the immediately prewar SP is James Weinstein, *The Decline of Socialism in America, 1912–1925* (New York: Monthly Review Press, 1967). A provocative criticism, with which I agree, of Weinstein's approach to SP history is Bernard K. Johnpoll, "The Socialist Myth," *Commentary*, LI (1976), 90–94. And see esp. Henry F. Bedford, *Socialism and the Workers in Massachusetts, 1886–1912* (Amherst: University of Massachusetts Press, 1966). Bedford's single-state study confirms several of the interpretations I derived from a national-level study.

8. Of these, only the Christian Socialists retained their distinctive identity within the party. This study will ignore them because they directed their main energies to propagandizing among clergymen and church members, not among the workers as a class. See E[dward] E[llis] C[arr], "The Reason for It," *Christian Socialist*, April 1, 1905.

9. The ensuing chapters will pay little attention to changes in doctrine and policy in the twenty-seven years covered, because their main subject is attitudes, which changed little because they grew out of a mode of perception that persisted throughout the period. For a perceptive account of doctrinal shifts in the SLP, usually considered the most stable of the three organizations, see (in addition to the Herreshoff chapter cited in note 7) Don K. McKee, "Daniel De Leon: A Reappraisal," *Labor History*, I (1960), 264–97.

10. Weinstein, *Decline of Socialism in America*, 27, 232.

11. For IWW statistics, see Dubofsky, *We Shall Be All*, 349.

12. An example of the approach I am arguing against is Kenneth McNaught, "Socialism and the Progressives: Was Failure Inevitable?" in Alfred F. Young (ed.), *Dissent: Explorations in the History of American Radicalism* (DeKalb, Ill.: Northern Illinois University Press, 1968), 253–71. NcNaught discusses everybody concerned but the ordinary worker, without whose conversion failure *was* inevitable. "Socialism," he says in his last sentence, "was very relevant," but his discussion shows it was relevant by his own criteria (the only ones he applies throughout the article), the main criterion being that in a class-ridden society socialism is natural and will grow unless betrayed, as it was then, by the errors of the intellectuals. In contrast, see Samuel P. Hays, "New Possibilities for American Political History: The Social Analysis of Political Life," in Seymour Martin Lipset and Richard Hofstadter (eds.), *Sociology and History: Methods* (New York: Basic Books, 1968), 198–209.

13. Herreshoff, *Origins of American Marxism*, 120.

14. The WFM membership apparently had decided by 1908 that these aims could best be achieved outside the IWW, and the WFM ended up back in the AFL. Many WFM leaders remained socialists, however. Their switch from the IWW to the AFL represented for them a change of radical tactics, not a repudiation of radicalism. See Vernon Jensen, *Heritage of Conflict: Labor Relations in the Nonferrous Metals Industry up to 1930* (Ithaca: Cornell University Press, 1950), 237–43.

15. Irwin Yellowitz, "The Origins of Unemployment Reform in the United States," *Labor History*, IX (1968), 356.

16. Cf. Joseph Robert Conlin, *Bread and Roses Too: Studies of the Wobblies* (Westport,

Conn.: Greenwood Press, 1969), 91: "the Wobblies were more like their contemporaries than either party cared to admit." True, but why did both parties refuse to admit the fact? How did each perceive itself and the other? The answer would probably tell us a great deal about what made the committed Wobblies Wobblies, for it would show that although they and their contemporaries shared many values and hopes, they differed profoundly in their perceptions. Another instance of the same phenomenon is the antisuffragists in the same period. They portrayed what they perceived as the horrors of woman suffrage in the states in which it existed and the threat it posed to the rest of the country. In fact, the antisuffragists and the suffragists shared far more than either group realized. Those common possessions certainly ought to be pointed out. But so should the reasons why they misperceived their society and their adversaries in just those ways. Their behavior is understandable only if we learn what it *meant to them.*

17. Not having investigated the private lives and personal histories of these people, I do not speculate about the possible psychological causes at work. Chapter IX includes conjectures concerning the implicit personal meanings of certain of their beliefs, but there is nothing in the hypotheses inconsistent with the normality of many or most of the people studied.

18. The most notable of these studies are A. William Hoglund, *Finnish Immigrants in America, 1880–1920* (Madison: University of Wisconsin Press, 1960); Josef J. Barton, *Peasants and Strangers: Italians, Rumanians, and Slovaks in an American City, 1890–1950* (Cambridge: Harvard University Press, 1975); Irving Howe, *World of Our Fathers: The Journey of the East European Jews to America and the Life They Found and Made* (New York: Harcourt Brace Jovanovich, 1976); and Edwin Fenton, *Immigrants and Unions, A Case Study: Italians and American Labor, 1870–1920* (New York: Arno Press, 1975).

19. In one respect they do assume a difference between themselves and the nonradical worker: when they add the influence of capitalist intimidation or the threat of unemployment. Such things often push a near-convert off the fence, completing his radicalization. No radical looking back to the period of his conversion recalls that intimidation had any other effect than to provoke him to hate the System. This may be one reason why radical historians' depictions of radicals put such great emphasis on their courage. At the same time they assume that capitalist threats have been partly responsible for the fewness of the converts. The workers' fear of suppression is, in fact, often given as the principal reason for their not following the radical vanguard. There are at least two problems with this hypothesis, however. First, it depends on inference, since in the nature of the case the data to support it must be few, and their typicality questionable. Hence the plausibility of the hypothesis must be judged by its consistency with what is known, and I believe that contrary hypotheses are by this criterion at least as tenable and probably more so. Second, let us assume that massive radicalization would encounter massive and violent suppression; it does not follow that the workers' belief that this would happen has been a motive for their refraining from becoming radicalized. Yet writers in this vein first impute to the workers their own belief as to what would happen and then give it as the workers' motive for not rebelling. In other words, the thesis is two steps removed from the evidence.

20. A similar point is made by John H. M. Laslett in his "Reply" to an essay by Philip Foner, in John H. M. Laslett and Seymour Martin Lipset (eds.), *Failure of a Dream?: Essays in the History of American Socialism* (Garden City, N.Y.: Doubleday Anchor, 1974), 246–47, 249. Other parts of Laslett's essay (pp. 244–51), as well as his major article, "Socialism and American Trade Unionism" (pp. 200–232), contain several points identical or similar to some that I make in this chapter. The "Comment" by Foner (pp. 233–43) exemplifies the kind of thinking produced when one judges past movements solely by one's own perceptions of reality: it criticizes this, that, and the other past radical leader and organization for various "errors," without recognizing that their actions and choices were correct and realistic in terms of their perceptions of reality. That is, if American society had been as they perceived it, then their policies would have succeeded. Foner's histories too all portray a

society in which radical movements "should have" flourished. Their failures therefore must have been due to errors or cowardice. In support of this assumption, radical historians sometimes offer (explicitly or implicitly) in evidence the alleged success of European radical movements in radicalizing their countries' working classes. This contention is part of the broader refutation of the theory of "American exceptionalism," and it presumes that the American capitalists have been exceptionally successful in propagating their ideology and that their government has been exceptionally skillful in suppressing radical movements. But what if the assumption that European workers converted en masse were wrong? Persuasive arguments to this effect have been offered by several historians; *e.g.*, Martin Diamond, "Socialism and the Decline of the American Socialist Party" (Ph.D. dissertation, University of Chicago, 1956), Chap. IV and pp. 116, 159; and Herreshoff, *Origins of American Marxism*, 16.

21. On the question of a public's active role in the transaction between it and those who would influence it, see Raymond A. Bauer, "The Obstinate Audience: The Influence Process from the Point of View of Social Communication," *American Psychologist*, XIX (1964), 319–28, the findings of which can be extended to include this chapter's subject matter.

22. The following tabulation of positions is grossly oversimplified, but it does summarize the present point. The chief tactical and structural dilemmas of the three organizations' positions were:

A	B
1) Bore from within unions	*vs.* Engage in "dual" organizing
2) Emphasize immediate demands	*vs.* Emphasize ultimate demands
3) Strive for popularity	*vs.* Strive for purity
4) Sign up as many members as possible	*vs.* Accept only the converted

The SLP chose 1B, 2B, 3B, and 4B; the SP chose 1A, 2A, 3A, and 4A; and the IWW chose 1B, 2AB, 3AB, and 4A. Other radical movements combined the positions in still other ways. That A and B were mutually exclusive did not prevent the IWW from trying to combine them in certain instances involving tactical issues 2 and 3.

23. A radical historian, in a letter to me, wrote that this hypothesis is deterministic. Although no radical historian would postulate total indeterminateness in any historical situation, the limits he postulates are always wide enough to accommodate the success of radicalism. Why? In fact, that approach is deterministic in that it rules out John Q. Worker's freedom not to agree with the radicals.

24. For the variety of theories within the IWW, see Supplement.

25. One editorial practically admits this: "The Spirit of Revolt," *IW*, May 22, 1913.

26. William D. Haywood, "Pick and Shovel Pointers," *ISR*, XI (1911), 458.

27. See Dubofsky, *We Shall Be All*, 313–17.

28. Fenton, *Immigrants and Unions, A Case Study*, 185–86. Fenton says that government raids on IWW halls in late 1917 merely dealt "the final blow to the tottering I.W.W. structure" (p. 187).

29. *Ibid.*, 259–87.

30. Dubofsky, *We Shall Be All*, does not mention this episode. This history was repeated in other cities and other industries; see Fenton, *Immigrants and Unions, A Case Study*, Chaps. VII–IX. It must be emphasized that the conflict was not between idealistic Wobblies (who repeatedly disclaimed idealism or love for the workers and insisted that their only aim was to "get the goods") and narrow-minded, materialistic workers. When the IWW leaders in the Lawrence strike were imprisoned the workers rallied to their support, and they defended Wobblies who were discriminated against by the bosses after the main strike had been won. According to Fenton, at least seventeen smaller walkouts occurred thereafter, under IWW leadership, and the organization flourished, with many language branches and shop committees. What finally alienated the rank and file was a series

of incidents that associated the IWW with atheism, violence, and permanent-confrontation tactics. "Like everyone else," concludes Fenton, "the Italians stopped paying dues to an organization which kept them constantly out on strike, and failed to improve their working conditions. By the summer of 1913, the I.W.W. was again a small organization with a few hundred members living on the memories of their days of glory. . . . The Paterson strike of 1913 administered the *coup de grace* to the I.W.W. textile union" (pp. 362–66). In Paterson the IWW leaders refused even to state their demands until the strike was in its sixth week. Even then they refused to enter into any agreement that did not include all the mills in the city. The millowners thereupon became more united than before, realizing that they were dealing not just with the representatives of their employees but with an organization dedicated to revolution. Whereas Wobbly theory portrayed a united capitalist class and proclaimed the need for the working class to unite, the organization's actions united the bosses and divided the workers. "Never again," says Fenton (pp. 371–75), "did immigrants in the East, particularly the Italians who had been the backbone of so many I.W.W. strikes, follow the Wobblies in a major foray." Moses Rischin, in *The Promised City: New York's Jews, 1870–1914* (New York: Harper Torchbooks, 1970), 190–91, describes an occasion on which the IWW, making no effort to organize the unorganized, at first had friendly contact with the United Cloth Hat and Cap Makers' Union in 1905, but then alienated it by its "destructive tactics." The radicals in the union then switched their union's affiliation to the United Hebrew Trades, "socialist in spirit if not in letter."

31. "Direct Action," *Sol*, December 18, 1909; untitled editorial, *IW*, May 6, 1909.

32. This last point was made by Charles Kerr, in "Industrial Unionism and the General Strike," *ISR*, IX (1909), 900, and by Robert Hunter, in *Violence and the Labor Movement* (New York: Macmillan, 1914), 275. Several historians have recognized the functional dilemma created by the no-contract principle. (See Supplement.) In "The Brotherhood of Timber Workers 1910–1913: A Radical Response to Industrial Capitalism in the Southern U.S.A.," *Past & Present*, No. 60 (August, 1973), 199 *n.* 152, James R. Green criticizes Dubofsky's discussion of the dilemma in *We Shall Be All*. "The IWW's inability to combine revolutionary goals with effective union-building tactics," says Green, "does not seem to have stymied the BTW." On the contrary, Dubofsky describes the un-IWW-like conservatism of the BTW and the tenuousness of its link with the IWW (pp. 214–18). It is true that, as Green says, the IWW's arrival on the scene revived union activity and strength; but for how long? His article covers only a few years. Unlike Green, Dubofsky does not extract this "radical, collective response to industrial capitalism" (Green, p. 200) from the historical context in which the "response" rose and then declined, thus showing itself to be a temporary response to temporary circumstances. The same criticism can be made of the closing paragraph of Garin Burbank, "The Disruption and Decline of the Oklahoma Socialist Party," *Journal of American Studies*, VII (1973), 150. Burbank lectures those who believe that American socialist movements could not "operate effectively in the American here-and-now," for, as he supposes, his account of the brief florescence of the Oklahoma SP proves the opposite. Certainly a very large number of Oklahoma farmers were genuinely radical; but their radicalism was as short-lived as the circumstances that engendered it. The effort to prove relevance in the here-and-now risks obscuring the real history of the there-and-then.

33. On the national SLP's demands, see SLP, *Proceedings*, 1896, pp. 56–57, 62; SLP, *Proceedings*, 1900, pp. 86, 93, 105–113, 253–56. On SLP municipal programs, see the typical one in "Albany Nominations," *P*, September 7, 1901. For the Milwaukee and Wisconsin socialists' demands, see Sally M. Miller, *Victor Berger and the Promise of Constructive Socialism, 1910–1920* (Westport, Conn.: Greenwood Press, 1973), 35–36.

34. Nevertheless it did on occasion bid for "popularity." White, "The Socialist Labor Party in America" notes the contradiction between the SLP's repeated rejoicing over the "purification" resulting from the expulsions and resignations, and its repeated attempts to

get accepted in large labor organizations. See, *e.g.*, p. 86. Other dilemmas, having to do with the party's inability to show what the function of the STLA was, in view of the theory that strikes and boycotts were useless, are perceptively discussed on pp. 175–80. See also pp. 228–29.

35. These will be discussed in Chapter VII below.

Chapter II

1. Werner Sombart, *Warum gibt es in den Vereinigten Staaten keinen Sozialismus?* (Tübingen: n.p., 1906), first published as articles in 1905.

2. D. H. Leon, "Whatever Happened to an American Socialist Party? A Critical Survey of the Spectrum of Interpretations," *American Quarterly*, XXIII (1971), 236.

3. William Z. Foster (or a ghost-writer), *History of the Communist Party of the United States* (New York: International Publishers, 1952), 542–44; Marc Karson, *American Labor Unions and Politics, 1900–1918* (Carbondale, Ill.: Southern Illinois University Press, 1958).

4. August C. Bolino, "American Socialism's Flood and Ebb: The Rise and Decline of the Socialist Party of America, 1901–1912," *American Journal of Economics and Sociology*, XXII (1963), 287–301.

5. Ernest Untermann, "Socialism Abroad," *ISR*, II (1901), 220, 222.

6. [Algie M. Simons], untitled editor's note accompanying Werner Sombart, "Why Is There No Socialism in the United States?" *ISR*, VII (1907), 420–25. The series had begun with Sombart's "Study of the Historical Development and Evolution of the American Proletariat," *ISR*, VI (1905), 129–36, 293–301 (the much-quoted passage is in the last installment).

7. John H. M. Laslett, "Reply," in John H. M. Laslett and Seymour Martin Lipset (eds.), *Failure of a Dream?: Essays in the History of American Socialism* (Garden City, N.Y.: Doubleday Anchor, 1974), 248. See also Leon, "Whatever Happened to an American Socialist Party?" 240–41.

8. See, for instance, Selig Perlman, *A Theory of the Labor Movement* (New York: Macmillan, 1928). The commonness of the question shows a way of thinking that would have existed even if Sombart had never lived. Since the proffered answers differ, it is the question, not the answers, that is significant.

9. Martin Diamond, in "Socialism and the Decline of the American Socialist Party" (Ph.D. dissertation, University of Chicago, 1956), offers cogent arguments against the common assumption that European workers—including most of those who belong to parties of the far left—have en masse converted to socialist ideology. Moreover, Diamond's central chapters in effect reverse the Sombartian approach by showing that the various factors cited as hindering American workers' conversion either existed in those European countries that did see mass conversions or did not play the role assigned to them by Sombartian historians. See esp. Diamond's discussion of feudal vestiges (pp. 71–75), social mobility (pp. 75–78), here explicitly refuting Sombart and Selig Perlman, and ethnic heterogeneity (pp. 81–85).

10. Leonard B. Rosenberg, "The 'Failure' of the Socialist Party of America," *Review of Politics*, XXXI (1969), 329–52. The inference that there are more than twenty-eight is based on phrases in Rosenberg's summary: "*Almost* all the explanations offered" can be placed in three categories; the "sociological (and psychological) factors *include*"; and "*among* the economic factors . . . are. . . ." (pp. 345–49; emphasis added).

11. The Platonic simile occurred also to Ronald Aronson; see his "Reply," *Studies on the Left*, VI (September–October, 1966), 60. Not all counterfactual hypotheses are of this sort, of course, and my argument should not be construed as applying to contrary-to-fact hypotheses per se. Some "if" questions are helpful in the reconstruction of historical situations—that is, those "if" questions that are based on courses of action that were possible. In the present context, the contrary-to-fact proposition is based on the ignoring of impor-

tant facts rather than on the possibilities created by the facts. See Sidney Hook, *The Hero in History* (Boston: Beacon Press, 1955), Chap. VII, for a cogent argument, which I agree with in general (with reservations concerning his discussion of the Civil War).

12. Howard Zinn, *The Politics of History* (Boston: Beacon Press, 1970), 11.

13. Foster, *History of the Communist Party of the United States*, 542.

14. Robert Skotheim, *American Intellectual Histories and Historians* (Princeton: Princeton University Press, 1966), 79, 131, 134–35, 137–38, 142, 150, 152–53. The reference to Parrington is on p. 140.

15. See Vernon Jensen and Melvyn Dubofsky, "The I.W.W.—An Exchange of Views," *Labor History*, XI (1970), 355–72. Jensen's portion, pp. 355–64, is a review of Dubofsky's *We Shall Be All: A History of the IWW* (New York: Quadrangle, 1969); the quotation from Dubofsky's reply is on p. 371. Jensen's critique is excessively harsh, in my opinion, and in one or two places unfair. But his accusation of teleology is generally correct, although Dubofsky's response to the review proves it much more clearly than the book does, for he is too conscientious a scholar to distort the evidence and write a mere tract with footnotes.

16. William E. Trautmann, *One Big Union: An Outline of a Possible Organization of the Working Class, with CHART* (Chicago: Charles H. Kerr & Company, Co-operative, n.d.), 25.

17. Foster, *History of the Communist Party of the United States*, 544.

18. *The Menace*'s circulation is given in John Higham, *Strangers in the Land: Patterns of American Nativism, 1860–1925* (New Brunswick, N.J.: Rutgers University Press, 1955), 180. In April 1915 it reached 1,507,923 (see Higham, p. 184).

19. For a similar argument, see Samuel P. Hays, "New Possibilities for American Political History: The Social Analysis of Political Life," in Seymour Martin Lipset and Richard Hofstadter (eds.), *Sociology and History: Methods* (New York: Basic Books, 1968), 197–98. On Marxist predictions in general, see George H. Sabine, *Marxism* (Ithaca: Cornell University Press, 1958), 1–15, which discusses how Marxism failed where it "should have" succeeded and succeeded where it "should have" failed.

20. See James H. Hutson, "An Investigation of the Inarticulate: Philadelphia's White Oaks," *William and Mary Quarterly*, 3rd ser., XVIII (1971), 3–25; the Lemisch articles criticized therein and listed in Hutson, p. 4, *n.* 3; Philip Foner, many books and articles, *e.g.,* his *History of the American Labor Movement* (New York: International Publishers, 1947—), and his "Comment," in Laslett and Lipset (eds.), *Failure of a Dream?*, 233–42; Laslett, "Reply," in Laslett and Lipset (eds.), *Failure of a Dream?*, 244–49.

21. Jeremy Brecher, *Strike!* (San Francisco: Straight Arrow Press, 1972). The quotation is on p. 238. See also review by Harold W. Currie, *American Historical Review*, LIX (1974), 593.

22. Brecher, *Strike!*, 238; Dubofsky, *We Shall Be All*, 189.

23. William M. Dick, *Labor and Socialism in America: The Gompers Era* (Port Washington, N.Y.: Kennikat Press, 1972), 79. Or, consider another recent comment, in William Preston, Jr., "By Life Possessed: The Dissenter as Hero," *Reviews in American History*, V (1977), 405. Explaining why Norman Thomas' "proper constituency" remained indifferent to the SP leader's message, Preston says, "Their political consciousness remained inert." This may be called "proof by the process of elimination," a method that depends on the historian's assumption that all the possible explanations he can entertain are all those there can be. If workers can, in a historian's own mind, be either radical (or radicalizing) or inert, and they are not radical (or radicalizing), then they must be inert. Why then investigate the actual thinking of Thomas' "proper constituency"? Those who do so, however, may discover that some people rejected Thomas' message on rational grounds. Since the method of proof by the process of elimination limits the range of possibilities to those that the historian can think of, the least imaginative historians tend to be the most certain that they have discovered the truth. (And vice versa, inasmuch as the certainty of the dogmatist, by ratifying the impoverishment of the historical imagination, constitutes a strong temptation to unimaginative minds.)

As to workers' being a radical's "proper constituency," this assumption creates the nonproblem of explaining why they do not respond to the radicals' message. Another instance of this assumption is in Russel B. Nye, "The Slave Power Conspiracy, 1830–1860," in Richard O. Curry (ed.), *The Abolitionists* (Hinsdale, Ill.: Dryden Press, 1973); see p. 136, where "the immigrant and the laborer" were "the two groups most likely to respond" to the abolitionists' propaganda. They were most likely to respond, of course, only because of Nye's a priori assumptions, and therefore their failure to respond is what requires explanation. So far as the radicals dealt with in this book are concerned, if one assumes that radicalism is the normal world view of the proletarian, one must explain not only the nonradicalism of the majority of proletarians but also the radicalism of many nonproletarians. These must then be "exceptions." That is about as logical as saying that roses are normally white and that the redness of the exceptions is what must be explained.

24. Clifford Geertz, "Ritual and Social Change: A Javanese Example," *American Anthropologist*, LIX (1957), 49, 53. In fact, historians, anthropologists, and sociologists have for many years been studying "the bottom," despite Lemisch's complaint, just as historians have written copiously and accurately about strikes, Brecher's text (although not his footnotes) to the contrary notwithstanding.

25. An excellent and all too rare analysis of the relationship of ethnicity to labor unity is Paul Buhle, "The Wobblies in Perspective," *Monthly Review*, XXII (1970), 44–53; most relevant to the present discussion is p. 50. See also Buhle's comment on certain radicals in his "Debsian Socialism and the 'New Immigrant' Worker," in William L. O'Neill (ed.), *Insights and Parallels* (Minneapolis: Burgess Publishing Co., 1973), 276.

Chapter III

1. William E. Bridges, "Family Patterns and Social Values in America, 1825–1876," *American Quarterly*, XVII (1965), 10; Ronald G. Walters, "The Family and Ante-Bellum Reform: An Interpretation," *Societas*, III (1973), 221–32; Nancy Cott, *The Bonds of Womanhood: "Woman's Sphere" in New England, 1780–1835* (New Haven: Yale University Press, 1977), "Conclusion"; Norman H. Clark, *Deliver Us from Evil: An Interpretation of American Prohibition* (New York: W. W. Norton, 1976), Chap. VIII.

2. Alexander Saxton, "Blackface Minstrelsy and Jacksonian Ideology," *American Quarterly*, XXVII (1975), 15. See also Dorothy Burton Skårdal, *The Divided Heart: Scandinavian Immigrant Experience through Literary Sources* (Lincoln: University of Nebraska Press, 1974), 272.

3. See Oscar Handlin, *Race and Nationality in American Life* (Garden City, N.Y.: Doubleday Anchor, 1957), 130–31; John P. Roche, *Origins of American Political Thought* (New York: Harper Torchbooks, 1967), 44.

4. See Arthur M. Schlesinger, "Biography of a Nation of Joiners," *American Historical Review*, L (1944), 1–25; Rowland Berthoff, *An Unsettled People: Social Order and Disorder in American History* (New York: Harper & Row, 1971), 233–34 and Chaps. XVII and XXVII. In addition, see Supplement.

5. See in general William Kornhauser, *The Politics of Mass Society* (New York: Free Press, 1959), and the minor revision of it suggested in Harry Eckstein, *A Theory of Stable Democracy* (Princeton: Princeton University Press, 1961), 42–45.

6. See David M. Potter, "The Quest for the National Character," in John Higham (ed.), *The Reconstruction of American History* (New York: Harper Torchbooks, 1962), 216–17.

7. Jeremy Brecher, *Strike!* (San Francisco: Straight Arrow Press, 1972), 241.

8. William Z. Foster (or a ghost-writer), *History of the Communist Party of the United States* (New York: International Publishers, 1952), 317.

9. William Z. Foster, *The Negro People in American History* (New York: International Publishers, 1954), 552. I do not know whether Foster actually wrote these two books and/or the third of his large histories, *Outline Political History of the Americas* (New York: International Publishers, 1951). It has been said they were ghost-written. The footnote cita-

tions imply a professional historian's familiarity with the literature. Whoever wrote the books was shockingly indifferent to the basic facts and to the historian's obligation to get them straight. The errors of even elementary fact demonstrate that the generalizations and theories offered were constructed independently of the data they purport to explain. But even if a historian wrote the books so that they could be offered to the public as Foster's, then the historian, Foster, and the CP were in effect telling the public what Foster would have been telling it if he himself had written them: that one does not have to study a scholarly discipline to understand it better than do those who spend years equipping themselves to write monographs on its subject matter. All one needs is the "science of Marxism-Leninism" and a list of secondary works written by scholars who lack understanding of their true meaning.

10. Herbert Aptheker, *The American Civil War* (New York: International Publishers, 1961), 5.

11. Paul Faler, "Working Class Historiography," *Radical America*, III (March–April, 1969), 63.

12. *Ibid.*, 65.

13. For other examples of the same genre, see Supplement.

14. See Antonio Gramsci, *The Modern Prince and Other Writings* (London: Lawrence & Wishart, 1957), *e.g.*, p. 124; John Cammett, *Antonio Gramsci and the Origins of Italian Communism* (Stanford: Stanford University Press, 1967), esp. pp. 204–206; Eugene D. Genovese, "On Antonio Gramsci," *Studies on the Left*, VII (March–April, 1967), 83–107; Eugene D. Genovese, *In Red and Black: Marxian Explorations in Southern and Afro-American History* (New York: Pantheon, 1971)—the article on Gramsci is reprinted as Chap. XIX, and other especially relevant passages are in Chaps. I, XVI, and XVII; Jerome Karabel, "Revolutionary Contradictions: Antonio Gramsci and the Problem of Intellectuals," *Politics & Society*, VI (1976), 123–72—an illuminating analysis and an introduction, via its footnotes, to the literature on Gramsci up to that time. Works about Gramsci have been pouring off the presses in such abundance in the past decade and a half as to induce nightmares about colleges' offering majors and degrees in Gramsci Studies. My references are solely to a few works that expound the ideological-hegemony theory as it has been or might be applied to American history. It has never been tested against the data of the social history of the American working class.

15. Aileen S. Kraditor, "American Radical Historians on Their Heritage," *Past & Present*, No. 56 (August, 1972), 141–42. I would now capitalize the *S* in system, for I no longer agree with what I wrote there. I went on to say that it followed that radical historians should pay more attention to the ideas and values of the population at large and should regard past dissenting movements as "limiting cases" of the prescribed consensus, that is, of the hegemonic ideology. I followed my own advice in the next few years, with the result that, after having tested the Gramscian hypothesis in the American context, I discarded it. This book is, in part, the result.

16. Howard Brotz, "Social Stratification and the Political Order," in Arnold M. Rose (ed.), *Human Behavior and Social Processes: An Interactionist Approach* (Boston: Houghton Mifflin, 1962), 310–11. To reject both overt force and ideological hegemony is not to deny all the bonds that hold a class-divided society together. Brotz's article, among other works by many social scientists, proposes a far more complex model.

17. The last twelve words refer to Marx and Engels, *The German Ideology* (New York: International Publishers, 1939), 39: "The ideas of the ruling class are in every epoch the ruling ideas: i.e. the class, which is the ruling material force of society, is at the same time its ruling intellectual force."

18. Michael Walzer, "Puritanism as a Revolutionary Ideology," *History and Theory*, III (1963), 75. The exception in the United States was the Slave South, in which the ideological hegemony of the large slaveholders over the slaves and the rest of the whites did prevail; that society was a System. What was true of the Slave South cannot, however, be assumed

to have been true of the North, despite radicals' references to free workers as "wage slaves." Even within the Slave South the Gramscian model probably fits only the older sections. It certainly does not fit the society described in J. Mills Thornton III, *Politics and Power in a Slave Society: Alabama, 1800–1860* (Baton Rouge: Louisiana State University Press, 1978).

19. Gwynn A. Williams, "Gramsci's Concept of *Egemonia*," *Journal of the History of Ideas*, XXI (1960), 587, quoted in Cammett, *Antonio Gramsci*, 204.

20. Quoted in Cammett, *Antonio Gramsci*, 9.

21. Genovese has rejected the notions of "consciousness raising" and "false consciousness." See Eugene D. Genovese, "Yeomen Farmers in a Slaveholders' Democracy," *Agricultural History*, XLIX (1975), 331–32. But *cf.* Genovese, *In Red and Black*, where the working class is "unconscious" of its interests and radicals must "bring the masses" to see this (p. 407) and "the masses . . . must be made to see" that (p. 408) and certain people are capable "of undergoing a revolution in consciousness" under the tutelage of Marxists (p. 413) and so on. He is careful to show that "we" do not yet have an adequate theory or organization to undertake this assignment. The radical vanguard seems to have as rudimentary an understanding as do those masses it must teach and lead because they do not understand their own interests.

22. Genovese, *In Red and Black*, 401.

23. *Ibid.*, 408.

24. On a related point, see Lester D. Stephens, "Proteus at Play with the Past: Historical Versus Mythical Thinking," *History Teacher*, VIII (1975), 412–13; Robert Tucker, *Philosophy and Myth in Karl Marx* (Cambridge: Cambridge University Press, 1961), 22.

25. See Fred Weinstein and Gerald M. Platt, *Psychoanalytic Sociology* (Baltimore: Johns Hopkins University Press, 1973), 94.

26. Karabel, "Revolutionary Contradictions: Antonio Gramsci and the Problem of Intellectuals," 143.

27. *Ibid.*, 146–56.

28. Sebastian de Grazia, *The Political Community: A Study of Anomie* (Chicago: University of Chicago Press, 1948).

29. See, *e.g.*, *ibid.*, 80–81.

30. *Ibid.*, 74–75, 215.

31. *Ibid.*, 115–19.

32. I shall not attempt to construct a model to replace the ones I have rejected. My purpose is negative: to refute concepts that cannot account for the pertinent data or that violate the meanings of those data. The interpretations that seem most faithful to those meanings are middle-level generalizations that may fit more than one model on a level of generalization matching that of the rejected ones. Certainly, hypotheses are necessary to research, but they need not be as all-encompassing as Marxism (any version) and de Grazia's.

33. Nancy Voye, seminar paper (Boston University, May, 1975). Voye's hypothesis is supported by Irvin G. Wyllie, *The Self-Made Man in America: The Myth of Rags to Riches* (1954; New York: Free Press, 1966), 86. I would add that not just any discrepancy between different elements of the social order can be constructive in Voye's sense. See Eckstein, *Theory of Stable Democracy*, for a discussion of which sorts are constructive and which destructive.

34. This term has been criticized as Europocentric. I am using it noninvidiously, as a convenient way to refer to a process that is not controverted in the literature.

35. Richard D. Brown, *Modernization: The Transformation of American Life, 1600–1865* (New York: Hill & Wang, 1976). E. A. Wrigley, in "The Process of Modernization and the Industrial Revolution in England," *Journal of Interdisciplinary History*, III (1972), 225–59, shows that the connection between modernization and industrialization "is contingent rather than necessary" (p. 225). In the present context, however, the two may be discussed together.

36. *P*, August 2, 1896. In addition, see Supplement.

37. See Peter Berger, Brigitte Berger, and Hansfried Kellner, *The Homeless Mind: Modernization and Consciousness* (New York: Vintage, 1973), *passim*, esp. Chap. I.

38. These same traits and the socioeconomic imperatives that foster them, however, have had long-term consequences that more recently have spread to other spheres. See *ibid.*, Chaps. IX–X.

39. Allan G. Bogue, "Social Theory and the Pioneer," *Agricultural History*, XXXIV (1960), 31. Another historian to whom the shake-up metaphor occurred is Rowland Berthoff; see his *Unsettled People*, 128, 240, both with reference to the Jacksonian era.

40. It may even be argued that the more the public-sphere roles require rationalized and bureaucratized relationships the greater need people have for the private sphere where their primordial needs can be satisfied. See Andrew M. Greeley, *Why Can't They Be Like Us?: America's White Ethnic Groups* (New York: E. P. Dutton, 1975), 98, 186–88.

41. The repeated assertion by Jeremy Brecher, in *Strike!*, that the inner logic of the period's mass strikes was revolutionary is not a testable hypothesis, and although he tries hard to marshal data showing that masses of workers consciously aimed to expel the capitalists from industries, he fails to show that they were typical. David Montgomery, in "Workers' Control of Machine Production in the Nineteenth Century," *Labor History*, XVII (1976), 485–509, also emphasizes the struggle of workers to control production, but he is discussing skilled workers only and the fact that the rationalization of production and the efficiency experts aimed in part to deprive these workers of control they had traditionally exercised. Furthermore, it should be recalled that one could acknowledge the industrialists' function in the economic sphere while denying their ideological hegemony in the political and social spheres. A more plausible view is that presented by Robert W. Smuts, *European Impressions of the American Worker* (New York: King's Crown Press, 1953), summarizing the observations of visitors at the turn of the century:

The frequency and the bitterness of industrial conflict was the most basic fault the foreigners found in American industrial life. Most of the visitors escaped the error of explaining American strikes as the product of exploitation. Although they were not blind to the poverty and degradation of some workers, they were more impressed with the prosperity, the welfare, and the honorable position of the majority. They realized, moreover, that American union members and, therefore, American strikers were mainly the skilled, highly paid workers—not the women and children and unskilled immigrants who were most obviously exploited.

Most of the European visitors explained industrial conflict as a result rather than a contradiction of the material and social democracy which typified the life of the American worker. The abundance of his life, they pointed out, added to the strength of his ambition for still more. His self-reliance made him sensitive to his rights. Industrial conflict in America was a man-to-man fight, with no quarter asked or given, unmitigated by the tradition of subordination on the one hand, or benevolence and responsibility on the other. For all its bitterness, the strike . . . was not a struggle against capitalism but against capitalists, not against the system, but for a bigger share of its benefits. . . . The underlying issue was the traditional American right of each man to determine for himself the basic terms of his life. The reward of industrial work was a greatly extended opportunity to remake the conditions of one's life off the job, but the penalty was the renunciation of control over one's life on the job. Europeans could not understand America's industrial conflicts because they emphasized the desire to increase the rewards of work but ignored the demand to reduce the penalties imposed upon the worker. . . . There was no precedent to help them understand a labor movement . . . which fought with all its means for power and control, without the slightest intention of using control to change the fundamentals of the economy (pp. 26–28).

42. Herbert G. Gutman, "The Worker's Search for Power," in H. Wayne Morgan (ed.), *The Gilded Age: A Reappraisal* (Syracuse: Syracuse University Press, 1963), 40. In addition, see Supplement.

43. The three previous sentences refer to the thinking of native-born Americans, not to that of the immigrant majority of the industrial working class.

44. Herbert G. Gutman, *Work, Culture & Society in Industrializing America* (New York: Knopf, 1976), 236. *Cf.* John M. Ingham, "Rags to Riches Revisited: The Effect of City Size and Related Factors on the Recruitment of Business Leaders," *Journal of American History*, LXIII (1976), 635. After describing iron and steel manufacturers in six cities, Ingham concludes that the data "indicate that there was a strong continuity of economic and social leadership." But his data show continuity of economic leadership and social *exclusiveness* among that group, not social *leadership*, for that requires followership. Ingham provides no evidence of this group's influence over others.

45. *Sol*, March 18, 1913. In one respect that picture is atypical: family life was not impossible for most native and many immigrant workers, but owing to the atypical constituency of the IWW, especially in the West, this theme received much more attention in Wobbly papers than in those of other radical organizations.

46. Zane L. Miller cautions against exaggerating the impact of ethnic diversity and ignoring that of the rapidity of urban growth. See his "The Ethnic Revival and Urban Liberalism," *Reviews in American History*, II (1974), 422.

47. John Higham, *Send These To Me: Jews and Other Immigrants in Urban America* (New York: Atheneum, 1975), 129.

48. On the latter clause, see Herbert G. Gutman, "Class, Status, and the Gilded-Age Radical: A Reconsideration. The Case of a New Jersey Socialist," in Herbert G. Gutman and Gregory S. Kealey (eds.), *Many Pasts: Readings in American Social History, 1865–the Present* (Englewood Cliffs, N.J.: Prentice-Hall, 1973), 139–40.

49. Skårdal, *Divided Heart*, 332.

50. Despite some employers' use of divide-and-conquer tactics, most seem to have been more inconvenienced than gratified by ethnic differences, which caused disruption, impeded communication of instructions, and raised the accident rate. For both responses, see, *e.g.*, Gerd Korman, *Industrialization, Immigrants, and Americanizers: The View from Milwaukee, 1866–1921* (Madison: The State Historical Society of Wisconsin, 1967), 42, 65–68.

51. See Gutman, *Work, Culture, and Society*, 43, 65, and *passim*.

52. See Thomas Luckmann, *The Invisible Religion: The Problem of Religion in Modern Society* (New York: Macmillan, 1967), 97; Sam Bass Warner, Jr., *The Private City: Philadelphia in Three Periods of Its Growth* (Philadelphia: University of Pennsylvania Press, 1971), 3–4 and *passim*; Peter L. Berger, *Pyramids of Sacrifice: Political Ethics and Social Change* (Garden City, N.Y.: Doubleday, 1976), 192.

53. Tamara Hareven, "The Laborers of Manchester, New Hampshire, 1912–1922: The Role of Family and Ethnicity in Adjustment to Industrial Life," *Labor History*, XVI (1975), 249–50. A related point, concerning Jewish immigrants, is made in David A. Hollinger, "Ethnic Diversity, Cosmopolitanism and the Emergence of the American Liberal Intelligentsia," *American Quarterly*, XXVII (1975), 138. See also Gutman, *Work, Culture, and Society*, 41.

54. *E.g.*, *P*, March 18, 1900. Radical papers enjoyed a much larger working-class readership at that time than they do now. See also de Grazia, *Political Community*, 117–18; citing various authorities (see pp. 121–22, 224), he suggests that when public outrage forced the rich to abandon their conspicuous extravagance and British upper-class affectations, and the public's anger died down, this meant that industrialists acquired a new, although incomplete, legitimacy. Its incompleteness was due to the persistent "simple anomie" that de Grazia sees as endemic in every competitive society. But legitimacy cannot be achieved that quickly or simply. I further doubt that the industrialists and financiers as a class have ever achieved legitimate authority in the United States in the traditional sense of the phrase, even during the 1920s boom (see Ellis W. Hawley, "Antitrust on the Defensive: The American Movement for a Cartelized Economy, 1918–33," *Reviews in American History*, IV [1976], 583–85); its apparently greater authority during the two World Wars was really the authority of the government, which lent its authority to businessmen in return for their loan of their power to serve the more inclusive goals of the government.

55. Quoted in Elizabeth Gurley Flynn, *The Rebel Girl: An Autobiography: My First Life*

(1906–1926) (New York: International Publishers, 1973), 243. *Cf.* the comments of British observers in 1950, quoted in Smuts, *European Impressions of the American Worker*, 55: "In short," concludes Smuts, "from the viewpoint of Europeans, American industry became civilized." Or, in terms of the present context, the shake-up period had ended by then, for the Britons contrasted the situation in 1950 with that of 1890, which had been characterized by "the ruthless exploitation of the weak, the refusal to recognize the cost to those who failed of the universal drive for private economic gain, the despotism of the employer," and so on.

56. Ronald Story, "Blacks, Brown, and Blood: The Hourglass Pattern," *Reviews in American History*, III (1975), 216.

57. Gutman, *Work, Culture, and Society*, 245–46.

58. As E. Digby Baltzell observes, in *The Protestant Establishment: Aristocracy and Caste in America* (New York: Vintage, 1966), 70, "power which is not legitimized tends to be either coercive or manipulative."

59. Korman, *Industrialization, Immigrants, and Americanizers*, 61. See also Robert Ozanne, *A Century of Labor-Management Relations at McCormick and International Harvester* (Madison: University of Wisconsin Press, 1967), 31.

60. As Peter L. Berger says, in *Invitation to Sociology: A Humanistic Perspective* (Garden City, N.Y.: Doubleday Anchor, 1963), 112, "The moral effort to lie deliberately is beyond most people. . . . The liar, by definition, knows that he is lying. The ideologist does not. . . . Most theories of conspiracy grossly overestimate the intellectual foresight of the conspirators."

61. On lack of confidence in the late nineteenth century, see Supplement.

62. Gary Dean Best, "President Wilson's Second Industrial Conference, 1919–20," *Labor History*, XVI (1975), 505–520. See also David Brody, *Steelworkers in America: The Nonunion Era* (New York: Russell & Russell, 1970), 220–23.

63. This was the case also in the mining patches described in Victor R. Greene, *The Slavic Community on Strike: Immigrant Labor in Pennsylvania Anthracite* (Notre Dame, Ind.: University of Notre Dame Press, 1968); I am, however, interpreting his data in my own way.

64. Frank Bohn, "After Ludlow—Facts and Thoughts," *ISR*, XV (1914), 115.

65. Robert Hunter, *Violence and the Labor Movement* (New York: Macmillan, 1914), Chap. XI.

66. Gutman, *Work, Culture, and Society*, 243.

67. This supposition seems plausible especially in the light of the public's reaction to the bombing of the Los Angeles *Times* building in 1910 by the McNamara brothers, who were union officials, as well as to an earlier series of exposures of union corruption. According to Joseph Rayback, *A History of American Labor* (New York: Free Press, 1966), 220–22, public opinion turned against the labor movement. Thus, both its sympathy and its hostility reflected judgments based on general social norms, not on specifically class biases or loyalties.

68. Ideological-hegemony theorists would cite this to support their thesis on the ground that the evolution of rules to regulate the class struggle legitimates the employer-employee relationship and hence the System that the employers rule. Wherefore it should be repeated that if a class struggle within the given economic system is a form of the ideological-hegemony relationship, so is every struggle or form of behavior that does not aim at revolution. But that thesis depends on the truth of the System paradigm and is therefore circular, as is any "proof" that depends on and includes the proposition it purports to prove. More to the point: what sort of evidence could be considered as disproving that hypothesis? It redefines all evidence that apparently contradicts it, by showing that such evidence means the opposite of what it seems to mean (struggle is a form of accommodation, the private sphere is really the carrier of public-sphere values, etc.) Proponents of this thesis do not show how it can be stated in a falsifiable form or suggest what kind of

data would disprove it. One is therefore free to hypothesize that the data that show rejection of the capitalists' claim to hegemony do show just that.

69. Edwin Fenton, *Immigrants and Unions, A Case Study: Italians and American Labor, 1870–1920* (New York: Arno Press, 1975), 201, 256; Brody, *Steelworkers in America, passim,* esp. 58, 96, 99, 108.

70. Greene, *Slavic Community on Strike.*

71. See John Graham Brooks, *American Syndicalism: The I.W.W.* (New York: Macmillan, 1913), 245–46.

72. Montgomery, "Workers' Control of Machine Production," 507. Daniel Nelson, "The New Factory System and the Unions: The National Cash Register Company Dispute of 1901," *Labor History,* XV (1974), 163–78, demonstrates that the danger to the workers was neither the employers' power nor arbitrary treatment but the combination of the two. It should be added that bureaucratization and legitimation are not the same; a bureaucratized power can be as lacking in legitimacy as personalized and arbitrary power.

73. The last clause paraphrases one in Hadley Cantril, *The Politics of Despair* (New York: Basic Books, 1958), 54. Other background for this paragraph includes Lewis Coser, *Greedy Institutions: Patterns of Undivided Commitment* (New York: Free Press, 1974), 4; Robert K. Merton, "Social Structure and Anomie," *American Sociological Review,* III (1938), 682; George Sabine, "The Two Democratic Traditions," *Philosophic Review,* LXI (1952), 472; Weinstein and Platt, *Psychoanalytic Sociology,* 93.

Chapter IV

1. Stephen Toulmin, *The Collective Use and Evolution of Concepts* (Princeton: Princeton University Press, 1972), Vol. I of Stephen Toulmin, *Human Understanding* (3 vols. projected; Princeton: Princeton University Press, 1972—), 348–50. See also Toulmin's review of Jacques Monod, *Chance and Necessity,* in *New York Review of Books,* December 16, 1971, p. 22: "Why do all our 'values' have to be linked together into a single 'system' . . . ? A truly Darwinian thinker would surely view the values, institutions, and social structures of a people as forming not a 'system' but a 'population'—a population which is more or less well adapted to the needs of the men concerned, and within which individual practices can change more or less independently in the face of new socio-historical situations in a pragmatic manner, and with more or less 'adaptive consequences.'" With respect to his remark about differing life-spans of various institutions, it should be recalled that current historiography has been disproving long-standing assumptions concerning the causal and temporal relationships among phenomena like the rise in population, the industrial revolution, changes in family structure, and the birth of modern science. Although the productive insights furnished by Marxism have been appreciated by many non-Marxist historians, what has been insufficiently noted is the effect of System-thinking on periodization in history. In this area the effect has been to assume causal and temporal relationships required by the theory rather than demonstrated by the evidence. See E. Anthony Wrigley, "Reflections on the History of the Family," *Daedalus* (Spring, 1977), 71–85, for a corrective in one area.

2. Toulmin, *Collective Use and Evolution of Concepts,* 356, 353. See pp. 328–40 for Toulmin's view that Marx had more in common, as an evolutionary thinker, with Lamarck than with Darwin. Thus it was, he says, no political accident that Lysenko's neo-Lamarckianism found favor with Soviet ideologists in the 1950s. Among the relevant points he makes, too numerous and extended to quote here, is that

when a historian reconstructs a particular social or political episode, he may retrospectively characterize it as involving a dialectical sequence of problems and solutions, by dissecting out the needs that were successfully met in each period by new political or social procedures from the more general background of unresolved socio-political difficulties. But . . . the appearance of "formal necessity" arising from the dialectical mode of exposition is misleading. This appearance originates in our retrospective judgement on the fruitful outcome of the events concerned; it points to no intrinsic feature in the events themselves. . . . In social and political history, as in the history of scientific thought, the "dialectic" lies primarily in our writing of history, rather than in the historical events about which we write. . . . Men demonstrate the "rationality" of their social and political procedures as much by their capacity to cope with unforeseeable problems as by their capacity to deal with problems that were already "implicit" in what had gone before.

But, he adds, we shall hardly recognize this process if we yield to "the temptation to project the logical structure of our historical analysis back on to the facts, and to construe its dialectical 'necessity' as a species of 'causality' inherent in historical events themselves" (pp. 330–32).

3. See in general, *ibid.*, 341–42, 350–53.

4. Herbert G. Gutman, "Work, Culture, and Society in Industrializing America, 1815–1919," *American Historical Review*, LXXVIII (1973), 582–83.

5. Michael Paul Rogin, *The Intellectuals and McCarthy: The Radical Specter* (Cambridge: M.I.T. Press, 1967), 192–93. In addition, see Supplement.

6. The best-known work that deals with this aspect of deviance is Lewis Coser, *The Functions of Social Conflict* (New York: Free Press, 1964). For a convenient survey of the evolution of the concept, see Lewis Coser, *Continuities in the Study of Social Conflict* (New York: Free Press, 1967), Chap. VI. An immensely suggestive discussion of how differently structured societies deal with deviance is Elliott P. Currie, "Crimes without Criminals: Witchcraft and Its Control in Renaissance Europe," *Law and Society Review*, III (1968), 7–32. My references to a society's "choosing" this and "discovering" that imply the danger of abstractionism and reification, and I must emphasize that such phrases in this chapter should be understood as shorthand references to real people. Examples of the real-life process of exploration are interestingly described by Morris Hillquit, *Loose Leaves from a Busy Life* (New York: Macmillan, 1934), 68–70, 81–91.

7. David Brion Davis, "Some Themes of Countersubversion: An Analysis of Anti-Masonic, Anti-Catholic, and Anti-Mormon Literature," *Mississippi Valley Historical Review*, XLVII (1960), 210.

8. See *e.g.*, Selig Perlman, *A History of Trade Unionism in the United States* (New York: Macmillan, 1922): In the coal strike of 1902, "the public identified the anthracite employers with the trust movement, which was then new and seemingly bent upon uprooting the traditional American social order; by contrast, the striking miners appeared almost as champions of old America" (p. 177).

9. See, *e.g.*, Max Hayes's speech at the founding convention of the SP; he said that hundreds of newspapers across the country were saying that the Morgans and Rockefellers were bringing socialism. SP, *Proceedings*, 1901, p. 33.

10. This is not to suggest that the radical movements should be studied *only* in terms of symbols. Their contributions to the debate over unionization and the proper structure of unions and the definitions of permissible free speech were functional in the most literal way.

11. Melvyn Dubofsky, *We Shall Be All: A History of the IWW* (New York: Quadrangle, 1969), 160–64; Joseph Robert Conlin, *Bread and Roses Too: Studies of the Wobblies* (Westport, Conn.: Greenwood Press, 1969), 75–78. But *cf.* Vernon Jensen, *Heritage of Conflict: Labor Relations in the Nonferrous Metals Industry up to 1930* (Ithaca: Cornell University Press, 1950), 346–47.

12. Conlin, *Bread and Roses Too: Studies of the Wobblies*, 76–77, 80. Conlin should take the advice he gives to historians of the IWW, and study the *prohibitionist* movement more carefully.

13. *Ibid.*, 82, 84. For Conlin's other evidence for the Wobblies' conventionality, see his Chaps. III and IV.

14. *Ibid.*, 108–111.

15. On the need for skepticism concerning a correlation between what people believe and what leaders and the media tell them to believe, see Melvin Small, "Some Suggestions from the Behavioral Sciences for Historians Interested in the Study of Attitudes," *Societas*, III (1973), 1–19, esp. p. 18.

16. Robert J. Goldstein, "The Anarchist Scare of 1908: A Sign of Tensions in the Progressive Era," *American Studies*, XV (1974), 55–56. One work that takes full account of both the discontent and the rational search for new answers is David P. Thelen, "Social Tensions and the Origins of Progressivism," *Journal of American History*, LVI (1969), 323–41. See also Maxwell H. Bloomfield, *Alarms and Diversions: The American Mind through American Magazines, 1900–1914* (The Hague: Mouton, 1967), 11, 67–69, 93, 96, and *passim*.

17. As James J. Martin shows, in *Men against the State: The Expositors of Individualist Anarchism in America, 1827–1908* (Colorado Springs: Ralph Myles, 1970), the terrorist variety of anarchism did not represent the main stream of anarchist thought. But since the public opinion dealt with by Goldstein did not distinguish between the different sorts of anarchists, qualifying adjectives will be omitted in this discussion.

18. Goldstein, "Anarchist Scare of 1908," 66–73.

19. *Ibid.*, 73.

20. Jensen, *Heritage of Conflict*, 70–71. According to "W.F.M. Joins A.F. of L.," *Sol*, July 9, 1910, the WFM's referendum showed a majority of 7,000 in favor of joining the AFL; only 5 locals out of 265 opposed.

21. Goldstein, "Anarchist Scare of 1908," 73.

22. *Ibid.*, 77 n. 33.

23. De Leon himself pointed this out, according to David Herreshoff, *The Origins of American Marxism: From the Transcendentalists to De Leon* (New York: Monad Press, 1973), 160–62. Denying that the government's violations of the constitutional rights of Haywood and Moyer amounted to war, De Leon observed, "The kidnapping and other outrages had taken place, and yet the convention of the . . . [IWW] met and worked in peace" (p. 62).

24. Goldstein, "Anarchist Scare of 1908," 72.

25. Robert Hunter, *Violence and the Labor Movement* (New York: Macmillan, 1914), 281.

26. Goldstein, "Anarchist Scare of 1908," 67. Although Goldstein says "even" the SLP's paper took this position, this was a fundamental belief of the party. De Leon, its chief ideologue, believed that the militant minority of the working class would soon convert to socialism and bring the passive majority along with it, and that violence could only harm the cause.

27. Elizabeth Gurley Flynn, *The Rebel Girl: An Autobiography: My First Life (1906–1926)* (New York: International Publishers, 1973), 227.

28. Quoted in David Brody, *Steelworkers in America: The Nonunion Era* (New York: Russell & Russell, 1970), 245. Similar statements abound in *IW* and *Sol*.

29. Flynn, *Rebel Girl*, 228. The Finnish socialists were IWW sympathizers, many of them belonging to both organizations.

30. See "Seattle's Red-Flag Incident," *Literary Digest*, August 2, 1913, pp. 160–61. They made the same distinctions after the McNamara brothers bombed the Los Angeles *Times* building in 1910. See also "The Common Welfare"; Paul U. Kellogg, "Conservatism and Industrial War"; and "Larger Bearings of the McNamara Case," a symposium; all in *Survey*, December 30, 1911, pp. 1407–1429, for a thorough examination of the issue and comments by many eminent observers.

31. Conlin, *Bread and Roses Too: Studies of the Wobblies*, 113–14.

32. See Robert L. Tyler, *Rebels of the Woods: The I.W.W. in the Pacific Northwest* (Eugene: University of Oregon Press, 1967), Chap. V, in which he contrasts the wartime suppression of the Wobblies with the good feelings between the government and the AFL.

33. "The Recall of Haywood," *Literary Digest*, March 15, 1913, p. 562. The sort of statements by Haywood that were the immediate provocation is epitomized in his Cooper Union speech early in 1912, when he declared, "I despise the law" and "I don't know of

anything . . . that will bring as much satisfaction to you, as much anguish to the boss as a little sabotage in the right place at the proper time." (William D. Haywood, "Socialism the Hope of the Working Class," *ISR*, XII [1912], 467, 469.)

34. If we compare the American public's reaction to the Wobblies with its reaction to Robert Owen's New Harmony experiment, we can perceive the reason for the rejection of violence. It was tolerant of Owen's economic plan but not of his irreligion. Similarly, John Humphrey Noyes's community of Perfectionists evoked no animosity on account of its economic arrangements but was run out of Putney, Vermont, because of its practice of "plural marriage." A sympathetic historian might be puzzled by the outsiders' perversity in focusing on what the historian considers secondary aspects of these experiments. But why did it focus on them? Public reaction to a movement or program is no less revealing of things the historian ought to know than is the movement's intentions. The American public in the early nineteenth century evidently did not feel communal economic arrangements to be a threat; it did feel irreligion and sexual deviance to be threats. Such experiments, like the upsurge of violence a generation later, were felt as invasions of the private sphere. As to the IWW, it evoked fear and hostility not only for its supposed approval of sabotage and violence but also for its defiance of community mores with respect to religion and sex. See Chap. VI below.

35. See the four articles cited in *n*. 63 to Chap. V below; one of them is quoted in *n*. 41 in this chapter. Also, items cited in press surveys in "Capitalist Press," *C*, November 28, 1910; and in several issues of *SDH* in the spring of 1905; and Marvin Wachman, *History of the Social-Democratic Party in Milwaukee, 1897–1910* (Urbana: University of Illinois Press, 1945), 63, 67–68, 71–72. Frederic Cople Jaher, *Doubters and Dissenters: Cataclysmic Thought in America, 1885–1918* (New York: Free Press, 1964), 69, points out that the Cleveland *Plain Dealer* panicked in 1887 when it thought the anarchists were threatening civilization, but when McKinley was assassinated in 1901 it remained calm, noting how few the anarchists were. Later, Jaher cites a press survey that shows American newspapers reporting fairly on the labor troubles in Cripple Creek and Telluride, the murder of former Governor Steunenberg of Idaho, the Moyer-Haywood-Pettibone trial, and the Los Angeles *Times* bombing. Those papers that did editorialize did not blame the labor movement. The comments on the Paterson strike show the same pattern. The IWW leadership there was not denounced; the editors emphasized the workers' grievances. See Jaher, pp. 225–26, *n*. 6.

36. Sally M. Miller, *Victor Berger and the Promise of Constructive Socialism, 1910–1920* (Westport, Conn.: Greenwood Press, 1973), 71. See also Henry F. Bedford, *Socialism and the Workers in Massachusetts, 1886–1912* (Amherst: University of Massachusetts Press, 1966), 119, concerning Massachusetts in 1899. This does not mean there were no incidents contrary to this trend. That a whole book could be constructed from a diligent collation of them is proven by William Preston, Jr., *Aliens and Dissenters: Federal Suppression of Radicals, 1903–1933* (Cambridge: Harvard University Press, 1963).

37. Hillquit, *Loose Leaves from a Busy Life*, 208–210.

38. See, *e.g.*, Robert E. Zeigler, "The Limits of Power: The Amalgamated Association of Street Railway Employees in Houston, Texas, 1897–1905," *Labor History*, XVIII (1977), 71–90. The episode described there did not involve the IWW, but the process of boundary-drawing was the same.

39. Irwin Yellowitz, "The Origins of Unemployment Reform in the United States," *Labor History*, IX (1968), 338–60, usefully distinguishes among different varieties of Progressivism and their views of the state's responsibility.

40. Thelen, "Social Tensions and the Origins of Progressivism," 341.

41. An editorialist at that time wrote:

The American Socialist is no longer a creature of hoofs and horns. . . . The growth of the creed measures the growth of the protest against the present economic and political order. . . . The strongest reason of all is what may be called the humane appeal of Socialism. Parks, playgrounds, medical examination of school-children, sanitary inspection of places where women and children work—all the comparatively new public activities that the old parties are slow to take up—these make a strong pull on all good men's sympathy, and men who wish these humane things done do not hesitate to vote for a Socialist mayor because a Socialist Congress, if we should have one, might try to abolish the Constitution. In fact it is silly to maintain that such helpful public acts commit a community to the state ownership of all productive industries. Thus Socialism has gained much from the conservative stupidity of its enemies. . . . [But all these reasons combined] give no reason to suppose that there is going to be a Socialistic party in the United States strong enough to hold the balance of power between the two old parties. Long before it reaches any such strength it will have so scared one or both the old parties into action against old abuses that much of the reason for protest will disappear. Such protests have a humanizing and liberalizing influence; and it may very well be that for this reason the Socialists are playing and will play a good part in preventing the fossilization of the old parties. This, in fact, is the reason why many men who utterly reject the creed see the party win minor victories with complacency—the reason why, too, the word "Socialism" no longer frightens them.

Ira Kipnis, in *The American Socialist Movement, 1897–1912* (New York: Monthly Review Press, 1972), 347, cites this article, along with three others—but he does not quote any of them—to support his statement "that popular magazines erupted in a barrage of articles on the seemingly irresistible advance of socialism in the United States." In fact, the authors of the other three articles considered socialism as resistible as this one did.

42. Jack L. Walker, "A Critique of the Elitist Theory of Democracy," *American Political Science Review*, LX (1966), 293–94. I do not know whether Walker would agree with my version of this model or my application of it to the shake-up period.

43. Jensen, *Heritage of Conflict*, 252–55, describes another such town, this one in South Dakota.

Chapter V

1. Robert Jay Lifton, *Revolutionary Immortality: Mao Tse-tung and the Chinese Cultural Revolution* (New York: Vintage, 1968), 54, 96. In addition, see Supplement.

2. V. I. Lenin, *What Is To Be Done?* (New York: International Publishers, 1929), 32–33.

3. *Ibid.*, 40.

4. Ira Kipnis, *The American Socialist Movement, 1897–1912* (New York: Monthly Review Press, 1972), 227. The footnote supporting the first sentence cites John Spargo, *The Substance of Socialism* (New York: B. W. Huebsch, 1911), 112–14, 140–42, and an editorial in the New York *Call* of August 18, 1912, entitled "Class Hatred and Class Consciousness." Neither of those documents contains a word relating to Kipnis' text; both discuss class hatred and disapprove of it. Kipnis' faulty logic and the discrepancy between his thesis and his documents are pointed out by Martin Diamond, "Socialism and the Decline of the American Socialist Party" (Ph.D. dissertation, University of Chicago, 1956), 103–106.

5. Carl D. Thompson, "Who Constitute the Proletariat?" *ISR*, IX (1909), 611–12.

6. This does not mean he never changed his theories after 1890. See L. Glen Seretan, "Daniel De Leon, 'Wandering Jew' of American Socialism: An Interpretive Analysis," *American Jewish Historical Quarterly*, LXV (1976), 245–46.

7. "The 'Intellectual,'" *P*, March 19, 1905, reprinted in Daniel De Leon, *Socialist Landmarks* (New York: New York Labor News Co., 1952), 21–25. See also SLP, *Proceedings*, 1900, p. 37, in which the Kangaroos comprise chiefly "women with churchly inclinations and a marked tendency for goody-goodiness" and "some reverends," and the split separated "the workingmen on the one side, the doctors, lawyers, reverends, and ladies on the other."

8. The noes had it. See IWW, *Proceedings*, 1905, pp. 65–70. For a discussion linking the cult of proletarianism with status ascription, see Daniel Bell, *Marxian Socialism in the United States* (Princeton: Princeton University Press, 1967), 82–85.

9. Remarks of William Knight of Colorado, in IWW, *Proceedings*, 1905, p. 173.

10. IWW, *Proceedings*, 1905, p. 203. Compare the second clause of the first sentence with the second sentence. The IWW's problem was, of course, different from that of the SLP and SP since it was a union as well as a radical organization.

11. Robert L. Tyler, *Rebels of the Woods: The I.W.W. in the Pacific Northwest* (Eugene: University of Oregon Press, 1967), 26.

12. "The Liquor Question," *IW*, May 27, 1909. For a debate within the SP over "booze-fighters," see SP, *Proceedings*, 1910, pp. 38, 49–51.

13. "The Unemployed and the IWW," *IW*, June 24, 1909. The italics are, in the original, in heavy roman type. In addition, see Supplement.

14. The designations "right" and "left" referred principally to policies regarding trade unions. On other issues individuals often divided and coalesced differently. I shall use these labels for the sake of convenience, but their restricted meaning should be kept in mind.

15. See also Henry L. Slobodin, "The National Socialist Convention of 1912," *ISR*, XII (1912), 808, on a denunciation by Spargo of the Wobbly street speakers in San Diego and of some delegates to the SP convention who spoke on a street corner in overalls so as to present themselves sympathetically to the crowd. Slobodin says that Victor Berger expressed similar opinions, whereas he himself disagrees with Berger and Spargo. Winfield R. Gaylord criticizes rabble-rousing in the same terms as Spargo, in "Remedies for Our Ills," letter to the editor, *C*, December 21, 1909.

16. "Ghent Discusses a Pressing Need," letter to the editor, *Worker*, November 23, 1907. See also Charles Dobbs, "Brains," *ISR*, VIII (1908), 533–37.

17. Kipnis, *American Socialist Movement*, 203.

18. See Morris Hillquit, "A Closing Word," letter to the editor, *Worker*, March 14, 1908. It is surprising to read, in that letter, the following statement: "The now famous terms 'chump' and 'yawp' were applied by him [Ghent] not to the proletarians in our ranks, but to those trouble makers who sought to create strife and to engender a low mob sentiment in our party." Kipnis, *American Socialist Movement*, p. 203, *n*. 25 cites this document but does not quote it.

19. Frances M. Gill, "Comrade Gill Replies to Ghent," *Worker*, November 30, 1907. Ghent replied to this and other letters in "The Function of Intelligence in the Socialist Movement," *Worker*, December 14, 1907.

20. On this issue, I agree with Michael E. R. Bassett and disagree with James Weinstein. See Bassett, "The Socialist Party of America, 1912–1919: Years of Decline" (Ph.D. dissertation, Duke University, 1963); Weinstein, *The Decline of Socialism in America, 1912–1925* (New York: Monthly Review Press, 1967). Among the sources there are many written before 1914 showing the party's failure to grow and periodic faltering in morale. See also John H. M. Laslett, "Socialism and American Trade Unionism," in John H. M. Laslett and Seymour Martin Lipset (eds.), *Failure of a Dream?: Essays in the History of American Socialism* (Garden City, N.Y.: Doubleday Anchor, 1974), 216–17.

21. Charles Kerr, "What Is the Matter with the Socialist Party?" *ISR*, IX (1909), 449–51. Kerr thought Local Denver should stay and try to oust the leadership and put wageworkers on the N.E.C.

22. Editor's comment following "W. J. Ghent's Reply," *C*, December 4, 1909.

23. George Allan England, "Our Hopeless Highbrows," *C*, January 30, 1911.

24. William D. Haywood, "Socialism the Hope of the Working Class," *ISR*, XII (1912), 462.

25. J. S. Biscay, "What Would Marx Say," *Sol*, March 19, 1910.

26. Louis Duchez, "The Revolutionary Proletariat," *C*, April 17, 1910. At the end he assures the reader that this is not a pipe dream but is the obvious conclusion from a study of modern industry in the light of Marxism. Another example is Duchez's "The Basic Industries," *C*, August 28, 1910, which toward the end slips into the oracular mode, prophesying—or rather, describing a vision of the future—in the present tense, apparently automatically. See also Duchez, "The Revolutionary Value of Strikes," *C*, August 7, 1910. When

reading these visions one of course recalls Marx's use of the same mode in Chap. XXXII of *Capital*, Vol. I (New York: International Publishers, 1947); up to p. 788 he has used the historical past and the normal present tenses, but then slips into the vision that ends with, "The knell of capitalist private property sounds. The expropriators are expropriated."

27. "Slobodin on Spargo," *C*, November 28, 1909. Wilshire was often criticized for the get-rich-quick investments he advertised in his *Wilshire's Magazine*. On this topic in general, see Bell, *Marxian Socialism in the United States*, 86–87. In addition, see Supplement.

28. See SP, *Proceedings*, 1904, pp. 178–83, 191–94, 197–98. The misuses of evidence by Kipnis referred to are only a few of those I discovered while following up source citations routinely. For one of the few that historians have pointed out, see his mention of SP contributions to strike and labor-defense funds in *American Socialist Movement*, p. 418, citing *American Labor Year Book 1916*, p. 122. *Cf.* that source and also Weinstein, *Decline of Socialism in America*, 37–38, and Bassett, "Socialist Party of America, 1912–1919," 53.

29. "The Discussion on Section 6," *C*, July 14, 1912.

30. The heresy involved in the loss of faith can be seen in letter to the editor, *C*, November 30, 1909, from Richard Kitchelt, the SP's candidate for mayor of Rochester, New York, in 1908; the editor entitled it "A Counsel of Despair." One of the few expressions of contempt for John Q. Worker by SLP members is J. H. Lewis, "Pennsylvania," *P*, December 22, 1895. Its tone is contradicted in "Socialist Trades and Labor Alliance. To the Wage Workers of the United States and Canada," *P*, December 29, 1905. Generally, members of the SLP deplored John Q. Worker's having been misled, implicitly assuming that he passively followed whatever leaders imposed themselves on him.

31. For references to such instincts, in addition to documents already quoted, see Supplement.

32. Robert Tucker, *Philosophy and Myth in Karl Marx* (Cambridge: Cambridge University Press, 1961), 228–30. For illuminating comments on the energizing function of the myth, see David F. Bowers, "American Socialism and the Socialist Philosophy of History," in Donald Drew Egbert and Stow Persons (eds.), *Socialism and American Life* (2 vols.; Princeton: Princeton University Press, 1952), I, 415–16.

33. Austin Lewis, *Proletarian and Petit-Bourgeois* (Chicago: I.W.W. Publishing Bureau, n.d.), 21–22.

34. "Tragic Pages. The Check-Off System," *P*, July 14, 1900.

35. For other expressions of contempt for the unawakened workers, some as extreme as those excerpted from the *IW* and all of them based on the assumption that his non-radicalism cannot be rational but must manifest either passivity, traitorousness, stupidity, or cowardice, see Supplement.

36. John Hallam Vonmor, "The Workingman to the Socialists" and "The Full Dinner Pail," *ISR*, VIII (1907), 107–108. Such poems were frequently used as space-fillers in radical newspapers and on occasion were in letters-to-the-editor columns. Another such poem is in John I. Kolehmainen, "The Inimitable Marxists: The Finnish Immigrant Socialists," *Michigan History*, XXXVI (1952), 397. Kolehmainen comments: "Pity, tinged with scorn, was manifested [by the Finnish immigrant socialists] toward those who in their stupidity had not learned of the new salvation." Kolehmainen is the only historian, so far as I know, who calls attention to this aspect of radical thinking in this period.

37. Forrest R. Edwards, "Sound Logic Is What Counts," *IW*, February 2, 1911. See also J. S. Biscay, "Boring or Building," *IW*, November 16, 1911.

38. See Phin[eas] Eastman, "Away with the Ranters," *Sol*, May 2, 1914; E. L. Dewar, letter to the editor, *Sol*, December 26, 1914; and "A Knock or Boost?" *IW*, July 15, 1916.

39. "No Moderation," *IW*, May 1, 1912. Both the *IW* and *Sol* were intended to be read by nonmembers as well as members. Many articles were addressed directly to the new, unconverted reader or potential convert, and, in the *IW's* issue of April 25, 1912, an editorial ("The Worker Press") explained that both papers had been trying to transmit information to members and also to be propaganda organs to reach nonmembers. It added that from then on the *IW* would concentrate on the latter function. There is, of course, no way

of knowing how many letters came in from the field complaining of the rhetoric that antagonized potential recruits, but indirect evidence suggests there were many and that such
attitudes were common among agitators in the field too. Elizabeth Gurley Flynn, in "As to
Leaders," *IW*, September 30, 1909, explained that editors of IWW papers wrote what the
rank and file wanted or were fired.

40. "Respect Will Inspire Self-Respect," *Worker*, May 25, 1907; Jos. Wanhope, "What
Are You Going to Do with Your Vote?" *Worker*, October 26, 1907. See also Charles Kerr,
"Publishers' Department," *ISR*, IX (1909), 559, lauding John Q. Worker's "instincts." The
one thing the radicals could not rely on John Q. Worker's instincts for was the judgment of
the correctness of radical doctrine.

41. Eugene V. Debs, *Industrial Unionism: An Address Delivered at Grand Central Palace,
New York, Sunday, December 10, 1905* (Chicago: Charles H. Kerr & Co., n.d.), 3. See also *The
Worker and the Machine* (Boston: n.p., n.d.), an SP leaflet, a copy of which is in the Boston
Public Library.

42. "Alliance No. 11," *SA*, II (February, 1898), 2.

43. Daniel De Leon, "What Means This Strike?" in De Leon, *Socialist Landmarks*, 110.
See also Document No. 5, p. 130 herein, where the cringing slave is despised by the boss
and by the radical in the same clause.

44. "Perseverance," *IW*, May 6, 1909.

45. *IW*, August 19, 1909.

46. *IW*, September 5, 1912. See also Debs's statement in Document No. 12, p. 133
herein, in which the exploiter's contempt is mentioned in the same sentence as his own
judgment that voting for a nonradical party is contemptible—one more example of the
merging of the radicals' and the mythical Capitalist's perceptions.

47. See several of the items in this chapter's Documentary Excursus I (pp. 129–34
herein) which support this inference: Nos. 1, 5, 6, 12, and 15 do so literally. This theme
suggests that the content of American radicalism may have differed slightly from that of
European radicalism, which developed in a milieu in which class subordination did not
conflict with a tradition that equated equality with virility.

48. J. O. Bentall, "Let's Have It Out," *C*, August 10, 1912. This essay is remarkable only
for its explicitness; its content is ubiquitous in radical articles and speeches. For other references to the omniscience, omnipotence, and malevolence of the capitalists, see
Supplement.

49. Eugene V. Debs, "Outlook for Socialism in the United States," *ISR*, I (1900), 135;
Lenin, *What Is To Be Done?*, 41. Both had, of course, been anticipated by a third authority
(see Luke 11:23) some years earlier; the original source did not, however, feel the need for
Debs's adverbs.

50. James Truslow Adams, *The Founding of New England* (Boston: Atlantic-Little,
Brown, 1949), 81–82.

51. Tyler, *Rebels of the Woods*, 26.

52. J. S. Biscay, "A (Bohn) Head," *IW*, July 27, 1911.

53. "The New Utopianism," *C*, February 11, 1912. Haywood's speech is in the issue of
February 11, 1912, and in *ISR*, XII (1912), 461–71. Among the passages that the *Call's* editorialist considered insulting to women was the statement that every boy had the right to
learn a trade and every girl had the right to learn some domestic art. Haywood had also
referred to a candidate for office in Colorado as the best man the state had ever produced
but added that he had been defeated by the newly enfranchised women.

54. George Charney, *A Long Journey* (Chicago: Quadrangle, 1968), 62. See also De
Leon's statement in 1896 that "the revolutionist is virile and self-reliant, in striking contrast
to the mentally sickly, and, therefore, suspicious reformer," in "Reform or Revolution," in
De Leon, *Socialist Landmarks*, 51–52.

55. "W. E. Trautmann's Report. As General Organizer, to the Fifth Convention of the
I.W.W.," *Sol*, October 29, 1910.

56. Quoted from Arturo Giovannitti, "Fighting Steel," *The Masses* (September, 1916), in William O'Neill, "Labor Radicalism and the 'Masses,'" *Labor History*, VII (1966), 206–208. For Giovannitti's pessimism, see, *e.g.*, "The Republic," *ISR*, XIII (1912), 21, and "The Bum," *Sol*, January 11, 1913. Giovannitti is included here, although he was an anarcho-syndicalist and not a Wobbly, because he was associated with Joseph Ettor and other Wobbly agitators in the Lawrence strike and elsewhere.

57. See [Charles Kerr], "A Change of Front in the Class War," *ISR*, XIII (1913), 626, predicting that representatives of capitalist interests will soon enact the socialists' immediate demands; William English Walling, "Capitalistic 'Socialism,'" *ISR*, XII (1911), 303–308, where omniscient capitalists are inaugurating reforms voluntarily, not forced by working-class militancy; and Robert Rives La Monte, "You and Your Vote," *ISR*, XIII (1912), 117–18: "The workers have no monopoly of the elementary social virtues. The upper class, cream or scum, knows more about the lower strata of society today than it ever did before. . . . And this increased knowledge begets increased sympathy." See also Charles Kerr, "Editorial," *ISR*, XIV (1913), 112–13. Kerr shows rare insight, in "Our Unconscious Allies," *ISR*, XII (1911), 111, when he recalls, "Some of us were Populists twenty years ago, and we had a curious superstition. We thought the Plutocrats were a compact, disciplined body of men with a baleful and relentless purpose to crush out the liberties of the American people," but he knows now that "it is not in the least true that the capitalist class as a whole is animated by an aggressive spirit of conquest, impelling it to crush out the working class." Its sole aim is greater profits. It should be noted that these attempts to explain Progressive legislation were made by SP left-wingers. Right-wingers had less explaining to do, and the SLP by now was too isolated to notice that there was anything to explain. Others on the SP left (like Debs) and Wobblies coped with the problem by exaggerating their own impact on American society.

58. Untitled editorial, *P*, November 10, 1900.

59. Max J. Hayes, "World of Labor," *ISR*, III (1903), 563–64.

60. See Bell, *Marxian Socialism in the United States*, 83. The brevity of Debs's working life is occasionally noted elsewhere but without examination of its implications. H. Wayne Morgan mentions it in "The Utopia of Eugene V. Debs," *American Quarterly*, XI (1959), 128, along with mention of Debs's gentlemanly taste in clothing, etc., and an assertion that he was an astute politician who understood the people. I suggest that the latter statement would be difficult to make (aside from the direct evidence against it) if what Morgan calls Debs's "utopian" vision of the future were understood as including a mythical perception of the present.

61. A similar point is made in H. Wayne Morgan, *Eugene V. Debs, Socialist for President* (Syracuse: Syracuse University Press, 1962), 24.

62. See *ibid.*, 82.

63. Morgan mentions Debs's inclination to believe what he wanted to believe, in *Debs*, 18. When Kipnis, *American Socialist Movement*, 347, *n.* 66, declares that popular magazines saw a "seemingly irresistible advance of socialism in the United States," he does not mention these unofficial ideologues of capitalism. Rather, he cites four articles: "Advance of Socialism in the United States," *Chautauquan*, LXIV (1911), 18–19; "The Tide of Socialism," *World's Work*, XXIII (1912), 252–53; "The Warning of Socialism," *Century Magazine*, LXXXIII (1912), 472–73; and Harry Farrand Grifflin [his correct name was Henry Farrand Griffin], "The Rising Tide of Socialism," *Outlook*, February 24, 1912, pp. 438–48. In fact, not one of these articles supports his text. References to Hanna especially, and also to J. P. Morgan and other authoritative spokesmen for capitalists, were very common in the radicals' writings. Surely if popular magazines had provided real support for Kipnis' statement he would have cited them. The most remarkable thing about these and similar articles is their calm, rational discussion of the pros and cons of socialist proposals and of the real grievances that made them (but not socialism) worthy of consideration.

64. But according to Ray Ginger, Debs sometimes used his platform style even in pri-

vate conversation, ignoring the individuality of the person he was talking to. See Ginger, *Eugene V. Debs: A Biography* (New York: Collier Books, 1962), 336. The gift of the overcoat is recounted on pp. 336–37, where Ginger shows that Debs gave it not to a particular shivering man but to a representative of the Oppressed Proletariat.

65. *Ibid.*, 425.

66. Morgan, *Debs*, 190.

Chapter VI

1. Needless to say, public-sphere phenomena affected the private sphere and vice versa; these exclusive-sounding terms are used for convenience. Public- and private-sphere questions are not equivalent to defining and nondefining issues, respectively. The tariff, for example, was a public-sphere issue but nondefining. The reforms that socialist administrations enacted in some towns were not defining issues. If they had been, those candidates would not have won. The following discussions will not recount the histories of the Negro and woman questions in the radical movements. For an excellent account of one, see R. Laurence Moore, "Flawed Fraternity—American Socialist Response to the Negro, 1901–1912," *Historian*, XXXII (1969), 1–18. Some of the essential facts concerning the other may be found in Mari Jo Buhle, "Women & the Socialist Party," *Radical America*, VI (February, 1970), 36–55. See also Sterling D. Spero and Abram L. Harris, *The Black Worker* (New York: Atheneum, 1968), Chap. XV.

2. In *The Ideas of the Woman Suffrage Movement, 1890–1920* (New York: Columbia University Press, 1965), I committed that error, accepting at face value certain nonsocialist suffragists' declarations that their reform was, in their own word, "bourgeois." Their motive, however, was to disassociate themselves from the more militant suffragists and from the free-love doctrines of some of those whom John P. Diggins calls "the Lyrical Left." See Diggins, *The American Left in the Twentieth Century* (New York: Harcourt Brace Jovanovich, 1973).

3. When Kelley, Ovington, and other socialists devoted most of their efforts to those other causes, they did not do so as missionaries from the SP, as Communist Party members later would go into "mass organizations" so as to enlarge their party's influence. These socialists formulated their own "lines" on their special reforms and acted independently of the party.

4. They had testified against Wobbly street speakers arrested in Seattle. The description called them "the petty larceny, cockroach, putty-faced, blind-pig, hole-in-the-wall, peanut political-merchants." It continued, "Three little snipes: A tonsorial whiskerite, a cabbage leaf cigar stand bilk, and a five-cent moving picture theatrical manager, all appeared in the role of a career that disgraced the name of man. When their epitaph is written by the workers, it should tell all that these vultures would do for a mouth full of the putrid carcass of SLAVERY and the forty pieces of silver. Judas had the manhood enough left to hang himself. These three Sheenies are squeezing the eagles on the forty pieces of silver." The court decision was postponed, whereupon: "The three little perjurors looked like sheenies at a sheriff's sale. A flood of bursted gall gave their hawkish faces a saffron hue as they snicker[ed] their way back to their skin game on Washington Street." This article is signed J. C. Conahan; the cartoon with the brogue-speaking Irish cop is signed "Schwartz" (tit for tat?).

5. Max J. Hayes, "The World of Labor," *ISR*, II (1901), 463. See also Max J. Hayes, "The World of Labor," *ISR*, V (1904), 376.

6. "About California," *P*, December 17, 1899. In the factionalism that decimated the SLP in the late 1890s, Jewish sections of the party and Yiddish-language publications played a large part. Yet that cannot have been the sole explanation for the occasional anti-Semitism in the *People*. Some instances seem to have manifested self-hatred. An article entitled "Charity" and signed "A Wandering Jew," in *P*, May 6, 1900, opens by asking why capitalists spend money on charity while begrudging their employees every cent, and con-

tinues: "Think of the capitalist Jews, who murder wage-slaves in sweat shops, contributing money to orphan asylums because they love Jewish little children." Later: "These over-fed Jew capitalists come out once in awhile to inspect the little children that they are fattening so that they can fleece them later." And so on at great length. Nothing in the portrayal of exploitation required the capitalist's Jewishness to be thus spotlighted. It seems to have had a personal meaning to the writer, who also seems to have felt the need to publish the screed along with his self-identification as a Jew who had "wandered" in a way that is quite obvious to the reader. What is equally obvious is that the writer's radicalism is inextricably bound up with his self-hate.

7. Stanislaus Cullen, "Uncle Sam Is Doing Business with the Chink," *P*, July 14, 1900. In "Letter Box," *P*, July 30, 1899, De Leon refers to Mexicans as "Greasers," placing the word within inverted commas.

8. Untitled editorial, *SDH*, November 30, 1901.

9. Moore, "Flawed Fraternity: American Socialist Response to the Negro," 6.

10. See, *e.g.*, many articles in *P* in mid-1899 concerning the SLP split in which the dissidents' German accents and beer-drinking are ridiculed. Some anti-Semitism appears too, including repeated mentions of "Hillquit (Hilkowitz)" and a reference to Henry Slobodin as "Slobodinoffsky." See esp. Jack Dorman, "What Happened Back of That Saloon on the 10th," *P*, July 23, 1899, for anti-Germanism.

11. On the future of ethnicity and the paramount importance of class, see Supplement.

12. Ida M. Raymond, "A Southern Socialist on the Negro Question," *NR*, I (1913), 990–91. Raymond was replying to an article three issues earlier (September) by Mary White Ovington. See the next few issues of *NR* for replies pro and con.

13. Theresa H. Russell, in *NR*, II (1914), 64; Mary White Ovington, in *NR*, II (1914), 178–79; Ida M. Raymond, in *NR*, II (1914), 179–80. Grace Potter, whom we met in Chap. V, noted Raymond's remark that a subordinate position is evidence of inferiority and observed that the working class must therefore be assumed to be inferior to the capitalist class (*NR*, II [1914], 180).

14. See, *e.g.*, SP, *Proceedings*, 1910, pp. 280–81; SP, *Proceedings*, 1901, First Session, 19–22; Hubert H. Harrison, "Socialism and the Negro," *ISR*, XIII (1912), 65–68; and I. M. Robbins, "The Economic Aspects of the Negro Problem," *ISR*, VIII (1908), 481, for the sharpest expressions of the various views. The divisions did not correspond to the races of the convention delegates or writers.

15. "The Birth and Progress of Disfranchisement," *P*, November 3, 1900.

16. "English Working Class," *P*, March 16, 1901.

17. Since the question of what if anything the turn-of-the-century movement should offer blacks was primarily a question of tactics, it is omitted here. Secondary sources cited in this chapter should be consulted for information on tactics—not only on the Negro question but on the immigration and woman questions as well.

18. See Michael E. R. Bassett, "The Socialist Party of America, 1912–1919: Years of Decline" (Ph.D. dissertation, Duke University, 1963), 19–20; David Shannon, *The Socialist Party of America* (1955; Chicago: Quadrangle, 1967), 50–52. Another left-wing socialist racist was Gaylord Wilshire.

19. An even more racist article was William Noyes, "Some Proposed Solutions of the Negro Problem," *ISR*, II (1901), 401–413. Editor Simons made it the lead article but prefaced it (p. 391) with a disclaimer, understandable inasmuch as Noyes omitted not one current stereotype. But *cf.* Simons' statement, shortly after the *ISR* began publishing, that he would print various views and thus strengthen the socialist movement, although he did not intend to compromise with capitalism. He later added that he did not agree with everything the magazine published. See [Algie M. Simons], "Editorial," *ISR*, I (1900), 317–19. The question is, how wide would disagreement become before he would consider an article as compromising with capitalism? A similar exchange took place in 1912. In April

Hubert H. Harrison published "The Black Man's Burden," the first article on the subject in the *ISR* for a long time. A Georgia socialist, W. N. Wertz, protested (see *ISR*, XIII [1912], 886). Charles Kerr, now editor, said Wertz's views were contrary to socialist principles and that Harrison's contributions would continue. The *ISR's* shift in position was doubtless linked to its sympathy for the IWW. In the next issue (July, 1912) it published an article by Wobbly organizer Covington Hall on "Revolt of the Southern Timber Workers" (pp. 51–52), recounting interracial cooperation.

20. See the fascinating debates on the resolutions in SP, *Proceedings*, 1901, First through Third Sessions, 18–19 (starting with the Fourth Session each session's proceedings start with p. 1); Ninth Session, 20–31; Eleventh Session, 3–4. William E. Costley of San Francisco, a black, presented a resolution calling upon American blacks to join with the SP for the emancipation of all workers. Blacks and whites were to be found on both sides in the ensuing debate.

21. Untitled news item, *C*, November 28, 1911; item under "Socialist News of the Day" on "Colored Socialist Club," *C*, December 16, 1911; Hubert H. Harrison, "Work among Colored People," *C*, July 11, 1912. According to Shannon, *Socialist Party of America*, 52, the party did not even know how many black members it had; he connects this fact to its general indifference to the Negro question.

22. See, *e.g.*, SP, *Proceedings*, 1901, First Session, 21–22.

23. See John Kerrigan's article excerpted as Document No. 14 in this chapter's Documentary Excursus (p. 172 herein); passages omitted there recount the Louisiana episode.

24. Some of the items cited in this discussion fit that description. Indirect evidence of the same unconscious image of the SP is the way documents dealing with the entire SP ignore the Negro question. See Supplement.

25. F. W. West, "The Negro and Socialism," *C*, January 28, 1911; Leo Weinstein, in *C*, February 1, 1911. See all the issues of *C* in this period for an outpouring of letters on the issue. More typical than West's and Weinstein's was that from Mary White Ovington, in "There Are Other Southern Socialists," *C*, January 30, 1911, in which she merely thanked the editor for his reply to "Southern Socialist" and said that fortunately many southern comrades did not share his opinions.

26. So did Algie M. Simons, who, in "The Negro Problem," *ISR*, I (1900), 204–211, gave an economic-determinist account of its history and then said, "The 'negro question' has completed its evolution into the 'labor problem.'"

27. Eugene V. Debs, "The Negro and Socialism," *ISR*, IV (1904), 392–93.

28. Spero and Harris, *Black Worker*, 405.

29. Eugene V. Debs, "An Up-To-Date Labor Class Movement," *SDH*, August 23, 1902.

30. See Moore, "Flawed Fraternity: American Socialist Response to the Negro," 9; and Document No. 8 (p. 170 herein).

31. I. M. Robbins, "The Economic Aspects of the Negro Problem," *ISR*, X (1910), 1116.

32. Thomas Potter, "Socialism and the Negro," *C*, January 11, 1911; "Colored Socialist Club" and Hubert H. Harrison, "How To Do It," both in *C*, December 16, 1911.

33. W. E. B. Du Bois, "Separate Organizations," *C*, December 26, 1911. For Du Bois' views on the larger question of the relation of the socialist movement to black workers, see his articles, "A Field for Socialists," *NR*, January 11, 1913, pp. 54–57, and "Socialism and the Negro Problem," *NR*, February 1, 1913, pp. 138–41.

34. "What Socialism Has to Offer the Negro," *C*, July 2, 1908. More evidence that the party could have recruited many more blacks if it had tried to is in Thomas Sweeney, "Socialism and the Negro," *C*, January 6, 1911.

35. "Race Prejudice," *IW*, July 15, 1909; untitled editorial, *IW*, June 3, 1909; IWW, *Proceedings*, 1906, p. 576. The Wobblies' colorblindness should not, however, be exaggerated. See Merl E. Reed, "Lumberjacks and Longshoremen: The I.W.W. in Louisiana," *Labor History*, XIII (1972), 58.

36. Alexander Saxton, *The Indispensable Enemy: Labor and the Anti-Chinese Movement in*

California (Berkeley: University of California Press, 1971), *passim*, esp. 266–67; Fred H. Matthews, "White Community and 'Yellow Peril,'" *Mississippi Valley Historical Review*, L (1964), 615, 616–18, 623.

37. IWW, *Proceedings*, 1907, Report No. 6, pp. 5, 8. Notice the "so-called" in the last sentence. This way of denying the AFL's legitimacy as a union was a Wobbly custom. In the ensuing discussion, a prominent Wobbly from California opposed the resolution, explaining that the anti-Japanese agitation was the work of small fruit-growers; they felt threatened by the ambitious Japanese who saved their wages to start their own orchards. The IWW in California had enough to do, he said, in the face of the prejudices against it, without provoking even more; Wobblies should stick to organizing "the men who are already in California." But the resolutions passed, slightly amended by De Leon: the word "ground" in the first sentence was replaced by "allegation." IWW, *Proceedings*, 1907, Report No. 7, p. 1.

38. Paul Frederick Brissenden, *The I.W.W.: A Study of American Syndicalism* (New York: Columbia University Press, 1919), 209.

39. "Silly Race Prejudice," *IW*, April 15, 1909; "Example of Japanese Workers," *IW*, August 26, 1909. These are but two of many such items throughout this period. See Supplement.

40. Morris Hillquit, "The Stuttgart Resolution on Labor Immigration," *Worker*, November 9, 1907; Shannon, *Socialist Party of America*, 48–49; see Shannon, pp. 49–50, for a good brief summary of the American SP's reactions at its 1908 and 1910 conventions. The following discussion will deal with the issue only in relation to the themes this chapter is concerned with.

41. See Ernest Untermann's remarks in SP, *Proceedings*, 1910, p. 84; those of James A. De Bell of Massachusetts in SP, *Proceedings*, 1910, p. 118; and those of Max Hayes of Ohio in SP, *Proceedings*, 1908, p. 121. Untermann was perhaps the leading orthodox Marxist theorist in the United States at that time.

42. SP, *Proceedings*, 1908, pp. 110–11.

43. SP, *Proceedings*, 1910, p. 90.

44. *Ibid.*, 121.

45. *Ibid.*, 132.

46. SP, *Proceedings*, 1908, p. 107. For information on Miller, see Vernon Jensen, *Heritage of Conflict: Labor Relations in the Nonferrous Metals Industry up to 1930* (Ithaca: Cornell University Press, 1950), 103, 340–43.

47. SP, *Proceedings*, 1910, p. 118. For Untermann's version, see p. 85. Another delegate's version is in SP, *Proceedings*, 1908, p. 117.

48. SP, *Proceedings*, 1908, pp. 106, 109, 110. The same comment can be made of Debs's statement in Document No. 9 (p. 170 herein), that the "real issue" was class and that the race issue was pure fraud. The entire flood of documents he was responding to proved that to many of his comrades the reverse was true. Once again Debs was mistaking his own opinions for the Voice of Truth.

49. SP, *Proceedings*, 1908, pp. 114, 116.

50. SP, *Proceedings*, 1910, p. 127.

51. *Ibid.*, 122–23.

52. The entire debate, at both conventions, is well worth close reading. See SP, *Proceedings*, 1908, pp. 105–122, and 1910, pp. 75–168. An interesting test of the supposed parallel between the opposing positions and the left-right division would be to try to predict, from the positions taken on this issue, what the same delegates' positions would be on the issue of SP policy toward unions and on the woman question. Some of the same delegates participated in one or more of those other discussions; the reader who expects to find the neat parallels that Ira Kipnis finds, in his *The American Socialist Movement, 1897–1912* (New York: Monthly Review Press, 1972), *passim*, has some surprises in store. In addition, see Supplement.

53. Kipnis, *American Socialist Movement*, 277–88, as usual portrays the left as the Good Guys and the right (and "center") as the Bad Guys. His "center" wing seems here, as elsewhere, to be a variable category invented to account for some comrades' taking the "wrong" positions for their wings. Herman Titus' leftism and racism were both too obvious to define away; that is the one "exception" that Kipnis notes. He calls Untermann a member of the center wing although he was definitely on the left; but then, Untermann was a racist. Kipnis does not mention Charles Kerr at all; Kerr, on the far left, advocated exclusion (see next note). In his account of the debates, Kipnis does not name many of the participants, so that their "wing" affiliations on defining issues must be sought elsewhere.

54. Charles Kerr, for one, based his argument on the need to appeal to John Q. Worker. The SP, he said, is the party of the working class, and if the workers want exclusion it is the duty of the SP to back them up with all its strength. Kerr, as a member of the party's left wing and strong proponent of vanguardism, never used that reasoning when the issue happened to involve a policy he believed in on principle. Working-class brotherhood, he added, "will come in the future as a result of the triumph of the working class, but we can not hasten its coming by acting in a way to divide the working class here and now. The capitalists are day by day giving the workers object lessons in the need of a political party of their own; it remains for us Socialists to show that ours is the party that they want." (Charles Kerr, "Editor's Chair," *ISR*, VIII [1908], 703.)

55. SP, *Proceedings*, 1912, p. 212.

56. *Ibid.*, 209.

57. In "Shall This Be All? U.S. Historians Versus William D. Haywood et al," *Labor History*, XII (1971), 442, William Preston criticizes Melvyn Dubofsky, in *We Shall Be All: A History of the IWW* (New York: Quadrangle, 1969), for drawing "a picture of homeless drifters, brutalized and degraded by 'character-debasing' employment patterns, and lacking even the benefits of 'normal sex,'" etc. Preston comments that the portrayal contains "many untestable assumptions and implied relationships (bachelorhood-radicalism, normal sex-conservatism, debased character-radicalism, etc.)," and remarks, "That stable personalities with wives and homes might be outraged by American capitalism and agree with the Wobblies['] analysis fades from realistic consideration." But Dubofsky's book is innocent of Preston's charge that it equates "family disruption and radical potential." Preston's animus is explained by the remark in the preceding paragraph of his article, that "there has been a predisposition not to accept the rebel's honesty and integrity. It has been easier to discredit the radical than deal with his criticisms of an unjust status quo." But the way a historian portrays the western Wobblies is not a *moral* question of honesty or discrediting; it is a *factual* question of reconstructing the situation revealed by the sources. Moreover, Dubofsky merely mentions this theme (on p. 148); he was right in giving it only passing notice in an institutional, not intellectual, history of the IWW. Yet Preston, in a short review, plays it up as though Dubofsky had spotlighted it.

But anyone who reads the *IW* page by page through its entire first year open-mindedly must be struck by the frequency of just this sort of article and its importance to the writers. If we view the western Wobblies as real people enmeshed in real-life situations, rather than as bearers of the torch of revolution, in a relay race called History, then concern with these questions becomes more understandable than the absence of such documents would be. The above quotation from Preston is part of a larger criticism of Dubofsky's adoption of the "culture of poverty" thesis to explain the western Wobblies. I agree with Preston that that thesis is inapplicable, but not for his reason—fear that it would discredit the Wobblies (see Preston, p. 442). A large percentage of the itinerant, articulate Wobblies whom Dubofsky is referring to were voluntary dropouts from respectable eastern families, as Wobbly writers themselves admitted, indeed boasted. The fact that so many, especially some of the educated writers for the *IW*, were dropouts from middle-class society surely helps explain that paper's ambivalence concerning family life, to be explored in the next paragraphs of this chapter. Perhaps also germane is that some of the relevant articles include references to (or are near articles that refer to) capitalists as cruel "fathers." This occurs often enough to notice but not, I believe, often enough to justify an assured psychoanalytic interpretation. Finally, the Wobblies themselves not only admitted that the familyless migrants formed the core of their committed membership but sometimes boasted of that fact. The article "W.F.M. Joins A.F. of L.," *Sol*, July 9, 1910, is only one of several documents that could be cited.

58. "The Social Evil," *IW*, April 8, 1909.

59. Walker C. Smith, "The Floater an Iconoclast," *IW*, June 4, 1910. See also John Pancner, "Men of the Woods," *IW*, December 15, 1910: "The most of us are not married. We are denied the pleasure of tenderly embracing our life comrade of the opposite sex. We cannot reproduce our own species, which is probably a good thing as things are now. We are huddled together in HE camps while thousands of young women in the textile industry of the East live in SHE towns. What happens to the few who do get married? Why, they sink deeper into slavery. They are always in fear of the boss. They dare not talk back. They must do as he says."

60. "Workers and Loafers," *IW*, May 28, 1910.

61. "Do You Like It?" and "The Non-Conformers," *IW*, June 18, 1910.

62. Cartoon, *IW*, January 26, 1911.

63. "Large Families," *IW*, June 1, 1911; "Birth Control," *IW*, April 1, 1916.

64. "Some Things To Consider," *IW*, April 10, 1913.

65. It is true that in some ethnic groups most immigrant workers for a time were single young men, even in the East. But a very large proportion of these returned to the Old Country within a few years. Generally, those who stayed sent for the wives they already had in the Old Country or started new families in the United States. The "birds of passage," as the sojourners were called, were understandably unreceptive to radical propaganda; they were interested in saving as much money as they could quickly.

66. *Sol*, June 25, 1910.

67. *Sol*, May 4, 1912. However, Wobbly theorist Justus Ebert was among the contributors to *Sol* who evidently did not subscribe to the back-to-the-home doctrine. See, *e.g.*, his regular column, signed "J.E.," in *Sol*, July 17, 1915; also, Elizabeth Gurley Flynn, "The I.W.W. Call to Women," *Sol*, July 31, 1915.

68. See, *e.g.*, Elizabeth Gurley Flynn, "Women in Industry Should Organize," *IW*, June 1, 1911. An unsigned article, "Where the Sexes Are Equal," *Sol*, January 8, 1910, was one of many diatribes against the woman suffrage movement for being an upper-class movement that would divide the working class on sex lines.

69. [Daniel De Leon], "Is There a 'Woman Question'?" *P*, January 14, 1900. See also "Letter Box," *P*, January 15, 1899; Olive M. Johnson, *Woman and the Socialist Movement* (New York: New York Labor News Co., 1918), which was written in 1907.

70. *P*, April 5, 1891; May 3, 1891.

71. Untitled article, *P*, June 9, 1895. See also "The Family," *P*, August 7, 1898.

72. *C*, July 6, 1908.

73. This is not to say that the party's official policies and unofficial attitudes did not change. See Mari Jo Buhle, "Women & the Socialist Party," for shifts between 1901 and 1914. The themes being explored here, however, persisted through those changes. See also Paul Buhle, "Intellectuals in the Debsian Socialist Party," *Radical America*, IV (April, 1970), 51, for suggestive hypotheses.

74. See, *e.g.*, "Woman Suffrage and War," *C*, December 17, 1908.

75. Franklin Wentworth, "The Degradation of Woman," *SDH*, March 12, 1904.

76. Joseph E. Cohen, "Socialist Philosophy," *ISR*, IX (1909), 966; Lida Parce, "Woman and the Socialist Philosophy: A Reply to Joseph E. Cohen," *ISR*, X (1909), 125–28. See also Theresa Malkiel, "Where Do We Stand on the Woman Question?" *ISR*, X (1909), 159–62.

77. "To Restore the Family, That Will Be the Effect of Socialism upon the Home Says Victor L. Berger," *SDH*, August 6, 1904. See also Padraig [pseud.], "Socialism, Christianity and Humanity," *Harp*, I (February, 1908), 3. Several socialists' forecasts are summarized and devastatingly criticized in Georgia Kotsch, "The Mother's Future," *ISR*, X (1910), 1097–1101.

78. An exception was Martha Moore Avery, who denounced such doctrine as insulting to women, portraying them as mere puppets of social forces. Furious that socialists' general denunciations of capitalism always included the statement that starvation wages drove women into prostitution, she declared that even those underpaid women had a choice, and most chose to keep their virtue. Such vicious doctrine, moreover, would drive strong-willed and self-respecting women away from the party. See "Working Women Defended," *SDH*, April 11, 1903. Her protest was never answered. Perhaps her insistence on free will had something to do with her decision, shortly thereafter, to rejoin the Catholic Church and become a crusader against socialism.

79. SP, *Proceedings*, 1908, pp. 300–306. Earlier a prominent delegate, Marguerite Prevey of Ohio, had said that the women wanted no special recognition (SP, *Proceedings*, 1908, p. 97). She and Payne were evidently in the minority.

80. Hillquit later called Simons "the only excitable lady that we have had on the floor here." SP, *Proceedings*, 1910, pp. 188, 193. For the entire debate, see pp. 177–211.

81. Hebe [pseud.], "The Suffragists and the Socialist Women," *C*, January 8, 1909. See also Bertha C. Howe, "Where Do You Stand, Brothers?" *C*, December 13, 1909.

82. See p. 179 herein.

83. Herbert M. Merrill, "Socialism and Suffrage," *C*, February 25, 1912.

84. "Woman and the Franchise," *C*, May 5, 1912.

85. Among those who explicitly repudiated that theory was Courtenay Lemon, in "Socialists and the Sex Question," *ISR*, IX (1909), 628–30.

86. In late 1908 and early 1909 articles on woman suffrage appeared more and more frequently in the *Call*, advocating it on most of the same grounds as the nonsocialist suffragist movement did. See Supplement.

87. See SP, *Proceedings*, 1912, pp. 118–19.

88. Malkiel, "Where Do We Stand on the Woman Question?" 161–62.

89. An exceptionally frank expression of this desire is Charlotte Perkins Gilman, "Should Women Use Violence?" *Pictorial Review*, XIV (November, 1912), 11, 78–79. Gilman was a socialist but her main interest was feminism.

90. My discussion of these themes in the next two paragraphs is indebted to Louise L. Stevenson, "The Anti-Suffragist Woman: Her Ideas and Activities in the Massachusetts Campaign of 1915" (graduate seminar paper, Boston University, Spring, 1975). It corrects several distortions in Kraditor, *Ideas of the Woman Suffrage Movement*, Chap. II.

91. Except when a didactic moral was to be drawn, as, *e.g.*, in Scott Nearing, "The Logic of the Indian," *ISR*, XVI (1915), 302–303. *Cf.* J. Howard Moore, "Savage Survivals in Higher Peoples," *ISR*, XVI (1915), 105–109, fourth in a series. Kerr published the book in December and highly recommended it to his magazine's readers. Savages, says Moore, are like modern infants; they cry easily, fear the dark, like pets and toys, have weak wills and reasoning powers, and so on (p. 108). See also George Allan England, "Modern Group Marriage," *C*, August 21, 1910. According to England, Australian aborigines' marriage customs are like our ancestors' and represent a step in the evolution of marriage toward civilized monogamy.

92. Stevenson, "The Anti-Suffragist Woman," 21.

93. See Kraditor, *Ideas of the Woman Suffrage Movement*, 34–35. Although I am not analyzing tactical problems, a few documents relating to them are relevant here, for they have implications for SP theory—esp. with respect to issues that were not clearly related to class. See Supplement.

94. There were no American socialist equivalents, so far as I know, of E. Belfort Bax's polemics against feminism. The English socialist was the author of *Fraud of Feminism*. His article "Socialism and the Feminist Movement," in *NR*, II (1914), 285–86, was a response to Mary White Ovington, "Socialism and the Feminist Movement," *NR*, II (1914), 143–47, which berated many male socialists for indifference to suffragism. Bax's blast at feminism two issues later is interestingly argued and explicitly consistent with the economic emphasis of the socialist movement, showing that feminism must be justified on its own merits. Floyd Dell rebutted Bax in "Socialism and Feminism," *NR*, II (1914), 349–53.

95. See, *e.g.*, William W. Freehling, *Prelude to Civil War: The Nullification Controversy in South Carolina, 1816–1836* (New York: Harper & Row, 1965), 346, *n.* 11.

96. Jesse Lemisch, "The American Revolution Seen from the Bottom Up," in Barton J. Bernstein (ed.), *Towards a New Past: Dissenting Essays in American History* (New York: Pantheon, 1968), 15.

97. Norman H. Clark, *Deliver Us from Evil: An Interpretation of American Prohibition* (New York: W. W. Norton, 1976).

98. Art Shields, "Why We Honor Jack London," *Political Affairs*, XV (April, 1976), 44–57, 43.

99. Perceptive suggestions are offered in Clyde Griffen, "The Progressive Ethos," in Stanley Coben and Lorman Ratner (eds.), *The Development of an American Culture* (Englewood Cliffs, N.J.: Prentice-Hall, 1970), 120–49, esp. 130–32.

100. James M. McPherson, *The Abolitionist Legacy: From Reconstruction to the NAACP* (Princeton: Princeton University Press, 1975), 375, mentions a *New York Times* article in 1908 that denounced the participants in an interracial banquet as socialists seeking "by revolution if necessary, to destroy society, and with it the home and religion." In view of the evidence (see Chap. IV above) that public opinion tolerated peaceful advocacy of socialism, this article is an excellent indicator of where the boundary of toleration lay. It lay at the interface of the public and private spheres. Race mingling was equated with destruction of the home and religion and therefore feared as much as violence was.

Chapter VII

1. See Frederick Cople Jaher, *Doubters and Dissenters: Cataclysmic Thought in America, 1885–1918* (New York: Free Press, 1964).

2. Another was Jack London; see *ibid.*, 199–200.

3. Victor Berger, "Are Socialists Practical?" *SDH*, March 21, 1903; Victor Berger, "A Word to the Rich," *SDH*, August 8, 1903; unsigned (but probably by Berger or at least representative of his views) reply to letter, *SDH*, November 26, 1904. See also Victor Berger, "A Few Plain Pointers for Plain Working People—by a Plain Man," *SDH*, March 17, 1906.

4. [Victor Berger], "Timely Thoughts on the Ballot," *SDH*, May 3, 1902; "While the Worker Sleeps, His Liberties Are Vanishing," *SDH*, May 20, 1905 (the latter article was evidently not by Berger, who was ill, but it did express his views).

5. Victor Berger, "A Big Weapon Left," *SDH*, June 25, 1904. See also Victor Berger, "Will You Vote to Establish a Kleptocracy?" *SDH*, November 3, 1906.

6. Victor Berger, "On the Question of Arming the People," *SDH*, November 30, December 7, and December 14, 1901. This series evoked heated controversy. See also Victor Berger, "Two Great Lessons from the Russian Uprising," *SDH*, January 6, 1906; he broached the subject on later occasions too. For one reply, by a Wobbly, see Justus Ebert, "Industrial Unionism," *Harp*, II (September, 1909), 5. The reader will note the similarity between Berger's portrayal of the cataclysm and that in Ignatius Donnelly's *Caesar's Column*.

7. Victor Berger, "Old Age Pensions for the People," *SDH*, August 9, 1902; "Old Age Pensions Just: Victor L. Berger Shows Why Society Owes Them to the Workers," *SDH*, March 18, 1905; item in "Editorial Etchings," *SDH*, January 20, 1906, refuting claims by

some radicals that the AFL unions could do nothing for the workers (this may have been written by Frederic Heath but expresses Berger's views).

8. Victor Berger, "Moving by the Light of Reason," *SDH*, April 15, 1905.

9. "Not 'Revolutionary' Humbugs. Victor L. Berger Shows Where Marx and His Compeers Stood on Tactics," *SDH*, April 22, 1905.

10. Ernest Untermann, "The Conquest of America. An Armed People Always Regarded with Respect," *SDH*, September 5, 1904.

11. [Daniel De Leon?], "The Birth and Progress of Disfranchisement," *P*, November 3, 1900; "Helpless Labor. Fettered by Misleaders and Sold in Bondage to the Enemy. De Leon's Speech in Detroit," *P*, October 11, 1896. In addition, see Supplement.

12. "As the Foe, So the Methods," *P*, December 10, 1899; "Letter Box," *P*, April 18, 1897. See also "Workingmen of Rhode Island, Strike Hard with the S.L.P. Hammer," signed "R.I. State Committee, S.L.P.," *P*, April 2, 1899; "Make Haste! South Carolina Leads the Way in the Disfranchisement of the Workers. If Not Ballots, Bullets," *P*, November 3, 1895.

13. "Letter Box," *P*, April 16, 1899.

14. "Russian Revolution Impossible! Victor L. Berger Shows That the Economic Basis Is Lacking," and "The Russian Revolt No Surprise! Eugene V. Debs Depicts Conditions in the Realm of the Czar," *SDH*, February 4, 1905.

15. Austin Lewis, "The Coming Unionism," *ISR*, XVIII (1917), 210–12. The "Manifesto of the Socialist Propaganda League of America" (extreme left), however, predicted that terrible things would be done to the workers after the war and that they would suffer worse conditions and spreading hunger. See *ISR*, XVII (1917), 483–85.

16. Charles Kerr, "A Campaign on Class Lines," *ISR*, XIII (1912), 172, and "Editorial," *ISR*, XIV (1913), 112–13; Roscoe Fillmore, "How to Build up the Socialist Movement," *ISR*, XVI (1916), 614–17; M[ary] E. M[arcy], "We Must Fight It Out," *ISR*, XV (1915), 627–28. In addition, see Supplement.

17. See, *e.g.*, SP, *Proceedings*, 1910, pp. 142–43, 198–99, 238, 297; "Illinois Socialists," *P*, October 13, 1900.

18. SP, *Proceedings*, 1901, pp. 38–40.

19. *Ibid.*, 22. On another occasion he implied that "the next generation" might make the revolution; see Morris Hillquit, Samuel Gompers, and Max J. Hayes, *The Double Edge of Labor's Sword* (New York: Arno & The New York Times, 1971), 78 (legislative testimony in 1914).

20. Eugene V. Debs, *Industrial Unionism: An Address Delivered at Grand Central Palace, New York, Sunday, December 10, 1905* (Chicago: Charles H. Kerr & Co., n.d.), 6; letter quoted in Sally M. Miller, *Victor Berger and the Promise of Constructive Socialism, 1910–1920* (Westport, Conn.: Greenwood, 1973), 73; "Hands That Lighted Ludlow Funeral Pyre Held Spade That Dug the Grave of Capitalism," *American Socialist*, July 25, 1914. In a letter to *ISR*, V (1904), 217, he says 1904 "will be an epoch-making year in the annals of the working class awakening and socialist party development." See Melvyn Dubofsky, *We Shall Be All: A History of the IWW* (New York: Quadrangle, 1969), 70, 75, for two more of Debs's prophecies.

21. Joseph E. Cohen, "Socialism and Reform," *C*, November 1, 1909; Frank Bohn, "The Middle Class and Progressivism," *NR*, II (February, 1914), 70–82; Berger, "Moving by the Light of Reason," *SDH*, April 15, 1905, in which Berger says, "It is ridiculous and criminal to talk about the Co-operative Commonwealth in 1908," which the impossibilists did (but *cf.* his warnings elsewhere about the imminence of catastrophe); Marvin Wachman, *History of the Social-Democratic Party of Milwaukee, 1897–1910* (Urbana: University of Illinois Press, 1945), 41. Wachman says that Berger's party believed, in 1901, that the revolution was a long way off. These statements can be reconciled with Berger's cataclysmic visions by means of his theory that the workers could stave off disaster by electing officials on local levels. Unlike the predictions concerning capitalism's life expectancy, many concerning smaller-scale events were correct, perhaps as often as those of nonradicals, who also failed to foresee what no one could have—the spectacular rise in productivity and living stan-

dards and other phenomena of our recent past. (Philip Taft, however, contends that "leaders of organized labor early in our history recognized that the American economy had within itself . . . a capacity for long-run growth" and "that the growing goods and services generated by an expanding economy could enable all workers to demand 'more and more.'" See his "Labor History and the Labor Movement Today," *Labor History*, VII [1966], 71.) I am stressing the wrong predictions only because the radicals themselves regarded their predictions as integral parts of comprehensive belief-systems such that, if several important predictions were wrong, so must be the science they were parts of.

22. "All Hail to the Doctors!" *SDH*, May 21, 1904.

23. Sometimes the writers said that a particular reform would require not the revolution but a very strong SP electing many judges and legislators. Others argued that if it could do that, the revolution was imminent anyhow. For typical documents on all these points, see Supplement. The phrase "'he' towns and 'she' towns" (in an article by Joseph E. Cohen cited in the Supplement) appears from time to time in De Leon's *P* also; see second paragraph in Supplement entry.

24. [Daniel De Leon], "Natural Again," *P*, July 17, 1898; SP, *Proceedings*, 1901, pp. 5–6 (report of platform committee). In addition, see Supplement.

25. Daniel De Leon, "Uncle Sam and Brother Jonathan," *P*, August 14, 1898.

26. [Algie M. Simons], "Conditions in Germany and Austria," *ISR*, VI (1905), 307–308; Ernest Untermann, "Socialism Abroad," *ISR*, II (1901), 221. In addition, see Supplement.

27. This metaphor and variations on it were quite common. See, *e.g.*, "Craft Scabbery," *IW*, April 15, 1909.

28. "Heaping Insult upon Injury," *P*, August 26, 1894.

29. Max Hayes, "World of Labor," *ISR*, VIII (1908), 789–90; Sidney Hook, "The Philosophical Basis of Marxian Socialism in the United States," in Donald Drew Egbert and Stow Persons (eds.), *Socialism in American Life* (2 vols.; Princeton: Princeton University Press, 1952), I, 440–41 (Hook's target is the Communist Party, but his statement applies to the earlier radicals as well).

30. John Graham Brooks, *American Syndicalism: The I.W.W.* (New York: Macmillan, 1913), 95.

31. Martin Diamond, "Socialism and the Decline of the American Socialist Party" (Ph.D. dissertation, University of Chicago, 1956), 5, 13; see also pp. 41, 43. Will Herberg, "American Marxist Political Theory," in Egbert and Persons (eds.), *Socialism in American Life*, I, 510. Several crucial exceptions were discussed in Chap. VI above.

32. On family, child-rearing, and the home under socialism, see Supplement.

33. IWW, *Proceedings*, 1907, Report No. 8, p. 3.

34. "Questions and Answers," *American Socialist*, July 25, 1914; William D. Haywood and Frank Bohn, *Industrial Unionism* (6th ed.; Chicago: Charles H. Kerr & Co., 1911), 55, 56.

35. Francis Marshall Elliott, "The National Strike," *ISR*, VII (1907), 426–28 (note that his last sentence neatly explains away John Q. Worker's indifference to socialism at the time Elliott was writing); Charles Kerr, "Socialist Unity in the United States," *ISR*, VIII (1907), 326; [Algie M. Simons], "Anarchy vs. Socialism," *ISR*, I (1901), 243. In addition, see Supplement.

36. "The Logic of the Situation," *P*, April 22, 1900. A few writers carried logic and inevitablism to the point of denying free will. The *ISR* contained several articles of this sort; see Supplement.

37. Morris Hillquit, "Candidates, Parties and Classes," *C*, October 10, 1908; "The Negro and Socialism," *C*, January 24, 1911.

38. Daniel De Leon, "Reform or Revolution," in Daniel De Leon, *Socialist Landmarks* (New York: New York Labor News Co., 1952), 41, 43, 57. See also Don K. McKee, "Daniel De Leon: A Reappraisal," *Labor History*, I (1960), 270–71.

39. The "order" that the radicals yearned for must be distinguished from the order

that grows organically out of a living culture. The former was an imposed order that a minority desired in response to its alienation from its communities and hence to the felt absence of true order. This need produced not only the highly systematic and comprehensive theories but also, among some Wobblies and SLP members especially, a fondness for diagrams and blueprints. The wheel, devised by Fr. Thomas Hagerty to illustrate the IWW's organizational structure, is the most famous; see Dubofsky, *We Shall Be All*, 84–85. Other examples are the STLA leaflet and De Leon's article in this chapter's Documentary Excursus III, items No. 25 and No. 26 (see p. 233 herein). Among the verbal rather than graphic blueprints in De Leon's description of the postrevolutionary society organized by industry, in "Socialist Reconstruction of Society," in De Leon, *Socialist Landmarks*, 216–17. See also Brooks, *American Syndicalism*, 203–207, for a perceptive discussion of William E. Trautmann's pamphlet *One Big Union: An Outline of a Possible Organization of the Working Class, with CHART* (Chicago: Charles H. Kerr & Company, Co-operative, n.d.), with its minute details of the future society all neatly arranged by industrial categories; Brooks regards it as a caricature of the present social order and observes that it contradicts the IWW's scorn for theory and glorification of action. Another fascinating datum is J[ustus] E[bert], "The Mormon Church Affords a Hint in Organization," *Sol*, July 25, 1914. Ebert disclaims admiration for theocracy but asks whether it is conceivable that a tightly organized, centralized, industrial union with interlocking subgroups—modeled on the Mormon church—could be defeated by a craft union. Many other articles in Wobbly papers discussing the Mormon and Catholic churches show this unwilling admiration for their order, in contrast to the IWW's lack of order. *Cf.* J. L. Talmon, *The Origins of Totalitarian Democracy* (London: Sphere Books Ltd., 1970), 31, a reference to Helvetius' fascination with the Jesuit order, evidently considering it a model for the vanguard he himself hoped for. In addition, it may not be fanciful to relate the theme of order to the radicals' fondness for military metaphors. Doubtless one source of them was the belief that the class struggle was war, with the implication that the stronger side's rules were not binding on the other. But this cannot fully account for the constant use of the verb "to drill" (the working class)—a prime duty of radicals—or for the imagery of battalions of workers and the rage for theoretical consistency and what De Leon called scientific intolerance, all suggesting that it was internal as well as external disorder that they felt threatening them. If Robert Wiebe is right in perceiving the shake-up period as characterized by a "search for order," then the radicals were the most responsive to that need (others succumbed to the threat and embraced anarchy and total rulelessness as a good, including Fr. Hagerty himself some years later).

40. For a similar point, see McKee, "Daniel De Leon," 269–70.

41. Kate Richards O'Hare, "The Land of Graft," *ISR*, VI (1906), 599–600. See also William English Walling, "Is a Socialist Party Desirable?" *C*, March 20, 1910.

42. See also, *e.g.*, Elsie Clews Parsons, "Ethnology in Education," *NR*, II (April, 1914), 229. *Cf.* P. L. Quinlan, "Reasons Why Irishmen Should Be Socialists," *Harp*, I (April, 1908), 4, exceptional in its explicit bucolic imagery and rejection of the mechanization of life. The *Harp* was also the only radical paper that fully appreciated the "primordial attachments."

43. Eugene V. Debs, "Socialism's Steady Progress," *SDH*, March 7, 1903; "A Living Force," *IW*, September 16, 1909.

44. Herman Whittaker, "Weissmannism and Its Relation to Socialism," *ISR*, I (1901), 519–20. For other "scholarly" discourses, see, *e.g.*, May Wood Simons, "Some Ethical Problems," *ISR*, I (1900), 336–46, and the same author's "The Economic Interpretation of History," *ISR*, III (1903), 530–36.

45. Algie M. Simons, "Evolution by Mutation" and "Science and the Workers," *ISR*, VI (1905), 172–75, 176–78. The *ISR* published a large number of articles on evolution; they can be found by random leafing.

46. "Supremacy of Environment," *C*, December 17, 1909.

47. Robert Rives La Monte, "Science and Socialism," *ISR*, I (1900), 166. In addition, see Supplement.

48. Giovanni Sartori, "Politics, Ideology, and Belief Systems," *American Political Science Review*, LXIII (1969), 402. Sartori's other four characteristics are also helpful in interpreting the radical theorists under discussion. See pp. 402–403.

49. "Direct Action," *IW*, April 1, 1909. This assumption explains why the radicals rarely pondered modes of propaganda. John Q. Worker's mind was like a sick body, needing merely the administration of medicine that worked almost automatically. Medicinal metaphors in fact were used from time to time, along with arguments that criminals and demoralized people were not responsible for what they did. "Awake" workers, however, were responsible. See, *e.g.*, F. Scrimshaw, "The Criminal," *P*, June 11, 1893; and A. R., "A Worker's View," *P*, June 3, 1894.

50. Hrolf Wisby, "Socialism in the Arctics," *ISR*, II (1902), 581; editorial note by [Algie M. Simons], 638.

51. *E.g.*, IWW, *Proceedings*, 1906, pp. 569–70. For the orthodox view, see "The Curtain Raiser," *IW*, March 18, 1909.

52. Louis Duchez, "Victory at McKees Rocks," *ISR*, X (1909), 300.

53. "Haywood Severely Criticizes A.F.L. Organization," *C*, December 19, 1910. See also Austin Lewis, *Proletarian and Petit-Bourgeois* (Chicago: I.W.W. Publishing Bureau, n.d.), 16.

54. De Leon, "Reform or Revolution," 57.

55. Untitled editorial on Jewish immigrants, *C*, August 1, 1908; recommendation No. 1 of Women's Committee report, SP, *Proceedings*, 1912, p. 160.

56. "Sources of Power," *Sol*, January 15, 1910; H. W. Bistorius, "A Workingman's Address to Fellow Workingmen," *SDH*, March 22, 1902; Daniel De Leon, *Preamble of the Industrial Workers of the World* (New York: New York Labor News Company, [1905]), 20; Eugene V. Debs, "The Western Labor Movement," *ISR*, III (1902), 264; [Charles Kerr], "The Socialist Party and the Revolution," *ISR*, XII (1911), 244; Daniel De Leon, "A Mission of the Trade Unions," in Daniel De Leon, *Industrial Unionism: Selected Editorials* (New York: New York Labor News Co., 1944), 16–20; Covington Hall, "The Only Hope," *Sol*, December 25, 1909. See also Daniel De Leon, "The Burning Question of Trades Unionism" (1904), in De Leon, *Socialist Landmarks*, 142. Another common expression of essentialism is typified in the statement of an SLP leader that the STLA "is not an experiment; it is the result of a growing conviction among the wage workers that the time has come in the economic as well as in the political movement to make an end of experimenting" (SLP, *Proceedings*, 1896, p. 25). The overgeneralization concerning "the wage workers," on the basis of what a mere handful believed, is plausible only on the assumption that that handful expressed the essence of working-class thought better than the majority did.

57. Morris Hillquit, "The Task before the Socialist Party," *C*, December 12, 1909; William E. Trautmann, "Fake Industrial Union vs. Real Industrial Union," *IW*, April 6, 1911 (at the head of the article Vincent St. John is named as author; the error is corrected in the April 20 issue).

58. Austin Lewis, "Organization of the Unskilled (Concluded)," *NR*, I (December, 1913), 961–62; Austin Lewis, "Syndicalism and Mass Action. I," *NR*, I (June, 1913), 576. See also "Alliance No. 11," *SA*, II (February, 1898), 2, presenting resolutions passed at meeting of STLA, including one that says the workers were uninterested in ownership of colonies—thus using the word "interest" in two ways at once. Debs does the same thing in "Outlook for Socialism in the United States," *ISR*, I (1900), 134. Another socialist, who became a prominent Communist, used the word "view" in the same double way; see Alexander Trachtenberg, "The Future of American Trade Unionism," *C*, August 14, 1910.

59. Joseph E. Cohen, "'When the Sleeper Wakes': The Car Strike and the General Strike in Philadelphia," *ISR*, X (1910), 982; "Not Racial But Class Distinction, Last Analysis of Negro Problem—Debs," *C*, August 27, 1908; Eugene V. Debs in SP, *Proceedings*, 1904, p. 255. In addition, see Supplement.

60. Peter Berger, *Pyramids of Sacrifice: Political Ethics and Social Change* (Garden City,

N.Y.: Doubleday Anchor, 1976), 114–15. His entire chapter, "Consciousness Raising and the Vicissitudes of Policy," is extraordinarily suggestive concerning aspects of radical attitudes toward nonradicals that seem to remain constant over the generations.

61. For examples of these metaphors, see Supplement.

62. Dubofsky, *We Shall Be All*, 169. For a dissenting voice see Elizabeth Gurley Flynn, "As to Leaders," *IW*, September 30, 1909.

63. See Joseph Robert Conlin, *Bread and Roses Too: Studies of the Wobblies* (Westport, Conn.: Greenwood Press, 1969), 26–27, for an interesting comparison of the Wobblies with French syndicalists. He quotes a paper, published by the latter, as referring to "the inert mass" that is goaded into action by the minority (the journal is *La Voix du peuple*; Conlin does not comment on the irony of the title). But he says, "While in practice the IWW leaders often accepted the principle of manipulation involved in this point of view, they were in theory inalterably opposed to it. The IWW espoused a participatory sort of democracy in which, while authority was centralized, all members shared in that authority. Their rhetoric illustrates a romantic's commitment to the inherent wisdom of the masses. It was a point of pride for the Wobblies to reply to the question, 'Who are your leaders?' with the answer 'We are all leaders.'" But the alleged equality of the *members* of the IWW implies nothing about the inherent wisdom of the *masses outside* the IWW. That some Wobbly writers did manifest that romanticism is undeniable (see, *e.g.*, the comments on Duchez in Chap. V of the present work); but that occurred where theory gave way to myth and is not incompatible with a thoroughly elitist attitude toward the unawakened masses. For a useful corrective, see Dubofsky, *We Shall Be All*, 261.

64. Untitled editorial, *IW*, March 26, 1910. This was a variation on the slogan, often used as a space-filler, "Get the goods!" or "We want the goods!" Sometimes a statement to this effect was included in editorials disclaiming idealism or love for the workers.

65. "From Our Friends (?) Deliver Us," *IW*, June 25, 1910.

66. "Leadership," *IW*, September 26, 1912, evidently written in response to protests against the militant-minority principle.

67. "The Strength of the Weak," *IW*, October 31 (misprinted November 31), 1912. In addition, see Supplement.

68. IWW, *Proceedings*, 1906, p. 609.

69. Henry L. Slobodin, "'Ballot or Bullet' Again," *P*, July 4, 1897. See also [Daniel De Leon], "Letter Box," *P*, April 18, 1897; and McKee, "Daniel De Leon," 270.

70. Isidor Ladoff, "Some Thoughts on the Crank in History," *SDH*, June 28, 1902; Morris Hillquit in SP, *Proceedings*, 1910, pp. 66, 64, 61, 62; "What Socialism Has to Offer the Negro," *C*, July 2, 1908.

71. Herberg, "American Marxist Political Theory," 504–505. For other expressions of vanguardism that did not explicitly deal with the militant-minority question, see Supplement.

72. IWW, *Proceedings*, 1905, 47; Max Hayes, "World of Labor," *ISR*, VII (1906), 311–12; "The 'Call' Editor's Nightmare," *Sol*, March 18, 1913.

73. "'Nothing to Lose,'" *Sol*, July 22, 1912. For other polemics against vanguardism, see Supplement.

74. "Trade Unions and the Socialist Party," *ISR*, III (1903), 426–27.

75. "Is the A.F. of L. the Labor Movement?" *IW*, January 16, 1913. Most SP members viewed the AFL differently; their essentialism was expressed in other ways.

76. IWW, *Proceedings*, 1905, pp. 55–57; Eugene V. Debs, "The Crime of Craft Unionism," *ISR*, XI (1911), 465–66. See also remarks of Delegate Richter in IWW, *Proceedings*, 1905, p. 222.

77. The fact that the SP rank and file was to the left of the leadership at the time the Third International was founded is a reminder that we must not assume that the rank and file was closer to the labor movement than was the right-wing leadership at that time. The opposite is closer to the truth. Once again it should be pointed out that the rank-and-file

working-class socialist or other radical was not merely a worker one step ahead of the rest of his class. He was an ideological deviant—with respect to his own class as well as to the capitalist.

78. Diamond, "Socialism and the Decline of the American Socialist Party," 165.

79. "A Negro Leader's Advice," *C*, August 28, 1910, p. 15 (this page is misdated August 25); IWW, *Proceedings*, 1906, p. 305; Eugene V. Debs, "The Western Labor Movement," *ISR*, III (1902), 264–65; Hugo Vogt, report on the STLA, in SLP, *Proceedings*, 1896, pp. 27, 29; George R. Kirkpatrick, "Just a Word with You, My 'Good' Socialist," *Worker*, February 2, 1907. See also IWW, *Proceedings*, 1913, pp. 38–39 (Koettgen's remarks).

80. Jos. Wanhope, "What Are You Going to Do with Your Vote?" *Worker*, October 26, 1907; "Respect Will Inspire Self-Respect," *Worker*, May 25, 1907.

81. Franklin Wentworth, "The Congressional Elections," *ISR*, VII (1906), 195. Wentworth's metaphors also answer a question that may have occurred to the reader: if the workers could vote in socialism any time they wished, as the SLP and SP believed, or inaugurate the Industrial Commonwealth by direct action as soon as they organized, as the IWW believed, why could they not use the same means to effect any other changes they might want, including changes short of revolution? None of the theorists seemed to consider the possibility that a large proportion of the working class might unite nationwide for any other object than the revolution (except for a very short time under misleaders soon to be exposed by the logic of the unity itself).

82. Linda K. Kerber, "The Abolitionist Perception of the Indian," *Journal of American History*, LXII (1975), 289.

Chapter VIII

1. Arthur Bestor, "Patent-Office Models of the Good Society: Some Relationships between Social Reform and Westward Expansion," reprinted from the *American Historical Review*, LVIII (1953) in Arthur Bestor, *Backwoods Utopias: The Sectarian Origins and the Owenite Phase of Communitarian Socialism in America, 1663–1829* (2nd enlarged ed.; Philadelphia: University of Pennsylvania Press, 1970), 231. See also p. 76 of the title work.

This chapter in general is indebted to the writings of several sociologists, esp. Georg Simmel, Lewis Coser, and Robert Nisbet.

2. Daniel De Leon, "The Burning Question of Trades Unionism" (1904), in Daniel De Leon, *Socialist Landmarks: Four Addresses* (New York: New York Labor News Co., 1952), 159.

3. IWW, *Proceedings*, 1906, p. 299; IWW, *Proceedings*, 1907, Report No. 8, p. 3.

4. Vernon Jensen and Melvyn Dubofsky, "The I.W.W.—An Exchange of Views," *Labor History*, XI (1970), 363.

5. See, *e.g.*, debate at the founding convention over whether standing committees should be elected or appointed, in IWW, *Proceedings*, 1905, pp. 42–54.

6. See, *e.g.*, "Decision of the Board of Arbitration on the Controversies in the Jewish Socialist Movement," *P*, April 12, 1896; and "Party News," *P*, April 25, 1897.

7. See almost every issue in the next few years for more of the same sort of intraparty acrimony. The same attitude was displayed toward socialists outside the SLP. In the same period, *The People* published increasingly frequent attacks on Debs. De Leon did not have a monopoly on the epithets or perceptions of secret plots.

8. Henry Kuhn, "To the Members of the Socialist Labor Party and the Friends of [the] Cause," *P*, July 16, 1899; "Three Cheers for the S.L.P.," *P*, July 16, 1899. For an explanation of the term "Kangaroo," see "Letter Box," *P*, July 30, 1899.

9. "The Class Struggle within the Party," *P*, July 16, 1899. "Pure and simple" was an epithet applied to those labor leaders who wanted their unions to work solely for economic benefits and avoid political alliances.

10. For another expression of the belief that a dissident had to have ulterior motives, see "Report of the National Executive Committee," in SLP, *Proceedings*, 1900, p. 11.

11. "Undivided Allegiance," *P*, December 24, 1899. See also statement issued by STLA

District 11, in *SA*, I (November, 1897), 3. I am ignoring changes in De Leon's thinking after about 1905. See David Herreshoff, *The Origins of American Marxism: From the Transcendentalists to De Leon* (New York: Monad Press, 1973), 163–66, for De Leon's growing willingness to accept differences of opinion within the socialist movement.

12. David Shannon, "The Socialist Party before the First World War: An Analysis," *Mississippi Valley Historical Review*, XXXVIII (1951), 288. See also Kent Kreuter and Gretchen Kreuter, *An American Dissenter: The Life of Algie Martin Simons, 1870–1950* (Lexington: University of Kentucky Press, 1969), 105.

13. A case in point is the small farmers of Oklahoma and vicinity, who brought the party far more than their proportional share of both members and votes. But what did their socialism consist of? Simons, the party's chief theorist on the farm question, said socialism would confirm the small farmers' ownership of the land rather than nationalizing it. Remarks by Thomas J. Morgan and Oscar Ameringer at the 1910 convention also suggest that the Oklahoma farmers' socialism was both a variant of Populism and a temporary (albeit authentically radical) consequence of their region's shake-up period. See SP, *Proceedings*, 1910, pp. 212–36. See also SP, *Proceedings*, 1908, pp. 178–84; and SP, *Proceedings*, 1901, seventh session 1–16. A good brief account of what socialism meant to those farmers is James Weinstein, *The Decline of Socialism in America 1912–1925* (New York: Monthly Review Press, 1967), 16–19. Another, from a contemporary left-wing socialist standpoint, is William English Walling, "The Socialist Party and the Farmers," *NR*, January 14, 1913, pp. 12–20. On Morris Hillquit's "reformism," see William English Walling, review of Morris Hillquit and John A. Ryan's *Socialism—Promise or Menace?*, in *American Journal of Sociology*, XX (1915), 534–37. But Richard W. Fox, "The Paradox of 'Progressive' Socialism: The Case of Morris Hillquit, 1901–1914," *American Quarterly*, XXVI (1974), 129 *n*. 4, argues that Hillquit was an orthodox Marxist, not a Bernsteinian.

14. William English Walling, "An American Socialism," *ISR*, V (1905), 577–84; Jack London, "Wanted: A New Law of Development," *ISR*, III (1902), 65–78; remarks of May Wood Simons, in SP, *Proceedings*, 1912, p. 42; alcohol resolution in SP, *Proceedings*, 1908, pp. 90–91; Charlotte Perkins Gilman, quoted in William English Walling, "State Socialism and the Individual," *NR*, I (1913), 515 (the last seven words quoted are in italics; Walling does not indicate whether the italics are his or Gilman's).

15. Arthur Morrow Lewis, book review, *ISR*, VI (1906), 438.

16. "Not Fifty-Seven Varieties," *C*, January 27, 1909.

17. "Municipal Ownership Again," *C*, April 22, 1909.

18. "The Game of Swat Each Other," *C*, September 1, 1912.

19. M. Baranov, "Tolerance or Mush," *C*, January 19, 1913.

20. "Confusion Worse Confounded," *C*, February 2, 1913. Other documents also discussed Haywood's refusal to plead his case.

21. See Martin Diamond, "Socialism and the Decline of the American Socialist Party" (Ph.D. dissertation, University of Chicago, 1956), 93–100, for arguments against the common assumption that the peculiarly nontheoretical bent of the American people is partly responsible for their failure to take to socialism.

22. See Jessie Wallace Hughan (an SP member), *American Socialism of the Present Day* (New York: John Lane Company, 1911), 245. An example with respect to the IWW is its papers' theories concerning wages. In "The Unemployed," *Sol*, May 21, 1910, the solution to unemployment is seen as the shortening of the hours of work to the extent of the labor surplus: since wages were governed by the law of supply and demand, they would rise because fewer would be job-hunting. But on most occasions the same weekly said that wages were governed by the cost of production; hence nonradical unions could win only limited increases within the capitalist system. Thus even basic economic theory varied according to tactical needs. That theory, having to do with the very structure of the System, must hence have had nothing to do with the "theorists'" motives for being anticapitalist.

23. An exception is J. E. C. Donnelly, editor of *The Harp*, organ of the Irish Socialist Federation, and most of his contributors; see esp. "Our Purpose and Function," *Harp*, I

(January, 1908), 6, and "How to Realise the Ideals of Thomas Dawes," *Harp*, II (July, 1909), 1. More typical are, *e.g.*, "These Are Valuable Days. Victor L. Berger Urges Practical Methods in Campaign," *SDH*, October 8, 1904; "Gleanings from Busy Socialistic Fields!" *SDH*, July 9, 1904; Finnish socialist quoted in John I. Kolehmainen, "The Inimitable Marxists: The Finnish Immigrant Socialists," *Michigan History*, XXXVI (1952), 398, 404–405; "Note, Comment, and Answer," *Worker*, February 16, 1907.

Donnelly and his co-workers made no inroads among the large Irish-American working-class community, despite their understanding—virtually unique among radicals then—of how important "primordial sentiments" are to individual identity. (On primordial sentiments, see Clifford Geertz, "The Integrative Revolution: Primordial Sentiments and Civil Politics in the New States," in Clifford Geertz [ed.], *Old Societies and New States: The Quest for Modernity in Asia and Africa* [New York: Free Press, 1963], 108–110.) It should be emphasized that recruitment to a union did not pose the problem of working-class universalism *vs.* ethnic particularism, as recruitment to a radical movement usually did. Paul Buhle hints at the reason when he refers to the left-wing socialists' expectation of the appearance "of a universal proletarian, the worker stripped of all his loyalties save that to his class. . . . No policy, however brilliant and diligently applied, could achieve what was a social and personal transformation." See his "Debsian Socialism and the 'New Immigrant' Worker," in William L. O'Neill (ed.), *Insights and Parallels* (Minneapolis: Burgess Publishing Co., 1973), 276. But if this hope is imputed solely to the left, its real significance is missed. (Moreover, Donnelly was on the left, and the melting-pot hope was expressed by many right-wing socialists.) The fact is, the contradiction was and is implicit in radical ideology.

24. This left-right scheme should not be given much weight, however, for some SP members of the right and center shared the views here associated with the Wobblies and the SP left. Here as on other issues the patterns are discernible only against the background of extreme variety of views. A revelation of the Wobblies' attitude toward democracy for the unawakened worker is described (the interpretation is my own) in Melvyn Dubofsky, *We Shall Be All: A History of the IWW* (New York: Quadrangle, 1969), 122. In 1907 the IWW had achieved enough power in Goldfield, Nevada, to try to act out its beliefs. It did so by demanding that the town's carpenters, members of an AFL union, join the IWW or (in Dubofsky's words) "be denied employment in and around the mines." They were evidently prepared to use the threat of starvation against fellow workers, even though the capitalists' power to do so was their chief grievance against capitalism. They would have argued that the policy was for the carpenters' own good; a carpenter might have replied that the question whether the Wobblies or the carpenters were the best judges of the latter's good should be answered by majority opinion and not by coercion. The difference between the IWW's and John Q. Worker's conceptions of democracy, exemplified in this incident, is that between substantive and procedural democracy; that theme is discussed later in this chapter.

25. "As to Violence," *Sol*, June 8, 1912; "As to Politics," *IW*, May 6, 1909; untitled editorial, *IW*, May 20, 1909; "The Final Aim of the I.W.W.," *IW*, May 20, 1909; untitled editorial, *IW*, July 22, 1909 (see also "We Are Selfish," *IW*, June 11, 1910; "Do You Like It?" *IW*, June 18, 1910; and "The Greatest Number," *IW*, August 12, 1916); "The General Strike" *IW*, February 5, 1910; "One Big Union," *IW*, March 7, 1912.

26. IWW, *Proceedings*, 1907, Report No. 3, pp. 5–6. If this theory is combined with De Leon's System-thinking, it means that all bad aspects of modern society are features of capitalism and all good things are outside the System; they are the achievements of humanity through the ages.

27. "They Throw Up the Sponge—We Grab It Firmly," *P*, December 15, 1895.

28. SLP, *Proceedings*, 1900, pp. 94–97.

29. John Spargo, "Literature and Art," *ISR*, IX (1908), 228–29.

30. For an SP member's views similar to De Leon's, see the remarks of Charles Dobbs in SP, *Proceedings*, 1912, p. 128.

31. "On the Question of Arming the People," *SDH*, November 30, 1901.

32. William Haywood, "Socialism and Law," *C*, November 29, 1911.

33. Henry L. Slobodin, "Concerning Violence," *C*, November 30, 1911; see also Robert Rives La Monte, "Shall We Be Law Abiding?" *C*, December 7, 1911, and other letters to the *Call* during November and December, 1911.

34. Victor Berger, "Suggestions for the Coming National Convention," *SDH*, April 23, 1904.

35. Victor Berger, "Some Thoughts for Labor Day," *SDH*, September 1, 1906.

36. "The Militant Minority," *IW*, October 3, 1912.

37. Quotation from the left-wing *Appeal to Reason*, in *Harp*, I (July, 1908), 3. See also right-winger Robert Hunter's *Violence and the Labor Movement* (New York: Macmillan, 1914), 174-79. Fear of regimentation by a well-meaning state is expressed also in Walling, "State Socialism and the Individual," 579-83.

38. William D. Haywood and Frank Bohn, *Industrial Unionism* (6th ed.; Chicago: Charles H. Kerr & Co., 1911), 50, 49.

39. "State Socialism," *IW*, October 3, 1912.

40. See, *e.g.*, Walter Lippmann, "The I.W.W.—Insurrection or Revolution," *NR*, I (1913), 702-704, 705; I. M. Rubinow, "Ballots vs. Cayenne Pepper," *C*, June 2, 1912.

41. Victor Berger, "There Are Many Socialisms," *SDH*, December 5, 1903. He went further in "Socialism Not Communism," *SDH*, July 15, 1905. For a perceptive discussion of the American socialists' attitudes toward democracy and their visions of the postrevolutionary society, see Will Herberg, "American Marxist Political Theory," in Donald Drew Egbert and Stow Persons (eds.), *Socialism in American Life* (2 vols.; Princeton: Princeton University Press, 1952), I, 511-17; Herberg's discussion covers a longer span of years than mine, and it therefore reveals how strongly the socialists' a priori, "scientific" theories were influenced by the pragmatic developments of and popular reactions to the American political system.

42. This contradiction was expressed in the radicals' opposition to checks and balances and the division of powers. See, *e.g.*, Marvin Wachman, *History of the Social-Democratic Party of Milwaukee, 1897-1910* (Urbana: University of Illinois Press, 1945), 27, for the Wisconsin party's demands for the initiative and referendum, abolition of the governor's veto, and abolition of the state senate. Such demands for simple majority rule abound and in combination point to a unitary electorate. The division of powers and the checks and balances were always seen as limits on popular sovereignty by the capitalists and never as protection of minority rights (including radicals') against potentially or actually oppressive majorities. (It is pertinent to recall here Justus Ebert's admiration for the centralized Mormon Church; see Chap. VII, *n.* 39 above.) This represents a triumph of principle over expediency, for it contrasts with the radicals' customary view of the voters as ignorant of their own interests and as having a propensity to vote as demagogues and misleaders told them to. It also throws light on the radicals' offhand attitude toward the private sphere, for the constitutional limits on majority power over minorities enabled democracy to be the formal framework within which private-sphere values could be acted out in limited milieux.

43. Eugene V. Debs, "An Up-To-Date Labor Class Movement," *SDH*, August 23, 1902.

44. Haywood and Bohn, *Industrial Unionism*, 61-62.

45. SP, *Proceedings*, 1910, pp. 42-43.

46. *Ibid.*, 49-57.

47. *Ibid.*, 56.

48. The disclaimers repeatedly linked the family with religion. They never explained why, but we may conjecture that both were linked with woman's "sphere"; woman was the center of the family and the mainstay of the churches. In that period there was widespread debate and uncertainty over what the proper sphere of woman was, and fear that the entrance of women into the public sphere would erode the walls protecting the private sphere. On a different level, the woman question and religion posed separate problems for the radicals. On blacks and women they theorized a good deal without much reference to

tactics; on religion they debated tactics at great length, without much reference to theory (whether God exists or the universe is material). This difference was due to the fact that their problems with regard to women and blacks arose from the contradiction between their perceptions of those two *permanent* distinctions and their unitary class theory; religion was a matter of *changeable* belief.

Chapter IX

1. An illuminating discussion is Hans H. Toch, "Crisis Situations and Ideological Revaluation," *Public Opinion Quarterly*, XIX (1955), 53–67.

2. Egon Bittner, "Radicalism and the Organization of Radical Movements," *American Sociological Review*, XXVIII (1963), 932; the phrase is italicized in the original. See also pp. 933–34.

3. "The General Strike" *IW*, February 5, 1910. See also William D. Haywood and Frank Bohn, *Industrial Unionism* (6th ed.; Chicago: Charles H. Kerr & Co., 1911), 39: "All the Democratic and Republican officials, from dog-catcher to President, are but the hired agents of the empire of industry."

4. William Kornhauser, *The Politics of Mass Society* (New York: Free Press, 1959), Chap. IV. Applying Kornhauser's definitions, we may say that the SP and SLP were not "mass" movements, although Debs and some other members were "mass men"; and that the IWW was, for its radical core, a "mass movement." Hence I believe it misleading to call the SP of that period "The Debsian Socialist Party." The type who would, with Debs, say "He who is not with us is against us" were only one component of the party. See Lewis Coser, *Greedy Institutions: Patterns of Undivided Commitment* (New York: Free Press, 1974), 104–105. *Cf.* R. R. Palmer, *The Age of the Democratic Revolution: A Political History of Europe and America, 1760–1800* (2 vols.; Princeton: Princeton University Press, 1959, 1964), I, 21, describing a "revolutionary situation." The subjective reactions, which Palmer lists, to the breakdown of legitimate authority, the fading of old loyalties, and so on, did not characterize the United States in the shake-up period, but they did characterize most of the radicals discussed in this book.

5. See Herbert Blumer, "Collective Behavior," in Alfred McClung Lee (ed.), *Principles of Sociology* (New York: Barnes & Noble, 1951), 213–14.

6. See Peter N. Stearns, "The European Labor Movement and the Working Classes, 1890–1914," in Harvey Mitchell and Peter N. Stearns, *Workers and Protest: The European Labor Movement, the Working Classes and the Origins of Social Democracy* (Itasca, Ill.: F. E. Peacock, 1971), 206–207, for related points concerning European workers and socialists. For other analyses of the "community" function of the radical organizations, see, *e.g.*, Wilbert E. Moore, "Sociological Aspects of American Socialist Theory and Practice," in Donald Drew Egbert and Stow Persons (eds.), *Socialism and American Life* (2 vols.; Princeton: Princeton University Press, 1952), I, 549, 553; Coser, *Greedy Institutions, passim,* esp. pp. 8, 126, 128.

7. On the process here summarized, see (among a large literature) Tamotsu Shibutani, "Reference Groups and Social Control," and William Kornhauser, "Social Bases of Political Commitment: A Study of Liberals and Radicals," both in Arnold M. Rose (ed.), *Human Behavior and Social Processes: An Interactionist Approach* (Boston: Houghton Mifflin, 1962); Theodore M. Newcomb, "Persistence and Regression of Changed Attitudes: Long-Range Studies," in Edwin P. Hollander and Raymond G. Hunt (eds.), *Current Perspectives in Social Psychology* (New York: Oxford University Press, 1967); Bittner, "Radicalism and the Organization of Radical Movements," 934–37; Lewis A. Coser, *Continuities in the Study of Social Conflict* (New York: Free Press, 1967); Hans Toch, *The Social Psychology of Social Movements* (Indianapolis: Bobbs-Merrill, 1965).

8. Dorothy Burton Skårdal, *The Divided Heart: Scandinavian Immigrant Experience through Literary Sources* (Lincoln: University of Nebraska Press, 1974), 184–85.

9. Among the Jewish immigrants in New York, socialism helped to orient many individuals to American society, according to Abraham Menes, "The East Side and the Jewish

Labor Movement," in Herbert G. Gutman and Gregory S. Kealey (eds.), *Many Pasts: Readings in American Social History, 1865–The Present* (Englewood Cliffs, N.J.: Prentice-Hall, 1973), 234–36. The same is true of Finns in the upper Midwest.

10. John W. Gardner, "Individuality, Commitment, and Meaning," in Hollander and Hunt (eds.), *Current Perspectives in Social Psychology,* 88–89; italics in original.

11. Kornhauser, *Politics of Mass Society, passim,* but esp. pp. 32–33, 60–62, 93, 192, 220–22.

12. These two functions are another form of the two functions described in Chap. I above: the IWW as a revolutionary organization *and* a union, and the socialist parties as revolutionary organizations *and* political parties; and, as explained there, the success of each *function* meant the failure of the other whereas the success of the *movement* required the success of both functions.

13. SLP, *Proceedings,* 1900, p. 87.

14. John Graham Brooks, *American Syndicalism: The I.W.W.* (New York: Macmillan, 1913), 175–76, 223.

15. "Stray Bullets," *Sol,* February 19, 1910.

16. Robert L. Tyler, *Rebels of the Woods: The I.W.W. in the Pacific Northwest* (Eugene: University of Oregon press, 1967), 27–28, 30–31. This statement excludes the miners who were Wobblies only through their membership in the WFM and the textile workers whose affiliation with the IWW was very brief. Neither group was typical of the members whom Wobbly writers themselves saw as their main constituency.

17. J. A. McDonald, "To My Class Brothers in the Harvest Fields," *Sol,* September 18, 1915. See also, *e.g.,* "Two Construction Workers!—Two Roads!" *IW,* February 17, 1917; "Why Dreams Become Nightmares" and "Hypnotized," both in *IW,* October 21, 1916. *Cf.* Andrew M. Greeley, *That Most Distressful Nation: The Taming of the American Irish* (Chicago: Quadrangle, 1972), 237: "for the lower middle class and working class, home, family, neighborhood, and community are indispensable extensions of the personality; a threat to them is a threat to the personality itself."

18. Charles S. Rathbun, "Socialist City Organization," *C,* November 30, 1910.

19. See, *e.g.,* W. L. Lloyd (evidently a rank-and-filer), "Our New Members," *C,* January 27, 1911. See also the article discussed in Chap. VI above, I. M. Robbins, "The Economic Aspects of the Negro Problem," *ISR,* X (1910), 1106–1117, esp. p. 1116, wherein Robbins maintains that the clubs' social functions discouraged blacks from joining. The more the party functioned as a surrogate community, the more resistance there probably was to equality of black members, and the less appeal the party would have had to blacks who would be left out of the social life. For discussions by prominent SP members of the social side of party life and its relation to recruitment, see, *e.g.,* Frank Bohn, "The Local Headquarters as a Social Center," *ISR,* XIV (1914), 420–22; remarks of May Wood Simons, in SP, *Proceedings,* 1910, p. 181.

20. See Dorwin Cartwright, "Achieving Change in People: Some Applications of Group Dynamics Theory," in Hollander and Hunt (eds.), *Current Perspectives in Social Psychology,* 520–29. *Cf.* Ernest Untermann, "Stand Up and Be Counted," *C,* September 18, 1908: "Who is your neighbor that he should have such influence over your soul?" Insights into the relationships between the deviant group and the environing society can be found in works cited in the Supplement.

21. Frank Bohn, "At Work in the Party," *ISR,* XIV (1913), 298. He inadvertently conceded how limited that family spirit was when he added that comrades should not interfere with one another's private affairs. Labor unions, he said, must keep political and religious differences in the background if they are to hold their members, and a member of the SP too should have the right to belong to any union and/or church and keep his private affairs private.

22. SLP, *Proceedings,* 1900, pp. 218–19. De Leon opposed the resolution. See also Malcolm Sylvers, "Sicilian Socialists in Houston, Texas, 1896–98," *Labor History,* XI (1970), 80, on expulsion of members for consorting with Populists.

23. Joseph Ettor, "I.W.W. versus A.F. of L.," *NR*, II (1914), 283 (*industrialist* meant *industrial unionist*).

24. Remarks of Mila T. Maynard in SP, *Proceedings*, 1910, p. 196.

25. Some members of the SLP and SP recognized this. See the debate in the SP convention in 1908 over whether to unite with the SLP. The full range of attitudes toward the SLP is displayed, from friendliness to hatred. One delegate acknowledged that doctrinal differences were minor. (SP, *Proceedings*, 1908, pp. 123–35.) Since each side believed unity was the natural condition of the working class, each therefore accused all others of dividing it. *E.g.*, see Julius Gerber, letter to the editor, *C*, December 26, 1910, which argues that the SLP survived only because the capitalists maintained it to injure the SP. And the IWW's tenets were too close to those of the AFL's industrial unionists for comfort; several socialists pointed this out (*e.g.*, Gerber's letter). The urge to distinguish themselves from those nonradicals closest to them had to take the form, ironically, of the rejection of certain symbols of community that Wobblies might otherwise have valued—in Brissenden's summary, "all rituals, signs, grips and passwords," all of which the decentralizers in the IWW wanted to abolish. (Paul Frederick Brissenden, *The I.W.W.: A Study of American Syndicalism* [New York: Columbia University Press, 1919], 167–68.) For the same reason—that such things were used by nonradical unionists—the Wobblies also adopted the term "fellow worker" after a long debate during which "comrade," "brother," and "gentleman" were rejected because other organizations used them. See IWW, *Proceedings*, 1906, pp. 418–20.

26. Untitled editorial, *SA*, I (August, 1896), 1; "The World's Labor Congress," *SA*, I (September, 1896), 1.

27. "The Logic of the Situation," *P*, April 22, 1900. The factionalism of the late 1890s produced many other examples of horrible epithets. See Supplement. Glen Seretan, in "The Personal Style and Political Methods of Daniel De Leon: A Reconsideration," *Labor History*, XIV (1973), 181–86, correctly notes that such rhetoric was common in the labor and radical movements. I do not, however, believe he succeeds in portraying De Leon as a rather mild controversialist. He is certainly right to emphasize De Leon's conciliatory behavior in debate on tactical questions relating to the IWW (pp. 194–99). One evidence of De Leon's lack of dictatorial power within his party is in the 1896 convention. He came in eleventh out of twelve candidates for membership on the Press Committee; the first five were elected (the fifth received 42 votes, De Leon 4). Earlier he had come in third in the election of the Committee on Constitution and Resolutions; here too the first five were elected. On other occasions delegates felt free to argue against positions he took. The proceedings show clearly that it was the party, not De Leon, that focused their feelings; the delegates wallowed in parliamentary procedure and details of the most trivial sort, and apparently needed minutely specified rules to rein in their belligerence. See SLP, *Proceedings*, 1896, pp. 7, 23–25, and *passim*. Charles M. White, "The Socialist Labor Party in America, 1890–1903" (Ph.D. dissertation, University of Southern California, 1959), *passim*, quotes many common epithets used in the SLP (*e.g.*, pp. 189, 192, 227–28). White contends that De Leon was motivated more by lust for power than by principle; I do not think he proves this.

28. The second favorite target of the Wobblies' epithets were small businessmen who exploited itinerant workers. In addition, they often referred to organized skilled workers as "reactionaries" by definition. An example of Wobbly vituperation is in "Daybreak in Lawrence," *IW*, March 14, 1912.

29. De Leon did not control the *SA*, which ran many articles expressing views contrary to his; see, *e.g.*, the interpretation of American history in "Chicago Public Schools," *SA*, I (February, 1897), 1–2. In addition, one thing that makes De Leon's writings so humanly appealing despite the dogmatism is that he occasionally spoke to and about real people, not historical abstractions. The *SA* always spoke to and about historical abstractions on principle. "Reference to individuals," it instructed the reader in the issue of October, 1896, p. 6, "is valuable only as their characters typify good and evil." The editor held consistently to this principle, which was of course perfectly compatible with the use of

epithets directed against the plotters and personifications of evil. See, *e.g.*, that article and also "Alliance No. 11," *SA*, II (February, 1898), 2.

30. Charles Dobbs, "A Question for the Agitator," *ISR*, III (1902), 462.

31. "Letter Box," *P*, August 14, 1898.

32. "No Idolatry," *P*, December 17, 1899. Defense of dogmatism as the guarantee of victory is combined with extreme vituperation against dissidents also in Henry Kuhn, *To the Members of Section Baltimore* (New York: n.p., 1896), a pamphlet. See also Georg Simmel, *Conflict and the Web of Group-Affiliations* (New York: Free Press, 1964), 38–43.

33. Daniel De Leon, "The Debs Movement," *P*, November 24, 1900.

34. Brissenden, *I.W.W.*, 146–48; see also pp. 238–40.

35. IWW, *Proceedings*, 1906, p. 610. For an account of Sherman's presidency, see Melvyn Dubofsky, *We Shall Be All: A History of the IWW* (New York: Quadrangle, 1969), 110–21. Note the apparent contradiction between the radicals' statements that their Truth was so obvious that a child could see it, and their perception of capitalists' secret plots against the people, their buying agents in the labor movement to hoodwink the workers, etc. If the truth were that obvious, what would be the point of the plots? And if the secret intrigues were so effective, as the propaganda insisted they were, how could the truth be so obvious?

36. IWW, *Proceedings*, 1907, Report No. 7, p. 7. The group-integrating role of the perception of ubiquitous threats is discussed in Coser, *Functions of Social Conflict*, 110.

37. "The Master Class Is Trembling with Fear," *IW*, June 1, 1911.

38. That the SLP attracted the sort of people who needed detailed rules as well as an authoritative Theory to restrain them from attacking each other as they did their political enemies is indirectly shown in the report of the National Board of Appeals, SLP, *Proceedings*, 1900, pp. 71–74.

39. "Varied Opinions on Varied Subjects," letter to the editor from Matthew F. Zych, *C*, July 16, 1912. More typical was the sort of calm rationality shown, *e.g.*, in "Socialism and Reform," *C*, October 12, 1908; remarks of Oscar Ameringer in SP, *Proceedings*, 1912, pp. 32–33. *Cf.* Courtenay Lemon, "Haywood, the McNamaras' Violence, and a Few Other Things," *C*, December 31, 1911, which complains that the paper expressed too little hatred for the capitalists and ridicules the socialists who wept over the coffins of the workers killed in the Los Angeles *Times* bombing—the workers who were "editorial harlots and scabs who happened to be wiped out" along with the plant.

40. Hadley Cantril, *The Psychology of Social Movements* (New York: John Wiley & Sons, 1963), 27–29. In addition, see Supplement.

41. These are, of course, not the only possible responses to disillusionment. Between these two types are those who accept the refuting data to one degree or another, break with the movement, and suffer lifelong anguish because they cannot relinquish their commitment entirely. (Those who restructure their egos and relinquish that commitment are outside this spectrum of reactions entirely.)

42. SP, *Proceedings*, 1901, fifth session, 40.

43. "Stray Bullets," *Sol*, February 19, 1910.

44. H. Wayne Morgan, *Eugene V. Debs: Socialist for President* (Syracuse: Syracuse University Press, 1962), 85.

45. "Eugene V. Debs on the Political Situation: His Opening Campaign Address at Milwaukee, Wis.," *C*, August 18, 1912.

46. This passage reveals a secondary aspect of ego-involvement—the focusing of intense feelings on the movement's theory. As several historians have noted, Wobbly writers and orators differed from most of their socialist counterparts in their much greater rage. Their movement enabled them to focus it on a hated object and justify it by means of their salvific mission. Emotion disguised as theory can be discerned in documents such as this editorial in *IW*, November 18, 1916 (in part): "Uneducated, the worker may emotionally believe in the necessity for the I.W.W. Uneducated, he cannot be a cool, determined, clear-

thinking clear-acting, fighting machine, seeing there is nothing for him but to fight coldly and calmly till the parasites of society are forced to go to work." The contrast between this Wobbly self-image as a cool thinking-and-fighting machine and the reality is too great to be explained in other than psychological terms.

47. Vulcan [pseud.], "Is Our Party Propaganda Effective?" *Worker*, June 8, 1907.

Chapter X

1. The chief critic of this approach is Herbert G. Gutman; see esp. his *Work, Culture, and Society in Industrializing America* (New York: Alfred A. Knopf, 1976), 9–11.

2. The four institutions mentioned are the recurrent concerns of Robert A. Nisbet's writings, to which I am indebted for insights into the importance of these social forms and their relation to the state on the one side and the individual on the other. See, *e.g.*, his *Tradition and Revolt* (New York: Vintage, 1970), 39–40.

3. See esp. Oscar Handlin, *The Uprooted* (Boston: Little, Brown, 1951); also, Donald B. Cole, *Immigrant City: Lawrence, Massachusetts, 1845–1921* (Chapel Hill: University of North Carolina Press, 1963), which admits that "the immigrants' yearning for security is deduced from their general situation," the sources themselves being "inconclusive."

4. See critique by Richard L. McCormick in "Ethno-Cultural Interpretations of Nineteenth-Century American Voting Behavior," *Political Science Quarterly*, LXXXIX (1974), 351–77.

5. Helpful to the nonspecialist who must rely on secondary literature are a number of works in addition to those cited in other notes in this chapter; see Supplement.

6. Francesco Cerase, "Nostalgia or Disenchantment: Considerations on Return Migration," in Silvano M. Tomasi and Madeline H. Engel (eds.), *The Italian Experience in the United States* (Staten Island: Center for Migration Studies, 1970), 232, *n.* 22. A similar point is made by A. William Hoglund, *Finnish Immigrants in America, 1880–1920* (Madison: University of Wisconsin Press, 1960), 53.

7. W. I. Thomas and Florian Znaniecki, *The Polish Peasant in Europe and America*, Vol. V: *Organization and Disorganization in America* (Boston: Richard G. Badger, 1920), section entitled "Disorganization"; Morris Hillquit, *Loose Leaves from a Busy Life* (New York: Macmillan, 1934), 24–25; William Hard and Ernest Poole, "The Stock Yards Strike" *Outlook*, May 13, 1904, reprinted in John Laslett (ed.), *The Workingman in American Life* (Boston: Houghton Mifflin, 1968), 60 (section entitled "As Sure as a Machine").

8. The variety of personal resources and hence of responses is emphasized in Dorothy Burton Skårdal, *The Divided Heart: Scandinavian Immigrant Experience through Literary Sources* (Lincoln: University of Nebraska Press, 1974), 327.

9. Cole, *Immigrant City*; this is the principal theme of the book. The portrait of the lone, bewildered immigrant is belied by facts such as the immigration official's observation that (in Fenton's words) "the typical Italian who arrived in New York was met by about five people"; Fenton adds that those without friends were helped by compatriots who had arrived earlier and established businesses and could provide essential services (Edwin Fenton, *Immigrants and Unions, A Case Study: Italians and American Labor, 1870–1920* [New York: Arno Press, 1975], 54 *n.* 82, 55–58).

10. See, *e.g.*, Michael Parenti, "Ethnic Politics and the Persistence of Ethnic Participation," in Edward C. Dreyer and Walter A. Rosenbaum (eds.), *Political Opinion and Behavior* (2nd ed.; Belmont, Cal.: Wadsworth, 1970), 208.

11. Humbert S. Nelli, "Italians in Urban America," in Tomasi and Engel (eds.), *Italian Experience in the United States*, 78. Mary Bosworth Treudley, "Formal Organization and the Americanization Process, with Special Reference to the Greeks of Boston," *American Sociological Review*, XIV (1949), 44–48, is especially perceptive on this question.

12. G. A. Dobbert, "German-Americans between New and Old Fatherland, 1870–1914," *American Quarterly*, XIX (1967), 673; Rudolph Vecoli, "*Contadini* in Chicago: A Critique of *The Uprooted*," *Journal of American History*, LI (1964), 412–13.

13. See Supplement. See also Victor R. Greene, *The Slavic Community on Strike: Immigrant Labor in Pennsylvania Anthracite* (Notre Dame, Ind.: University of Notre Dame Press, 1968), 97, 108, 137. Greene emphasizes the spontaneity of the Slavs' decisions to strike but does not speculate on why they lashed out so suddenly and, as he says, "viciously," in contrast to other ethnic groups' more deliberate behavior. I believe his own evidence suggests that the difference was due to the fact that these Slavic miners did not constitute a true community with differentiation of functions. They had a less developed institutional structure than most other immigrant communities and produced no continuous indigenous leadership. This may be why they revered the UMW's John Mitchell; that adulation Greene calls "enigmatic and indefinable" (pp. 163, 199–203), but it could be explained by the absence of locally produced leaders. The extraordinary solidarity of these miners during their strikes and marches seems to have been due more to blind rage finding an outlet and brooking no resistance, than to rational planning. (See also Greene, pp. 148–49 and *passim.*) Greene claims that his findings "weaken the generalization of the Slav in America as thoroughly conservative and tradition oriented. In a strike, change was his goal, and his methods were radical; at these times the 'simple peasant' forgot the status-quo nature of his past" (pp. 213–14). Greene seems to be equating "radical" methods with fury and violence; but there was nothing radical about the miners' objectives. This behavior can be found in peasant history from time immemorial.

14. Irving M. Levine and Judith Herman, "The Life of White Ethnics: Toward More Effective Working-Class Strategies," *Dissent*, XIX (Winter, 1972), 291.

15. Gareth Stedman Jones, "Working-Class Culture and Working-Class Politics in London, 1870–1900: Notes on the Remaking of a Working Class," *Journal of Social History*, VII (1974), 485–87; Jon M. Kingsdale, "The 'Poor Man's Club': Social Functions of the Urban Working-Class Saloon," *American Quarterly*, XXV (1973), 485–86.

16. See Nancy F. Cott, *The Bonds of Womanhood: "Woman's Sphere" in New England, 1780–1835* (New Haven: Yale University Press, 1977), 197–206, and Daniel Scott Smith, "Family Limitation, Sexual Control, and Domestic Feminism in Victorian America," in Mary Hartman and Lois W. Banner (eds.), *Clio's Consciousness Raised: New Perspectives on the History of Women* (New York: Harper, 1974), 119–36, for excellent summaries of the new interpretative trend.

17. Barbara Sicherman, "American History," *Signs*, I (1975), 481; Maxine S. Seller, "Beyond the Stereotype: A New Look at the Immigrant Woman, 1880–1924," *Journal of Ethnic Studies*, III (Spring, 1975), 59–60; Rudolph Vecoli, "European Americans: From Immigrants to Politics," in William H. Cartwright and Richard L. Watson, Jr. (eds.), *The Reinterpretation of American History and Culture* (Washington, D.C.: National Council for Social Studies, 1973), 104.

18. A brilliant exception is Fenton, *Immigrants and Unions, A Case Study*, 46, 469–70, 491–92, 502–508, 576, contrasting Italian and Jewish women workers.

19. Vecoli, "*Contadini* in Chicago," 404–417, is the best-known early challenge to the historiographical emphasis on the disorienting effects of immigration. Among the outstanding contributions to the newer interpretation are essays by Tamara K. Hareven; see, *e.g.*, "Family Time and Historical Time," *Daedalus* (Spring, 1977), 57–70, and "The Laborers of Manchester, New Hampshire, 1912–1922: The Role of Family and Ethnicity in Adjustment to Industrial Life," *Labor History*, XVI (1975), 249–65.

20. John Bodnar, "Materialism and Morality: Slavic-American Immigrants and Education, 1890–1940," *Journal of Ethnic Studies*, III (Winter, 1976), 11, mentions that the Yugoslav Socialist Federation was torn by ethnic conflicts among Serbs, Croats, and Slovenes. If even those who had demonstrated their commitment to socialism by joining the organization could not behave consistently with their own tenet that ethnic animosities were due to capitalist instigation, those animosities must have had other sources. They could also sometimes impair efficiency, wherefore employers often discouraged them; see, *e.g.*, Gerd Korman, *Industrialization, Immigrants, and Americanizers: The View from Milwaukee, 1866–*

1921 (Madison: State Historical Society of Wisconsin, 1967), 65–66. The complexity of the problem, producing ambiguous responses from some employers, is succinctly set forth in Hareven, "Laborers of Manchester," 260–62, and William M. Leiserson, *Adjusting Immigrant and Industry* (New York: Arno & The New York Times, 1969), 92–94.

21. Contrary data and arguments have been available for some time; *e.g.*, Margaret F. Byington, *Homestead: The Households of a Mill Town* (New York: Charities Publication Committee, 1910); Herbert G. Gutman, "Work, Culture, and Society in Industrializing America, 1815–1915," first presented at a conference in 1968 and published in *American Historical Review*, LXXVIII (1973), 531–87; Peter N. Stearns, "The European Labor Movement and the Working Classes, 1890–1914," in Harvey Mitchell and Peter N. Stearns, *Workers and Protest: The European Labor Movement, the Working Classes and the Origins of Social Democracy* (Itasca, Ill.: F. E. Peacock, 1971), 173; Howard P. Chudacoff, "Mobility Studies at a Crossroads," *Reviews in American History*, II (1974), 180–86; Michael Novak, *The Rise of the Unmeltable Ethnics* (New York: Macmillan, 1972), 210. For a summary of the literature, see Thomas Kessner, *The Golden Door: Italian and Jewish Immigrant Mobility in New York City, 1880–1915* (New York: Oxford University Press, 1977), Chap. VII and its endnotes.

22. John E. Bodnar, "Socialization and Adaptation: Immigrant Families in Scranton, 1880–1890," *Pennsylvania History*, XLII (1976), 147–62; Josef J. Barton, *Peasants and Strangers: Italians, Rumanians, and Slovaks in an American City, 1890–1950* (Cambridge: Harvard University Press, 1975), *passim*; Byington, *Homestead*, *passim*; Irving Howe, *World of Our Fathers: The Journey of the East European Jews to America and the Life They Found and Made* (New York: Harcourt Brace Jovanovich, 1976), 154–68 and *passim*. For other traits peculiar to particular ethnic groups see Supplement.

23. Many wanted to earn more money to send to relatives in Europe; the evidence that they sent large amounts conflicts with the contemporary radical depictions of unrelieved misery. *Solidarity* did not notice the contradiction; it reprinted without comment an article from another periodical on "Immigrant Workers in Peabody Tanneries" (*Sol*, December 27, 1913) about the large sums sent. References in secondary works to the immigrants' saving part of their wages either in banks or to send to Europe include Fenton, *Immigrants and Unions, A Case Study*, 94, and Greene, *Slavic Community on Strike*, 43, 48, 187.

24. Bodnar, "Materialism and Morality," 1–19; David Brody, *Steelworkers in America: The Nonunion Era* (New York: Russell & Russell, 1970), 96; Iris Saunders Podea, "Quebec to 'Little Canada': The Coming of the French Canadians to New England in the 19th Century," *New England Quarterly*, XXIII (1950), 365–80; Skårdal, *Divided Heart*, 59–60, 84–88, 105; Vecoli, "*Contadini* in Chicago," 410 *n*. 25; Virginia Yans McLaughlin, "Patterns of Work and Family Organization: Buffalo's Italians," *Journal of Interdisciplinary History*, II (1971), 299–314; Jon Wefald, *A Voice of Protest: Norwegians in American Politics, 1890–1917* (Northfield, Minn.: Norwegian-American Historical Association, 1971), 10–13; Thomas and Znaniecki, *Polish Peasant*, V, 119.

25. Victor R. Greene, "For God and Country: The Origins of Slavic Catholic Self-Consciousness in America," *Church History*, XXXV (1966), 446–60; quotation on p. 460.

26. Howe, *World of Our Fathers*, 114.

27. In fact this "discovery" is very old. Byington, in *Homestead*, depicts the astonishing range of choices among the ethnic and racial groups as to how to spend even the money that went to bare necessities; their very definitions of "necessities" differed (see, *e.g.*, pp. 70, 101).

28. We must distinguish between skilled and un- or semiskilled workers here, for this instrumental attitude toward the job did not exist among craftsmen; means and ends were inseparable where work and the private sphere remained integrated. See, *e.g.*, Paul Faler, "Cultural Aspects of the Industrial Revolution: Lynn, Massachusetts, Shoemakers and Industrial Morality, 1826–1860," *Labor History*, XV (1974), 367–94. On p. 388 he says, "Equating dependency with shame deepened the shoemakers' determination to fight for their

rights." Here and there the primary sources for the present study show this equation and suggest that it was one of the emotional sources of radicalism. The integration of work with other aspects of life did not, of course, die out for all occupational groups; not only have some blue-collar occupations retained it, but many professional groups—*e.g.*, academics—have also. See also Faler's "Working Class Historiography," *Radical America*, III (March–April, 1969), 56–60, for his and E. P. Thompson's hypothesis as to how historiography should relate the public and private spheres. Although their approach repudiates the older custom of ignoring the workers' culture, it is the opposite of the approach I am suggesting. Theirs investigates culture in terms of workers' adjustment and resistance to industrial capitalism. But it ignores the workers' long-range motives and goals by considering their culture only in the capitalist-System context and therefore implicitly equates resistance to unacceptable conditions in the public sphere with resistance (perhaps unconscious) to capitalism. In my hypothesis both resistance and accommodation can be tactics instrumental to independent goals not subsumed under the System rubric. If it be answered that objectively there is no difference in the resulting course of history, one can only reply that "subjective" meanings are the essence of the history of people, as distinguished from capitalism or animals or rocks.

29. For arguments against the assumption that unskilled and semiskilled workers have generally defined themselves mainly in terms of how they earned their living, see Supplement.

30. Not all the immigrants, of course, had been peasants. John T. Cumbler, "Labor, Capital, and Community: The Struggle for Power," *Labor History*, XV (1974), 396, and other recent works correct the older tendency to ignore the many immigrants who came from industrial cities in Europe. My point is not affected by this fact, since it refers to the tradition and legitimacy of class per se in Europe, regardless of changes in the forms it took.

31. On the Finns, see Donald G. Sofchalk, "Organized Labor and the Iron Ore Miners of Northern Minnesota, 1907–1936," *Labor History*, XII (1971), 214–42. On the Jews, see Howe, *World of Our Fathers*, 251 ("almost everyone regarded himelf as something of a socialist"—perhaps meant as hyperbole, although it depends on how *socialist* is defined) and pp. 101–102 (concerning Old World roots of Jewish radicalism). On both groups, see also Supplement.

32. See Gale Stokes, "Cognition and the Function of Nationalism," *Journal of Interdisciplinary History*, IV (1974), 542.

33. There is a large literature on this subject; sufficient for present purposes are Howe, *World of Our Fathers*, 15–17, 61, 101–102, 112, 251, 309–310, 358, 514, 600 (and see the primary and secondary sources cited in his bibliography); Bernard D. Weinryb, "The Adaptation of Jewish Labor Groups to American Life," *Jewish Social Studies*, VIII (1946), 219–44; John Higham, *Send These to Me: Jews and Other Immigrants in Urban America* (New York: Atheneum, 1975), Chap. V. Arthur Goren, "A Portrait of Ethnic Politics: The Socialists and the 1908 and 1910 Congressional Elections on the East Side," *Publications of the American Jewish Historical Society*, L (1961), 236, however, shows how the very similarity of ethnic and socialist universalisms could divide as well as blend them: "Of all the parties in the ghetto, the Socialist party was least responsive to the ethnic interests of the residents of the ghetto. Cosmopolitan in outlook and faithful to its class allegiance, the party was hostile to what it considered to be the conflicting loyalties invoked by 'nationality.'" The crucial variable was religious belief, which is perhaps why the secularized Jewish radicals were sometimes deliberately provocative in their atheism.

34. Moses Rischin, "The Jewish Labor Movement in America: A Social Interpretation," *Labor History*, IV (1963), 235. See also p. 236.

35. See *ibid.*, 234.

36. Howard P. Chudacoff, "The New Immigration History," *Reviews in American History*, IV (1976), 102. See also Irwin Yellowitz, "American Jewish Labor: Historiographical Problems and Prospects," *American Jewish Historical Quarterly*, LXV (1976), 207–209; and

John H. M. Laslett, "Socialism and American Trade Unionism," in John H. M. Laslett and Seymour Martin Lipset (eds.), *Failure of a Dream?: Essays in the History of American Socialism* (Garden City, N.Y.: Doubleday Anchor, 1974), 214.

37. East European Jews formed enclaves in other American cities, but it is the very large East Side and its Brooklyn offshoots that produced a disproportionate number of radicals, successful businessmen, professionals, entertainers, gangsters, and writers.

38. Higham, *Send These to Me*, 158.

39. Nathan Glazer, *The Social Basis of American Communism* (New York: Harcourt Brace & World, 1961), 93.

40. See Howe, *World of Our Fathers*, 309. It should be added that most Jewish immigrants seem to have wanted to rise from the working class. Scholars are still debating why. Among the reasons may have been that, in a period in which the six-day work week was universal, a Jew had to be either self-employed or a schoolteacher if he was to avoid working on Saturday. Unless, that is, he worked for a Jewish clothing contractor, in which case he had both the incentive and the chance to become one himself.

41. Michael A. Gordon, "The Labor Boycott in New York City, 1880–1886," *Labor History*, XVI (1975), 184–229; Moses Rischin, *The Promised City: New York's Jews, 1870–1914* (New York: Harper Torchbooks, 1970), 182; and esp. Herbert G. Gutman, "Work, Culture, and Society," *passim*.

42. "Religion," rather than "the church," is the subject of this generalization. The immigrant workers' attitudes toward their churches were as varied as their ethnic cultures. The differences included the degree to which they accepted the leadership of their clergy in secular affairs and even the degree to which they accepted it in religious affairs. All such variables flourished more in the United States than in Europe, owing to the multiplicity of sects and the separation of church and state. For data on these topics, see, *e.g.*, Vecoli, "*Contadini* in Chicago," 514–17; Skårdal, *Divided Heart*, 95, 130–33, 166–67; Thomas and Znaniecki, *Polish Peasant*, V, 40–44; Andrew M. Greeley, *Why Can't They Be Like Us? America's White Ethnic Groups* (New York: E. P. Dutton, 1975), 82–86.

43. The immigrants freely criticized some values and practices of the host society; see, *e.g.*, Bodnar, "Materialism and Morality," and Wefald, *Voice of Protest*, 11–13. Robert W. Smuts, in *European Impressions of the American Worker* (New York: King's Crown Press, 1953), 22, points out that Pullman, Illinois, attracted so much attention because it was exceptional, "as alien to the well-developed independence of the American worker as it was to the business sense of most employers."

44. Among non-Protestants only, of course. The author's mother recalls that the missionaries "tried to entice the [Jewish] children with free lunches, gifts, various forms of recreation in their beautiful building" in the Williamsburgh section of Brooklyn, in the early years of this century (Henrietta L. Kraditor to author, May, 1976). They had meager luck among children whose parents might have prospered in the Old Country if they had been willing to convert. Some studies of ethnic groups tell of similar proselytizing efforts. For missionary efforts, mostly unsuccessful, among Italo-Americans, see Silvano M. Tomasi, "The Ethnic Church and the Integration of Italian Immigrants in the United States," in Tomasi and Engel (eds.), *Italian Experience in the United States*, 170–71; Nelli, "Italians in Urban America," 94–95; Humbert S. Nelli, "Ethnic Group Assimilation: The Italian Experience," in Kenneth T. Jackson and Stanley K. Schultz (eds.), *Cities in American History* (New York: Alfred A. Knopf, 1972), 204.

45. See Edward G. Hartmann, *The Movement to Americanize the Immigrant* (New York: Columbia University Press, 1948), first few chapters and Chap. X.

46. The settlement-house workers comprised a separate category, for some did not consciously aim to get John Q. Worker to change. Yet they shared with the Americanizers and radicals the ideal of the eventual withering of all strong group bonds in favor of an undifferentiated humanity. Note Jane Addams' views, as summarized in Daniel Levine, *Varieties of Reform Thought* (Madison: State Historical Society of Wisconsin, 1964), 20.

47. For an interesting comment see Lewis A. Coser, *Continuities in the Study of Social Conflict* (New York: Free Press, 1967), 227.

48. Thomas and Znaniecki, *Polish Peasant*, V, 127.

49. Silvano M. Tomasi, "The Ethnic Church and the Integration of Italian Immigrants in the United States," 102.

50. Thomas and Znaniecki, *Polish Peasant*, V, 266–67.

51. I hope I shall not be misunderstood as advocating government cognizance of ethnic, racial, and sex categories; such policy, even for "good" objects, I consider abhorrent. If, in Thomas and Znaniecki's example, the government had intervened to uphold the marriage, the consequences would have been only somewhat less destructive of the community's vitality, and in the long run more so. Public-sphere institutions' recognition only of individuals is consistent with—and in the ethnically heterogeneous United States is necessary to—the viability of true communities.

52. Hoglund, *Finnish Immigrants*, 127–28.

53. See, *e.g.*, Goren, "Portrait of Ethnic Politics," 239.

54. Clifford Geertz, "Ritual and Social Change: A Javanese Example," *American Anthropologist*, LIX (1957), 53.

55. Herbert Blumer, "Society as Symbolic Interaction," in Arnold M. Rose (ed.), *Human Behavior and Social Processes: An Interactionist Approach* (Boston: Houghton Mifflin, 1962), 180.

56. See exchange between Karson and Henry J. Browne, in Laslett and Lipset (eds.), *Failure of a Dream?*, Chap. V. Gerald M. Grob, in *Workers and Utopia: A Study of Ideological Conflict in the American Labor Movement, 1865–1900* (Chicago: Quadrangle, 1969), 166 *n.* 8, criticizes Karson's thesis but errs in a different direction. Grob suggests that the Catholic workers' antisocialism was due to their "essentially middle-class psychology" which "tended to parallel" the Church's position "although for somewhat different reasons." Grob neglects to consider ethnocultural values and ideals which may have "tended to parallel" middle-class aspirations "although for somewhat different reasons" such as an aversion to then-current working-class conditions. In fact, Grob contradicts his statement when he notes (p. 168) that these same Catholic unionists had begun to accept their wage-earner status as permanent. *Cf.* Andrew M. Greeley, *That Most Distressful Nation: The Taming of the American Irish* (Chicago: Quadrangle, 1972), 85. For a nativist view contemporary with John Q. Worker, note Josiah Strong's complaint that "the Roman Catholic vote is more or less perfectly controlled by the priests" (quoted in Robert H. Wiebe, *The Search for Order, 1877–1920* [New York: Hill & Wang, 1967], 54). It seems that whenever John Q. Worker did something that some observer disapproved of, it was because he was "controlled" by some Power that that observer also disapproved of; and this is true of observers of all political and religious views.

57. See Supplement. On the immigrant's ability to select among proffered messages on the ground of their content rather than the authority of influentials: *e.g.*, at least some East European Jews in New York who read the socialist *Forward* every day remained totally uninfluenced by its political message because it conflicted with their religious self-identifications (letter from author's mother, May, 1976, concerning her parents).

Index